The Complete Barbel Angler

THE COMPLETE
BARBEL ANGLER

ROGER MILLER

The Crowood Press

First published in 1996 by
The Crowood Press Ltd
Ramsbury, Marlborough
Wiltshire SN8 2HR

British Library Cataloguing in Publication Data

A catalogue record for this book is available from the
British Library.

ISBN 1 85223 980 8

Dedication
To the memory of John William Martin – 'The Trent Otter' –
who understood the ways of the species before anybody
else, and who influenced many great post-war anglers to spend
days among the barbel. Without the inspiration of those
subsequent writings this book could not have been written.

Picture Credits
All photographs by Roger Miller
All line-drawings by Paul Groombridge

Printed and bound by BPC Consumer Books, Aylesbury

CONTENTS

PREFACE

The relatively recent surge in popularity of the barbel, as well as its rise in status, is undoubtedly linked to the national increase in its numbers and its availability to far more anglers than seemed possible as recently as the mid 1970s. The mass defections from the ranks of disillusioned carp anglers have certainly helped. What angler can resist that heart-stopping moment when a group of summer barbel enter the swim, flashing over the gravels before beginning to feed on the bait?

This new appreciation of the barbel is also fuelled by the unmistakably raw, rod-wrenching bite that is so quickly followed by a majestic and unparalleled fighting ability so typical of our favourite adversary, as freedom is contested in either clear summer streams or in the coloured water of the autumn floods. To crown the renaissance of barbel fishing, there is that wonderful sense of accomplishment when a mid-winter barbel is unhooked by frozen, excited, trembling fingers beneath slate-grey skies and on bleached, dead sedge banks with a sullen and swollen, hitherto lifeless river sliding silently by.

Surely, and as if we do not already have reason enough for our grand obsession with the species, its absolute uniqueness is completely uncontested. Do big barbel not carry the awesome presence and regality of any carp? All barbel have the beauty and grace of the daintiest roach and, certainly on frequent occasions, the cussedness of the wariest chub. And surely barbel have an ability to bring out the strange primeval hunting instinct that so motivates the big pike and ferox hunters.

Modern barbel fishing certainly has a dimension that so many of today's stillwaters lack. It offers challenging fishing for wild, untamed and magnificent fish in a wonderfully natural environment. The barbel angler can enjoy fishing in a private space, away from the crowded areas that are full of equipment and where the fish are known by name. The beauty of barbel fishing is that it is often just angler against a visible fish, with no external distractions.

To cap it all, there are countless barbel, certainly some of them genuinely massive, that are just waiting to be caught for the very first time. The potential of many barbel rivers and their tributaries is still relatively unexplored. There has never been a better time to be a barbel angler than right now. We have more barbel in the UK than at any time before, and never have so many huge barbel been reported than today.

Week-long marathons and motionless inactivity are no part of the barbel angler's repertoire. Days spent on the river are all about innovation, mobility and watercraft – if properly adhered to, these will bring their own rewards. How many forms of angling are there where there is a constant possibility of the rod being wrenched into the river with the fleeing adversary hell-bent on reaching the nearest snag and with the power to do so should it be given the slightest opportunity?

This work is about catching barbel; no angler who has yet to catch one can fully understand how fundamentally important this is to those of us who have. Barbel fishing is a return to the very roots and meaning of angling, a meaning that has been sadly obscured for far too long. It is an intensely personal pursuit, with every single barbel angler having a private, secret reason for this passion. When a barbel is eventually, and thankfully, beaten and in the net, we find our own private heaven.

All barbel anglers should join the Anglers Co-operative Association so that the habitat vandals and polluters of this world can be brought to justice and that their prosecutions can deter other would-be despoilers of our wonderful rivers and all that lives in and around them.

Furthermore, no barbel angler can afford to ignore the ever-growing Barbel Society, which has produced an excellent handling code for experienced and inexperienced barbel anglers alike. By meeting and talking with other barbel anglers so much can be learned and enjoyed. Never afraid to say things that need saying, the Barbel Society is ideally placed to take the best interests of barbel fishing into the next millennium.

To paraphrase that great modern angler James A. Gibbinson: 'Let us be quite honest about it – barbel are barbel; the others are just fish!' The barbel revolution continues unabated; as with any voyage of discovery, the more we learn about barbel the less we find we really know at all.

1 HOW BARBEL BEHAVE

When it comes to barbel fishing there is nothing to beat a low, clear river in summer with the sun beating down. Most barbel anglers will shudder at such a thought, but these conditions are absolute paradise. This is the time that you really can see the fish, study them properly and get to know (as much as you ever can) what is happening beneath the surface.

There are several aspects to this: you might want to know the exact size of the barbel in a particular stretch of river; you might want to look out for and locate a target fish; you might want to discover new barbel-holding areas; you might be intrigued to know the make-up of the bottom and the snags that cause such problems in the winter floods. Most importantly, you will probably wish to learn as much as possible about the reactions of your quarry to baits and rigs during such visible periods. Whatever the reason, barbel spotting in summer is a magnetic and highly educational occupation.

While most people will find an otter, badger or buzzard enchanting and fascinating, they are quite unaware of the delights of the barbel, and fail to enjoy its grace and beauty as it swims in its environment. There have been days that I have spent sitting on a favourite piece of riverbank watching barbel flashing, feeding and displaying themselves in gleams of gold and coral pink. Then I have looked up and enjoyed watching a buzzard, spiralling on the thermals. I have never seen any difference between the two: both are magnificent creatures.

Does watching barbel help the angler? My belief is that it does, without any shadow of doubt. Far too many barbel anglers – dare I say the vast majority? – are content to unload whole bootfuls of gear, waddle to the waterside,

tackle up at the nearest point and spend the rest of the day watching a motionless quivertip. If pleasure is achieved by this then so be it; I am the last person to condemn anything that gives an angler enjoyment. However, all too frequently the angler is disgruntled and blames the weather or the fish, rather than this very limited approach.

The committed barbel watcher is constantly alert, constantly thinking, constantly trying to lift the veil that obscures the quarry. The more secrets the barbel watcher witnesses the more barbel will be caught as a result throughout the season.

Another of my passions is badger watching – without some knowledge of the badger and its habits the watcher is doomed to hours of boredom and failure. However, once the watcher knows when the badger stirs, where its paths lead, what it feeds on and where, then watching becomes a quite different business altogether. It is just the same with the barbel: I can think of several examples of fish caught because their habits have been read and properly interpreted.

How accurately can any human being, however practised, say what a fish is doing or how it is reacting to its environment? Can any human being interpret the mind and movements of an animal? I feel that to an extent we can. While it is impossible to know exactly how every barbel is reacting, experience can give strong guides and fairly reliable pointers on most occasions.

What I have seen and what I have interpreted from these sightings can easily be challenged. I hope it will be: it would be a very dull world indeed if there was no new knowledge to be discovered and there were no controversies to set us alight. All I can say, quite truthfully, is

A big barbel ready for the weigh-sling.

that this chapter is built on years and years of barbel-watching on clear-water rivers around the UK and on the Continent.

Of course, what I have witnessed the barbel doing in clear water might not tally with larger, murkier rivers like the lower Thames. It could well be that the way a barbel behaves on, say, the Teme might be different to barbel behaviour on the Great Ouse. You cannot say what a barbel is doing if you cannot see it in the first place! All I can repeat is that years of barbel-watching, I am sure, have helped me put more fish on the bank. And that holds for waters where I have not been able to see them. At least I have been able to imagine where they would be and what they would be doing and that, I am convinced, has always helped me. I hope this chapter helps you too!

WATER TEMPERATURE

There is probably no branch of fishing where the thermometer seems to play so big a part. On established barbel rivers most of the good anglers are dunking thermometers all through the day and night in an effort to find out exactly what turns the barbel on or off. This is praiseworthy endeavour and pictures are slowly emerging. Every shred of evidence built up is of use not just in catching barbel but, more important, in really getting to know how these complex and fascinating fish behave.

The most significant temperature is the minimum at which barbel feed, and this has been the subject of a great deal of discussion over the years. Most anglers now agree that once the water temperature drops sharply to below around 40°F (5°C) the barbel move into pretty much a comatose state and feeding barely takes

Although caught during a frost, this barbel fed in a steady water temperature.

We must consider the other end of the scale: when air temperatures are particularly high, say mid-sixties (about 18°C), feeding activity during the day slows down. It is wrong to say that it ceases altogether. It may well be that the bulk of their feeding takes place during the dark hours but that does not mean to say that barbel are blind to opportunities during the day, however warm the water may be. After all, when we consider that the barbel extends as far as southern Europe, we can see that the species is quite capable of dealing with the warmest weather.

The barbel is quite happy feeding through a great range of temperatures and it is only in very cold winter weather that they stop – and there is even doubt about that. The barbel is a hardy and adventurous fish and there is not much that puts it off.

Taking water temperatures is a fascinating subject. Is the temperature of the river the same in the margins, where water temperatures are generally taken, as in the middle, or in a deep hole, or in a weir-pool? Or can we say that a margin temperature at least gives some indication of a rising or falling mean? It is extraordinary just how rarely the temperature of a river will remain constant through the course of the day. For example, a few hours of sunlight will raise it by half a degree Fahrenheit or so. Equally, a warm river can really plummet in temperature in the evening if there is a frost and a clear sky. A thermometer is a fascinating tool to have and it really does make for a great deal of added interest on the barbel river.

Most successful barbel anglers will own either a digital thermometer or a traditional Reuben Heaton mercury thermometer, which is not only robust but comes in a protective carrying case. A cord of some type has to be attached – preferably several yards of the strongest braid in your tackle box. One of the many qualities of the Reuben Heaton thermometer is that it reads temperatures in both Fahrenheit and Centigrade. The Fahrenheit scale gives a more sensitive and accurate reading of water temperature than the larger Centigrade divisions. The angler who watches

place. Every time you discover a rule you will find instances that break it, but by and large it is true that barbel do not like feeding when water temperatures drop sharply to below 40°F (5°C).

It is also very well known that if the water temperature is low but rising, barbel will tend to shape themselves up and stir out of their lethargy. So, a water temperature of around 46°F (8°C) can produce a lot of barbel activity if the temperature has risen a little over the past day or so. Conversely, if the water temperature has been 50 to 52°F (10 to 11°C) and drops to 46°F (8°C) the barbel's metabolism will be slowing down and feeding will be much more spasmodic. So, it is not the temperature that is important but whether it is climbing or falling.

Autumn days on barbel streams are rarely wasted.

and understands those winter temperatures will learn to become quite excited about an increase of a single degree of Fahrenheit, let alone one degree Centigrade (1°C equals 1.8°F, so 10°C is 50°F and 11°C is 51.8°F). It therefore pays to take readings in Fahrenheit for a more accurate picture.

Modern technology has recently blessed us with the far more informative and accurate digital thermometer, which also produces readings in both Centigrade and Fahrenheit. The two major advantages of the digital thermometer over the more traditional variety is that its readings are given in tenths of a degree and that the probe can be left in the water with the digital temperature reading permanently visible through the entire session. This is certainly much better than dunking a conventional thermometer in and out of the water all day and having only a rough estimate of any slight water

temperature alteration during the session. Digital thermometers are readily available through Seer Rods.

By taking a temperature reading you will instantly know more about the state of play than all those who choose to ignore it put together. For instance, spate rivers are notorious for their erratic as well as their dramatic temperature changes and while barbel anglers can often luxuriate in mild, seemingly perfect conditions at the lower end of the valley, the hills can often see a completely different story in the form of sharp overnight frosts or squally, cold-water showers. The effects of these events quickly find their way downstream to kill off the sport that those not conversant with the temperatures are expecting. Upstream frosts and other adverse weather conditions do not only occur on spate rivers, but on lowland rivers too. Being swelled by rain water is not the only manner in which rivers can increase

The only fish of a hard day, significantly as the water temperature began to rise slightly.

in temperature; air temperature also exerts a heavy influence.

While anglers believing that conditions are ideal are baiting heavily with meat or pastes, a handful of maggots or a lobworm tail fished with patience and finesse will often prove to be the downfall of barbel that are not particularly keen on feeding because of the deceptively cold water flowing in from the hills or the higher ground. They will certainly not be at all interested in hoovering up carpets of bait.

Other highly valuable information imparted by the thermometer during a day's fishing is the sudden but often slight rise in the water temperature that sometimes occurs at the end of the day when many anglers have had enough after a blank day's fishing and are keen to get home. Under the conditions of a rising temperature at dusk or just before, it is well worth fishing in the dark after everybody else has gone

home and left all those baited swims for you to explore. Or you can return at dawn the next day. The previous evening's slight rise in temperature may well have prompted the barbel into wanting to sample a few hookbaits! Given the choice, it always pays to fish late on in the dark on a rising temperature as the early hours of the morning can often bring it down again.

With one or two notable exceptions, all rivers in England and Wales are controlled artificially by sluices and weirs, with water often being released for short periods at a time. This water has usually been stored and can consequently become slightly warmed. This slightly warmer run-off has been known to last for no more than half an hour on the Great Ouse, for instance. The barbel have fed voraciously for that half an hour and at no other time of the day. Without constantly keeping the thermometer in the water and checking it this crucial but fleeting event can easily be missed.

If you catch barbel under these circumstances it is important to be aware why you did, so that you can learn to recognize these circumstances should they recur. The very moment the water and temperature levels have risen slightly, with the temperature edging up by just a tiny fraction, is the time to cast out a fresh bait and concentrate on the quivertips. The bite may not be big but you will be ready for it when it comes!

FLASHING

One of the most common barbel activities is the well-known, easily recognized and often commented on flash. This occurs in good weather – say from May to September – when the water is clear enough for barbel to be seen. Then, every day, the gleam of a barbel turning on its side and catching the light with its flank will be a common occurrence. There are many swims on some rivers where barbel seem to flash constantly throughout the daylight hours – and probably in the dark as well. Flashing is an established behaviour pattern known to virtually every river angler and it has been com-

mented upon for decades.

The first theories about this go back into the nineteenth century and were propounded well into the twentieth. What everybody has always agreed on is that the flashing barbel is a very dramatic beast indeed and that the gleam of flank really does light up the whole river in a most awe-inspiring way. Furthermore, flashing barbel do tend to give the game away: nothing reveals a fish more instantly than that dash of gold and ivory beneath the surface, often in quite coloured water. Many is the barbel swim that has been found in this way. But why do barbel flash at all?

Perhaps the most common theory is that the barbel are cleaning themselves after spawning. This has probably come about because barbel are very visible in the early summer, as they are on the shallow gravels preparing for spawning. Observers have been able to see them easily and have noticed a lot of flashing activity. They have, understandably, linked this with spawning activities.

It is true that barbel flash a great deal in May and June when they are about to spawn or have just finished spawning. But they also flash at other times of year, and often just as frequently.

A barbel flashing, that distinctive beam of ivory catching the stomach. The question is why the barbel flashes in the first place.

I have watched barbel for hours at this time when they have been on the spawning beds and I am still not at all sure what they are cleaning from themselves. Older writers used to say that they were trying to free themselves of milt or eggs stuck to their flanks. This is a neat theory but I am not convinced about it – I have rarely if ever seen a female barbel waddle past with a coating of milt or eggs attached.

Another theory to do with spawning is that barbel are cutting redds, rather like salmon do. This has slightly more sense to it though I have often seen barbel spray their eggs out amidst *Ranunculus* weed or among the gravel in a quite haphazard way. I am not at all sure that barbel are redd cutters – certainly nowhere near to the degree of salmon or trout. This is another theory that sounds very nice in a book but does not really seem to hold the water by the riverside. So, my conclusion to all this is that barbel do flash around the spawning beds but that there is nothing really special or unique about this: barbel flash nearly all their lives and the act of spawning does not stop them.

Another hypothesis is that barbel are cleaning themselves of parasites. Here there could be something of truth. On many rivers the argulus or freshwater louse can be a problem to the barbel population. This rather horrible little parasite can move freely from host to host and

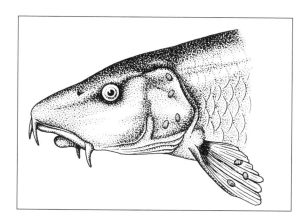

Argulus cause a good deal of damage.

from host to stone, where it lays its eggs. Possibly because the barbel tends to spend a lot of its life on the bottom, amidst stones, it is particularly attractive to the argulus, which is a really nasty customer and often leaves open sores behind it that can become infected.

It would make a great deal of sense for the barbel to scrape its flanks along the bottom gravel, attempting to free these lice. Barbel do seem to flash rather more frequently in rivers where they are affected than in rivers where they are not. This would be difficult to prove, but if we are looking for a sensible, down-to-earth explanation of flashing, the presence of argulus in the river could well be a signpost.

Some flashing barbel might be territorial. There are different types of flashing and it is wrong to lump all flashers together. For example, a barbel that might be flashing to get rid of a water louse will often scrape its body in a dramatic and pronounced fashion, often repeating the process ten or fifteen times in a little over thirty or forty seconds. It looks as though the barbel is very irritable and aggressive, desperately trying to free itself of an irritation, and flashing is the only way it knows. It is much the same with a territorial fish: I have noticed on many occasions that a single barbel will flash along a particular route several times an hour. It looks as though it is marking out some sort of territory and alerting other species to its presence. This is often quite a small patch and it is noticeable that very few fish will move into an area when a barbel has marked it in this way. This flashing is very deliberate and again quite aggressive; it differs from the possible parasite flashing only insofar as it follows a precise route on each occasion; parasite flashers tend to be quite haphazard in their course across the river.

It could well be that a shoal of flashing barbel is doing the same sort of thing on a mass basis: perhaps a tight group of barbel that live together flash to warn intruders off their patch. This is backed up in more than theory: it is very rare to see a new fish in among the established group. Occasionally the odd big fish will stay with the shoal for a while before moving on but it is rare to see new smaller fish join. There is a lot of work to be done here, but I still think territorial ambition is at least one reason for the flashing barbel.

We also ought to consider if barbel flash through simple fun. The impression most anglers have of the barbel is of a dull fish, a bottom-grubber with a hangdog expression and a rather dull mind. Any barbel watcher will immediately dispel that image! The barbel is a very joyful fish, really exploring its environment and taking obvious pleasure in it. Barbel will often hang in the sunlight, as though enjoying the feel and the warmth. Flashing, too, I feel could be an expression of contentment or excitement – rather like a whinnying foal or a playful cat. Not all flashing will be an expression of pleasure, but a happy barbel could well become a flashing barbel.

Flashing is a habit of many fish species. Chub will flash at times and so will gudgeon, minnows, dace and roach. Salmon are great flashers too and sometimes a shoal of sea trout can look like a whole school of flashing barbel! So this is not purely a barbel idiosyncrasy – perhaps all fish species like to feel the current roll them about and even turn them on their sides. It looks like a moment of relaxation and laziness that the salmon enjoys as much as the roach and almost certainly the barbel. There are times when we loll, lie down or lean against a lamp post; why should fish be any different?

One commonly promoted explanation of flashing is that the barbel is feeding. This is at least partly correct. There is no doubt – and many anglers have seen this – that the more bait introduced into a swim the more the fish begin to feed and the more flashing activity takes place. This could just be an example of high spirits, as already mentioned, but it is likely that the flashing is more than this.

Feeding barbel seem to flash in a slightly different way. The flashing is slightly slower and more controlled than the flash of a territorial fish. The flashing will also tend to follow a distinct upstream pattern, probably following the line of the food. So, what you tend to see is a methodically flashing barbel, flashing in a definite direction and at a fairly steady pace. Moreover, when barbel are flashing because of feeding, there are often shoal members following the fish. It is possible that the flashing process dislodges items of food from the gravel bed and makes them easier for the fish to eat. Perhaps flashing barbel are showing elements of team work and are following each other in a long trail up the swim, each profiting from the flashing activities of the fish in front.

So, looking for flashing barbel is vital to the observant angler. They will certainly indicate where fish are and where a possible swim exists. A flashing barbel could very well be a feeding barbel and it pays not to start fishing but to settle down and watch where, how and at what pace the flashing is taking place. I have seen an angler observe one flash and then remain fruitlessly glued to that spot all day. By watching just a little longer it would have become clear that the fish was probably a territorial one and that it lived a short distance upstream from where all the fishing was taking place. With just a little bit more time watching and thinking, this angler could have had a successful day.

ROLLING

The action that most anglers mean by this term is a head and shoulders movement – as is so common with tench and carp. This movement is not common with barbel, so when I see it I am always excited and intrigued. The traditional roll is a lazy, quiet movement and you tend to see the tip of the snout, the top of the head and the eye – and, quite clearly, the back and the dorsal fin – before the fish disappears again. It is graceful and beautiful, and leaves you with a sense of awe.

Many years ago I talked to Martyn Page, who felt that barbel rolling like this were travelling and they carried out this manoeuvre as they were moving up or down the river.

However, I am now far from happy with this explanation. When barbel roll like this it is often

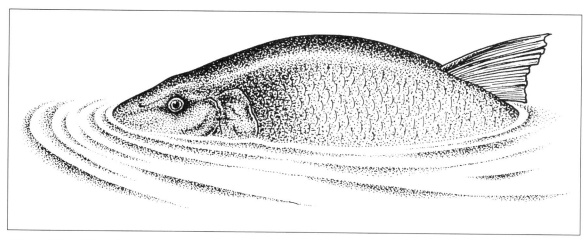

The traditional barbel roll.

quite continuous and may go on for two or more hours. Moreover, the rolling seems to be concentrated in one specific area. I do not therefore think that we can associate rolling with travelling. Often only one, two or perhaps three fish are rolling at any one time – even though the shoal they are members of might number ten, twenty or even forty fish. When tench roll like this it is often associated with feeding but I do not think in the case of barbel it is quite so simple.

There are other types of barbel roll that can be linked with feeding. With the tail flap all the angler sees, rather momentarily, is the distinct tail of a barbel and perhaps its root. It will wave for a second or so before disappearing. After many years of thought about this and a good few close observations I believe that what is happening is the sub-surface roll. The barbel is coming close to the surface but swirling away just before its head breaks out. It is probably taking food in the upper layers of the water.

What this food is can vary. Hatching nymphs are an obvious favourite but I also have proof that small fish are also taken (but more of that later). Never think that barbel are solely bottom feeders – especially in good weather, up to a quarter of their feeding takes place off the bottom.

Most anglers will have heard splashes in

their barbel swims and seen a fleeting glimpse of a large jumping fish. In a river like the Wye this is often put down to a salmon or a trout – rarely a barbel. But if you look very carefully you will recognize that unmistakable shape hanging above the surface of the river a fraction of a second before splashing back.

There are times when the barbel are just showing evidence of rowdy behaviour but there are many other occasions when the reason is much more subtle and productive. I now have many sightings of barbel clearing the water close up and often they are pursuing minnows or small fry. A barbel moves into an area and sees, above it, a shoal of small fish of one sort or another hanging in the surface layers. The barbel pauses, positions itself, steadies its fins and accelerates up to the surface layer, mouth open, taking one or two small fish in as it clears the surface. Sometimes the strength of the leap is such that the barbel will cartwheel in the air.

Here we go again – predatory barbel! They eat small fish in far greater quantities than most anglers appreciate. Many is the time small fish have showered out of the swim during the course of a fishing session and perch or pike are suspected as the culprits. As often as not, barbel are behind the activity. The inference to the angler is obvious.

The jumping fish.

BODY LANGUAGE

It is important for the angler to be able to tell the difference between a relaxed barbel and a stressed one, because a relaxed fish is far easier to catch. A relaxed barbel is easy to recognize. By and large, its movements will be easily placed: they will possess serenity and they will not be erratic or rushed. If the fish are moving round the swim, they will not deviate much to the left or right but they will sweep along well-defined lines. You will begin to notice distinct patterns of movement around the swims that will not alter much through the course of a barbel-watching session. It is as though the fish

have total confidence in their environment and are relaxed within it.

Though relaxed barbel will often enjoy the shelter and shade offered by a snag – especially on a warm day – they will still be quite unafraid of moving out into open water. A relaxed fish will not apparently feel the need to hug cover or snags as though in fear of its life.

These relaxed barbel will indulge in what seems to be very calm behaviour. For example, they may well hang just under the surface among weed or submerged branches. It seems as though they enjoy the feeling of being caressed by the loose fronds in the current. Very relaxed barbel will often tilt onto their side for thirty seconds or more, not flashing but just letting the current push them around as it flows past. Everything about the barbel in this mode is gentle, graceful and unhurried. Body, fin and eye movements are all executed with ease and unhurried precision.

Stressed fish are very much the opposite. One typical characteristic will be their desire to cling to any sort of cover. You will very rarely see the fish move out into open water and if they do it will be in a fast, darting manner. They show a fear of the open and a loathing of going out in it more than is absolutely necessary.

When they do move round a swim they will not follow any prescribed course but jig here and there, moving quickly left or right, always looking on edge and very quick to turn and swoop away with the current behind them, back into refuge. This movement is erratic and frequently violent, generally suggesting fear and a desire to escape.

The attitude of the different fish to baits is also interesting. A confident fish will generally take a bait in its stride, as it works its way up the swim, feeding here and there as it goes. However, a wary fish may well react very differently. I can think of many occasions when I have seen a stressed fish approach a bait and study it for anything up to two minutes before sweeping away with obvious anxiety. This process may well be repeated by the same fish at least six or seven times with intervals of anything up to twenty minutes between each inspection. At the end, the fish may well take the bait but as soon as the decision is made it will bolt in obvious panic, pulling the rod tip right round and virtually into the water.

The stressed fish often gives away its mental state through its fin movement. The fins will often be particularly active, not just outstretched but fluttering and flickering constantly.

Barbel also show signs of stress on the bank. I have noticed on frequent occasions when observing weighing and photography that a certain type of reaction takes place. In certain circumstances the body of a stressed barbel begins to lose colour. There are also frequent muscle spasms along its flank. These really are danger signs to watch out for. If they appear, everything must be curtailed at once and the fish returned to the water and held very carefully until it is ready to swim off – however long that might take. I have known a barbel that has

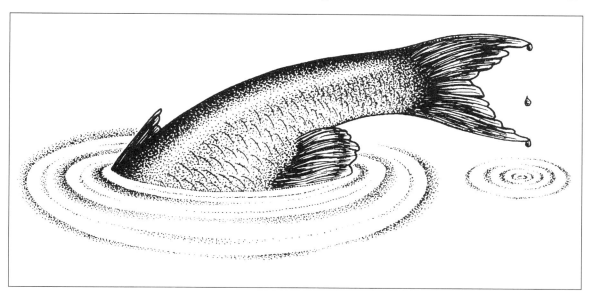

The tail flap.

suffered particularly – in warm weather after spawning – take as long as 25 minutes before recovering the energy to make its own way safely back to the swim.

CURRENT SPEED AND DIRECTION

One of my favourite angling stories is that of Dick Walker, when called upon to make a film for television about barbel fishing on a stretch of river that he had never seen before. Apparently,

Dick walked the river endlessly, just looking, not putting up his tackle, taking ages to decide where to concentrate his efforts. He knew what the crew could never know: that there are give-aways to the exact position of barbel and that to cast blind is a waste of time and effort. At last Dick picked out his swim – apparently purely on the strength of current speed – put in a little bait, cast out and almost immediately was into a good fish. The film was finished and they all went off to the pub to celebrate a short day's work!

A nice fish is ready for return.

All sorts of features attract barbel, notably rafts, underwater snags and specific bottom make-ups. However, one of the most important considerations in any discussion on the where-abouts and location of barbel must be an analy-sis of current speed. If you ask an experienced barbel angler what current speed barbel favour they will probably feel they know exactly, in their bones, what the barbel like. But that does not mean they would find it easy to put into words. The perfect barbel current is something that with experience you can recognize instinc-tively without exactly knowing why. You just look at a stretch of river and feel that you know where the barbel will be, an intuition – though not infallible – based purely on previous experi-ence of current speeds.

So it is important to try to understand what that perfect current speed is. Ideally, it will be not too fast and not too slow, though barbel can live happily in both very fast and almost static water if they have to. There is, however, an ideal that Walker had taught himself to recognize and in general it is true to say that barbel like that area where fast water is easing off before it becomes too slow. I know that there will be

many exceptions to this vague statement, but at least it is a basis. I can think of scores of prime barbel swims that fall into this category – beginning at that point where streaming water becomes steady and tapering away where steady water becomes sluggish. I cannot quote exact current speeds because rivers vary from each other, and in the same river the current speed will differ according to the season and the amount of rainfall. Barbel will also stray into fast and slow water at specific times as conditions and their own desires dictate.

You must look very carefully at not just the speed of the current but what the water surface is telling you. I like the water to be moving briskly, indicating a good steady push of water beneath. I also like it if the surface is slightly indented – not vigorously boiling but just dim-pling here and there, enough to suggest that there are stones on the bottom just breaking up the general push of the water. Creases are good signs too – anything that indicates that you have not only the correct speed of water but also some objects of interest on the river bed, where it really matters.

To get the very best out of a swim you have

A miniature stream, but big barbel reside beneath these weed beds.

also to consider exactly the direction of the current. This might sound easy but it is not. Currents do not follow the river downstream in a completely logical fashion. Each river will have its own little twists and turns that deflect the current here and there and push the barbel slightly off the course that you would expect.

There is one particular swim that I know just beneath a bridge where the water seems to progress quite amiably in an uncomplicated downstream direction. However, if you get up on top of the bridge you see that a depression upstream in the river bed shifts the current so that it flows from the right bank slightly towards the left. The current swings diagonally across the river and this is how the barbel lie. They are not, therefore, sitting on the bottom pointing directly upstream but rather across the river bed towards the right hand bank.

This is very important when it comes to catching those fish. They are quite used to food approaching them in this rather unexpected direction. If an angler tries to trot a float directly downstream the bait will look unnatural and be rejected. The fish are quite aware of any aberrant behaviour by a bait and the angler really must know exactly what the current is doing to any particles of food before being able to present the bait in a natural fashion. Otherwise, the barbel will be aware that something is not quite right with the presentation and will ignore the bait.

Rivers are fascinating places because they have the added dimension of the current. Barbel love to push themselves against it and enjoy feeling the moving, muscular water. The true river angler will identify with the river as much as possible, seeking to understand it, know its moods and appreciate this very significant dimension. Ignore the current at your peril.

2 THE LEARNING FISH

Barbel are a big, long-lived species and are often easily recognized by shape, colouring or body marks visible either in or out of the water. All this makes it a good deal easier to follow a particular fish or shoal of fish and guess at how they are reacting to pressures building up on them.

Virgin barbel are as naive and as easy to catch and fool as any other fish. The only problem in catching them is probably to get them to recognize the bait that you are using if it is not natural. While they might immediately switch onto a lobworm, for example, it might take a while to initiate them into the joys of sweetcorn. However, once this is done catches can be spectacular. Indeed, any angler lucky enough to find an untouched shoal of barbel will have a very good time for a short while at least. However, things change rapidly and barbel have proved over and over again that they are as capable of learning as any other fish. And they learn quickly too.

A barbel has only to be caught or hooked a couple of times to make it an educated and aware fish. This is all the more apparent if it has had sightings of shoal members also hooked or lost. Even a fish that has not been hooked can become educated and wary from what it has witnessed.

At this comparatively early stage, barbel are still not uncatchable by any means, but they do demand increasingly sophisticated and different approaches. New baits and new terminal rigs may be required. The fish may very well, for example, become alarmed by the sound or the sight of a feeder. Naturally, the richer the river and the lower the number of barbel the less need there is for them to rely on anglers' baits and the more their natural caution can have an impact.

After three or four catchings in a rich river with comparatively low barbel stocks, it is possible that the fish will switch off altogether and become quite impossible for the average angler to catch. An expert will continue to make inroads but it will still be hard work and all manner of tricks and stunts will need to be resorted to – including fishing at unsocial hours of the day.

On rivers where there is almost constant angling pressure there will be some anglers who are always one step ahead – especially if big fish are involved. That is why certain barbel are caught over and over again. A perfect example is that of Bo, a female on the River Wensum. Bo was a big, beautiful fish that lived in a very small, clear river and was the object of desire of many very good anglers. Consequently, though very shrewd, she had little or no hiding place. As a result Bo was caught at the very least forty times over a long and colourful career.

In nearly all cases, after the first few, Bo was caught by very excellent angling. However, the sad fact remains that the average angler will probably go to any length to catch a barbel that is well up on the learning curve. For example, many anglers will fish with line that is far too fine to land more than a small proportion of the barbel hooked. This has been a problem on many rivers and even if the barbel is not lost the inordinate length of time spent playing it can often prove disastrous. I remember in my days on the Severn it was not unusual to see a competitor play just two fish during the course of the whole five-hour duration.

On the Wensum, on the other hand, anglers went to extreme lengths to disguise gear strong enough to land a big fish. It was not at all unusual for anglers to bury the line by hand under weed or bottom debris to fool a fish coming out of hiding later on to find bait. Hair-rigs, bolt-rigs, long-stay sessions and all the other trappings of the modern coarse fishing scene also have been used to combat the wary barbel. None of it is particularly pleasant but answers are difficult to find.

The life of the average British barbel is far from easy and anglers must be aware of this and make things better for the barbel that they do catch. For example, keep-nets are completely out of place on the barbel scene. We all know the damage they do to the fins in particular but the mental stress, while less obvious, is much more fundamental. There is no doubt that a fish kept in a keep-net is traumatized severely: catching is bad enough but subsequent incarceration only increases the horror of the experience and accentuates the learning curve. Put the barbel back at once.

The same goes for keeping a barbel for long periods on the bank. I am never convinced about the wisdom of weighing average-size fish unless it is for some scientific purpose. Why an angler who has taken several over 10lb needs to weigh an obvious seven-pounder is quite beyond me. Weighing takes time and once again the fish has to be put in a sling, again an unpleasant process. It should be possible to play a fish, unhook it in the water and let it go without even exposing it to the air. The more this is done the less rapidly the learning curve will develop.

A barbel is a sentient creature and the more we abuse it the more its defence mechanisms will build up. The last thing anybody wants, surely, is rivers full of stressed or terrified fish.

FEEDING PATTERNS AND METHODS

We have tended to build up an image of the barbel as a vampire-like fish that leaves the gloom of its daytime lair as the dusty shadows reach over the valley, a fish that feeds with the owl and the badger and settles to sleep with the sunrise. The Victorians began to think and write like this and the message was taken up and expanded throughout the 1920s and 1930s. Indeed, there is a lot of truth here as every barbel-watcher will know: a river that is dead all day long can explode into life as the sun sinks and the night silence is shattered by a big fish crashing at the moon. Swims that are useless by day can become electrifying by night and the rod tip is never still as the long, lean bodies flick the line and the coral-shelled pectorals stir the tackle.

It is true that you can see the crumbs of the feasting being mopped up at first light when the sky is as grey as the heron and there is barely a breath of wind on the shallows, just upstream of the barbel hole. If you watch carefully you will see the heavy, slow bow-waves and, as the light grows, a dorsal fin or a tail breaking the surface as the fish drives into the gravel, dislodging caddis, leeches, nymphs and loaches from the shelter of the stones.

The sun strikes, and the barbel are fleeting shadows, blurs of gold sinking into the pool, sliding into the weed, lost till the bats return.

But as with all fish-watching the image, however appealing, rarely tells the whole truth. There are still many issues that need settling. Do barbel feed right through a short summer night but just for spells in the long winter ones? Do first and last light see the height of feeding activity as we all like to suppose? How great an impact do water temperature and colour make? Is daytime feeding entirely precluded by this nocturnal bingeing and how do bait-induced feeding spells differ from natural ones in length and intensity?

I believe that a barbel is much like a carp or a trout – an opportunistic feeder quite aware of everything its environment can offer and happy to feed when the river sends food of any kind. I do not see the barbel adhering to a rigid timetable in the least.

They do feed at night, though in part this is something that man has forced upon them. Fishing pressure has done extraordinary things and one of them is to make the barbel a night hunter – exactly like the badger. In the distant past the badger was just as happy to feed by day. Like the barbel, it learned.

There are other, more subtle incentives. If you have your thermometer constantly at the ready, you will probably find that water temperatures often rise a fraction towards dusk. This is probably quite enough to spark such a finely tuned instrument as the barbel into life.

Other considerations revolve around food. For example, some caddis become increasingly active at night as do loach, bullheads and crayfish. The barbel are aware of the nocturnal wanderings of such important foods and are bright enough to plan to intercept them. So, security, water temperatures and food availability can all at times make nocturnal feeding seem an attractive option – but not, by any means, the only one.

In their natural state, barbel are still quite happy to feed during the day – and of this we can make sense also. We know that barbel do feed a lot by touch and vibration but eyesight still plays an important part. Daylight helps to some degree. Further, a great deal of favoured barbel food is diurnal: nymphs are the perfect example and barbel will often take them deep down in the water as they begin to emerge in the late morning, through the afternoon or in the early evening. They will hunt them on weed stems, rocks, submerged obstructions and even take them just below the surface. I have even seen barbel on occasion go quite mad for mayflies on the top. (I have never seen this described before, but most barbel anglers are inactive on the river at that time of the year and most game anglers would not recognize a barbel.) When it comes to minnow-hunting, daylight is probably essential.

It is also important to look at feeding

At least twenty-five barbel are working over the hemp and caster fed swim here, and two minutes later the left-hand rod was nearly dragged in by a nine-pounder.

rhythms. The natural pattern is surely relaxed and steady. There are peaks when feeding is uppermost in the barbels' mind, and they will work to some sort of controlled climax. However, their eyes are always open to food and even when the feeding urge has worn off, something particularly attractive is always liable to be taken.

What anglers see of the barbel's feeding rhythm is often quite unnatural. The modern barbel method is to pile in vast quantities of addictive particle baits – especially hempseed, casters, maggots and sweetcorn. The effect of this enormous windfall is to cause unnatural behaviour. This is why anglers who have baited swims to the brim see such frenetic activity by the barbel, combined with not a little aggression. It is quite typical for barbel to indulge in anything between three and six hours of gluttony when such a feast arrives.

The introduction of vast amounts of particles must surely upset the natural feeding rhythm of barbel and therefore probably does little for their growth rates or health. There was one well-known swim on the river Wensum where angling was banned for a couple of years. The frustrated anglers complained that the barbel were so dependent on their baits that without them they would deteriorate in weight and condition. The opposite was true. Known barbel often put on 10 per cent of body weight and their whole appearance was much more sleek and attractive. What happened – and I studied the barbel during this non-angling period – was that the fish reverted to their natural foods and relaxed feeding rhythms, with beneficial results.

It is important to consider the barbel's feeding methods. The four barbels that decorate their mouths are used to burrow in gravel and

Dusk, the barbel angler's hour.

among bottom weed to seek out the natural food on which they naturally exist. The barbel's mouth is also an interesting creation, being low slung with lips that can protrude. Certainly, they can give a fair impression of a vacuum cleaner, able to suck light food items in from several inches. Their lips are also rough and rubbery, as you would expect with a fish that has to spend a great deal of time grazing on stones that can be far from smooth.

The shape of the barbel is often described as designed to combat swift currents. It also looks as if it was designed to be a feeding aid, as many of the barbel's natural foods take some dislodging. A crayfish does not give up easily and often the barbel has to drive into the gravel to dislodge the food that it seeks. The long, lithe, streamlined body of the barbel allows it to do this with far more ease than, say, would be possible for a fat-bellied mirror carp. There are

times when this battering ram of a body is used against chub or other invaders in the swim, and it is a fearsome tool.

Every angler has seen the barbel feed in its normal mode – sweeping up the swim, hoovering the gravels, securing a good pouchful of food and then drifting downstream to chew, swallow, regroup and repeat the process. There are all manner of variations and the barbel can show itself to be extraordinarily athletic.

For example, I have seen them hoover the underside of rock ledges, hanging on their backs in the most fierce of currents. These have often been big fish but still have proved quite capable of keeping their balance and position under such difficult circumstances. Their muscular bodies and huge fins can be used for many purposes.

Mentally, too, the barbel shows extraordinarily adventurous vision. There has been

Late season is always such a problem: unfortunately the barbel are usually feeding like crazy.

occasional comment about barbel feeding from the top of weed beds where bait has collected. I have often seen barbel take flies from the surface as well as floating bait – perhaps casters that refuse to sink. Certainly, they are quite happy to comb fallen branches or weed beds that ripple near the surface. Barbel will investigate the margins, the shallows and the deeps of the middle of the river. They will comb rocks and sunken features for food. If any part of their environment seems to offer something of interest they will investigate it.

PREOCCUPATION WITH FOOD

Every fish species becomes preoccupied with a certain type of food at some time and barbel are no exception. The type of food that barbel become preoccupied with rather depends on the season.

In the early summer – say from June onwards – certain fish may well become preoccupied in hunting fry or minnows or any other small fish that inhabit the shallows relatively near to spawning grounds. You will often find in mid summer that many fish become preoccupied with caddis grubs. Once the autumn gales have broken and the rivers begin to flood – probably for the first time since the preceding winter – you will probably find a noticeable preoccupation with lobworms. A large number of worms are washed into a river after a few days of heavy rain. The creatures burrow into the surface and so are very vulnerable to run-off.

The inimitable Bob James once told me that after a storm on the Avon the sluice gates were packed with dead, dying and bloated worms. He said that at this particular mill there must have been several thousand washed up, waiting to be taken off downstream. Had barbel not taken their share upstream, goodness knows how many more thousand would have been added to this grisly scene!

There is plenty of evidence for the fish-watcher for barbels' preoccupied feeding, as excitement is very often evident. The fish will frequently flash and they will follow feeding routes quickly and systematically with hardly any deviation and delay.

Preoccupied feeders can show very little concern for possible dangers around them. I have found a big school of barbel feeding with their backs out of the water around dawn. I am sure that an infestation of small, black leeches had drawn them into very shallow water and no hazard was deterring them from this luscious feast.

I suspect that – like trout during the mayfly hatch – the barbel become more or less blind to other potential food sources. Certainly, barbel are always open to preoccupied feeding and they can be led to it by a bonanza of food of almost any sort. So perhaps when the angler concentrates on feeding a concoction of sweetcorn, maggots or casters, then preoccupying the barbel with these foods is not harmful.

The problem probably begins to rear its head when various seeds – some uncooked, and particularly hempseed – are used in large quantities. Some anglers arrive at the riverbank with pints or even gallons of hempseed. Barbel love this little black seed and will devour it. However, it is apparently not a beneficial food. It is not easily digested and tends to pass through the fish almost intact. Whether this does the fish any good or any harm is not clear, but when they are preoccupied with hempseed it means that they are not taking the time to feed on more beneficial foods. Hempseed will preoccupy them and dominate their energies when they could and should be eating more nutritiously.

3 TRAVELLING BARBEL

It has been suggested that a barbel can travel up to 5 miles (8km) a day. I do not doubt this, especially if there are no water mills, weirs or other obstructions. I once saw a school of barbel move 4 miles (6.5km) along a river between 10am and 4pm – though I have never seen its like before or since.

The tendency to migrate is not deeply rooted in all barbel. Generally, they choose to remain more or less static. Most anglers are aware that there are well-documented barbel holes that can hold anything between ten and forty fish. It is possible that on big rivers, in deep holes where observation is impossible, the numbers could even be higher.

The same school of fish might very well be present in a barbel hole for many years. The fish have found an area that they like and they see no reason to move. They might be edged out by extremes of weather, swim destruction or angling pressure but there has to be a sound and extraordinary reason for moving.

It is likely anyway that, for a good barbel hole, the swim is generally unaffected by extremes of weather and dramatic water conditions. In all probability the barbel hole will be deep enough to provide adequate shelter in high and low water conditions.

When it comes to dealing with angling pressure, barbel are certainly quick to build up their own defence mechanisms. I have repeatedly known a new barbel hole to be discovered and to deliver fish very quickly over a matter of weeks. Then, the fishing will suddenly slow down and abruptly cease. It seems that the barbel have discovered what terminal tackle, hooks and baits look like, and will have no more of it. A very skilled angler, fishing light or at night, can still occasionally winkle a fish out but the days of bounty are long past. The static shoal of barbel in a well-known hole can often go for several days without making a single mistake, even though very skilled anglers are pursuing them and gallons of bait are going through the swim.

Some barbel are undoubtedly periodic movers. They will inhabit one area of the river in the summer but perhaps drift a few hundred yards up or downstream as the winter approaches. I can think of many such examples, although the fish appear only to use a quarter of a mile (400m) of river or so, and find within that area everything that the seasons dictate they will need.

In the summer, one group of fish I know are quite content to live in a long, reasonably shallow run that is gravel-bottomed but with large stones here and there. They seem to move in there after spawning and stay until the first floods. Once the higher water arrives they move together about 150 yards (140m) downstream to a long, slow, deeper stretch that gurgles its way under a number of alder trees. There they remain until about April, when they begin a drift towards the spawning grounds. Thus they do move a little, but within strict confines and according to a clear annual pattern.

Most of the barbel in any river will make the move to spawning gravels around May. However, they do not stay on the gravels nearly so long as several of the older writers used to suggest – perhaps there is more pressure on our rivers nowadays and they hurry out of the shallow, vulnerable areas. It is certainly a dramatic sight to see large numbers of barbel – often a hundred or more – congregating in the shallows and milling around in small groups. It is a very good time for fish-watching and for marvelling at the size of barbel that you had previously never guessed were in the river!

Some barbel are true nomads and their river habitat allows for their idiosyncrasies. It is often said that the truly nomadic barbel are the large pioneering fish that push their way upstream, exploring new water, spreading the species. This is an appealing theory, yet often when I have caught barbel in unexpected places they have been small ones. Undoubtedly some of the nomads are big fish – perhaps they are easier to watch or cause more excitement when they are caught.

SPAWNING

Spawning time for barbel is generally con-trolled by the temperature of the water. If the spring has been particularly warm they begin to assemble from mid May and stay in the shallows until mid June. If the water is cooler, spawning can take place throughout June and occasionally into early July.

Before spawning, most barbel begin to migrate up or downstream, looking for a stretch of lively water flowing over clean stone and gravel. A little *Ranunculus* weed is also helpful. Barbel will certainly travel a great distance to find the exact area that they require; my own observations suggest that each fish returns to its own favoured spawning site.

It is not at all unusual to see groups of twenty, forty or even sixty barbel together at this time of the year – on the biggest rivers with the biggest barbel populations this could be increased. Activity can be quite frenetic and the barbel will spurt around the area in small

Perfect therapy for a child-minding, daytime barbel angler.

groups, rolling, splashing and often jumping clear of the water altogether.

Older writers suggested that there is some type of orderly procession, with the bigger males to the front, followed by ripe females and small fish on the outskirts. I have never seen anything as neat and orderly as this. Barbel of all shapes and sizes seem to mingle in together.

The barbel is a prolific egg-layer – females of 2 to 3lb (0.9 to 1.4kg) will apparently produce nine thousand eggs. These are yellowish and sticky, about 1/16in (1.5mm) across, and they adhere to the surface of the stones. The alevins, the tiny barbel, hatch out in 7 to 14 days, depending again on water conditions and temperatures. It seems certain that females mature at around four to five years old and possibly the males a little earlier.

Quite frequently I have found barbel spawning in the middle of June and watched anglers trying to catch them – with precious little success. It seems that at this time of the year their interest in food is minimal. Compared with carp, they show very great restraint. Nor do they switch onto the feed immediately after spawning; there is often a 24 to 72-hour time lag before feeding starts again. Even then, they may not be ravenous and will often be surprisingly picky.

Anglers should treat barbel caught after spawning with even more consideration and care than at other times. The fish are tired and are particularly vulnerable to bad or over-prolonged handling. Recently spawned fish should never be kept in nets or sacks but released as quickly as possible – preferably without being taken from the water. A barbel caught at this time of the year should be held in a gentle current for as long as it takes to recover its strength and make its own way back into deeper water. Never hurry this process: it is not unusual to see the fish waddle off a couple of yards, roll over and find it impossible to regain its balance and position in the stronger current.

TERRITORY

An ideal barbel swim will have a steady current over a clean gravel, sandy or stony bottom. There might well be a few decent-sized stones dotted around, and some decent overhead cover – especially if the swim tends to be close to the bank. There might also be a noticeable depression on the bottom, with the key area of the swim a few feet deeper than the surrounding stretches.

Acknowledged barbel holes are generally built up around a swim that includes most of these features. However, there are many variations and often many unexpected places on the river can hold barbel in plenty. So, what are these unexpected territorial requirements of the barbel?

There can be a noticeable difference in the winter and summer requirements of the fish. In the winter a good number may move down to slower, deeper stretches of water. Presumably these areas offer an easier life in the winter, especially when the barbel are not feeling par-

The smooth water between the rocky island and the near bank holds barbel galore.

ticularly energetic. Floods and frosts will probably be less keenly felt.

It is not just in winter that odd, often larger than average fish prefer these deep, slack areas. You would think that the slow current and the dirtier bottom would deter them, but from time to time they will be found in these places. Perhaps they find less competition from other fish or perhaps it is sheer laziness. Maybe these big barbel have not travelled upstream to spawn or they are just content to keep away from any current and drift where they wish. There could well be extensive seams of gravel or chalk that the fish enjoy feeding on. And even in the deepest, slowest stretches there will still be some current, possibly enough to satisfy the requirements of some fish. So do not write these sections off in the summer without careful investigation.

According to tradition, barbel should adore undercuts, but we should not always assume that they are obvious barbel swims. One long and deep undercut that I know is perfectly placed next to some gravels. I have often waded in and even had a poke around but never once disturbed a fish in there. Nor have I ever seen a fish either enter or leave the undercut.

Big rocks are often linked with barbel. There is something about a really large rock in the middle of the river that will always prove a magnet. It could well be something to do with the food that collects there or the way that the rock provides interesting deflections of current. Perhaps it provides shade from the sun. It need not just be boulders that provide the sort of underwater obstruction that barbel like. I have even seen the skeleton of a cow, lodged in the middle of the river and festooned with weed, proving to be very attractive to a number of fish.

Ruined walls and fallen masonry seem to be particularly sought after, even in swims that do not look particularly promising from other angles. I do not know what it is about them that is so appealing, apart from the build-up of food that might gather on the various angles and old brick faces. Again, perhaps the deflections in the current might prove attractive.

Mill-pools offer the complete list of requirements for any barbel – different current speeds, varying depths, clean bottom, fallen masonry and virtually everything that any barbel could want. Bridges – including remains of old bridges – are particularly attractive because the river is squeezed and narrowed and the current is slightly speeded up. Beneath the bridge there will generally be a fairly deep hole, which often proves irresistible to at least some fish. Whereas a mill-pool might be quite enough to satisfy barbel most of their lives, a bridge pool will probably need a fairly large feeding area around it. It is unlikely that barbel will want to spend their lives exclusively in a bridge pool and they will probably need to wander quite frequently to scout out new food sources.

Barbel paradise. Gravel, streamer weed and clear summer water.

4 BARBEL-WATCHING

I have reported what I have witnessed over six-teen years of watching barbel. I might have misinterpreted what I have seen, or what I have observed might not have been typical barbel behaviour. It could also be that barbel in murky waters where visibility is not so good behave differently.

The barbel is always quite capable of doing something that you would never expect, and dumbfounding even someone with good experience of the species. That is one of its attractions: you can just never say that you know it well. In the summer of 1995, I was walking a pretty featureless, placid stretch of river not expecting to see anything in the way of barbel until I came upon rapids further up-river. The light was not nearly as good as I might have wanted. However, the bank was high, the river reasonably clear and it was well worth being out with sunglasses, binoculars, chest-waders and all the rest of the kit.

I had walked half a mile or so when, way out beyond the middle of the river, I noticed a great stain on the water. I put up the binoculars, focused and to my total amazement saw a bar-bel tail waving out of the water. Quite what that fish was doing I did not know but what was even more surprising was that it was part of a group of about fifty entwined together. This was long after the end of the spawning season.

For most of that first day I watched the group of fish. They hardly moved at all from an area where the river suddenly became shallow, with a rocky ledge, but still offered a quite noticeable depression that attracted this indi-visible shoal. Not once in all the time I watched did the shoal break up – although odd mem-bers sometimes moved 1ft (30cm) or so away

and occasionally an erratic flasher would disap-pear off. The fish were feeding to some extent, judging by the amount of bottom silt that was disturbed and drifted off downstream – this was a very slow stretch with hardly any clear gravel or sand exposed.

The next day I decided to fish, though the method took a little working out. The barbel were about 50 yards (45m) away but I knew that if the bait was not placed exactly on them there would be no chance of a bite. I fished from the high bank where I could see the group, which added another 10 to 15 yards (9 to 14m) to the cast. The weather was quite windy. I opted for a 12ft rod with a 6ft line straight through to a bomb, bead, swivel, hook-length, size six hook and a large lobworm. I assumed that no pre-baiting would be neces-sary and that they would respond immediately to a large juicy food item that they would rec-ognize at once. I cast beyond the fish, drew the line back over them and let it drop as quietly as possible. The line tweaked and tightened with-in about thirty-five seconds and I was playing the first fish from the shoal.

Once that first barbel was safely unhooked and returned, I went back up the bank prepar-ing to make another cast. The shoal had gone. It had disappeared. Nevertheless, the sun was on my side and I looked up and down until I found them around 100 yards (90m) beneath the original shoaling point. The group was still quite compact but what was interesting was that it was now feeding in earnest. All the fish were flashing, throwing up silt and behaving in a most energetic way. They seemed very easy to catch at that particular point and altogether during the course of the day I took a further

Peanuts accounted for this magnificent specimen.

twelve, of which two were over 10lb.

The next day I returned to the same spot, to find the barbel back in the original position just on the shallow ledge. This time it was an hour and a half before the line tweaked, even though my worm had been lying amid this huge number of barbel for so long. Again, as soon as the first barbel was returned, the shoal moved to the same position downstream and started feeding in earnest. It was just like the first day and once more I landed about another eight fish. Most of them were between 6 and 8lb (2.7kg and 3.6kg) but another of over 10lb came out and I had the impression there were one or two quite enormous fish there. I visited the area once or twice in the next few weeks and each time the shoal behaved in exactly the same way.

Some years ago and for no apparent reason a huge shoal of barbel – at least eighty fish – appeared on the gravels of a mediocre swim on the Wye. Although not so tightly shoaled as the former group, they were together for about ten days and I caught a number of fish, including some good ones. This great shoal then split into groups of five or six fish, which made their separate ways up and down the river. There is no obvious explanation why the fish came together in the first place and then split up so dramatically and quickly. The action had nothing to do with spawning, so perhaps a huge food source attracted them to this particular area of the gravels. If I had not followed my habit of walking and watching and really scanning the water, I would never have found these fish and would never have caught a beautiful 11lb (5kg) barbel.

Some observations can be rather depressing. One March day on the River Kennet I worked myself into a nice position where I could see a barbel of 8 to 9lb (3.6 to 4kg) comfortably holding the bottom and apparently quite at ease with the world. I put three grains of sweetcorn 2 yards (2m) or so upstream. The grains hit the bottom 4ft (120cm) from the barbel and travelled perhaps 6in (15cm) towards the fish when he bolted. I discussed this with the bailiff, who confirmed that there had been an angler in

that particular swim every day of the season. This apparently had also been the case with every swim along the whole stretch of river. Night fishing had recently been introduced and most swims had been occupied for twenty-four hours a day.

The only way to guarantee success was to fish with casters over hempseed, using size 18 hooks and 2 or 3lb bottoms. The bailiff estimated that one fish in six was landed. It is obvious that the fish were becoming more and more spooked, and the anglers were increasing the stress and trauma that the barbel were experiencing. We must find an answer to this sort of situation on our heavily fished rivers.

On a lighter note, I was once wading and fishing in some very fast water – it was so quick that I was having trouble keeping a foothold. There was a group of barbel in the swim before me, which was a deeper channel running between shallow rocky margins. One or two were quite big fish. Although I did not catch any that day, what I saw more than made up for the lack of rod-bending. The barbel were behaving like this: they would move towards me in a tight phalanx feeding quite traditionally and heavily as they approached. Once they got to the head of their beat, close to where I was, they would lift their pectorals, turn their heads and let the current wheel them back down to the starting point of their patrol route. They rolled over in the current, on their backs and on their sides, a tumbling mass of bodies with their stomachs catching the light as they cartwheeled. Once back at the bottom of their route they would stop, stick their pectorals out and the whole sequence would start again. If anyone suggests that barbel are sad, gloomy fish this sighting will confound them. The species is amazingly able in the water and it must know and ride the currents better than any other fish.

Barbel are supposed not to have particularly sharp eyesight, especially beyond a short range. It certainly is very acute within a few inches from the snout – but the fish are clearly aware of things going on much farther away. They can see a bait at least 5 or 6ft (1.5 or 1.8m) away in clear water. A barbel will see a worm from at least 6ft and begin to position itself to intercept it if it is in the mood, so do not underestimate its eyesight.

Smell is rather more difficult to gauge. The barbel has a strong sense of smell and natural smells can be great stimulants. For example, if sweetcorn has gone off just a little, it seems to work just that little bit better. The same goes for cheese or hempseed – anything that is just a little bit high – and I do think there is a difference between using this type of bait and pouring in chemical flavourings.

The question of barbel colour is of interest. It is possible to watch a big shoal of fish and see at least four or five different shades of back and flank. Barbel can be coloured through a whole spectrum of gold and bronze, even to very dark brown. It is not clear why this is the case – especially with fish in the same shoal and therefore inhabiting the same area.

I once saw what appeared to be a completely albino barbel lying deep down in clear water. I failed to catch it, though I am sure it would have made a stunning photograph. It is the only white barbel I have seen.

At times barbel seem happy to coexist in a swim with other species – roach and chub, for example – but there are occasions when they seem to bully chub out of any swim they want to inhabit. I have seen them push chub with their snouts or bang against them with their flanks. It is very physical: the smaller, lighter chub tend to lift higher up into mid water and then vacate the swim altogether. Of course, this does not happen all the time and there are swims where the two species do coexist.

When it comes to dishing out a bit of muscle in the river, barbel do seem to be the kings. I have even seen an 8lb (3.6kg) barbel budge a pike of about the same size – and the pike was no match whatsoever!

GIANT FISH

Great barbel, real leviathans, are every barbel angler's dream – deep down in us all is the romantic and the eternal optimist. However, many years of barbel-watching have taught me that there are distinct problems with judging the size of a fish in the water. It is one thing to see a long fish but it is quite another to know exactly what its breadth or depth will be. Also, a large-framed fish can be very hollow, especially in the early summer, and weigh a pound or two less than it would in February or March. A rather shorter, deeper, thicker fish probably weighs a good deal more than a long, lean one.

Barbel are probably as hard to judge for weight in the water as any other species I know. It is difficult to make any judgement on a fish a long way from the bank in clear water. Water can magnify a fish greatly, especially if you are looking down from a high bank. Flashing fish take some getting used to: the flash is such a dramatic movement that it is easy to become over-excited about the size of the fish. Keep an air of realism about you when you spot what you think is a monster!

Dick Walker recorded seeing barbel approaching 20lb in the Avon many years ago. They were seen by other experienced anglers as well. I have heard rumours of colossal fish recently from the Teme, the middle and lower Severn and from Poland. I am sure that leviathans do exist in these places, but I have not seen them myself.

I did see a stunning barbel in France in 1973. I stopped at a café in the Loire region and on the wall there was a colossal stuffed barbel. The weight given was something in excess of 9kg (almost 20lb). I saw a huge barbel leap clear of the water in a river in southern Austria in 1990. It was an amazing creature, but was at least 50 yards (45m) from me in mid stream and I would not be able to guess accurately at its weight.

In June 1994 on the Wye I was wading in some shallows, eager to get to a run where I could put a float or freeline bait down to some barbel. The light was quite good and the water was crystal clear. I disturbed the occasional fish of 6 to 8lb (2.7kg to 3.6kg) on my way across.

When I reached the point where the water began to lap dangerously towards the top of my thigh boots I stopped and began to bait my hook. I looked down and coming towards me was a barbel that I will never forget. It did not notice me for the first thirty seconds or so as it worked its way up-river towards my green rubbery legs and I had a good while to see it at very close quarters. I guess that it came to within 4 or 5ft (120 to 150cm) before it was aware of my presence and then it accelerated explosively upstream, creating quite a bow-wave as it left. I talked about the sighting of this fish with friends, and have frequently been asked its weight. I would not even hazard a guess.

I also observed a big barbel in the hot, clear summer of 1995. There had long been rumours of a big fish in this particular area, and in late June I decided to put in some fish-watching from the high bank over the snag. I saw many ordinary fish including quite a few just over 10lb (4.5kg) – exciting and beautiful but nothing to back up the rumours – until a quite colossal shape glided darkly into view down-river. This fish hung around a while, even fed for a short period and then disappeared back in the direction from which it had come. I saw it very briefly twice again that summer, as did two other friends, and it must have weighed 14lb (6.4kg) or more.

Specific techniques for targeting big barbel are described in Chapter 8.

5 TACKLE

RODS, REELS AND QUIVERTIPS

All discerning barbel anglers will require their rods to possess a number of indispensable characteristics, if they are not to be found wanting at some stage. First, the ideal barbel rod should have power yet not be unwieldy or heavy. It should be capable of casting large baits, weights or feeders and yet have sensitivity in the form of a quivertip for delicate bite detection. It should also be capable of handling a lunging and violent barbel. A good barbel rod should take nylon lines of up to 12lb b.s. and ultra-thin braided HPPE lines of up to 30lb b.s. and should have the highest quality rings – silicon carbide or titanium – to protect against sustained feeder fishing or wear from the HPPE line.

A great many perfectly adequate yet compromised rods in this class are marketed as feeder rods. One of the better equipped is the Drennan 13ft IM8 Super Feeder. These rods come with two quivertips in 2 and 2.5oz test curve strength, but there are several occasions when stiffer quivertips are essential. Although these rods perform well in most barbel fishing situations where quivertips are required – particularly when feeder fishing – they are not designed specifically for barbel fishing and therefore lack versatility as well as outright muscle.

Given that very few rods are manufactured specifically for barbel fishing it is refreshing that there are at least a couple of small companies making them. Seer and Graham Phillips lead the way in design and choice. Seer offer two excellent quivertip rods: an 11ft 4in model with a 1lb test curve and a 12ft 3in rod with a 1lb 8oz test curve for heavier work. Both

This rod has just subdued a double-figure barbel, with plenty 'in reserve'.

models are known as the Barbel Quiver. These rods come with tapered quivertips, which are more versatile than the Drennan models as their finer tips are sensitive in slower water but their taper allows their use in stronger flows without having to change over to a stiffer tip. Their action is somewhat superior: they have much more power in reserve in the lower third than any other current barbel rod.

Also from Seer are the Specialist Rover rods – 10ft 6in and 11ft 8in models, both of which have a 1lb 4oz test curve. Both come with a removable tip ring and push-on carbon quiver. These are designed to allow both rod top legering and quivertipping from the same rod, a valuable ability for the roving angler who wishes to travel as light as possible. Seer rods are hand made to order and cater for individual angler's tastes. They offer optional extras that newcomers and experienced barbel anglers alike will find indispensable. For example, they can have ready-made Isotope or Beatalite housings, which allow the owner the advantage of fishing in the dark. No other rod manufacturer carries such housings, which are a necessity given the barbel's propensity to feed at night the whole season through.

Each individual rod is made precisely to the angler's requirements. The owner's name, as well as a personalized number if required, is painted and sealed onto the rod, a superb security measure in these days of frequent tackle thefts. These rods are designed and manufactured by Andy and Jill Orme, both highly regarded barbel anglers.

In the same league is the Graham Phillips Onstream series. Their basic 11ft Barbel Quiver is similar to the Seer Rover rod in that it comes with an interchangeable tip ring or quivertip. The Onstream series includes the Stepped-up Barbel Quiver – a 1lb 8oz test curve quivertip rod for snag fishing. This rod really does have the capacity to bully the barbel out and is also ideally suited to heavy feeder work. It is a very welcome addition to any barbel angler's armoury.

If your rod does not come with an Isotope or

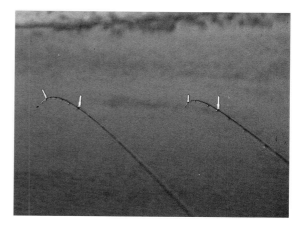

Quivertips with correctly positioned Beatalite housings.

Beatalite housing you will have to fix one on yourself. Most confirmed night owls prefer the attachment of two Isotopes, one 3in or 7.5cm from the tip (positioning the housing there reduces the opportunity of the line, especially HPPE, to tangle with it) and a second at the base of the quivertip. While a vigorous bite is easily visible on a single Isotope the inclusion of two Isotopes makes smaller, gentler night bites much easier to discern, as well as taking out much of the eyestrain involved in concentrating on a single Isotope.

The addition of these housings is quite easy to construct. Some whipping thread, a green Drennan swivel sleeve, a Stanley Knife blade and Humbrol clear polyurethane are the only items required. Begin by slicing the sleeve in half at a sharp angle to create a point onto which the whipping can be started, with the sleeve itself pressed against the appropriate position on the quivertip. Continue the whipping up the sleeve to a point where the sleeve begins to stand proud of the quivertip. Continue behind the sleeve to create a slight ridge, which forces the sleeve to sit somewhat prouder still. An angle nearing 90 degrees is perfect. Re-whip over the original whipping, seal liberally with the clear polyurethane and leave to dry and harden overnight.

The choice between Beatalite and Starlite inserts is up to the individual. Beatalites will glow for at least a whole season before beginning to fade. Starlites glow much more brightly but last only for one night, so they can become quite expensive if you plan a few nights' fishing using two rods. Starlites are also available in clip-on form: they can be clipped onto rod tops and, at a push, quivertips without the aid of quivertip housings.

Within the context of barbel fishing, reels are a relatively minor subject. Centrepins probably have more practical applications in barbel angling than in any other area of coarse fishing. Barbel are capable of tearing a rod off its rest in an instant, especially when the clutch of a fixed spool reel is clamped down too tightly. Centrepins are far more suitable when this occurs with any degree of regularity as the ratchet can be engaged, allowing a violent barbel bite to take line directly off the spool and acting as a form of shock absorber.

A long cast that is beyond the capability of a centrepin is relatively rare in barbel angling – so the angler using centrepins will not be at a disadvantage on many occasions. Perhaps the only real disadvantage with a centrepin is the comparative slowness of its line-retrieve ability, which can put the angler on the back foot should a barbel suddenly decide to shoot off towards the rod. Under these circumstances it can be difficult to keep up with the fish.

There is a compromise between conventional fixed spools and centrepins. The double-handled Shimano Aero Baitrunner GT 5010 reel carries 280yds (255m) of conventional 10lb b.s. nylon line, more than enough for barbel fishing. These reels have the ability to disengage their spools, allowing line to be taken off the spool at a pre-set drag setting. For barbel fishing this usually means just enough to prevent the force of the current from taking line off the spool.

This feature is particularly useful when bolt rigging for barbel as we are all aware of how quickly a barbel can pull a rod off its rests when bolt-rigging baits. The Baitrunner system acts as a buffer as much as anything. By snapping over the bale arm as a barbel begins tearing line off the spool, the spool is re-engaged and allows the barbel to be played conventionally against the clutch. The Baitrunner system was originally designed for predator fishing but the system can be incorporated in the barbel angler's repertoire quite successfully, although centrepins remain the best option under these circumstances.

Centrepins are in a league of their own when it comes to the much-neglected practice of trotting for barbel, as well as freelining and trundling for them. Although centrepins are disregarded by many as being aesthetically pleasing but rather impractical for most of the time, more and more barbel anglers are finding them to be not only highly pleasing to use, but also that their practicality often outshines fixed spool reels under a surprisingly large number of circumstances. If you have never played a big barbel on a centrepin using braided, non-stretch line in an autumn spate, you have denied yourself one of barbel angling's greatest joys.

MAIN LINES

The importance of making the correct choice of line for barbel angling is without doubt greater than in any other branch of coarse angling. The days of seeing line purely in terms of breaking strain are over; so much more is possible with modern lines.

Barbel anglers must consider the effect of the current on the choice of line. We have to consider its visibility and colour, its diameter, strength, abrasion resistance, memory, tensile strength and wet knot strength. Modern technology has blessed us with great advances in the quality, choice and adaptability of lines. If used in the correct circumstances they can revolutionize your barbel fishing.

Line falls into two distinct categories: nylon and HPPE. The best nylon (or mono) lines are made in the United States and the qualities so vital in a good line for barbel are all to be found in these: Berkley Big Game, XL (extra limp), XT (extra tough) and Silver Thread AN40.

Correct line choice is vital for a swim such as this.

Abrasion resistance is a much used term when discussing quality line. Abrasion resistance means the ability of a line to withstand nicks, friction, flat spots and general wear. Lines with a high abrasion resistance such as Berkley or Silver Thread were originally developed for the rigours of constant casting and retrieval by hard-working American lure anglers, but have since been used in the UK for the same kind of fishing, as well as for fishing snag-ridden swims, casting and retrieving leads over gravel bars or fishing in any sort of rocky or snaggy terrain. Barbel anglers would be wise to use such a line for all their fishing as any swim is capable of damaging line.

The Berkley XL line also has its place in the barbel angler's tackle bag since its extra limpness lends itself far more readily to freelining or trundling large baits through known barbel runs as well as to presenting smaller offerings on the float. The limpness of this line allows it to peel off the spool more readily than its stiffer contemporaries and it also makes a useful hooklength. Berkley XL line will not offer a major advantage under the circumstances outlined but it will give you an edge that might put one or two

Fishing with Berkley Trilene XT in a fast swim.

extra fish on the bank for you. When manufacturers talk of line possessing a low 'memory' they mean the line's lack of ability to kink, curl up or react to stress. For instance, if nylon line is pulled between a tightly clamped finger and thumb nail it will curl. HPPE lines do not react in this way and therefore possess no memory. All nylon lines have some degree of memory and the less they have the better they will perform.

Tensile strength refers to the ability of a line to maintain its strength under tension. Many cheaper lines are short of this ability and will snap if they are jerked under even a small amount of pressure – for example, when playing a big barbel close in.

The diameter of a line can have a profound effect on whether a barbel-holding area can be fished or not. As the barbel fisher's year progresses into the autumn, with the subsequent increase in river levels and flow, the line diameter that was suitable for the summer swims ceases to be so as the increase in flow pulls the terminal tackle out of position because of extra pressure on the mainline. Many anglers will increase the weight of their feeders or leads in an effort to hold position. On many of the larger rivers leads of up to 5oz (140g) have been used with some success but these tactics can be modified with a lower diameter line.

What many anglers fail to appreciate is that an increase in current velocity does little in the way of directly moving a dead weight such as a lead bomb. It is the pressure of the increased velocity of current on the line that causes the angler's terminal tackle to move out of position. To underestimate the importance of line diameter can be the difference between catching barbel or not for several weeks. The reason for this is simple: barbel feed with greater gusto in high, warm, coloured water than in any other condition. This does not necessarily mean that they will move swims and so what was an easily fishable swim during normal summer conditions might become unfishable using the same line when the river rises by a couple of feet. This problem is due solely to the increase of water pressure on the line.

On many occasions such as these the current will move a lead fished on a 12lb b.s. main line away from where you want to fish, whereas an 8lb b.s. line will offer substantially less resistance to the current and can often allow you to fish exactly where you wish. It is the decrease in line diameter, not breaking strain, that is offering less resistance. The thinner the line, the less pressure there is on the submerged part of it. It therefore offers less resistance and has less chance of dragging the bait away from your chosen fishing position. The merest fraction of a millimetre taken off 10 yards (9m) or so of submerged line strung out in the current will amount to a substantial area of resistance that has immediately been removed.

There comes a point where it is not possible to decrease further the diameter or breaking strain of the line. Most barbel anglers would feel unhappy about fishing with a line of less than 6lb b.s., but there are some options for the angler who cannot hold position with a large feeder or lead on a line of this strength. First, there are the manufactured nylon lines with a very low diameter. Drennan Double Strength was for a long time the brand leader. On an 8lb b.s. spool it has the equivalent diameter of a standard 4lb b.s. nylon line. It does have the disadvantage that it is non-stretch and can

One of the incredibly strong small-diameter HPPE lines now available to the barbel angler.

therefore be very unforgiving when you are playing a powerful fish close in. Its knot strength is also suspect and great care has to be taken when knotting it. Lines such as Diawa Shinobi or Ashima tend to be a good compromise between Double Strength and a conventional Maxima-type line in terms of diameter and performance.

While a reduction in line diameter is a far more efficient way of holding a bait in position than increasing the size of the lead, it is not advisable if the line choice is suspect. The answer is to use an HPPE (ultra-thin diameter braid) line. These modern braids open up a whole new world in presenting a bait in fast, high water where conventional nylon cannot be used. No nylon line can compete with the toughness of these braids, which are made from Spectra (the material used for bullet-proof vests). Neither can any nylon compete with their abrasion resistance, limpness and total lack of memory. There are many varieties on the market, with Newtech Power Cable perhaps combining these features with value for money better than any. Other excellent brands include Iron Thread and Gorilla Braid. These HPPE lines are only to be used as main lines and not hooklengths, as the extremely tough and almost wire-like HPPE can cause damage to the mouth of a fish.

The table below compares the different types of HPPE line with nylon line of equivalent diameter. The total amount of resistance to the 10lb b.s. Power Cable is one-third of the resistance that the current exerts upon 6lb b.s.

Breaking strains of Newtech Power Cable HPPE compared with nylon lines of similar diameter.

- 10lb b.s Power Cable – equivalent in diameter to 2lb b.s nylon
- 20lb b.s Power Cable – equivalent in diameter to 6lb b.s nylon
- 30lb b.s Power Cable – equivalent in diameter to 7lb b.s nylon

---

nylon line – the minimum that sensible barbel anglers would use. On large, powerful rivers this makes a great difference and otherwise inaccessible areas in high water conditions become fishable again. This has put many extra barbel on the bank for those anglers who have had the foresight to exploit this new form of line.

Using flat (as opposed to circular) braid is a mistake. In river fishing the action of the current always causes the line to flip round and show its flat side to the flow, rendering it ten times worse than nylon. Check that the HPPE line you buy is not flat, like Leeda Outcast for example.

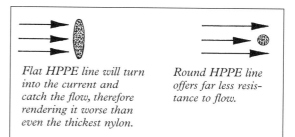

Flat HPPE line will turn into the current and catch the flow, therefore rendering it worse than even the thickest nylon.

Round HPPE line offers far less resistance to flow.

The small diameter of these lines is only one of their advantages. Their resistance to any form of abrasion is perhaps their greatest attribute. Try this simple experiment. Select a length of ordinary, everyday nylon line as used by most anglers, some equivalent breaking strain Berkley Trilene XT and finally some Power Cable or any other brand of HPPE. Begin by rubbing the ordinary line up and down something like the edge of a workbench or a desk and count how many times you can do this before the line breaks. Repeat the process with the XT line and you will see that it takes a lot longer to break it than the standard nylon line, a lot longer. Repeat the process once more with an HPPE of the same breaking strain and be prepared for a long wait. The results of this experiment speak for themselves – it is no surprise that barbel anglers are finding these HPPE lines increasingly useful. The final advantage of braided lines is their lack of stretch, which can be used to considerable

The strength of braid can give so much confidence when playing barbel close to snags.

benefit under the correct circumstances. HPPE lines stretch to a maximum of 5 per cent whereas traditional nylon lines fluctuate between 25 and 30 per cent.

The development of braided lines for lure fishing in the United States demanded a more direct contact with a taking fish. Nylon line with its 25 to 30 per cent stretch does the angler no favours in setting the hook. There are occasions where the elasticity of nylon acts as a very useful shock absorber – for instance, those vicious bites close in, or when hooking a barbel on a small river with the subsequent fight occurring close to or beneath the rod tip.

On larger rivers this elasticity can work against the angler as it not only cushions the strike but helps to mask the original bite as

well. Many barbel bites are missed because the angler did not know that there was a bite in the first place. In the autumn and winter when the rivers carry extra water and debris, detection can become impossible. HPPE significantly reduces this problem for the simple reason that it does not stretch to any great degree and puts you in more direct contact with the fish.

HPPE also helps on occasions when bites appear bold but are unhittable. There can be any number of reasons for this but the most common one is that the angler is attempting to straighten out a large bow in a line caused by the current. There is little or no pressure on the hook point because of the springiness of the nylon line and barbel that are wary will drop the bait as soon as they feel the slightest drag. A non-stretch HPPE line becomes a considerable advantage here, as the strike sets the hook and does not stretch the line. Try fishing a standard nylon line alongside a braided one – conditions permitting – and keep a count of which rod gives the more exaggerated bites and subsequently hooks the more barbel. It will be the HPPE line.

When you are playing a barbel on HPPE the whole sensation takes some getting used to and may at first feel a little wild! Every head shake, every twist of the body, every thrust of the tail is transmitted onto the rod top. A springy nylon takes a lot of this away. With HPPE you are head to head with the barbel, which is extremely exciting. You will need to set your clutch somewhat softer than with nylon because of the absence of the nylon shock absorber.

Another extremely important aspect of non-stretch HPPE is the profound effect that it has on the art of touch legering. One American reviewer of the new breed of braid went a little over the top by stating that you will be able to feel it if a fish breathes on the line! However, HPPE does transform touch legering and brings the barbel a lot closer to you in the sense that you are in direct contact with what is occurring at the other end of the tackle. It is again a useful experiment to fish with nylon and then with HPPE. Wait for an occasion where the

This barbel snagged me three times in a sunken tree, yet still the HPPE held out.

barbel are feeding hard, touch leger for a while with nylon and then switch to HPPE. If you originally thought nylon was sensitive, then you will be amazed at the phenomenal sensitivity that HPPE offers. You will feel things that do not even register themselves on the most sensitive of quivertips, and many barbel are caught by anglers who strike at the merest flicker to the quivertip or the faintest tremble on the line.

Nylon tends to lend itself more to summer angling when the rivers are running lower and clearer, and the diameter of the line is not working against your presentation. Lack of line colouration and visibility becomes the most important consideration here, as the summer rivers will mostly be running low and clear. What appears bright and highly visible on the bank will not necessarily be so to barbel in their aquatic environment. Many American imports appear quite garish but whereas a bright white line will become invisible under the water one of their bright greens, for example, is barely visible when fished among a weed-bed.

A line will usually be off the bottom, so it is important to consider its appearance to the fish. Carp anglers can pin their line to the bot-

tom by using a back lead but this is not always an option open to the barbel angler. Line camouflage and colour are often of prime consideration, especially when the fish are jittery. Barbel in general might not be particularly tackle-shy but there are many individuals that have developed an extra awareness – perhaps because of angling pressure or superior intelligence. The relative invisibility of modern nylon lines is a great aid to presentation in clear water and in this situation gives them the edge over HPPE. As the rivers begin to colour up and their levels rise, not only does the diameter become relevant but the high visibility of HPPE, sometimes a disadvantage during the summer, becomes far less of a drawback.

HPPE is far more buoyant than nylon and takes a lot longer to sink. This behaviour does not help the barbel angler, who might well need to present a bait hard on the bottom and will want the line to sink and settle as quickly as possible. This can be achieved by treating the line with a sinking compound, which is sprayed onto the spool of line.

The importance of line cannot be underestimated; for barbel fishing it can often be the

Granite Juice is essential for line care and coats the line with an abrasion-resistant skin.

Selection of proven hooklengths. Braid offers many advantages.

most important decision to be made on the day. While an angler will think nothing of switching baits, methods or swims in an effort to improve results, very few consider a change of line, which can not only give a massive improvement in presentation, but make previously inaccessible areas eminently fishable.

While modern day lines require almost no maintenance they should nevertheless be stored out of direct sunlight when not in use. The most successful barbel anglers change their lines on a regular basis.

HOOKLENGTHS

Hooklengths are of no less importance than the main line. The correct choice of hooklength will dictate whether a barbel will accept the hookbait as safe. A line is only as strong as its weakest point, and this point is usually somewhere in the end rig section of the tackle, so it pays to take as much care as possible in choosing correctly. It makes little sense to fish with HPPE line and then to use a nylon hooklink, which not only weakens the set-up but hinders good bait presentation as well. All anglers require the best possible presentation of their bait. As nylon line is much stiffer than braid, a braided hooklength will allow a bait to behave far more naturally than a bait attached to a nylon hooklength. A bait behaving differently to all the free offerings surrounding it will be eyed suspiciously by a barbel who has felt the steel of a sharp hook before.

The most commonly used hooklengths are those marketed by Kryston Advanced Angling under the name of Merlin or Silkworm. They have breaking strains of 4 to 25lb. Coupled with their amazingly fine diameter, subtlety, abrasion resistance and high knot strength, these attributes allow them go a long way in presenting a bait in the most natural way possible.

KNOTS

It is imperative that the correct choice of knot is made for tying hooks and swivels as well as nylon to these hooklengths and HPPE. The old-fashioned blood knot, never the most reliable of knots for nylon, is virtually useless for knotting braided hooklengths and HPPE. Known as a strangulation knot, the blood knot, if tied in braid, cuts into itself and will break at a considerably lower breaking strain than the main line.

Two proven alternatives exist for braid: the Double Grinner or Uni-knot and the Palomar knot. Both these knots are well known for their reliability. However, they still require checking as sometimes tying them can for some unknown reason render them not quite as strong as they should be. The best way of testing a knot, as well as bedding it down, is to grip the shank of the hook tightly with a pair of pliers and exert pressure on the hooklength with a steady and slowly increasing pull. By gripping the shank of the hook all the pressure is concentrated on the knot, and this will reveal whether it is reliable and ready for use.

A final touch to these knots, which are equally as reliable in nylon, is to dab on a tiny blob of rig resin. This not only makes the knot almost totally reliable, it also seals it and protects it from damage, stress and wear. Prolonged immersion in water can cause some glues to soften, so a tiny blob of Kryston Rig-a-Mawtis resin applied over the glued knot increases the protection and strength still further. This solution takes six to eight hours to set properly.

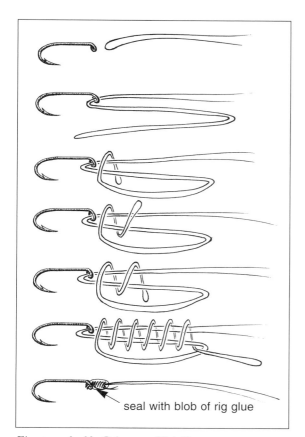

seal with blob of rig glue

Five turn double Grinner or Uni-Knot.

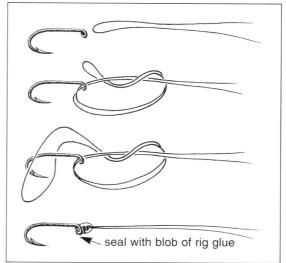

seal with blob of rig glue

Palomar Knot.

When tying these knots in nylon, the friction caused on the line can often damage or weaken it if the line is not moistened first. Also remember that tying a knot damages pre-stretched lines more than conventional ones, so always take extra care.

LINE ACCESSORIES

The technical advances made in improving line quality and choice in recent years have spawned a number of line accessories that can be of immense use to the barbel angler. Line floatants sold in a spray-on form are useful for trotting baits through beds of streamer weed and over gravel runs.

While the wonderful subtlety of the modern braided hooklengths greatly enhances bait presentation, the limpness of the line can cause such hooklengths to tangle. Many barbel anglers will be in a position where they need to make an accurate cast to a visible feeding area and know that they will only have one chance before spooking the fish. There is nothing more frustrating than making an accurate cast that does not spook the barbel only for the braided hooklength to tangle on its way to the hot spot. It therefore pays to treat the hooklength with an anti-tangle gel. This stiffens the braid of the hooklength, but once submerged it dissolves leaving the hooklength in its original limp form.

Another particularly useful line accessory available to the barbel angler is another Kryston product: Granite Juice. Barbel love snags and snaggy swims, which can sometimes be a little off-putting. Granite Juice coats the line with a layer of protection that increases the abrasion resistance considerably (up to 300 per cent, it is claimed). Just as a small diameter HPPE can make unfishable areas into fishable ones, this product can swing the possibility of extracting a barbel from a veritable jungle into a likelihood. Many barbel live behind sharp rocks and boulders in certain rivers, which are a waste of time trying for with nylon, but a strong HPPE coated with Granite Juice will give you the best possible chance of landing such barbel, even if they do take you round and behind a boulder hell-bent on parting the line. These days I treat all my lines with generous amounts of Granite Juice, simply because there is no reason not to. One again it is that all-important edge that we have to strive for; Granite Juice gives that edge in all barbel fishing circumstances.

HOOKS

Barbel should be fished for using carp hooks; do not forsake strength in design for lightness. There are a number of exceptionally strong and reliable carp hooks in sizes 4 to 10 that are ideally suited for barbel and will cover all eventualities. These are sold under the names of Partridge (Jack Hilton's), Owner, Gold Label Penetrator 1 and 2, Fox Specialist Carp Series 1, 2 and 3, Drennan Starpoints and Drennan Continental Boilie Hooks. The lightest of these is without doubt the Starpoint, the only one to have been designed with a fluted point, which is said to increase penetration. The relative lightness of the hook works as an advantage when presenting small particle baits but its chemically etched point renders it not quite as reliable in snaggy hook-and-hold situations.

Chemically etched needle point hooks, as well as the Starpoints, which are undoubtedly extremely sharp, are not quite as reliable as the manufacturers would have us believe. Barbel hooked at close range, as many are, will often come off because of the hook tearing out. It has taken a lot of lost barbel for this to sink in, but a number of disappointed anglers now shun such hooks. Whatever the precise cause, chemically sharpened hooks cause unreliable hookholds for close-in scraps with angry barbel.

The Partridge-made Jack Hilton carp hooks are solid and reliable and made to a classic design. They have landed countless barbel and carp over the years and have no obvious flaws. They have straight eyes, are black in colour and exceptionally strong, and are the most versatile barbel hooks currently available. These and the other hooks listed are a little thicker in the wire than chemically sharpened hooks and all are undoubtedly more suitable to general purpose barbel fishing than the chemically etched models.

Hooks such as the Gold Label Penetrators, Fox Series or Drennan Continental Boilie Hooks are designed to stay in and rarely pull out. Gold Label Penetrator 1 hooks are not as thick in the wire as the Penetrator 2. The Fox Series 1, 2 and 3 follow the same increasing thickness and strength scale. Hooks from these two stables in the over 1 class are perfectly matched for hit-and-hold situations and do not straighten or come adrift without good reason.

Many anglers are reluctant to use big, thick in the wire, heavy hooks for fear of marring bait presentation because of their seemingly excessive weight. However, it is easy to counterbalance the weight of a hook by using Superglue to fix a tiny piece of black rig foam onto the shank to negate the hook's excessive weight.

All these hooks are manufactured to be exceptionally sharp but a few casts and retrieves over typical barbel gravels can cause terrible damage to the points. Constant atten-

tion must be paid to ensuring that hookpoints have not bevelled over. Check every hook as it is taken from the packet, as the odd dud manages to get through the factory checks.

Basic stone hook sharpeners leave a lot to be desired and it is better to use one that requires the hook to be passed through two sharpening surfaces at once. These handy little items are sold in game fishing shops and designed for the constant maintenance of trout and salmon flies, but there is no reason why barbel anglers should not be equally hook conscious. These little hook sharpeners can be hung from a waistcoat or jacket or worn round the neck.

While sharpening a hook is the most obvious way of increasing its efficiency it is by no means the only way of doing so. Flattening the barb with a pair of pliers so that only a tiny hump remains will permit the hook to penetrate the mouth of the fish cleanly and easily. A conventional barb not only stops the hook coming out, it also impairs its ability to penetrate in the first place. Nipping down the barb is a perfect compromise, and the removal of a hook modified in this way causes less damage to the mouth of the fish than a standard hook.

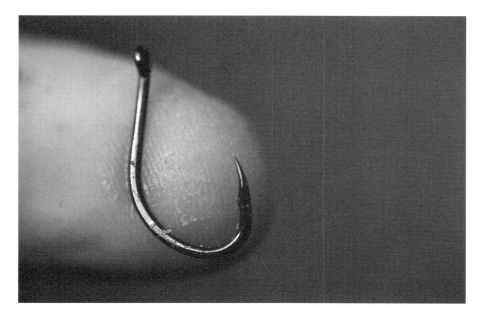

A de-barbed Drennan Continental Boilie Hook – a lethal weapon!

The modern barbel angler will take with him a very large lead selection to the water – all have their place.

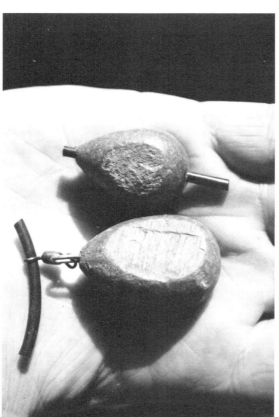

Leads, flattened with a hammer, hug the bottom far better than the ordinary round shape.

LEADS AND BOMBS

The main purpose of a lead is to anchor a bait in the area where the bait is to be fished. The lead should be of sufficient weight and design to do this, despite the pressure of the current on the line.

Most anglers use the standard Arlesey Bomb or variations of it. These are quite unsuitable and were never designed for river fishing in the first place. Most thinking barbel anglers flatten standard bombs and derivatives with the aid of a hammer. There seems little point in fishing a river with a conventionally shaped, rounded Arlesey Bomb because you will need a far heavier lead if it is round and you can never be certain that it will remain precisely where you want it because of its tendency to roll along the bottom.

The best leads for this purpose are the dumpy Korda Pear leads, which graduate from 1 to 4oz (30 to 110g) in half-ounce divisions. The shape of these leads is less prone to tangling than round leads, and they have a smooth finish that reduces wear on the line or the hooklength. When these leads are flattened they sit on the river bed better than any other lead I know. I am also particularly fond of Korda's In-line Pear leads – they come in the same sizes and are practically tangle-free. Provided no snags are close to hand, they make a better and certainly simpler rig than the standard breakaway. Care needs to be taken when flattening these in-line leads as it is easy to close the hole that runs through the centre. Insert a thick piece of wire into the tubing to make sure that the line can be threaded through when the time comes to mount the lead on the main line. Both these sets of leads come with their weights imprinted on the side, so vital when a lead quickly needs switching in the middle of the night.

The use of rounded Arlesey bombs is less of a problem during the summer, because of the lower current velocity, but as the rivers rise it takes far less lead to hold the bottom consistently with a flattened lead than a standard rounded lead. Ideally, all river leads that are intended to hold their position in the flow, in summer as well as winter, should be flattened. By law, however, leads of under 1oz (28g) should be made of an alternative material to lead. Many bombs of under an ounce are made of steel, which is far harder to flatten than lead – though small weights of this class can only be fished close to the near bank or in water often slower than average where it does not matter what shape the lead is. Flat, circular-shaped weights manufactured by Dinsmore are available in weights under 1oz and remain more versatile than conventional rounded bombs.

Given the clear water and often close proximity in which barbel are fished for, particularly in the summer, it can be very useful to camouflage the lead with a coating powder. The best available is distributed by Gold Label in black, green, brown and mottled colours. Wary barbel will know that a lead spells trouble in a swim, and the simple expedient of disguising it will prevent that from happening. This little edge can mean the difference between a barbel and a blank day.

BAITDROPPERS

This item of tackle is extremely important to the barbel angler. From the precise positioning of hempseed and sample baits in the summer to the introduction of larger quantities of meat and paste baits in high, coloured water, the baitdropper is indispensable.

Standard shop-bought Thamesley baitdroppers work quite well but are too small. They need to be cast into the swim on too many occasions to allow sufficient bait to be introduced. The capacity of the largest Thamesley baitdropper is 14 to the pint (24 to the litre) – far too small for barbel work. Apart from the extra work in casting and retrieval, particularly when a number of swims are being prepared, there seems little point in disturbing a swim any more than necessary. For barbel, the fewer casts that it takes to introduce the bait into the swim the better, regardless of the size of the dropper itself.

The answer is to build a baitdropper yourself. Made from tuna cans of 100 or 200g capacity, these home-made droppers will contain 6 and 3 to the pint (10 and 5 to the litre) respectively. To be able to deposit hempseed in significantly fewer casts is a major advantage in time and in minimizing swim disturbance.

The larger the baitdropper the heavier it is when full of bait, especially hempseed. It is therefore advisable to use a separate rod – a piking rod or something similar is ideal, especially for the 200g size – with a few yards of the strongest line you can obtain on the reel to make sure that you get the dropper back every time.

A loaded baitdropper ready to hit the swim.

Not only is this set-up easier to use, it also allows the angler to continue introducing bait at will throughout the session without having to break into the rigs that are being fished. If it is necessary to introduce bait into a swim while the swim is being fished, the spare rod allows this to be done without having to retrieve the hook-baits.

How to Make a Baitdropper

Components:
- 200g or 100g empty tuna can
- 2mm stiff plastic sheet
- 3mm welding rod
- Five 3mm pop rivets
- Old car tyre inner tube
- 2oz (55g) in-line carp fishing lead bomb
- Size 1/0 swivel

Tools:
- Hammer
- Heavy-duty scissors
- Hole punch
- File
- 75mm nail
- Drill with 3mm and 4mm drill bit
- Pop rivet gun
- Matt black or olive green paint and small paintbrush
- Pliers
- Wire cutters
- Emery paper

2. *Place the open end of the tin onto plastic sheeting and using a felt-tip pen draw round the edge of the tin and then cut out the impression with heavy-duty scissors thus creating the lid of the dropper.*

3. *Drill two 3mm holes 1cm apart at a point 5mm down from the rim of the tin and then drill two further holes into the plastic disc 1cm apart and 5mm from the edge.*

1. *Discard the top of an open tin, remove the paper wrapping and with a hammer and nail puncture the tin with several holes.*

4. *Take a piece of inner-tubing and cut out with the scissors a rectangle 3cm x 2cm and round off the corners. This will become the hinge.*

5. Push out four holes in each corner of the hinge with a hole-punch for later attachment to the tin with rivets.

6. Attach the tin to the round plastic disc by pop-riveting the hinge to both tin and plastic through the previously drilled holes.

7. Snip off a 23cm length from the welding rod and drill a 4mm hole through the top and bottom of the tin at exactly half depth for later insertion of the welding rod.

8. Insert the welding rod through both holes and flatten over the top end of the rod.

9. Bend the rod to create two right angles so that it overlaps the plastic disc therefore keeping it closed.

10. Slowly drill out the centre of the 2oz lead with a 3mm drill bit and slide the 2oz lead onto the bottom of the rod. Flatten the end of the rod and push the bomb back so that it jams onto the flattened end.

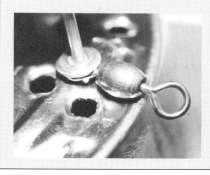

11. Pop-rivet a large 1.0 size swivel onto top of tin on the perforated side which is the attachment for the line when in use. With the emery paper smooth off any rough edges or sharp sides and then paint the dropper with two or three coats of paint ensuring that the paint, having dried, does not effect the smooth operation of the device. Finally paint on the dropper measures of capacity for future reference.

The dropper finally sees the hemp bucket.

A barbel safely gathered in the soft mesh of a deep net.

These home-made baitdroppers, made and designed by the exceptionally successful barbel angler Colonel Goram, are worth their weight in gold and fully justify the time and trouble that is required in their construction. An evening spent in the close season making up a few of both sizes is wisely spent and the panel shows how it is done.

LANDING NETS

There are three major considerations: strength, size and appropriate mesh. Clearly the barbel angler requires a robust design, but because of the nature of barbel fishing it should not be too large and therefore too heavy in the current. A large net with too fine a mesh is very awkward to use in a strong flow – especially when a barbel is being drawn over a submerged net, only for the angler to find that it wants to go on another searing run! Choose a net with the largest, knotless mesh you can find but with a finer mesh at the bottom to protect the fish, especially the vulnerable dorsal fin, which is prone to catching in too large a mesh as it writhes for its freedom at the bottom. Also, try to find a net with the longest handle available, as barbel often fight their hardest when they are being brought from their deep glides into shallower water near the bank. A long telescopic handle will allow the angler to net them just that little bit sooner, which is certainly good from the angler's point of view – and even better for the fish, given their habit of exhausting themselves during a long fight.

The 'Rods High Tripod' in action.

ROD RESTS

One item of tackle taken for granted is the rod rest. The barbel angler should not only see this device as a means of supporting rods, but also as a means of elevating as much line as possible out of the water to reduce pressure on the line. By far the most suitable device for this purpose is the Leeda Rods High Tripod. A cross between a Rod Pod and a Swimfeeder Rod Rest, the Rods High Tripod was designed for still-water carping in an effort to combat marginal weed, close in gravel bars and anything else that required rods to be fished high.

At its tallest setting this tripod allows the rods to be placed so that the reels can sit at shoulder height. This lifts a tremendous amount of line

out of the water and this device has been directly responsible for my being able to fish a swim and catch many barbel from it, when someone fishing at a conventional height was having his line constantly swept away from several ravenously feeding barbel. This unfortunate soul fishing with the usual bankstick and quivertip rod rest head was fairly tearing his hair out as eighteen barbel of up to 9lb were grassed in four hours. On that occasion the barbel were caught by the tripod, not by me.

Furthermore, the tripod is very versatile and can act as a conventional rod rest for two quivertip rods when it is not necessary to point the rods skywards. It is an item of tackle for larger rivers, but its value is also significant on smaller rivers when they are in full flow and causing presentation problems.

More conventional rod rest heads are perfectly suitable for most summer barbel fishing. The unique quality of the Drennan Quivertip Head, which falls into this category, is that numerous positions are available so that the quivertip can be positioned with just enough of an arc to indicate the sensitive pulls and plucks so typical of a nervous, edgy barbel.

THERMOMETERS

A thermometer is an essential addition to any barbel angler's tackle box during the autumn and winter. Its importance to the year-round barbel angler is so vital that to fish without one for much of the season makes as much sense as fishing without bait. The practical application and use of the thermometer is discussed in detail under 'Water Temperature' in Chapter 1.

UMBRELLAS, CLOTHING AND CHAIRS

There is no question that the warm and comfortable angler is not only inclined to fish longer, but will almost certainly fish much more effectively. Some creature comforts will

The multi-grooved rod rest allows for many rod positions – very useful when quivertipping.

An umbrella makes winter fishing so much more comfortable.

My one-piece made the ten-hour wait at least warm and comfortable.

undoubtedly help the angler to put more barbel on the bank.

Few anglers enjoy fishing beneath an umbrella. However, an umbrella is an important item of equipment for the autumn or winter barbel angler whose optimum conditions are wind and rain. There are a lot of cheap and inadequate umbrellas on the market; the most robust is probably the 50in Steadfast Wavelock. This model is rather large and therefore catches more wind than smaller umbrellas. To counteract this, the insertion of two storm rods to stabilize the umbrella in strong winds is the answer. A bit of thought here can make or break a fishing session and two banksticks screwed into the storm rods, together with two adjustable bankstick stabilizers, will support the umbrella through thick and thin. Further consolidation can be made by the replacement of the rather inadequate standard central pole

with a far more robust one made by Gardner. Apart from keeping the wind and rain off, fishing behind an umbrella is always warmer and the rods are more stable in windy conditions.

Appropriate clothing is of vital importance and will have a bearing on the amount of barbel that the prospective night fisher will catch. A good quality one-piece such as that marketed by Wychwood or Rod Hutchinson and a standard pair of Skeetex Moon Boots are essential for a comfortable winter day or night of fishing.

Choosing appropriate gloves or mittens is also vital. Cold, numb and wet fingers make it difficult to tie reliable hooks, fiddle around with complicated rigs and touch leger effectively. Woollen gloves or mittens are worse than useless, as they will not dry once they are wet and consequently make your hands colder than they would be without any covering at all. Some of the best are Efgeeco neoprene mittens, which are made from the same material as divers' wetsuits. They insulate not only against the cold, but against the wet too. There are several designs available; those with the thumb and forefinger coverings replaced by fold-over flaps are the most practical for barbel fishing. These mittens also come with small grips on the palms, which aid your grasp of the rod handle in wet and windy weather.

Carrilon gloves (also made from neoprene) are a good alternative. Carrilon also make neoprene socks, which are particularly useful for anglers who do not like wearing moon boots or who spend a long time in the river wearing thigh boots.

Lengthy hours spent fishing should be done from a comfortable chair. Fox International make extremely comfortable and fully adjustable chairs that are ideally suited to the uneven and often inhospitable environment of the river bank. Very often a match-fishing tackle box cushion serves as a perfectly adequate substitute where it is not possible to find a site for a chair. A cushion placed on the ground in each swim is certainly a lighter and more portable option than a large chair.

TERMINAL TACKLE AND ACCESSORIES

What we have discussed thus far forms the backbone of our approach. Whilst this framework is essential for consistent angling efficiency, it is all the seemingly minor tackle items that give the true edge and deadliness that separates successful barbel fishing from failure.

Inside the Complete Barbel Angler's Tackle Bag

The ideal tackle bag is a large, capacious rucksack that enables the barbel angler to carry all the necessary tackle long distances and between numerous swims with the minimum of effort and comfort. Kevin Nash, Fox and Wychwood Tackle make luggage of sufficient quality to last and of sufficient size to carry all the tackle and bait the barbel angler is ever likely to need.

The table below gives a list of tackle items that the discerning barbel angler should always have to hand. They will cover virtually all barbel fishing situations. References to particular brand names and manufacturers are made solely because of their quality and proven track record.

- Tubs of split shot containing BB, AAA and SSG shot for trotting or added weight for trundling or very light legering links
- Rig tube of 1, 1.5, 2 and 3mm for anti-tangle rigs, attaching bombs to main lines or bolt rigs
- Hook sharpening stone
- Line floatant spray for applying to line intended for trotting
- Kryston Heavy Metal Rig Putty for weighing down pop-up baits
- Kryston Snag Free Super Putty for snag fishing
- Kryston Silkworm Braided Hooklength 8lb b.s and 12lb b.s for neutral buoyancy hook lengths
- Kryston Super-Nova Ultra Braid Hooklength 15lb b.s for all-purpose hook lengths
- Kryston Meltdown Dissolving Cord for PVA stringer rigs
- Gold Label Rig Foam in black, green, yellow and red for particle or boilie pop-up rigs
- Gardner Polystyrene 5 and 10mm Rig Foam for critically balancing meat baits and boilies
- Kryston Bogey Particle Fixer for presting hempseed or tares on the hook
- Starlite or Drennan Night Light Isotopes for night fishing with quivertips
- Size 20 hooks to nylon for deadbait snatching
- Optima 10lb b.s Power Gum for feeder rigs and stop knots

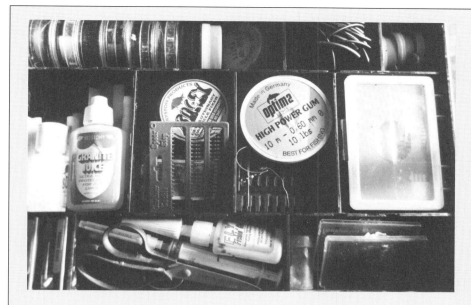

A typical tackle box for terminal tackle components.

- Rubber beads for knot protection and hard plastic beads for feeder rigs
- John Roberts low-resistance leger rings for free-running leger rigs
- Rig board for pre-tied rigs of assorted lengths of braided and nylon hooklengths
- Selection of swivels in sizes 7 to 10 for basic rigs
- Drennan swivel beads for bomb and feeder attachment
- Four spare Beatalites for quivertips
- Tape measure for measuring barbel
- Fine stitching needles for hempseed and hair rigs (back up to Bogey in case of bait or hands becoming wet)
- Shrink tube for hair rigs and sleeving off swivels
- Float stops for creating a 'bite' for Heavy Metal rig putty
- John Roberts or Gold Label Helicopter rigs
- 1lb b.s hair rig line (thinner and less damaging to hempseed, maggots and tares than braid)
- Selection of darning needles for mounting above
- Drennan swivel sleeves
- Plummets
- Float rubbers

- Selection of flat leads to 5oz (140g) or more in a Gold Label Paddy Bag
- Large disgorger (usually for nuisance chub)
- Drennan long baiting needle for stringers
- Scissors for cutting braid
- Syringe for balancing lobworms with air and precise flavouring of bait or groundbait mixes
- Rig resin for sealing knots and stiffening braid
- Superglue for any quick repairs to equipment
- Gardner hair rig needle
- Scissors for trimming nylon line
- Gardner boilie drills of 5 and 10mm for making buoyant boilies and meat baits
- Kryston anti-tangle gel for braided hook lengths
- Kryston Greased Lightning for protecting and improving nylon line for float fishing
- Kryston Klin-ik for treatment after hook removal
- Kryston Multi-strand for combi-links
- Maglite torch with red filter for rig changes at night
- Assortment of Drennan Loafer floats and balsa-bodied Avon-style floats for trotting
- 3 to the pint and 6 to the pint (5 and 10 to

the litre) home-made baitdroppers
- Gold Label Ulti-mat for safe unhooking of barbel
- Gold Label weigh or photography sling for the big ones
- Gold Label pike or barbel tunnel for safe retention of the record!
- Kryston Rig-A-Mawtis for permanently stiffening braids and knot protection
- Two spare spools each of 6, 8 and 12lb b.s Berkley XT or Silver Thread AN40 nylon line for main lines
- Spare spool of 6 and 8lb b.s Berkley XL nylon line for trotting and hooklengths
- Two spare spools each of 20 and 30lb b.s Power Cable HPPE line
- Thermometer for taking autumn and winter temperatures
- Can opener (for cans of sweetcorn, hot dog sausages)
- Large torch for packing up and safety at night
- Hook wallet
- Nut drill for hair-rigging pellets
- Rod Hutchinson PVA tubes for mass particle introduction
- Drennan Leger Stops
- Stanley knife blades for trimming off rig foam for perfectly balanced rigs
- Note book and pencil for recording of barbel caught and multi-swim preparation notes
- Drennan or Fox brass rings as alternatives to swivels
- Mobile phone for emergencies
- Digital weighing scales
- Selection of Drennan quivertipping rod rest heads

6 BAITS AND ATTRACTANTS

A bait selection for a winter's day.

While barbel can be choosy when it comes to bait and are capable of being caught on almost anything, their activities in relation to bait tend to occur within the parameters of the following. It is very rare for a barbel to ignore all these baits yet be caught on something else:

- Pastes and boilies
- Meats
- Lobworms
- Sweetcorn
- Hempseed
- Maggots and casters
- Cheese
- Deadbaits
- Caddis

The general tendency with barbel baits is that in the summer months, with clearer and warmer water, the best response is to natural baits and particles. In the autumn and winter, with coloured, cooler water, the non-natural, larger, flavoured and aromatic baits tend to be more successful. In this chapter each of these major baits will be reviewed in turn, as will some lesser used but potentially excellent baits.

It is a mistake to generalize about baits. While you might find that on one river, for instance, sweetcorn is by far the best bait, do not assume that sweetcorn is the best bait on any other river. Treat each individual river as an unknown quantity and experiment accordingly. Although rivers do have many bait traits in common, no two rivers are exactly the same and nor do they all respond in exactly the same way to baits and methods; a successful bait presentation method or combination on one river does not guarantee success on another. Some barbel anglers, for example, experience serious problems with eels constantly taking the bait, and their whole approach to baits is geared around trying to avoid eels by using hempseed-based baits. On the other hand, there are many rivers where eels barely exist in sufficient numbers to trouble the barbel angler at all; what is necessary on one river is often not needed on the next.

If you treat each river as unique and keep an open mind, you will be more successful as a barbel angler than you will be by believing all barbel rivers to be exactly the same. Even the generally accepted qualities of hempseed will not necessarily work on all rivers – barbel can even be seen to bolt at the mere sight of it on some over-fished stretches. Barbel are often a rule unto themselves when it comes to bait – one day all they will feed on is sweetcorn and the next day they will want something completely different, even if they have not been fished for, let alone caught on it. It is vital that the barbel angler rings the changes and is always in a position to use as many alternative baits as possible if sport is slow. The more baits you have access to, the more successful you will be over the course of a season.

PASTES AND BOILIES

Non-natural – requires prior introduction

The effectiveness of many pastes and boilies

relies heavily on the state of mind of the angler using them. If you believe you are fishing with the best bait available, you will naturally fish a lot better with it than with one you have less confidence in. There are many successful users of extremely high quality baits that are wholly complete in the barbel's dietary requirements. These anglers believe that they have the edge – and that is what makes them successful – but an angler with an equal belief in, say, flavoured meat, will never be far behind when fishing for barbel.

All boilies start life as a paste until they are boiled to form the skin that prevents nuisance fish from pecking them to pieces. Baits intended for barbel should not be boiled for more than 15 seconds and often much less. Barbel tend to switch onto soft paste baits more quickly than boilies and certainly barbel prefer soft pastes to hard boilies. Depending on the amount of small nuisance fish around, the softer we can fish a bait the better as far as barbel are concerned.

Barbel will respond to pastes and boilies as well as any species and a growing number of big barbel are being caught on these baits every season. Although not as quick onto a boilie as, say, a carp, the barbel is not far behind and certainly its ability to recognize pastes and boilies as food is in a league above many other species such as the tench, which requires a considerable amount of weaning before fully accepting them as a food source. While barbel do take a little longer than carp to recognize these baits as food, once they do, they take them as avidly as any other bait and the various flavours that appear palatable to barbel seem to take longer to become ineffective than with carp.

Barbel that are used to meat baits in particular, and to a lesser degree cheese or cheesepaste, appear to progress onto boilies quite smoothly, whereas very naive barbel do tend to take a little longer. Barbel tend to respond only to certain flavoured pastes or boilies with any degree of enthusiasm, while many of the most popular carp and tench flavours – especially those that are sweet or fruity – are hopeless bar-

This barbel took an ill-advised liking to Madras flavoured paste.

bel baits. An initial introduction of mini (6mm) or midi (10mm) boilies usually ensures that the barbel switch on to the baits far more quickly than to the introduction of standard (14 to 16mm) or larger sized boilies (18mm or 22mm).

Barbel continue to respond to the same spicy flavours in pastes as they do in any other baits. It is doubtful whether barbel will select one paste or boilie over another because of nutritional content alone; indeed, many is the time that barbel make their selection on the size of the boilie in preference to anything else. There have been many occasions where I have observed a shoal of barbel ignore good-quality standard size boilies of high nutritional value and appear to prefer identically flavoured semolina-based baits (commonly known as crap baits) in a mini or midi boilie size. And many is the time that barbel have ignored pastes or boilies completely in favour of a natural bait, so it pays to keep

pastes and boilies in perspective and be receptive to what the barbel want.

Buying ready-made boilies, bait ingredients and flavours from many tackle shops is a hazardous business, and many of the available products are of poor quality. Trustworthy suppliers, on whose goods I have caught many barbel, include Rod Hutchinson, Nutrabaits and Richworth. Some other suppliers market flavours, baits and ingredients that are on a par with these, so shop around to see what works for you or, more important, what works best where you fish.

A very simple and straightforward mix, using the ingredients given overleaf, makes a superb barbel bait. I have based many of my paste baits on this recipe and it is one in which I have complete confidence. Variations on this basic mix can be the inclusion of an appropriate measure of a flavour in place of the Marmite or Bovril or the proportionate inclu-

---

Straightforward Recipe for Paste Bait

- 1lb of Richworth 50/50 base, Rod Hutchinson Pro Mix 50/50 or Nutrabaits 50/50 Boilie Mix
- 8oz (225g) of ground cat pellets (liver)
- 2 teaspoons of Marmite or Bovril
- 8 size 2 beaten eggs

---

sion of any of the listed powdered flavours or bait ingredients. This bait mix is an excellent basis on which to build and develop using any of the ingredients known to be attractive to barbel. This bait, at least on the rivers I tend to fish, is for some reason comparatively ignored by the chub; while I have indeed caught chub on it I would never consider using it for chub fishing. Its appeal to barbel and its anti-chub qualities make it a very valuable bait indeed on rivers and swims where chub are a nuisance. The baits produced from this mix require no more than about 15 seconds of boiling time; if at all possible I do not boil it at all.

Proven flavours, effective ready-made boilies and other highly attractive bait ingredients that will appeal to barbel are listed in the table opposite, together with their manufacturers. They should be available from all good tackle shops. All these bait ingredients have caught barbel, though some flavours appear to work better on some rivers than others. A good example is that turmeric is superb on the Great Ouse, while barbels' reaction to it on the Wye is lukewarm at best.

Boilie dips made up of two tablespoons (30ml) of Richfish or Feed Inducing Oil and a teaspoon (5ml) of a liquid or powdered flavour of your choice (or a blend) are a further option. See under 'Attractants' at the end of this chapter for more details.

Atomizing neutral boilies – flavouring them with any flavour of your choice – is a superb way of giving ready-made Richworth boilies a flavour that you believe in, whether it be Madras curry, garlic or a blend of anything else. Flavouring neutral boilies gives us the scope to give our own baits a distinctive appeal, and to ensure that the bait is working for us and no-one else. For 1lb (450g) of bait, adding ten 1ml squirts with an atomizer of normal strength liquid flavour to the bag of boilies before freezing them will ensure that the flavour is fully absorbed by the baits as they thaw. It is far better to let baits thaw as slowly as possible, rather than microwaving them. I prefer to let mine thaw slowly in the fridge the night before a session. This ensures a more flavoursome bait.

Powdered flavours available from supermarkets or other spice outlets – such as paprika, turmeric, cayenne pepper, chilli, garlic powder or any form of curry powder – make wonderful additions to the bait. A heaped teaspoon of any of these powdered flavours (or any others along these lines) introduced to the base mix will improve its appeal immensely. Further ingredients that certainly liven up the basic mix are the powdered ingredients – virtually powdered flavours – that are available from bait companies and can be included into the base mix by subtracting 2oz (55g) from the 50/50 base mix and the cat biscuits respectively, and replacing it with 4oz (110g) of liver powder or roast peanut meal. These two powdered ingredients are far superior to all the others, although fish meals now appear to be more appealing to barbel than was first thought.

All these flavours benefit from the use of flavour enhancers, otherwise known as palatants or appetite stimulators. The various types available are all compatible with whatever flavour we intend using: some are compatible with sweet flavours (not of much interest to barbel anglers) while others are designed for more savoury or spicy flavours. I particularly value the inclusion of fish feed oils into a barbel bait as the flow of the river does a wonderful job carrying the enticing, oil-borne flavour of the bait downstream to the barbel.

For the angler who does not have the time or inclination to make pastes or boilies, the shop-bought varieties I have listed do catch a lot of

Proven Bait Ingredients that Appeal to Barbel

Rod Hutchinson

Liquid flavours Shellfish, Madras Curry, Red Hot Chilli, Garlic, Superspice, Ultraspice, Megaspice, Amino Blend Swan Mussel, Crayfish, Hemp, Smelly Cheese, Megawhite Spice, The Liver, Spicy Liver Sausage.
Powdered flavours or bait additives Squid Extract, Mussel Extract, Ultimate Spice Blend, Savoury Liver Powder.
Flavour enhancers (sense appeal concentrates) Savoury, Shellfish, Spice.
Ready mixes Original Ultra Spice, Super Savoury, The Liver Mix, Pro Mix 50/50.

Nutrabaits

Liquid flavours Peanut, Liver, Cheese, Garlic Mint, Caviar, Strawberry Nutrafruit, Tutti-Frutti Nutrafruit.
Powdered flavours or bait additives Green-lipped Mussel, Shrimp, Liver Powder, Liver Attract.
Flavour enhancers (cajouser) and essential oils Spice Cajouser, Clove Terpenes, Madagascar Clove, Black Pepper, Mexican Onion, Spanish Gage, Madagascar Basil, Leek.

Richworth

Liquid flavours Tutti-Frutti, Spice Oriental, Strawberry Cream, Cheese, Blue Cheese, Curry, Hazelnut, Liver, Luncheon Meat, Peanut, Roast Beef, Worm Extract, Freshwater Mussel, Shellfish.
Powdered flavours or ingredients Liver Powder, Roast Peanut Meal, Hazelnut Meal, Robin Red.
Flavour enhancers and oils Multi Flavoured Enhancer, Worm Extract, Hemp Oil, Richfish Oil, Feed Including Oil, Garlic.
Impact boilie dips Liver and Marine, Blue Cheese and Garlic.
Ready mixes Fish Meal Mix, Nut Meal Mix.
Shelf life boilies Minis (6mm): Hemp, Strawberry Cream, Tutti-Frutti. Midis (10mm): Cheese, Fish Meal Mix, Luncheon Meat, Strawberry Cream, Tutti-Frutti. Standard (14mm): Fish Meal Mix, Meatymix, Peanut, Tutti-Frutti, Marine Mix.

barbel. The main drawback is that everyone else has access to them as well. That is why I prefer flavouring my paste baits with a flavour or blend of flavours of my choice or atomizing neutral boilies with the same, virtually unique flavour concoctions.

One recent bait development worth a try has been from Solar Tackle, marketed under the name of The Pellet. These baits come in pellet form in three different sizes as well as a powder. The powder can be used for making the bait up as a boilie or a paste with eggs or water, or as a groundbait or feeder base mix. The three sizes of pellet are 5mm (small), 10 to 12mm (medium) and 16 to 18mm (large) and all three sizes are suitable for barbel at certain times of the year. The manufacturers claim that The Pellet gives fish the total dietary requirements that they require. These pellets have a neutral buoyancy, which is considered to aid presentation.

As well as the three different sizes, The Pellet comes in three flavours: Dairy Cream, Quench and Squid/Octopus. Of the three the last is undoubtedly the favourite among the barbel and several big fish have already been caught on it. The 5mm pellet makes an effective mass particle bait and attractant for summer fishing and an increasingly popular method is to fish a ball of pellet paste over a carpet of 5mm pellets. Pellet paste and the pellets themselves also have many applications in feeder fishing.

There are countless permutations of flavours, powders and mixes available from bait outlets, supermarkets, delicatessens and tackle shops and the scope for experimentation is endless. Anything meaty or spicy will appeal to barbel – it is just a question of finding the right flavours. Catalogues produced by the bait companies listed in the Further Reading section, although rather biased towards carp, certainly make excellent and interesting reading for the barbel angler who wishes to make progress in this fascinating area of bait and bait ingredients.

MEATS

Non-natural – instant

Meats have perhaps accounted for the capture of more barbel than any other bait in recent years and are without doubt the most popular bait in use. The more expensive, better quality tinned meats (such as Chopped Ham with Pork, Bacon Grill and to a lesser extent Spam) are certainly more effective than cheaper luncheon meats. I have found garlic sausage to be an extremely under-rated meat bait and certainly superior to any form of luncheon meat (with the possible exception of Bacon Grill, which still has the ability to out-fish garlic sausage on occasions).

Plumrose's Bacon Grill and Chopped Ham with Pork can be fished very successfully straight from the can, and should be diced into uniformly square cubes on the day of the session. They offer a very effective, relatively cheap and durable bait that works best in coloured water. Such is the popularity of this basic bait that there are a lot of stretches that do not produce quite as many barbel on it as they once did, due mainly to the quantity of barbel that have been caught on it. Where this is the case we have so many other options available to us with meat that its effectiveness can be prolonged for a considerable length of time.

Quite often, barbel that have become wary of conventional, cubed lumps of meat will begin to take meat avidly again if its shape is changed. Tearing a segment from a block pulled straight from the tin and producing a ragged edge to a strip of meat is one very effective alternative, while meat in a flat, circular shape or in a short cylindrical form ⅔ to ½in (1 to 2cm) long, made with the help of an apple corer, is another.

Meat introduced in particles – diced up into

Barbel love any smoked, flavoured meat like this.

tiny squares – is a particularly effective method, especially in the summer, with a slightly larger lump of meat fished over a bed of the tiny cubes. A flavoured meat or garlic sausage hook-bait amidst all the particles probably produces more barbel than an unflavoured bait.

Garlic sausage is one of the very best meat baits for barbel. It can be easily obtained from the delicatessen section of a supermarket in whatever quantity is required. The stronger French versions are vastly superior, so make sure that this is what you are given. Ask for the meat in a block as most assistants will slice it up without asking.

As garlic sausage starts to become less effective it is a good trick to fish with a few layers of sliced meat on the hook, as the different shape and softer texture of the sliced meat can extend the life of the bait. Beware when experimenting with garlic sausage as some of the varieties will float. These floating meat baits appear to carry an over-abundance of fat and gristle; they are useless for free offerings as they will float away!

There is also the hot dog sausage, sold in cans in brine. These are good, but not as popular as they should be, due mostly to their softness and their habit of flying off the hook. This problem can be overcome by wrapping a diced segment with a short bristle of stiff nylon or something similar about ⅖in (1cm) in length. Chipolata sausages diced into segments are also superb baits. Their texture is stiffer than hot dog sausages although their flavour is not quite so evident.

Pepperami sticks make an excellent alternative bait. They are sold in pre-packed lengths in a standard version (green wrapper) and a hot version (red wrapper). Pepperami is rather a hard bait, so it needs to be cut into small segments. It is generally regarded as more of a summer bait than a winter one, although the hot Pepperami has caught the odd barbel for me even in the depths of winter.

Similar pre-packed spiced sausages in much thicker and slightly softer form are also available from some supermarkets, with some being quite a bit more spicy than others, especially those imported from Spain and Hungary. These can be diced up and the hook point just nicked through the rubbery outer skin for a deadly presentation.

After a while, plain tinned meat in any shape will start to lose its effectiveness, but flavouring and colouring can begin to give it a new lease of life. Without doubt the best means of flavouring the meat at this stage is by using shop-bought spices such as Madras curry

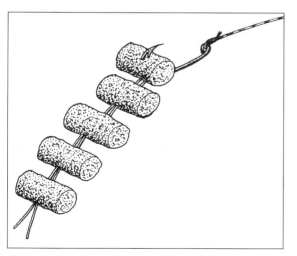

Stringer Rig with cylindrical meat sections.

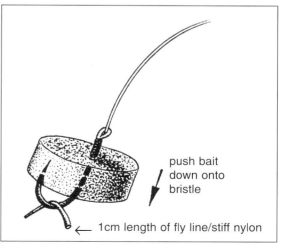

push bait down onto bristle

← 1cm length of fly line/stiff nylon

Method of attaching hot dog sausage to hook.

A modern super-bait for barbel.

Some modern flavourings – all guaranteed to send the barbel wild.

powder, turmeric, cayenne pepper or Rod Hutchinson's Megaspice, or a liver-based flavouring. Experiments have shown the hotter spices tend to be the more effective, especially in winter; barbel really appear to enjoy these hot spices more than any species.

Flavouring and colouring meat is not only a very effective method of giving a tired bait a new lease of life, it is also very easy. Begin by dicing up the equivalent of a pound of Bacon Grill or chopped ham with pork into whatever shape you wish. In an old mug, blend three teaspoons (15ml) of Richworth Nutritional Mixing Oil with a teaspoon (5ml) of a powdered or liquid flavour and a teaspoon of a powdered bait dye of your choice. Pour the oil and spice mixture into a medium-size freezer bag. Add the diced meat, blow air into the bag until it is fully inflated and trap the air. Shake the bag gently until all the baits appear to be evenly covered with the blend of ingredients. Release all the air from the bag, seal it and freeze immediately. The subsequent thawing of the bait draws the flavour into the meat, allowing it to be released gradually as it is being fished. An alternative is to get the frying pan out and fry cubes of meat in a flavour of your choice. The powdered cooking spices and curry powders are ideally suited for this method of flavouring; superbly aromatic baits are

Perfect lobworm fishing conditions.

produced by frying at a low heat in a little cooking oil with a flavour of your choice.

Using a different flavoured meat on the same hook or PVA stringer – such as alternate cubes of Rod Hutchinson's The Liver and a hot curry flavour – is a very effective way of fishing flavoured meat combinations. The choices and options are virtually endless.

LOBWORMS

Natural – instant

Lobworms are possibly the best and most consistent barbel bait of all. From a lobworm tail flicked out into the path of a feeding barbel in summer to a ball of three or four legered in autumnal floods, their versatility and year-round effectiveness are unsurpassed.

The lobworm should not be confused with the common earthworm: it is larger, with a flat tail. It has three great strengths as a barbel bait. First, it is a natural bait, so it takes a lot longer to become ineffective than, say, sweetcorn. Second, a lobworm is an instant bait: barbel require no education to recognize lobworms as food. Third, it can be used with devastating effectiveness over a bed of another bait: hempseed, casters, maggots or sometimes sweetcorn.

A lobworm is capable of taking barbel on those hot, bright summer days when all the fish want to do is rest and doze in the current. A lobworm, either freelined or trotted, will often get them excited when all else fails. Many is the time that I have watched a shoal of big barbel sitting over a bed of bait, including hempseed, and completely ignoring it, only for one of them violently to take the first lobworm moved very slowly through.

Lobworms are at their most effective during high water or flood conditions. Barbel have always responded well to pre-baiting; at times of flooding nature is pre-baiting for you as lobworms are deposited in the river in large quantities. This process appears somewhat patchy and some stretches appear to respond better to lobworms during a flood than others.

Lobworms are easy to obtain when the weather is wet and mild; they can be plucked from the surface of a lawn or football pitch in darkness as long as you have a dimmed torch and can creep up to the worms without scaring them back into the soil. Worm gathering during the summer months can be a problem so it pays to have facilities to store them. Use a wooden box at least 12in (30cm) deep filled with compressed molehill soil with some turf on top – this can be provided by sprinkling a handful of grass seed over the surface, which will quickly germinate in the shade. The box can be kept in a garden shed or garage for months, provided it is not placed directly on the floor. For autumn and winter storage a 1in (2.5cm) thick square of polystyrene cut to the same size as the box should be placed between the box and the floor

for insulation. Lobworms hate extremes of weather, and a frost or excessive heat can prove fatal. In summer the box of worms is best kept in a refrigerator at its lowest setting. Check for dead worms as one dead one can kill the lot. Do not feed the worms with kitchen waste (such as old tea bags) as the fitter they are the more they wriggle!

Dendra worms are virtually unknown to anglers: they inhabit woodland and are slightly smaller than lobworms. What makes them so unusual is their incredible liveliness. Put a dendra on the hook and it will wriggle and curl in a manic fashion that is highly attractive to barbel. For storing purposes soggy, rotting leaves and rich compost are what they thrive in; they are best kept separate from lobworms. Dendra worms can be purchased by mail order from Wiggly Worms, a supplier that specializes in these and grade A lobworms. Their address is given at the end of the book.

Lobworms can be injected with air for improved presentation, but they can also take a flavour. The injection of a liquid flavour or palatant into a bait can give it a remarkable new lease of life in situations where the barbel are beginning to eye static lobworms with suspicion. Natural bait essences (such as shellfish, mussel, shrimp, fish or worm extract) tend to blend better with the natural aroma of the bait than meat and spice flavours, especially during the summer, with flavours such as Rod Hutchinson's The Liver or Super Savoury being the more effective during the autumn and early winter. A 70/30 combination of oil and flavour is an effective balance, and 1 to 1.5ml of the chosen flavour and oil injected into the head of the worm is about right. Shop-bought syringes are adequate for this, though larger gauge models cope better with the thick viscosity of the oil.

SWEETCORN

Non-natural particle – requires prior introduction

Sweetcorn is perhaps the finest particle bait for

This barbel was totally preoccupied by corn, ignoring every other bait.

oily flavour i.e. shrimp or mussel

Inject oil-based attractant to head of lobworm to draw suspicious barbel upstream.

summer barbel. Sweetcorn has many good qualities: it requires no preparation, is easily available, has an attractive aroma, is cheap, highly visible to fish and angler, and has the ability to get fish preoccupied with it. Sweetcorn is a bait well loved by all fish of the *Cyprinidae* family, with barbel being no exception; it contains an unusually high quantity of fish-attracting amino acids, which many other seed baits do not. This feature may go some way to explaining its astounding success as a bait.

While barbel can take a little time to recognize sweetcorn as food, once they do, they usually become very easy to catch on it. For all its advantages, sweetcorn does have a tendency to become less effective more quickly than virtually any other bait. It is also very easy to spook barbel if too much sweetcorn is introduced into a swim at once. The little-and-often principle is the one to follow; barbel are extremely prone to bolting at the sight of a mass of sweetcorn on the bottom. A single can will sometimes be too much, so go easy and if possible watch the way the barbel respond to the sweetcorn once it has been introduced.

As sweetcorn begins to become less effective the angler can exploit its ability to take a flavour or colour quite easily. This can be achieved in the same manner as with meat, using the same flavours and the same colours. Commercially flavoured and coloured sweetcorn is readily available under the brand name Pescaviva. It comes in resealable tins and certainly helps to extend the life of the bait. As cans of Pescaviva are not cheap, it may be advisable for baiting-up and weaning barbel onto the new flavour to buy a catering-size can of standard sweetcorn and flavour and/or colour it yourself.

Eventually, even dyed and flavoured sweetcorn will be no good, but its life can be extended by using it with another bait – maggot, caster, dead minnow, lobworm tail, tiny squares of meat; indeed any bait you can think of works well as a cocktail with sweetcorn. Combinations of colours can sometimes work, as can different flavours fished on the same hook.

HEMPSEED

Non-natural – instant

Barbel find the smell of hempseed more attractive than anything else and many barbel anglers centre their entire approach around it. Hempseed has in the past been more of an attractant than a hookbait; there is hardly a barbel angler who has never caught a barbel using it as an attractant. Barbel will move a considerable distance upstream to intercept and feed on hempseed. Any bait fished over a bed of hempseed is instantly more attractive than when fished on its own, not least because the magical seed has probably brought barbel into the swim in the first place.

Prepare the hempseed the day before a barbel trip. Soak it for about ten hours, and in the evening pour the soaked seeds and the water in which it has been soaking into a pressure cooker. Simmer it under pressure for five minutes before releasing the steam and pouring the hempseed and the water into a watertight bait container and leaving it to stew overnight.

Some barbel anglers advocate sweetening hempseed with intense sweeteners from bait suppliers and even flavouring it with something else, though I believe that this is not necessary. Others claim that introducing a spoonful of bicarbonate of soda gives the hempseed a blacker, shinier lustre following preparation. Others insist that it is best to drain the residue away after boiling and let the hempseed soak in fresh, clean water, but this is a mistake as the residue left following the boiling process is also highly attractive to the barbel.

The only practical and cost-effective way to buy hempseed is direct from seed or grain merchants in half hundredweight (25kg) or hundredweight (50kg) sacks. Kept in the dry and shade of a garden shed, hempseed will not spoil and can be used throughout the season.

Until recently it has been very difficult to present hempseed on the hook in a way that is acceptable to barbel. The advent of the hair rig aided this presentation considerably, with the cooked seeds being threaded onto the hair using a fine darning needle. This was very fiddly and never worked in practice as well as it did in theory, as a cooked hempseed tends either to split in two, with the kernel being knocked out of the shell, or the shell splits and the whole seed flies off the hair.

Then, anglers started to use Superglue. The hempseed was glued to the shank of the hook or onto other materials such as rubber bands,

It took six pints of casters for this barbel to eventually make its mistake.

which were in turn hooked. The strong petrol-like aroma of Superglue masked the scent of the hempseed and was not as successful as was suggested.

Another of the old methods was tying tiny hooks-to-nylon onto the eye of the main hook, with the hempseed itself being hooked by the smaller hook, a size 20 or 22 for instance, and fished in that fashion. All these methods worked to a degree, but hempseed as a bait never really blossomed as it should have done.

Modern developments of hempseed rigging are described in Chapter 7. Like most particles, hempseed works rather better in the summer and autumn than in the winter but on an exceptionally mild winter's day a small introduction of hempseed into the swim can often work wonders.

Tares are very similar to hempseed but are a little larger and jet black in colour. While not possessing anything like the attracting qualities of hempseed, tares fished either on a Bogey ball or threaded on hair rigs over a bed of hempseed make a deadly bait as they resemble big, fat hempseeds. There are occasions where tares can be used as a substitute for hempseed on stretches of river where barbel have begun to associate hempseed with danger.

While tares in their own right do not appear to be particularly attractive because of their inert lack of smell, they can be made to resemble large hempseeds if they are flavoured with a liquid hempseed flavour easily obtainable from good tackle shops or bait suppliers. Tares look more appetizing than hempseed on the bottom and because of their larger size are possibly more visible as well. Barbel can often be seen feeding on hempseed-flavoured tares with abandon when their reaction to hempseed itself is far more guarded.

MAGGOTS AND CASTERS

Natural particle – instant

Both these baits have two distinct aspects to them – they make wonderful barbel baits but using them as bait invites trouble from eels and other nuisance fish. However, once a few barbel move onto a bed of maggots or casters all the nuisance fish get pushed out. To get the best from maggots or casters it pays to get the barbel preoccupied with them. By introducing a lot of maggots or casters into a barbel swim the activity of the nuisance fish together with the constant trickle of the bait drifting down and around them will often stimulate the barbel into feeding. Where it is possible to fish for barbel without the presence of other fish, quite often a couple of pints of maggots or casters is sufficient to get them going. There is nothing that barbel love more than hoovering maggots or casters off the bottom, and they appear to have a limitless appetite when doing so.

It can be a good idea to introduce hempseed into a swim first. By introducing maggots or casters on their own the whole process is prolonged as barbel will take longer to respond to their introduction than hempseed, which apart from anything else allows the nuisance fish to start on the maggots or casters well before the barbel switch on and start on the bait themselves. Casters and hempseed appear to be a more successful combination than maggots and hempseed.

While maggots and casters are generally more popular with barbel anglers during the warmer months, the success of maggots during winter is somewhat less appreciated. There are considerable advantages with winter maggot fishing: the activities of eels, minnows, bleak, gudgeon and bream are absent, and although dace and chub can still be a problem, the quivertip spends much less time being twitched and plucked by nuisance fish than it does in the summer months. Nor is it necessary to introduce as many to prompt a response from the barbel as it is in summer, when as much as a gallon of maggots might be required.

Maggots will take flavour and colour as well as any other bait; in fact it makes no sense to use maggots unless they have been flavoured. Most shop-bought maggots will do little to attract barbel in comparison to flavoured ones. They usually smell of ammonia, so you need to flavour them unless you can buy good quality, fresh maggots (which still need cleaning with maize meal to remove their pungent smell).

An effective way of flavouring maggots is by adding a teaspoon (5ml) of liquid or a level teaspoon of any powdered flavour to a pint (0.5 litre) of maggots. Maggots can also be flavoured very effectively by inserting a Richworth atomizer into one of their bottles of liquid flavours. There are countless permutations possible, with the blending of different flavours being used to give the maggots virtually your own personal flavour. Do not worry about blending, for instance, strawberry cream with hot Madras curry powder – the barbel will still love it. Maggots flavoured with hot, spicy flavours work exceptionally well with barbel, as do all the other flavours mentioned above under 'Pastes and Boilies'.

While maggots used in large bunches are often particularly effective, a single maggot, especially in the winter, will often take a barbel where all else fails. Another way to extend the life of maggots as a bait is to use them dead. Dead maggots are best fished with a flavouring and can be surprisingly effective; this works in both winter and summer. Quite why dead maggots should be effective in a river is not clear. Dead maggots fished over the silty bottom of a stillwater where maggots can wriggle out of sight of the fish makes sense, but not on the hard gravelled runs so popular with barbel where there seems no hiding place for live wriggling maggots. Nevertheless, dead maggots catch barbel on occasions where live ones do not. Maggots can be killed by pouring boiling water over them or by putting them in a bait box in the freezer. If you wish to fish dead, flavoured maggots, flavour them while they are still alive.

The proof of the pudding.

CHEESE AND CHEESEPASTE

Non-natural – instant

While protein pastes and certain other non-natural baits require varying degrees of prior introduction, cheese and its associated pastes do not. Quite why cheese should be an instant bait is a mystery, but you can use any number of the varieties that are currently available in supermarkets. Soft, wrapped, triangular cheeses (Dairylea, for example) are favourites, and any blue cheese (such as Danish Blue) makes a superb barbel bait. The stronger flavoured cheeses are the more attractive to barbel; milder varieties are definitely inferior. Cheese tends to work better during winter than summer, probably because of its smell.

Plain cheese goes very hard during the winter months, which not only makes it a less attractive bait but also prevents the angler from setting the hook with any degree of regularity. To overcome this problem it is advisable to mix the cheese with pastry, or even a stiff breadpaste. Three parts blue cheese to one part pastry makes a good bait for the colder months.

COARSE FISH DEADBAITS (FRESHLY KILLED)

Natural – instant

Deadbaits are undoubtedly the most under-used and under-rated barbel bait. Barbel are extremely fond of very small fish, especially minnows, even becoming preoccupied with them on occasions. Even in rivers that do not boast large stocks of minnows, these little fish

Mounting fat minnows in this fashion reduces missed takes considerably.

still make great bait.

A high proportion of barbel are semi-predators on rivers overflowing with minnows, gudgeon and even bleak, as well as those little fish of pure rivers and streams, loach and bullheads. Almost any barbel will take a properly presented, freshly killed minnow deadbait. A live minnow should be taken from the bucket, killed by tapping it on the head and cast out immediately. It is this freshness that is the key to successful deadbaiting. It makes the bait so much more appealing to the barbel.

As when fishing for perch, the fresher the deadbait the more appealing it is. For further reading on deadbaits refer to *The Book of the Perch* (see Further Reading section). How strange that barbel and perch have such similar palates!

This predatory trait has been somewhat misunderstood over the years and it has been gen-

erally supposed that barbel enjoy feeding on fry in the very early part of the season; they will in fact feed on very small fish of any species well into the late autumn and beyond. The barbel is an omnivore and will exploit any food source that it can. What is seldom noticed when one observes a shoal of barbel is the masses of minnows and other tiny fish of all species that stay alongside them. Barbel are large fish and spend much of their time grubbing around on the bottom, flashing, twisting and turning over the gravels for all manner of reasons. Masses of tiny fish are attracted to a shoal of barbel because of the food made available by the disturbance they cause to the bottom. Barbel will often exist in a cloud of such fish, which are no larger than a decent caddis and a lot smaller than a lobworm, and will feed on the small fry accordingly. Many is the time that a shower of minnows or fry-sized fish will explode from the water with the blame virtually always being linked to pike or perch. Closer inspection will reveal the predators to be barbel on more occasions than is generally appreciated.

Deadbaits for barbel can be fished on a basic leger rig and treated like any other bait. A large minnow fished on its own or three or four small ones fished on the same hook can be extremely effective. Barbel will take deadbaits with more violence and more savagery than any other bait. Oddly, these strong bites are often missed, especially if a large single minnow deadbait is lip-hooked. The way to hook a single deadbait, and therefore increase the bite ratio, is to thread the hooklink through the mouth and out through the vent with a hair-rigging needle. Tie on the hook – a size 6 or 8 Drennan Continental Boilie hook appears to be the most compatible – and draw the eye and shank of the hook back into the bait. For smaller deadbaits, say under 1½in (4cm), hook them in the mid-dle and thread them up the hook like a lob-worm.

Like many other barbel baits, deadbaits work exceptionally well over a bed of hempseed or a small carpet of sweetcorn. They are also wonderfully effective when used to tip other more conventional particle baits that are beginning to lose their initial effectiveness. The secret with deadbaits is to make sure they are fresh and fish them just as you would any other natural bait.

The drawbacks are pretty obvious – perch and eels love them and the odd jack pike puts in an unwanted appearance – but these problems with nuisance fish are no worse than with maggots or worms. Deadbaits certainly do not cause the quivertip to be twitched all day by small fish as maggots and casters do.

Catching suitable bait can be a problem but where minnows abound it is a simple case of throwing a ball of groundbait into a submerged, fine-meshed landing net, lifting it sharply after a

Smaller deadbaits are best presented thus.

few minutes and tipping all the minnows into a bait bucket. The removal of a few minnows for bait does not upset anybody and does no harm to the river's ecology in the way that mass pike bait removal did in years gone by. It is a good idea to collect a number just before the start of the season and freeze them for occasions when the minnows cannot be found. Get them into the freezer as soon as you can, to preserve their freshness. While freshly killed baits are the more effective, frozen baits still have the ability to out-fish all the alternatives.

Perhaps the most important thing that the prospective deadbaiter will require is complete confidence in the bait itself, and true confidence will not come until a barbel or two have been landed. The best approach for a deadbaiting sceptic is to fish with two rods in the modern, quivertipping style. One rod should be baited with whatever bait the angler feels confident in using and the other rigged up with a dead minnow hooked in the manner described. Both baits can be used over a bed of hempseed and it is very rare indeed for the minnow to be out-fished by any other bait (except perhaps lob-worms occasionally).

To assist in the presentation to barbel that are ordinarily cautious, it pays to neutralize the natural weight of the deadbait (usually the swim bladder will have been burst while mounting the bait) and the hook with the aid of a small sliver of rig foam that can easily be inserted into the fish through its mouth. Alternatively, a buoyant hook can be employed to counterbalance the weight of the hookbait. It is possible to mount a mature minnow without puncturing its swim bladder, and with a little bit of practice the natural buoyancy of the bait can be counterbalanced by the natural weight of a non-buoyant hook. A deadbait presented pop-up style with its tail off the bottom – apparently feeding on the bottom in a vertical position – works better than one laying hard on the bottom, as a herring would be presented for pike.

One of the great advantages of deadbaiting is the ease with which free bait samples in the form of minnows and the rest can be attracted into the swim as well as the barbel themselves. An extremely effective way of doing this is by priming a small cage or frame feeder with a mixture of grilled or crushed hempseed and some Sensas or Van Den Eynde groundbait. Some loose hempseed included into the mix not only tends to draw in the barbel, but minnows and other small fry as well. While the barbel will in all probability not be looking to feed on the swarms of minnows that are fighting to get at the groundbait, a large dead minnow or three or four little ones will tend to provoke an immediate response in the form of a vicious take.

While legering deadbaits on the bottom in the manner described catches a lot of barbel, we should not be blind to the tremendously exciting method of trundling deadbaits through known barbel glides, searching out the stream-er weed runs, depressions, gradients, rocks and snags. Barbel love to take trundled deadbaits and will happily move several yards across the stream to intercept such a bait. Nor should we be blind to stalking individual barbel. There is little to beat drawing a barbel out from under-neath its shelter, watching it approach the deadbait and then seeing the fish take it with a force that no other fish can match.

As with all other baits, even deadbaits can

The caddis larva, so under-used yet so deadly in summer.

eventually start to fail, and by flavouring them with the usual flavours their longevity can be enhanced. Many fish flavours do not seem to appeal to barbel, although seafood flavours (such as prawn) certainly do. Whitebait is much less successful for barbel than it is for chub. Frying minnow deadbaits in a household spice, whitebait style, also works exceptionally well for barbel that are under pressure.

CADDIS

Natural – instant

Caddis grubs are a wonderful barbel bait yet long forgotten and virtually unused nowadays. They make up a high proportion of the barbel's natural diet, as do nymphs and freshwater shrimps. It is quite large enough to be presented on a respectably sized hook and is a superb summer bait that barbel cannot resist. Strictly a summer bait, a caddis is at its most effective when trotted through the swim just tripping the bottom. They are also very effective when fished hard on the bottom over a bed of hempseed.

The caddis is the larva of the sedge fly. Colonies of these creatures can be found in clear, shallow streams beneath rocks and flat stones. They look like small lengths of twig adhering to the underside of the stone. If you squeeze them gently the caddis will emerge, presenting itself as a succulent bait. Once the larva has been extracted from its case it should be used immediately, or the grubs can be kept for a day or so in a bait box shaded from the sun and filled with wet moss.

Caddis grubs are not the easiest baits to obtain, but where you find one you can find several and they really are worth the effort of collection. Many different species of fly larvae make up a large proportion of what a barbel eats and, given the ease with which the caddis can be presented on the hook, it really makes no sense to ignore their long-forgotten qualities. There is much to learn in the pages of old angling publications, perhaps more about barbel than any other species, and the effectiveness of caddis is one such gem.

OTHER BAITS

Bread, nuts, seafood and wheat have all taken barbel and many have had periods of popularity. On some hard-fished waters where all the basic baits have been exploited, these alternatives can be successful. A lump or flake of bread resting on the bottom will often frighten barbel, who refuse to recognize it as food. A better bet is breadpaste, and where established flavours such as Marmite or Bovril can be worked into the paste to give it more appeal. Breadpaste is undoubtedly more successful where it can be introduced beforehand, but it does not have the ability to maintain its consistency for long and is extremely susceptible to the attentions of nuisance fish who will soon tear it to pieces. Using flavoured crusts fished pop-up style 1 to 3in (2.5 to 7.5cm) from the bottom is perhaps the most effective way to fish with bread for barbel and will sometimes succeed when all else fails. Crusts are best flavoured with aerosol spray flavours and frozen to enable the flavour to be drawn into the bait when they thaw.

Many of the most effective carp fishing baits, such as tiger nuts and black-eyed beans, have never appealed to barbel in the same way as they do to carp. The only exception to this apparent indifference towards nuts is the barbel's liking of peanuts. Barbel will switch on to peanuts very much more quickly than to many other particles. Like all seed and nut baits, peanuts require a little preparation before becoming palatable to fish. Soak them for up to three days in a bucket of water, allowing them to ferment somewhat; they can in fact double their size. Peanuts will fill fish up very quickly, so make sure that only a small quantity of peanuts is introduced into a swim at any one time. A properly soaked peanut becomes a relatively soft bait, but sufficiently large to present to a barbel either directly on the hook or

A barbel that displayed a liking for a prawn.

hair-rigged in the normal way. It is not clear whether it is the protein contained within the peanuts that makes them so attractive to barbel or the distinctive smell after they begin to ferment, but peanuts are an extremely under-rated barbel bait.

Given widespread use, seafood – prawns, cockles and sea shrimps – could well elevate themselves to join the favourite barbel baits. While barbel continue to ignore whitebait, both loosefed and as hookbaits, the seafood menu continues to delight them. Prawns appear to be the pick of the bunch, with an instant appeal to barbel. The same cannot be said for cockles and sea shrimps; though after a degree of prior introduction they sometimes rival the deadly prawn. The fact that salmon anglers have given up using prawns on certain stretches of British rivers for the simple reason that they catch too many barbel on them perhaps gives the best possible endorsement of the bait. But barbel love prawns in rivers that have seen no salmon for centuries. Peeled, frozen prawns are readily available from supermarkets, but if you buy them fresh and prepare them yourself you will end up with a more effective bait.

Similarly, cockles have been big fish catchers for decades. By buying them fresh (not pickled in vinegar!) you will have a superior bait, although they usually require prior introduction. Sea shrimps mirror the effectiveness and pre-introduction requirements of cockles and are used even less often. As with all barbel baits their effectiveness is enhanced by presenting them over a bed of hempseed.

Wheat is a classic roach bait, at one time immensely popular but today hardly ever used. It is also a bait for the enterprising barbel angler in circumstances where many of the more traditional barbel baits are being ignored. A very small number of wheat enthusiasts have recently been taking a number of barbel from hard-fished stretches using wheat, both loosefed and as a hookbait. Although obtaining wheat is seasonal, its use and effectiveness certainly are not. Like any bait, wheat is at its most effective when fresh and of the highest quality. Good quality wheat is fat, round and large. It cannot be used in its raw state and must be prepared using the same treatment as hempseed. It needs less boiling than hempseed and if it is over-boiled it will turn into a gooey mess. The moment the kernels split is the time to turn the heat off. Wheat swells up much more than hempseed, so allow room for it to do so during preparation.

Because of its absorbent nature wheat takes flavour and colour exceptionally well. Dyed, flavoured and frozen wheat makes a wonderful alternative bait and once barbel latch onto it they become as preoccupied with wheat as they are with any other more established particle. Years ago, roach anglers were conscious of wheat over-filling their quarry because of its dense, heavy nature. With barbel this is less of a problem but barbel will not tolerate wheat introduced into a swim in the same quantities as hempseed. While wheat is an easier bait to use directly onto the hook than hempseed, the best form of presentation is as described under 'Hair-rigged and On-hook Pop-up Rigs' in Chapter 7.

GROUNDBAITING

Groundbaiting is another recently developed area that has passed too many barbel anglers by and a better understanding of the subject can certainly lead to better catches. Not so very long ago, anglers from continental Europe were the best pole anglers in the world, but by studying their methods British anglers, willing to learn, were soon competing on a par with them. While poles have little application to barbel angling, groundbaiting certainly does and a working knowledge of groundbaits, especially for feeder fishing, is vital.

It is possible to go into a good tackle shop and buy exactly what you need. Pre-packed groundbaits that bind – as opposed to those that cloud or explode on impact – are preferable given the flow rate that most barbel tend to prefer. It is possible to blend many of these groundbaits, and as barbel are attracted by coloured water as well as many other things, a cloud or exploding ingredient that fizzes and releases particles on the bottom is no bad thing. These modern groundbaits are infinitely preferable to the old fashioned stodgy white breadcrumbs, which apart from anything else fill the fish up. One of the great advantages of many of these groundbaits is their ability to work for you when used inside the feeder and not just lie on the bottom doing nothing.

Mixing an even-textured groundbait is essential; if one or two rules are followed you should get perfect results every time. Use a shallow, round mixing bowl and blend the dry ingredients together with hookbait samples of the particle variety, such as casters or sweetcorn. Introduce the water or flavour with the aid of a sponge and mix thoroughly with the other hand as the liquid trickles in. It pays to take a little bit of time with this: you can always add a little extra water to a mix if it is on the dry side, but you cannot take it out if it is too wet. A sponge allows an even distribution of the liquid and prevents an uneven consistency, which is to be avoided. Mix groundbait thoroughly and it will be ready for use in the feeder. For how to use it see under 'Feeder Fishing' in Chapter 8.

ATTRACTANTS

Attractants give us the means to carry the flavour of the bait we are using downstream to any awaiting barbel. This can be done with feed-inducing rig tablets or, better still, feed-inducing oil bait dips.

Rig tablets are small and round, with a hole in the middle for easy attachment to the rig. They are soluble and can be attached to leads

Proven groundbaits for barbel.

A shallow yet wide mixing bowl is essential for a consistent mix.

or hooks using PVA, interspersed between bait samples on stringer rigs, or placed inside a feeder. Rig tablets carrying flavours that work for barbel include hempseed, luncheon meat, strawberry cream and tutti-frutti.

Bait dips are another preserve of those of the carp fishing world that have transferred their effectiveness to barbel fishing, especially when used with any of the meats or boilies and pastes. Commercially bought bait dips from the carp fishing counters of tackle shops are adequate but I prefer to create and blend my own, not least because I can copy the flavour or blend of flavours that I am using in a bait at any given time. To make my own bait dip I take 30ml (two tablespoons) of Richworth's Richfish or Feed Inducing Oil and blend in either 5ml (one teaspoon) of a liquid flavour or a teaspoon of powdered flavour of my choice. By then dunking a lump of flavoured meat into the dip for a few seconds, an extremely attractive barbel-drawing bait is created. By previously flavouring the meat using the standard polythene bag and freezing technique with an identical oil and flavour mix, the bait maintains its identity for the barbel to move up to and feed on whenever they like, often after dark.

Bait dips work so well because the current gradually washes the flavoured oil off the surface of the bait and downstream towards any barbel in the vicinity. Barbel often find the oil-borne flavour hard to resist. Bait dips by no means limit themselves to boilies and meat baits; there is no reason why you cannot dip a lobworm in worm extract or a minnow in a green-lipped mussel based dip. The permutations are endless and are just waiting to be tried. Without doubt the effectiveness of bait dips is increased during the winter months when fewer free samples are introduced because of the propensity of the barbel to feed in shorter, sharper bursts than in summer.

The effects of the bait dip are such that the barbel are attracted by the scent of the hookbait more than the cumulative flavour of a mass baiting exercise. Beware of overdoing the dipping process, and adhere strictly to the instructions on the bottles of commercially available dips or the measures quoted above for the home-blended variety. Rig tablets and bait dips are little used as yet for barbel, but if you are looking for that little edge this is another area waiting to be exploited.

7 PROVEN RIGS

Discerning modern barbel anglers usually use rigs that draw heavily on two sources: carp fishing and match angling. The origin of most leger rigs used by barbel anglers comes from the carp fishing world, while many of the feeder fishing rigs borrow heavily from match fishing. The more enlightened barbel anglers fuse both schools of thought, often coming up with a dual approach. Under the correct circumstances this can be devastatingly effective.

What follows is a sequence of diagrams and explanations, which have been developed in conjunction with the learning curve of the barbel and are applicable to a number of barbel fishing situations. Beginning with suitable rigs for that first cast to a completely naive shoal of

barbel, through to gradually more refined set-ups for cautious to educated barbel and ending with sophisticated rigs suitable for highly pressurized fish, I hope to cover most, if not all, the barbel fishing situations we are likely to encounter. I have deliberately omitted feeder rigs from this section; these are discussed under 'Feeder Fishing' in Chapter 8.

THE STANDARD LEGER RIG (FLAWED)

To begin a section of proven rigs with a flawed rig may appear to be a contradiction, but this standard and seemingly very popular barbel

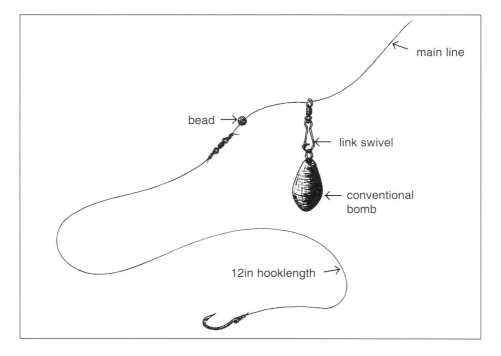

The flawed standard leger rig.

rig, usually used for presenting baits hard on the bottom, is included to show all that is wrong with it! Most barbel rigs depict bombs attached to the main line, as shown, by way of the wholly inappropriate link or snap swivel, which is a mistake. The eye of the swivel, which is often attached to a large lead, causes wear and tear to the main line because of its lack of flat contact with that line. Also, the rough edges and protrusions of the snap or link swivel will catch and tangle a braided hooklength as it is cast and retrieved. The swivel attachment will also tangle with a nylon hooklength in the same way. Finally, there is no breakaway mechanism should the bomb become tangled in weed or snagged elsewhere. I abandoned this rig many years ago as wholly unsuitable, and I advise you to do the same.

THE STANDARD BREAKAWAY LEGER RIG

A practical and simple basic barbel rig with none of the disadvantages appertaining to the flawed rig shown previously, this rig is suitable for most barbel fishing situations where the sole objective is to present a static bait on the bottom. The impractical link or snap swivel has been discarded and replaced by a loop of 11lb b.s. Optima Power Gum threaded through a John Roberts low-resistance leger ring and knotted once. The bomb is attached by pushing the loop through the eye of the bomb swivel, bringing the bomb through the loop and pulling tight.

Power Gum is essential for the breakaway leger rig.

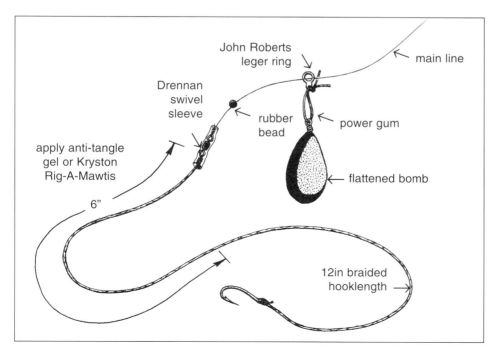

Standard leger rig for general legering.

The reasons why these simple modifications have been used are:

• The low-resistance plastic leger ring causes far less damage to the main line than the metal of the swivel eye.

• The large bore of the leger ring does not get choked up by river debris that would otherwise render the rig inoperable and a danger to the main line.

• The hole of the leger ring used for attaching a link to the bomb is perfectly sized for a knotted loop of 11lb b.s. Power Gum to secure the bomb to the rig, but is not too large to prevent it from pulling out under pressure if the lead becomes snagged.

In addition, should a change of bomb be required, it is a simple matter of pushing the bomb back through the loop and pulling it back through the swivel or, alternatively, pulling the knotted Power Gum back through the smaller second hole to change the lead.

Every bomb used for this rig should be flattened so that it holds the bottom better and requires less weight to do so. Apart from the obvious breakaway advantages created by using the Power Gum link in the rig, this rig does not catch the main line or hooklength in the same way as the link or snap swivel does and is therefore perfectly suited to its task. To complete the construction of this rig, sleeving the Power Gum with either a Drennan swivel sleeve or stiff rig tubing pushed onto the top of the bomb helps prevent the hooklength tangling around it.

The concept of allowing potential snagging devices, such as bombs, a breakaway mechanism has never really been accepted for some bizarre reason, and equally bizarre is the obsession with including superfluous lumps of metal in rigs such as extra snap or link swivels. Barbel love snaggy areas and this rig makes fishing them much safer for the angler as well as the barbel.

BOMB LEGER RIGS

These rigs apply to the same fishing circumstances. I probably prefer the in-line leger rig to all the others for basic barbel fishing. I find that an in-line lead casts with a great deal more accuracy than a lead hanging off the line, and I also like the simplicity of the rig, which causes no damage to the line. A flattened in-line lead is virtually tangle free and is far less likely to snag than an off-line lead. I will always use this rig when I am confronted with snag-free swims. If I have one complaint, it is the bother of having to break down the rig to change a bomb to a different weight.

Another snag-free rig is the tubed bomb arrangement, which has its uses where an accurate cast is not as essential. By slipping a short length of rig tube through the eye of the bomb's swivel as shown in the diagram, we again create a tangle-free rig, especially if braided hooklengths are being used. I tend to use this rig when I have run out of in-line leads or where I want the option of creating a quick bolt rig by

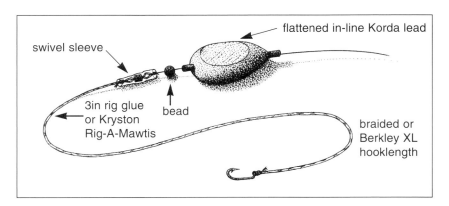

In-line flattened lead rig.

swivel sleeve

flattened in-line Korda lead

3in rig glue or Kryston Rig-A-Mawtis

bead

braided or Berkley XL hooklength

Free-running tubed boom rig.

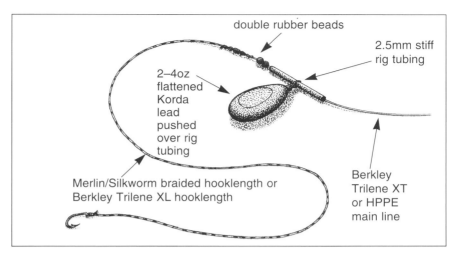

Trundling rig.

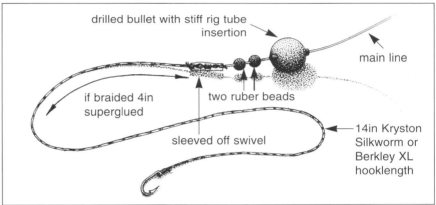

removing the bead and pushing the rig tube onto the eye of the hooklength swivel.

TRUNDLING RIGS

I have devoted a whole section to trundling and its principles, and the rigs for use with the method are very simple. The ideal situation in summer is where a couple of SSG shot are sufficient to hold the bait down yet allow it to trundle downstream in a natural fashion. If we are confronted with a river carrying extra water, in summer as well as autumn, a two or three SSG shot arrangement may not be sufficient to prevent the whole rig being swept away. On occasions when the river is really fast flowing I find that small in-line leads are perfectly equipped for the job; when the river is between these two extremes, good old fashioned drilled bullets are quite adequate for the task. In the case of drilled bullets, I always insert small lengths of stiff rig tubing inside them to protect the main line from the wear and tear caused by continuous contact with the edges of the lead. On the rare occasions that drilled bullets appear in the tackle shops with this tubing already intact, I buy as many as I can find.

PLASTICINE AND PUTTY RIGS

This rig is for those barbel swims where bombs becoming snagged is the norm rather than the exception. Standard shop-bought Plasticine is perfectly suitable for these rigs but Kryston's commercially produced Snag Free Putty is manufactured for this particular purpose and is perhaps the better choice owing to its lack of smell and greater density. The idea behind the rig is a simple one. If the putty or Plasticine becomes snagged it slides off the rig, allowing direct contact with the fish again. Given the barbel's love of snaggy swims it is no surprise that this material is rapidly becoming an indispensable item of equipment.

The rig shown is a variation of the standard breakaway leger rig with the Snag Free Putty used as a substitute for the original lead. The putty bites into the Power Gum stop knot and holds firm. Avoid using a swivel to mould the putty round, as a bare swivel can still catch on snags whereas a stop knot does not, or at worst will slide off.

LONG TAILED RAFT OR ROCK RIGS

Barbel often inhabit swims that appear impregnable, often weed and debris rafts caught up on snags, but by looking at them from a different angle, quite often from the opposite bank, such swims can suddenly appear more accessible and more fishable.

To attack these swims, which are often full of barbel, requires courage, confidence and appropriately strong tackle. This rig is nothing more than a long tailed in-line rig but with Snag Free Putty acting as the weight rather than a conventional, potentially snagging lead. The length of the tail depends purely on the distance between the point where it is possible to cast the rig for the weight to settle, and whatever distance it may be downstream to the precise location of the barbel. A buoyant hook is essential and the hookbait must barely sink, so the hooklength must be a braid of neutral buoyancy, for instance Kryston's Super-Silk. This virtually weightless hookbait will then be pushed downstream by the current, to a distance set by the hooklength. Such a perfectly balanced bait will not only end up precisely where you want it but will do so in the most natural way possible. Quite often such a bait will be taken prior to the long hooklength being fully extended.

Takes from barbel when fishing in this way can be savage, usually because they have already turned, and owing to the proximity of the snag they have to be shown who is boss and

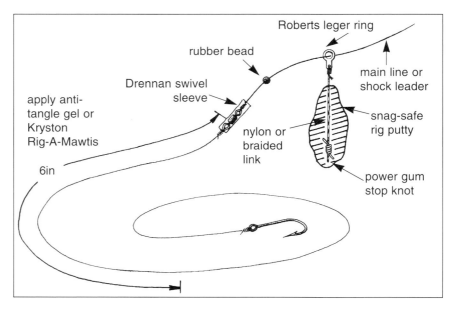

Plasticine or putty rig for snag fishing.

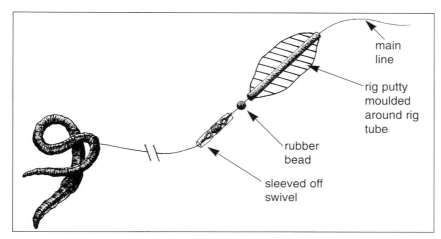

Long tailed raft or rock rig for reaching inaccessible barbel.

main line

rig putty moulded around rig tube

rubber bead

sleeved off swivel

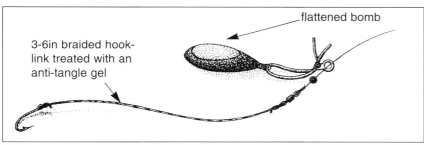

Short link semi-fixed bolt rig.

flattened bomb

3-6in braided hook-link treated with an anti-tangle gel

played hard from the outset. This is not such a suicidal tactic as one might think, as they will often surge downstream, occasionally up-stream, and not use the snag as a possible way of breaking free from the tackle. A barbel often prefers to fight with sheer power rather than with guile. If the angler allows the barbel to kite in the middle of the river and not plough into the snag, the fish can probably be landed.

BOLT RIGS

The bolt rig is almost as effective for barbel as it is for carp, and should only be used when the standard barbel rig begins to produce sharp, unhittable plucks and pulls – which tell you that the barbel are getting decidedly edgy. The concept behind bolt rigs is exactly the same for bar-bel as it is for carp: to get suspicious, nervous fish to turn, hook themselves and bolt. The angler must make sure that a conventionally

mounted bait has the hook point protruding to catch the mouth as the barbel turns and bolts.

There are three main rigs that will achieve the bolt effect. The diagrams depict the stan-dard legering rig but with a Korda (previously pear-shaped) flattened bomb of not less than 2oz (55g) and a hooklength dramatically short-ened to, say, 3 to 6in (7.5 to 15cm). Although this rig is free running, the shortness of hook-length and the weight of the bomb will still cause the barbel to bolt as a result of it feeling the resistance as it takes the bait fished hard to the rod top. The use of this simple rig is a prime example of how a gradual, ordered progression through the whole range of recognized barbel rigs does not educate the barbel into being wary of sophisticated rigs too early.

The next step is the semi-fixed bolt rig. This rig works on a different principle, with the bolt-ing barbel pulling directly against the bomb, as opposed to through it. This rig is a harsher, cruder rig but nevertheless an extremely

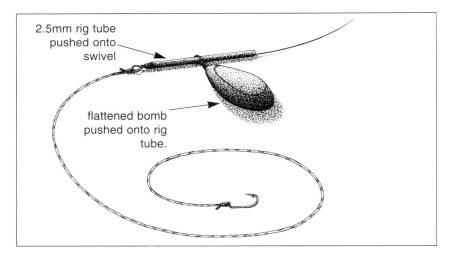

Standard barbel bolt rig.

2.5mm rig tube pushed onto swivel

flattened bomb pushed onto rig tube.

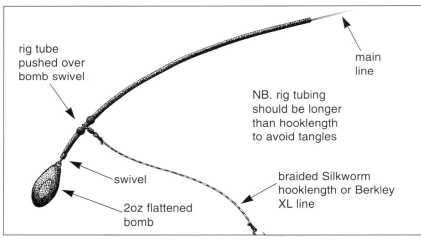

Fox helicopter rig.

rig tube pushed over bomb swivel

main line

NB. rig tubing should be longer than hooklength to avoid tangles

swivel

braided Silkworm hooklength or Berkley XL line

2oz flattened bomb

efficient method of hooking nervous, suspicious, finicky barbel. Although the bomb is fixed to within the rig itself, it will release if the rig is lost and attached to a barbel, hence its description.

The safest way of doing this is with a tulip or bolt bead that is attached to the bomb. The bead is pushed onto a short length of rig tube that is itself then pushed onto the swivel. This arrangement is very efficient and works exceptionally well.

The angler who prefers to buy rigs ready-made will be pleased to learn that semi-fixed bolt rig kits intended for carp fishing are available in most tackle shops and will fit the

bill adequately.

The helicopter rig is rapidly superseding the semi-fixed bolt rig as the standard bolt rig for barbel anglers. It is every bit as effective in its ability to bolt a taking barbel as the semi-fixed and in addition does not tangle; indeed this was one of the reasons for its invention. Ready-made helicopter rig kits are also available from tackle shops and are superbly suited to bolt rigging for barbel.

BUOYANT HOOK BOGEY RIGS

Where hair-rigging is distrusted, ineffective or

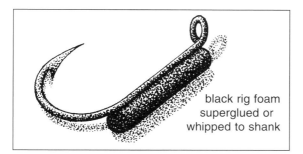

black rig foam
superglued or
whipped to shank

rejected as unethical by the angler there is a very simple and effective alternative: to counterbalance the natural weight of the hook. This can be done in a number of ways but the most effective appears to be gluing or whipping a thin strip of hard textured black rig foam to the outside shank of the hook. This method does not impede the successful hooking of a barbel, nor does it work loose. Rig foam glued to the hook in this way will stay in place for weeks. At this stage the unbaited hook intended for hempseed or tare presentation should float, so it pays to err on the side of too much buoyancy rather than too little, as the foam can be whittled down far more easily than it can be added to.

For seed bait presentation we are blessed with a brilliant new product marketed by Kryston under the name of Bogey Particle Fixer. This is without question the only way in which hempseed and tares can be presented suf-

ficiently well on the hook in modern barbel fishing. The product resembles a stiff, sticky, rubber like jelly and is an aroma free, transparent, adhesive substance that was specifically designed for fixing dry particles as small as hempseed and tares directly onto the shank of the hook, as well as onto hairs, cork or polystyrene balls, rubber bands or any other item that can be smeared with Bogey and then in turn be placed onto a hook and fished with.

It is undoubtedly a better idea to prepare a number of baits at home, as such work is fiddly, time consuming and unnecessary on the bank. There is always a risk of getting moisture or grease onto the Bogey while on the bank, which will render the whole operation extremely difficult to manage.

Whenever Bogey Particle Fixer is used, all the surfaces that are to be stuck must be clean and dry. I always prepare mine at home for this reason. With clean, dry hands roll up some small balls of Bogey or wrap it around the shank of the hook with a cocktail stick or something similar and then roll it in dry, uncooked hempseed. The resulting little balls of hooked yet unsoaked seeds can then be soaked for a day or so, together with the rest of the raw seeds, in the usual way. They should not be included in the boiling process as neither the Bogey nor the foam takes particularly kindly to it.

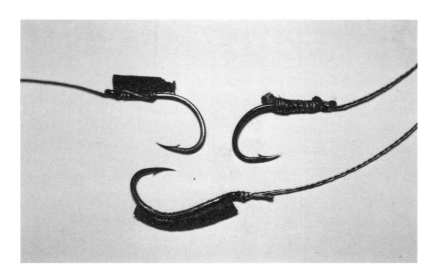

A selection of buoyant hooks – often something that makes the difference.

These hempseed cluster baits can then be used in a conventional manner; if presented over a bed of fully prepared, loosefed hempseed with split kernels it can prove to be highly effective. While barbel prefer freshly prepared hempseed to hempseed that has been frozen, it appears to make no difference whether the little Bogey balls of hempseed have been previously frozen, provided the loosefed hempseed it is being fished over is fresh.

A bait that refuses to rise off the bottom along with any of the free samples will almost certainly be ignored by any educated barbel feeding in the swim. The main objective when fishing tiny particles such as hempseed or tares is to match the action of the hookbait to the free samples. The ways in which this can be achieved are numerous, with the more effective rigs appearing in the diagrams below.

For fine-tuning purposes, it pays to keep a tub of tiny black polystyrene balls resembling the seed baits to hand as they can easily be used to increase the buoyancy of the bait should the doctored hook be weighed down by an over-abundance of seeds.

Another popular method – and a useful alternative to the buoyant hook idea – is to smear a small cork or polystyrene ball, either ¼ or ½in (6 or 12mm) in diameter, with the Bogey until it is completely covered, before rolling the coated ball in dry hempseed or tares and soaking as usual. These little seed balls can be used in the same manner as any other bait – impaled on the hook or hair-rigged if conducive conditions prevail.

Buoyant hooks are not only effective for seed rigs but indeed all baits. Any bait that has a hook embedded within it is automatically heavier than a free bait, and whether or not the bait is fished hard on the bottom a presentation is always improved with a buoyant hook. I have heard it said that most barbel cannot differentiate between a bait fished on a buoyant hook and one that is not. However, a hookbait is often ignored, not because it is eyed with any form of suspicion, but because it behaves differently from those around it. The differing action of the hookbait will not usually in itself spook the feeding barbel; they do not deliberately ignore the bait but appear simply to overlook it, because it does not rise off the bottom as they suck at the free samples of bait from a

Mould Kryston Bogey to required shape and roll in dry, unprepared hempseed/tares. Prepare seed as normal. The bait can then be hooked the same as any other.

Apply Kryston Bogey around shank of hook with aid of sausage stick or something similar. Then roll hook in dry seed and soak as normal.

Ideal barbel hooks for many occasions.

few inches away. They are not preoccupied; they are feeding in a certain way that prevents the hookbait from being taken because of the offsetting natural weight of the hook.

The importance of buoyant hooks cannot be over-estimated as they give the hook bait presentation a completely fresh dimension. Supergluing cork or hard-based rig foam to hook shanks may appear somewhat crude, but the results of its use speak for themselves. Eventually, I am convinced, this will be understood commercially with manufactured buoyant or counterbalanced hooks being readily available, at which point there will be no looking back, at least for a time anyway!

Hair-rigs fished hard on the bottom have never been as reliable for barbel as they have for carp and tench. The effectiveness of the rig appears to be very erratic with barbel, as on too many occasions all the angler succeeds in doing is missing bite after bite and finding the hair broken or stripped of bait. This is not because of any superior intelligence or caution on the part of the barbel but is more likely to relate to the manner in which they feed. While the hair-rig does present hempseed or tares in an extremely natural way, the rig is not generally efficient enough for feeding barbel to be hooked consistently. This trait does change from river to river,

with some appearing to be slightly better hair-rigging venues than others. While a non popped-up hair-rig works extremely well on still waters, its whole action is different in strong flowing water; it is quite frequently impeded and does not work as well. That is why still-water roach and chub succumb to it while their river-dwelling counterparts do not.

HAIR-RIGGED AND ON-HOOK POP-UP RIGS

All is not lost for those wishing to hair-rig for barbel however – baits that are presented off the bottom, commonly known as pop-ups work particularly well when fish become preoccupied with particles such as hempseed, tares or sweetcorn. The hair-rigged pop-up is a much more effective presentation that a hair-rigged bait that is resting on the river bed.

A popped-up bait is technically a buoyant bait that is fished, generally speaking, between 1 and 3in (2.5 and 7.5cm) off the bottom and is anchored to the river bed with rig putty. A properly fished pop-up is one that is perfectly balanced so that the bait and the counterbalancing of the buoyant hookbait cause the rig barely to sink.

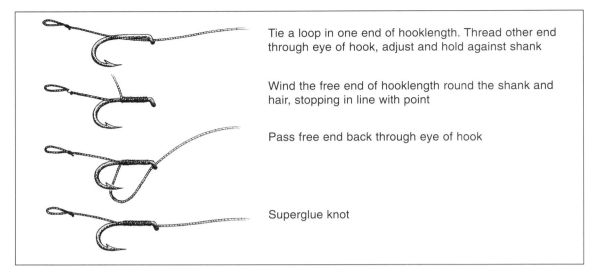

Tie a loop in one end of hooklength. Thread other end through eye of hook, adjust and hold against shank

Wind the free end of hooklength round the shank and hair, stopping in line with point

Pass free end back through eye of hook

Superglue knot

Tying a braided hair directly onto the hook using the hooklength.

Nervous and suspicious barbel are often said to fan at particles, particularly hempseed, but I have watched them do the same with other particles such as wheat, tares, peanuts, maggots, casters, sweetcorn, mini boilies and mini meat cubes. They fan, quite vigorously at times, at the particles with their caudal, anal and pectoral fins to lift the particles off the bottom to test their safety. In addition to this the barbel will also push particles off the bottom by jetting water out through their gills and then fanning away. I have often watched completely naive barbel fan at baits so they do not have to be either nervous or suspicious for this to occur. This behaviour appears to be a perfectly natural feeding technique among naive as well as sophisticated fish.

I have also witnessed barbel under these circumstances appearing to work for each other's benefit, with one barbel feeding on the suspended particles thrown up by the fish in front of it. I have then watched them swap round, and work with several others, on more than one occasion during the feeding spell. Fishing a hair-rigged popped-up hempseed or tare presentation when the barbel are in this mood certainly puts the bait exactly where the barbel expect it to be – just off the bottom, acting like

all the other seeds and seemingly untethered.

The most effective way to re-create these underwater events is to fish a hair-rigged hempseed pop-up, and this is relatively simple. A small Bogeyed-up cork or polystyrene ball covered in hempseed or tares is particularly effective here. The balls can be mounted onto a very short hair with the natural buoyancy of the bait then counterbalanced by a small amount

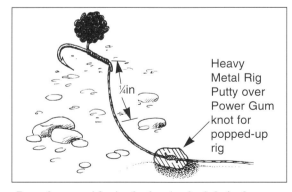

Heavy Metal Rig Putty over Power Gum knot for popped-up rig

Popped-up particle rigs for fanning barbel. Apply Bogey to cork ball and roll in dry hempseed. Soak hempseed as normal. For presentation whip a 12in braided hooklength, looped at one end, to a Gold Label Penetrator or Fox Series I or II ensuring that the braid emerges through the eye of the hook towards the inside. Bait then attached to looped hair.

of rig putty moulded onto the hooklength, so that the hookbait, once again, barely sinks.

The Bogey ball mentioned previously can also be fished in this style by fine-tuning the bait with black polystyrene balls so that it rises off the bottom, as opposed to only just resting upon it as in previous diagrams. The use of Heavy Metal Rig Putty will again counterbalance the buoyancy of the hookbait and create the popped-up presentation, as with the Bogied cork or polystyrene ball.

So that the rig putty does not slip it needs something to grip onto, and float stops or Power Gum stop knots are both perfectly adequate. The easiest way to balance a buoyant bait for a pop-up is to put on too much putty initially and then keep nipping tiny segments of it off until the desired effect of the bait only just sinking is achieved.

One of the most effective ways of extending the life of maggots on the hook is to Superglue them to a pea-sized polystyrene ball or, better still, a cork ball of similar size. A tiny blob on the blunt end of the maggot is all that is required before it is pressed against the surface

of the ball. The maggot will wriggle a bit at this stage and the technique is to keep its blunt end pressed against the surface of the ball for several seconds before it is secured firmly. The best way of doing this is with a small pair of tweezers. This process does take time but it is time well spent as several maggots can be attached in this way. The best way of presenting this creation, known fondly in barbel circles as a 'Medusa Rig', is on a short hair. It can be very useful for heavily pressurized barbel.

Another highly effective way in which to fish a writhing mass of maggots is with the aid of a fine darning needle and very fine hair-rigging nylon. By threading the line through the lip of the blunt end of the maggots any number can be so attached. One end of the line can, for instance, be tied to the eye of the hook with the remainder wrapped around the shank before being secured on the hook bend. This is a useful alternative for those anglers who distrust the hair for barbel or for those who fish rivers where the hair does not work.

Hair-rigging popped-up particles such as hempseed, tares, maggots, sweetcorn or mini-

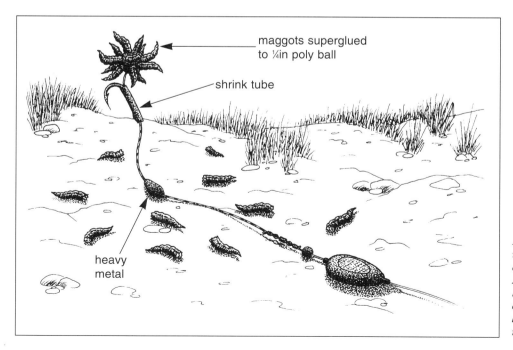

maggots superglued to ¼in poly ball

shrink tube

heavy metal

Poly ball pop-up maggot rig or the Medusa's head fished over carpet of loosefed maggots.

boilies appears to work slightly better than hair-rigging presentations involving larger baits such as meat or midi to standard sized boilies. All hair-rig presentations appear to work better for barbel when the braid is whipped onto the shank of the hook. By then applying some Kryston Hawser Rig-a-Mawtis to the first quarter of an inch of the braid, the hook will sit nicely over the rig, thus increasing its hooking capabilities. The Gold Label Penetrators and Fox Series all have in-turned eyes and were designed for this type of bait presentation, albeit originally boilies for carp, yet for this type of barbel fishing they are equally effective.

Conventional canned sweetcorn, as well as the Pescaviva variations, can all be fished pop-up style with a small piece of appropriately coloured rig foam cut to the necessary size. I find Gold Label's rig foam to be very durable as well as being easy to work with and it is available in red, yellow, green and black, which covers most bait eventualities. The two diagrams show at least two proven sweetcorn variations.

The effectiveness of popped-up baits for barbel does not stop at particles but covers all baits, although some of the larger baits are easier to pop-up than others. Boilies, Bacon Grill, garlic sausage and most of the other meats can be made buoyant with the aid of a Gardner Bait Drill and foam plug kit or with a Marvic Boilie Punch and foam. For those anglers who will not use the hair rig on principle, the diagram overleaf shows a very effective substitute.

Barbel will fan any bait that they can manoeuvre off the bottom. Given their immense strength this just about covers any bait you care to mention. Baits of a size that fanning barbel are not inclined to lift off the bottom, for reasons best known to themselves, are often inspected with the aid of their sensitive barbels. If the bait appears to be unduly heavy and does not react in exactly the same way as all the other free offerings, it will generally not be taken. The presentation of a popped-up lump of paste or meat to a fanning and wary barbel will very often deceive it into believing the bait to be genuine. An imperfectly balanced hookbait will always be different in its behaviour from all the rest of the loose feed, large or small, and the more the angler can imitate the natural action of

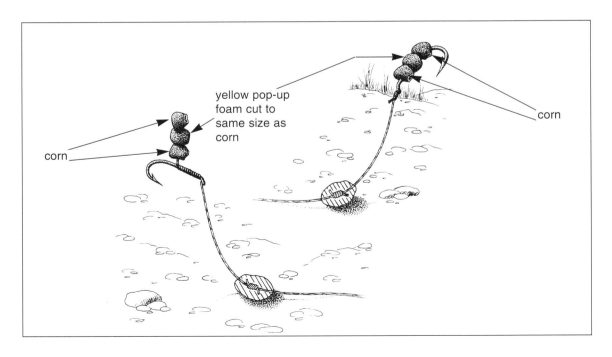

yellow pop-up foam cut to same size as corn

corn

corn

Autumnal rivers such as this place tremendous pressure on the mainline.

A braided hook-length scores yet again.

Mainly Loafers and Avons, ideal barbel fishing floats.

Flattened bombs for all conditions.

Meat fished with a hemp based feeder mix rarely fails in autumn.

A swim full of snags, and barbel.

Barbel are often to be seen swimming up and down these Ranunculus *beds.*

Baiting up a gravel run beneath an overhanging tree.

Winter sunlight reflects off a pristine paste-caught

A bait to appeal to the predatorial instincts within barbel.

This long glide always fishes well as the sun begins to sink into it.

As the sun sinks more open swims can be fished with greater confidence.

The features in this swim made it an obvious choice. The good judgement is endorsed by the action.

An evening caught barbel attracted by a hemp flavoured rig tablet.

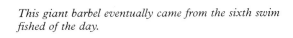

This giant barbel eventually came from the sixth swim fished of the day.

This barbel moved the quivertip no more than an inch in the middle of the day.

If a barbel gets snagged in a swim like this panic not, let the barbel swim straight out again.

I matched the current speed at this flooded river to summer flows and caught immediately.

Flat lead, Power Gum Breakaway and barbel, standard fare!

a free offering with the hookbait, the more successful will be the result with cautious fish.

Lobworms too can easily be counterbalanced against the weight of the hook by an injection of air close to the point where the worm is hooked. A lobworm wriggling half on and half off the bottom often makes this irresistible bait even more so.

STIFF HAIR POP-UP RIGS

This is a rig that works extremely well for big baits on rivers where the hair-rigging of such baits does not seem to work at all. Quite why this is so is unclear, but work it most certainly does. Fishing with a conventional soft hair tight up to both the bait and the hook shank should work but it does not. This stiff hair rig is excellent with barbel that display caution even in coloured water, and popping the bait up off the bottom by as little as ⅖in (1cm) can prove to be the difference between catching barbel and not doing so. I particularly favour this rig during the autumn floods when a lot of dead and dying weed is swirling around and catching on the tackle. Taking the exposed hook off the bottom goes a long way in preventing the hook and bait from catching on anything lying on the rubbish-strewn river bed, which potentially renders the reaction of the bait to a taking barbel wholly unnatural. Angling the hair, or perhaps more accurately the bayonet, to sit at 60 degrees enables the hook to sit at its most deadly angle. This is not a rig for all rivers but was devised for educated barbel on a particularly difficult non-hair river, where it worked.

PVA STRINGER RIGS

This is a very important rig, especially in autumn and winter on a coloured river when the angler can never be sure where the introduced bait is ending up. PVA is a form of dissolvable cord and the stringer rig is highly successful on several counts, not least because free

Popped-up meat bait with aid of Gardner bait drill and foam bait plug.

Lobworm critically balanced just off bottom by injection of air near to hook hold.

Hempseed Bogeyed to bouyant hook. Critical balance can be fine-tuned by adding black polystyrene balls to bait cluster until neutral bouyancy is achieved.

offerings are deposited adjacent to the hookbait as accurately as they are with any feeder. The beauty of the PVA method of introducing bait is that all the evidence dissolves, unlike the obvious physical presence of a feeder that can frighten wary barbel out of the swim.

Another, perhaps less appreciated, advantage of the stringer rig applies particularly to suspicious barbel. Such barbel will often approach a line of stringered baits very cautiously and take the one closest to them (the bottom bait on the stringer) after much examination and prevarication. They will then repeat the process and gradually work their way up the line, before finally getting to the last bait in the line, the hookbait, by which time most of their suspicions will have been allayed. Stringered baits are often taken in a very confident manner, even by quite pressurized barbel, when a

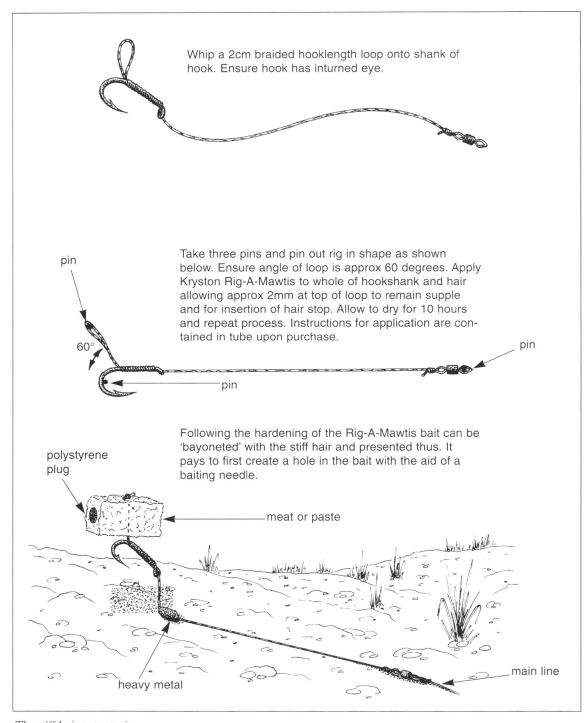

Whip a 2cm braided hooklength loop onto shank of hook. Ensure hook has inturned eye.

pin

Take three pins and pin out rig in shape as shown below. Ensure angle of loop is approx 60 degrees. Apply Kryston Rig-A-Mawtis to whole of hookshank and hair allowing approx 2mm at top of loop to remain supple and for insertion of hair stop. Allow to dry for 10 hours and repeat process. Instructions for application are contained in tube upon purchase.

60°

pin

pin

Following the hardening of the Rig-A-Mawtis bait can be 'bayoneted' with the stiff hair and presented thus. It pays to first create a hole in the bait with the aid of a baiting needle.

polystyrene plug

meat or paste

heavy metal

main line

The stiff hair pop-up rig.

single bait would have been examined and ignored with the angler none the wiser.

There is a lot of sub-standard PVA on the market that takes far too long to dissolve, much of it ending up as an unwanted gooey mess right next to the bait, which does far more harm than good. The best choice is supplied by Kryston who market PVA stringer under the name of Meltdown. Capable of dissolving in water right down to freezing point, as well as being very strong, Meltdown will not leave any residue on or near the bait or the hook.

For barbel work, which means using either meat or pastes or boilies, thread four to six baits onto a long Drennan Stringer Needle, hook a double length of the Meltdown onto the needle and slide the baits off the needle onto the Meltdown. Avoid knotting the Meltdown, as a knot takes far longer to dissolve than a loop. This loop of Meltdown is sufficient to hold the baits in place without the aid of knots, boilie stops or anything similar. Ensure that the baits have a distance of at least 1in (2.5cm) between them so that the Meltdown dissolves more quickly, as well as being presented on the bottom as a line of individual baits and not some long sausage-shaped whole, which the barbel will usually see as suspicious and consequently ignore.

Also available are PVA bags or tubes, which will deposit bait as effectively as the PVA string. Where large baits such as boilies or pastes and lumps of meat are introduced with the aid of the bag or tube, the element of gradually increasing the barbel's confidence as it works up the line is lost. PVA bags or tubes are therefore more suitable for the introduction of particles, provided they are dry, than anything else. One of the more effective methods is to include the hookbait within the bag itself and secure the top of the bag around a float stop after moistening it. Good-quality PVA bags or tubes are sold by Kevin Nash and Rod Hutchinson.

PINNED DOWN RIGS

The principle behind backleading rigs for carp is to pin the line to the bottom of the lake to render it less visible than it would be if it were stretched through the swim in mid water. Given the increased use of HPPE main line in carp fishing circles, backleading has become a common method of line disguise. Because of the nature of many barbel swims, not least because of the running water, backleading for barbel is often impractical. While barbel do not possess

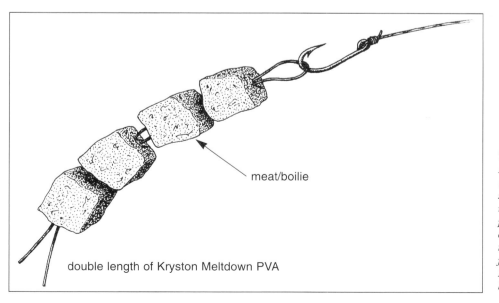

meat/boilie

double length of Kryston Meltdown PVA

The stringer rig. Hook bait (omitted for simplistic reasons) is pressed down onto hook therefore jamming the PVA onto the hook bend.

the line awareness of large carp their tendency to swirl and charge around baited swims, especially those of the hempseed-laden variety, often causes lunging line bites, which if struck at in error will either spook the fish or even temporarily foul-hook them, which can ruin a day's sport. An alternative to backleading is applying small blobs of Kryston's Magma Liquid Tungsten at regular intervals up the line. This method seems to work better on smaller rivers than large ones as the greater current velocity of the larger rivers has a tendency to lift the line off the bottom whether it is pinned down with Magma or not. This is particularly true in higher water conditions and it is a matter of fishing and finding out.

Backleading for barbel can be possible where bolt rigs are being employed and a direct contact with the hookbait for striking purposes is not essential.

COMBI-LINK RIGS

The combi-link is a part braid and part Kryston Multi-Strand (KMS) rig for ultra-wary barbel and a natural progression from braided hooklengths where certain situations prevail. Multi-Strand has several separate strands of material that terminate at the hook. KMS offers the ultimate in bait presentation, but owing to its high degree of tangling it should be used in conjunction with a Kryston Merlin or Silkworm braided hooklength. The most effective combination is 7in (18cm) of braided hooklength to 3in (7.5cm) of KMS. The knot required for joining the two components together is the four-turn water knot. The combi-link is not so much a rig as a presentation and can be used for hair-rigging hempseed as well as presenting large lumps of meat on the hook.

Once in the water all the multiple strands of the KMS separate and lie very flat and invisible on the gravels. This is not a rig for pop-ups or weedy waters as the numerous strands will conspire to tangle and mar the overall presentation. It is not an easy rig to use at the best of times, especially on rivers, but the natural action of the bait, together with the manner in which the strands merge into the gravels, has made it a

Pinned down rig. Normal or bolt rig with small lumps of Magma Liquid Tungsten on line.

superb barbel taker on highly pressurized waters where the barbel have begun to associate conventional braided hooklengths right up to the hookbait with suspicion. The application of an anti-tangle gel to the braid of the hooklength gives the whole presentation a better chance of working properly in the flowing water of a typical barbel swim.

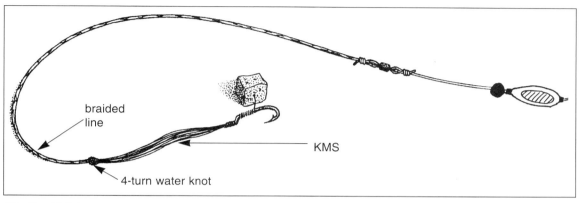

The Combi-link.

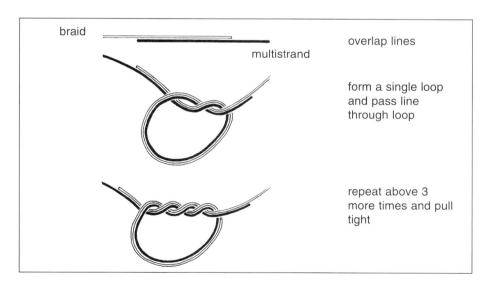

Four turn water knot.

8 TECHNIQUES

TROTTING

Trotting is an under-rated method for barbel as they love to take moving baits and can be compared to pike in that they will often take such a bait out of instinct whereas a static bait may be ignored, sometimes indefinitely. Trotting baits through barbel glides is a summer method with natural baits heavily outscoring the non-naturals. The reason trotting is so neglected by barbel anglers is unclear but perhaps it does come down to using incorrect baits. Meat, sweetcorn, paste or boilies and cheese are nowhere near as successful trotted as they are legered, but maggots, casters, minnows, caddis, lobworms and even prawns certainly are.

The table shows suggested tackle for trotting. One of the essentials on the way to becoming successful at this technique is to fish

Suggested Tackle for Trotting

- Graham Phillips 12ft Stepped Up Barbel Trotter
- Dave Swallow centrepin reel
- Selection of balsa-bodied Avon floats or clear plastic Drennan Loafer floats
- SSG and AAA shot
- Berkley Trilene XL line 6lb b.s.
- Drennan Starpoint hooks sizes 6 to 10
- Line floatant spray
- Plummet
- Baitdropper

over-depth and to ensure that the hookbait precedes the float and the line throughout the

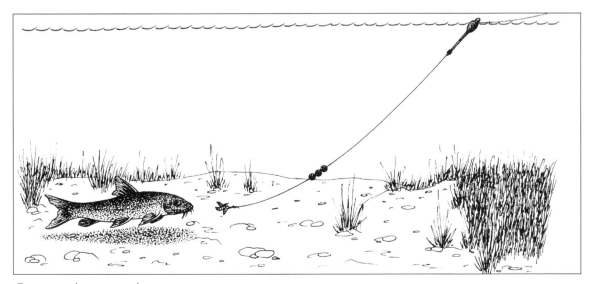

Correct trotting presentation.

A float-caught barbel – always a lovely sight.

whole of the way down to the shoal. Barbel will usually ignore a trotted bait if it is not held back slightly. The current velocity is slower nearer to the bottom than it is on the surface because of the braking effect that the bottom of the river exerts on the flowing water. Barbel will steadfastly refuse to take a bait that travels faster than the current in which they are sitting. Neither will they accept a bait that has the line billowing out in front of it caused by a lack of proper control from the angler. This telegraphs the whole deception to the waiting barbel before the bait even reaches them!

Another essential is not to use the same line for trotting as for conventional quivertipping as many anglers do. To trot successfully the line must float. Any line that sinks pulls at the float and consequently at the bait and renders it in the eyes of the barbel exactly what it is, a fake. Line can be made to float with the aid of a line

floatant spray. Berkley Trilene XL line is perfect for barbel trotting: it peels off the spool beautifully and yet is capable of withstanding the rigours of a hard day's barbel trotting with no ill effects. Commercially available float-fishing lines are inferior – while for roach and chub this may not be so important, for barbel your line must be the most robust as well as the best.

Large balsa-bodied Avon floats or clear plastic Drennan Loafer floats fished double rubber and carrying two to four SSG shots are ideal for this kind of work and their weight will draw line from a fixed spool very easily should you not be in a position to use the superior centrepin. By fishing the run 1ft (30cm) or so over-depth and holding back slightly, the perfect presentation is thus achieved. The humble plummet is a vital part of the approach here as a bait fished too deep or too shallow will be ignored. Sadly for the keen barbel float angler, the choice of rod is somewhat limited with Graham Phillips 12ft Stepped Up Barbel Trotter perhaps the pick of a very small bunch, which includes the Drennan Tench Float and the Seer Trotters.

One of the delights of trotting is the enthusiasm with which barbel take the bait. Often with a shoal of feeding barbel the float will disappear, with the line racing off the spool before the angler has time to react. This is not only a marvellous form of barbel fishing but is exceptionally effective too.

Totally natural baits such as caddis or minnows require no prior introduction and will catch barbel on the first trot through a shoal whereas maggots, and to a lesser extent casters, fish better if a baitdropper or two full of bait is introduced into the run first. As with most forms of pre-introduction of bait, it pays to rest the swim for an hour or two before beginning to fish.

The most successful trotting swims appear to be those with pace, presumably because the barbel has less time to inspect the bait, thereby allowing its competitive instincts to take over for the second or so that it sees the bait drifting past. Runs where wary barbel hide beneath streamer weed are perfect for trotting as this is often the only way the barbel can be enticed out to take a hookbait.

During the summer months, particularly when the barbel are visible, it can be quite disconcerting to see barbel apparently flee in panic at the sight of the oncoming bait. This reaction is not always what it seems, however. Barbel are excitable creatures and the mere sight of food can often stimulate them into all sorts of strange antics, which can be misconstrued as fear. Although a barbel will appear to turn from a perfectly presented bait this can often be the sign that a bite is imminent. At times, barbel in shoals react to outside influences as one; these traits are discussed in Chapter 1. Trotting baits through a shoal of barbel can easily spook the lot of them, but a barbel that turns away from a bait may not necessarily be panic stricken. It is probably doing one of three things: bolting in fear, allowing another member of the shoal first crack at the bait, or displaying natural caution amidst its recognition of a bait as food prior to taking it. Often the next bait trotted down will be taken by the same barbel that appeared to bolt at the mere sight of the previous presentation.

Trotting through a summer barbel glide.

TOUCH LEGERING

Modern technology has brought this ancient method of bite indication into a completely new realm, and its effectiveness is perhaps unsurpassed as modern methods go. As with trotting, most anglers accepted that it had potential but only a few had the belief to persevere with it. Fortunately an increasing number of anglers are matching the latest line technology with the old skills and reaping the rewards.

Most successful barbel anglers appreciate that any barbel is capable of inspecting and rejecting a bait without any indication at the quivertip. While touch legering may not always convert such bites into fish on the bank, the angler will at least have a chance to hit them, and pulls and plucks that barely move the quivertip are magnified when the line is resting in the angler's fingers. Most barbel anglers with experience of touch legering have only used nylon line. While this is still a wonderfully sensitive and indeed thrilling way to catch barbel, the advent of the new fine-diameter braids has improved the effectiveness and excitement of this method. There are two rules that the touch leger specialist must follow to get the best from the method immeasurably. First, the rod tip should be pointing towards the bait as much as possible and the quivertip should be dispensed with. The more conventional 90-degree angle and the cushioning of bites by the quivertip should be abandoned and the rod top pointed at the bait as suggested so that every nudge, no matter how slight, is transferred directly up the HPPE line and communicated to the fingertip of the angler and not the rod or quivertip. The versatility of the Seer Specialist Rover Rod allows its quivertip to be removed and a tip ring pushed on in its place – this rod is the perfect tool for the barbel angler who is always looking for an opportunity to touch leger.

Each angler will formulate a preference as to how to feel for the bites and with which finger. The fact that HPPE does not stretch amplifies the bite to the fingertip as well as indicating any prevarication by the barbel beforehand. The

> **Suggested Tackle for Touch Legering**
>
> - 10ft 6in or 11ft 8in Seer Specialist Rover rod
> - 15 or 20lb b.s. Newtech Power Cable HPPE line
> - Hooklengths of 8lb b.s. Kryston Merlin braid or 6lb or 8lb b.s. Berkley Trilene XL nylon line
> - Gold Label Super 'V' rod rest head
> - Solar Tackle 20ft extending steel bank stick

committed touch leger angler will always hit more bites than the angler who watches a quivertip all day. The fact that you can feel the bite first is not the only reason that more bites are hit; the simple fact that you are forced to hold the rod to touch-leger gives you that all important edge, in that the bite is hit that split second sooner. Too many barbel anglers slouch behind two rods on their rod rests waiting for a powerful bite; this is a one-dimensional approach and will never be as effective as the angler who is in a position to strike at the smaller, gentler bites with rod in hand.

What if the barbel are not prepared to play the same game as the lazy barbel angler, and they pull the rod in? Again, it is the angler who has the ability to interpret underwater events and then formulate the appropriate tactics who is the most successful. There are many occasions where one rod fished touch-leger style will catch more barbel than two quivertip rods sitting idly in the rests just waiting for something to happen.

If there is one disadvantage with HPPE line as a touch-legering line then it is its rather painful habit of cutting into the indicating finger upon the strike. One of the most popular ways of holding nylon line when touch legering is to nip it between the index finger and the handle of the rod. To strike at a barbel with HPPE line held in this fashion will ensure that

A close-up of the line over the sensitive finger – the perfect indicator of bites when touch legering.

you have a very sore cut to contend with for the remainder of the session. A less masochistic method is to press the middle finger against the braid as shown in the photograph. On the strike the braid will not cut into the flesh but be drawn down and away from the indicating finger. In theory, you should be able to release the index finger grip at the time of the strike, but in all the excitement of a take this is often forgotten, at least by me anyway.

Over the course of the barbel season two quivertip rods fished intelligently will of course catch more barbel than the single touch-leger rod but there are certainly many sessions when the opposite is true. What the angler who fishes with rods permanently in the rests will never know is the spine-tingling sensation of feeling the line react to a taking barbel, which at night is quite something.

FREELINING AND TRUNDLING

The table lists suggested tackle for freelining and trundling. These are in many ways an extension of touch legering but with a moving bait as opposed to a static one. The rod is held in much the same way, with the bites being felt by fingertip or by the tightening or slackening of the line. It is not often that a static bait can be freelined for barbel given their preference for a pacey current in the summer; therefore freelining is more suited to a moving bait.

Trundling, as the name suggests, is the same method but with a little weight added to keep a bait down and on line. A moving bait, either freelined or trundled, is an effective method on hard-fished waters as well as neglected ones.

Suggested Tackle for Freelining and Trundling

- Seer 11ft 8in Specialist Rover or Graham Phillips 12ft Stepped Up Barbel Trotter
- Dave Swallow centrepin or Shimano GT 5010 baitrunner reel
- 15 or 20lb b.s. Newtech Power Cable HPPE line
- SSG shot and selection of drilled bullets
- 8 to 10lb b.s. Merlin hooklength braid or Berkley Trilene XL nylon

---

Many barbel anglers go to great lengths flavouring baits and using complicated rigs while fishing static baits on hard-fished stretches, whereas by switching over to a moving bait just freelined or trundled through, the bait will be taken immediately. This method of fishing perhaps works better in higher water temperatures when the barbel are more inclined to move for a bait than in the lower temperatures of winter.

As with most moving baits for barbel, it is the naturals that tend to do better in the clear waters of summer, but when the rivers begin to colour up at the onset of autumn, freelined and trundled baits such as the meats become more effective.

As a general rule fishing a moving bait by way of trotting does appear to lend itself to summer fishing rather better than freelining or trundling, possibly because of the way line can be prevented from preceding the bait much more easily with the aid of the float. When the river is carrying some colour this appears to matter less, and the rather inferior presentation of the freelined bait in clear water is somewhat negated by the less visible conditions.

For truly effective freelining or trundling it is wise for the angler to have observed the swim in clear water conditions when the gravel runs, weed-beds and snags could be seen but which are no longer visible. On smaller rivers it may well be possible to swim a large bait through a run without the aid of any weight at all (freelining), whereas a larger river may well require several SSG shot pinched onto the line so that the bait bounces along the bottom and through the run in a natural manner (trundling).

One of the major advantages of these two methods is that they can be fished both upstream and down. The upstream method requires the bait to be cast to the head of the run and allowed to bounce back along the bottom towards the angler. There will be occasions when the bait will settle momentarily; this is perfectly natural and can be allowed to happen but for only a short time, say two or three minutes, before the bait is gently eased back downstream and the trundle through continued.

Bites will be indicated by either an acceleration of the line towards the angler or a sharp tightening away. Sometimes a gentle pluck may be felt without the line going anywhere; in any event hit such things hard. The HPPE line will tell you much of what is happening and, with a little bit of practice, differentiating between a natural stoppage of the bait and one that has been taken by a barbel will become second nature.

Freelining or trundling baits downstream tends to work along the same principles with bites sometimes appearing as a slackening of the line (barbel coming towards you) or the more common rapid tightening (barbel swimming away from you) as well as the bait staying where it is (barbel doing likewise).

Many freelining or trundling specialists prefer the upstream approach as the bait can be eased and rested on its way down the run. This action may well appear more natural to a barbel and certainly seems to be the more effective. The bale arm will be closed when upstreaming a bait as line is regained when the bait returns to you. This is a big advantage in saving that split second when fishing for nervous barbel that require the quickest possible strike so that they are not missed. Trundling a bait downstream requires the bale arm to be left open, and the angler is forced to strike and snap over the bale arm to set the hook. The substitution of a centrepin for the fixed-spool reel immediately makes the whole method more efficient and the angler better equipped.

This approach, coupled with the line resting against the preferred finger (in this case the index) in true touch-legering style makes it a truly effective method as any barbel, even one smelling the bait, will be felt through the HPPE mainline.

Nothing could be simpler for trundling as the necessary amount of SSG shot is nipped gently onto the main line about 1ft (30cm) from the bait and just above the hooklength and swivel or Drennan ring. The freelining rig requires nothing more than the hook.

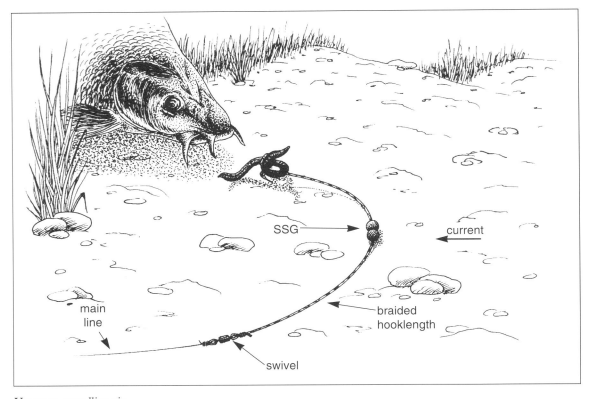

Upstream trundling rig.

This barbel moved ten yards to intercept a pair of trundled minnows.

QUIVERTIPPING

Suggested tackle for quivertipping is listed below. Quivertipping a straight leger rig is the backbone to the approach throughout the season, be it in a small summer stream or a large winter river in flood. The barbel angler's requirements when it comes to quivertips and their modifications were described in Chapter 5 and here it is proposed to study their most effective deployment.

Quivertipping is by far the most widely used method of bite indication by barbel anglers and it is indeed rare to see anglers using the rod top to indicate bites as they did in the old days. The sensitivity of the quivertip is decided by two things: the angle at which it is being fished and the stiffness of the quivertip in relation to the current speed. The optimum angle at which to fish the quivertip is 90-degree. When fished in this manner the bites will be emphasized and more readily hittable. If too soft a quivertip is used in too heavy a flow the current will pull the tip too far round thus eliminating the 90-degree sensitivity. Too many anglers are content to sit behind too soft a quivertip in too powerful a current and in extreme cases the tip will point straight down the line with the backbone of the rod taking the strain, rendering all but the most positive bites extremely difficult to spot. A quivertip perfectly matched to the flow in which it is being fished should take on a slight arc whether the quivertip is of a half or four ounce test-curve strength.

Probably the most versatile range of quivertips available to the barbel angler comes as part of the Drennan range of feeder rods. The quivertips are interchangeable from 1 to 4oz test curve, are clearly marked and obtainable separately. The Super Feeder IM8 rod does not come with either 3 or 4oz test curve quivertips, which are so useful in high water conditions; these will have to be bought in addition to the standard 2 and 2½oz models that come as part of the rod. But 2 and 4oz test-curve quivertips do come as standard with the Heavy Feeder

---

Suggested Tackle for Quivertipping

- Drennan 12ft Heavy Feeder Rod
- Seer 11ft 4in (1lb 4oz test curve) or 12ft 3in (1lb 8oz test curve) Barbel Quiver or Graham Phillips 11ft (1lb 8oz test curve) Stepped Up Barbel Quiver
- Drennan quivertip rod rest and butt rest heads

The perfect quivertipping angle.

rod, and are interchangeable with the Super Feeder IM8.

These quivertips come stored in the butt of the rod but after whipping on the two Beatalite housings to each of the quivertips it is best to store them elsewhere. Together with the extra tips required throughout the year quite a collection is built up, especially if you fish regularly with two rods. The safest way of storing the selection of quivertips is to cut off a suitable length of rod tube, cut an appropriately sized circle of polystyrene and stick it to one of the end caps. The thick ends of the quivertips can be pushed into the polystyrene and then placed inside the tube.

Bites can manifest themselves in many ways on the quivertip: a conventional pull, or a sharp drop back, right down to the merest tremble. Anything out of synch with the rhythmic nodding of the quivertip should be struck at. If HPPE is used as a main line the bites given on the quivertip will be exaggerated and between them they become an extremely sensitive form of bite indication. While this is not always necessary in barbel fishing the more the quivertip can tell you the better, especially when the slightest nudge alerts the angler to the impending possibility of a typical rod-wrenching barbel bite. It certainly gives an edge to be prepared,

particularly in tight, snaggy swims where the upper hand must be gained at the earliest possible moment.

Suitable rod rest heads are needed for conventional quivertipping and Drennan Quivertip rod rests are essential if a 90-degree angle and a slight arc are to be maintained. The front rod rest head has a series of positions along its length to enable the rod to be placed in exactly the position required. The rear rest is angled and cupped. It holds the rod in position even if it becomes necessary to point the rod upwards to avoid debris or extra current.

FISHING IN AND AROUND SNAGS

Fishing in or around snags occurs more with barbel fishing than perhaps any other branch of angling. A summer pursuit in which visibility is of the essence, snag fishing for barbel has developed into a method in its own right. Although it can be regarded as a high-risk activity, an intimate knowledge of the snag itself, a confident approach, appropriately strong tackle and a correct fishing position will all combine to change the extraction of barbel from snaggy swims from a possibility into a probability. The blind panic most anglers experience on hooking a barbel

A barbel swim at dusk; note Beatalite and angle of quivertip.

close to a substantial snag and playing the whole situation, as well as the barbel, by ear is a foolish enterprise.

The option of attempting to draw barbel out from their snaggy residence a suitable distance upstream by way of introducing a few bait-droppers of hempseed should always be explored. This ploy can often work but can never be as prolific as taking the mountain to Mohammed and fishing right in their lair. Barbel can be relatively easy to catch from snags because they feel confident within them, as opposed to being quite jittery when being tempted out into the open by the nearly irresistible hempseed. It is one thing attracting barbel out of snags, but another thing entirely putting them on the bank.

It is no coincidence that many of biggest barbel reside in these underwater jungles. While some snags are unfishable and will forever remain so, the lure of snag fishing in slightly less difficult terrain in an attempt to hook one of the monsters is compelling. Snags can be sunken tree roots trailing in the margins, wholly sunken

Suggested Tackle for Fishing in and around Snags.

- Seer 12ft 3in (1lb 8oz test curve) Barbel Quiver or Graham Phillips 11ft 4in (1lb 8oz test curve) Stepped Up Barbel Quiver
- Shimano Aero GT 5010 Baitrunner Reel
- 30lb b.s. Newtech Power Cable HPPE line
- Hooklengths of 25lb b.s. Kryston Super Nova Braid
- Gold Label Penetrator, Fox Series 2 or 3 or Drennan Continental boilie hooks
- 25lb or 35lb Kryston Quicksilver shock leader
- Kryston Magma Liquid Tungsten
- Kryston Snag-Free putty
- Kryston Granite Juice

or semi-submerged trees, rafts (usually associated with the latter), sunken boats, old river walls, bridge buttresses and large boulders. Vehicles, garden sheds and even bedsteads have all been barbel-infested snags at times and, depending on which river you fish, any of these features can be responsible for creating barbel swims.

No matter what the snag is the barbel will usually be in residence for two reasons: cover and food. Barbel make much more use of cover than is generally supposed but the main reason for finding barbel among snags is that they are food traps. Exposed tree roots, for example, are usually exposed by the current undercutting the bank upon which the tree is growing.

Trees that have toppled over into the river offer cover as well as breaking up and deflecting the current, leaving relatively slower, smoother, eddying water in the wake of the tree. Such a feature tends to accumulate food and therefore barbel. Submerged or semi-submerged trees often tend to gather the assorted jetsam and flotsam that comes down a river and therefore creates a raft of weed or debris. These rafts increase cover – where they exist so do barbel.

Sunken boats, bridge buttresses and old river walls all create similar swims to sunken or semi-submerged trees. The current will hit the obstacle and be deflected from its natural course, creating a crease to one side, sometimes both sides of the feature, and a relative slack or hole behind it. These swims are often very easy to spot during the summer months and this is the time to get out and start noting the location of a few of them.

When one comes across a snaggy swim in the summer it makes sense to study it and if possible ascertain precisely where the barbel reside within the swim. By spending an hour or so studying it an attack plan can be formulated and if necessary work done on the swim to improve it from an angling point of view. Wherever possible, the best way of learning about a snag swim is to get in the river and wade up to it with the aid of a pair of thigh boots, or better still chest waders.

My snag swim, nobody else ever fishes it. I wonder why?

Some tree-based snags do not contain barbel because they do not form food traps. These swims usually occur in very slack or even still water well off the main pace. In addition, the river bed beneath the snag may be littered with other debris and associated river rubbish. Barbel do not mind what rubbish they live under but they do like a clean bottom over which to graze. If the bottom beneath a tree-based snag is not only clean but shelves away from the snag and the bank towards midstream, then it is probably a very good barbel swim indeed.

Once the precise location of the barbel within the snag has been established by bankside observations, it is the time to don the boots. Once in the water, study the snag and the distance to the barbel from the nearest point where the tackle may get caught. Getting in the water gives the angler a better perspective of the swim from the bank, which is particularly useful for baiting-up purposes and especially when a barbel is finally hooked.

Establish where the tackle should be cast and imagine what the barbel will do once one of their number is hooked. It is far easier to play a barbel with a picture of the snag in your mind than to do it blind.

Maintenance work on such swims is often beneficial but care should be taken not to alter the features of the swim. Odd trailing branches or dead or dying tangled lengths of weed, for instance, can often prevent the bait being placed precisely where you want it as well as being extra snags for the barbel. An odd bit of pruning here and there can make tree-based snags much easier to fish. In semi-submerged tree snags the branches that protrude out of the water can easily catch on the line while fishing and mar a successful presentation. Removal of an odd strategic twig or two above the water line will not alter the characteristics of the swim, nor will such work lessen the appeal of the swim to the barbel.

Tree-based snag swims, like all other barbel swims, benefit greatly from the introduction of bait with the aid of a baitdropper a few hours before starting to fish. This can be done from either bank or by wading out to the snag. Baitdroppers are just as prone to getting snagged as rigs so it pays to wade out and do it from a better vantage point, not least because half a dozen baitdroppers festooned in or around a snag neither do the swim any good nor promote any confidence in the barbel.

Exposed roots and fallen tree snags are often fished from an upstream position on the same bank, but whenever possible they should be fished from the opposite bank. The angler who fishes downstream to a tree snag on the same bank is instantly put at a disadvantage. A barbel hooked by an angler on the same bank can do anything it likes because all the angler can do is to apply pressure and attempt to pull the barbel against the current in an effort to get the fish out. This encourages the barbel deeper into

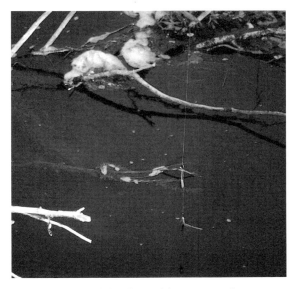

A breakaway rig being lowered into a pruned snag.

current. The current does not hinder the playing process from the opposite bank but helps it, provided the clutch is clamped down hard on the barbel, whose natural reaction, in all probability, will be to make for the snag. By applying maximum pressure the barbel will be forced to kite downstream, away from the snag and out to midstream and relative safety. If a barbel is determined to get into the snag straightaway then it may well do so and escape but the chances are that it will not.

Should your barbel behave as it should and kite downstream and away from the snag, allow it to do so and, if your fishing position allows it, follow the fish a little way downstream and ensure that the barbel is played out well away from the snag. This not only increases the chances of landing the barbel in snag free water, it prevents the other barbel from becoming spooked. While a shoal of barbel in free water appear to be unaffected by a fighting barbel in their presence, a fish that is crashing around in a confined sanctuary area such as a tree based snag will soon disperse others that will not return for some considerable time.

Large rocks or boulders can certainly be classed as snags and will often have several barbel in residence. While most sunken and semi-submerged trees are relatively temporary, large rocks and boulders can often remain in place for decades.

Nothing deflects the current like a large lump of rock and, because of the length of time that they tend to remain in the same place, large craters are often gouged out by the current immediately behind them. These holes act as excellent food traps. In low water conditions it is often possible to see a large rock in the water, while on other occasions a rippled or broken surface will indicate the presence of a rock or boulder just beneath the surface. There will usually be a crease running downstream of the snag with slacker water immediately behind it. Barbel often tend to sit tight behind large rocks in the slacker water as well as along the crease and an amazingly large amount of them appear happy to do so.

the snag as it is its nature to pull directly against the force of the hook. The angler is attempting to draw the barbel either through the snag or along the edge of it before attempting to net it. Although barbel are not renowned for their guile during a fight, but for their power and stamina, they can still get snagged up quite easily because of the direction from which they are being played.

By casting upstream from a downstream position to a snag you can create a better vantage point from which to attempt the extraction process, but the reality of playing a barbel is much the same with less opportunity of placing a bait precisely where you want to from the downstream as opposed to upstream position.

When a snag is being fished from the opposite bank and a barbel is subsequently hooked, it is a better option for the angler to hit and hold and allow the barbel to swim or kite directly away from the snag (usually downstream but occasionally upstream) as opposed to through it, which is usually the case when the snag is being fished from the same bank.

Another advantage of fishing across to an opposite bank snag is that any barbel that is hooked will not be played directly against the

A double rock swim, a suicidal proposition without correct tackle.

As with the tree snags, a good wade around the rock will be of immense benefit and, while it is not always possible to reach a rock in thigh boots or chest waders, such a view as afforded by getting as close as possible to the rock will at least allow the angler a much closer view than is possible from the bank. While there is not much maintenance work that can be done to rock snags they do on occasions collect rubbish such as branches and trailing weed. These can hinder a successful presentation and are best removed. Bridge buttresses create much the same environment for barbel as rocks and can be treated in the same way.

Tackle for snag fishing is of a highly specialized nature and no compromises should be entertained. The Graham Phillips Stepped Up Barbel Quiver Rod was designed for snag fishing and the Seer 12ft 3in Barbel Quiver is also an ideal tool for these situations. The coupling of either of these rods with 30lb b.s. Power Cable HPPE line makes a very powerful combination. The reason behind using such high breaking strain line is not to drag the barbel out of the snag, although the stronger the tackle the harder the fish can be played, but because of the line's ability to withstand the rigours of playing a barbel in and around snags. Once a

hook is put into a barbel the angler has a responsibility to that fish to net it and remove the hook. Forget giving it a chance, just land it!

An alternative to an HPPE main line is a short shock leader. Shock leaders are commonly used in carp fishing to absorb the shock of long casts and give added protection for snag fishing. In the context of barbel fishing it is the latter quality that we are interested in. A shock leader is a short length of line tied to the end of the main line (carp anglers make their leaders about twice the length of the rod) with the leader substantially stronger than the main line and therefore capable of absorbing more abuse.

Kryston Quicksilver is perhaps the finest and most robust shock leader available and comes in 25lb, 35lb and 45lb b.s. spools, more than strong enough for most barbel fishing situations! Quicksilver is best tied to a nylon main line such as Silver Thread or Berkley Trilene XT of between 12lb and 15lb b.s. The nylon line and the leader can be improved with a liberal coating of Granite Juice line protection, which further increases the chances of landing a barbel.

The thickness of the leader would ordinarily make it stand out more than conventional lines, but when fished adjacent to tree snags the barbel appear to tolerate it. Should this not be the case a couple of blobs of Magma Liquid Tungsten at 2ft (60cm) intervals up the line will pin the leader down onto the river bed, reducing its visibility to virtually nil.

The terminal rig for fishing in tree snags should without question incorporate Snag Free Putty, as described in Chapter 7. Often when a barbel becomes snagged it is the lead that has been caught up and nothing else. In the event of the putty getting snagged it will pull off the rig with ease; 4lb of pressure is said by the suppliers Kryston to be required for this to happen.

In the end, though, it is the quality of the hook and hooklink that will make the difference between the barbel being landed or not. A 30lb b.s. HPPE mainline or a similar leader strength is futile if the hooklength is weak and the hook unreliable. Whereas an 8lb b.s. hooklength is perfectly adequate for most barbel fishing situations, for snag fishing it is not. A hooklength of 10lb b.s. or more is a suitable choice. Hooks must not open up; those described in Chapter 5 are all capable of extracting barbel from snags – the Gold Label Penetrator Two and Fox Series 3 are ideal.

Fishing by rocks and boulders requires a different approach from tree snags. Rocks are, generally speaking, fairly clear of debris but a barbel getting round to the wrong side of a rock can part any nylon or braided line in seconds. A rock snag can be read quite easily and the best way to approach one is to cast the long-tailed raft or rock rig with an unbaited hook to a point a few feet upstream of the rock from a downstream position and allow the putty to settle just in front of or beside the rock. (Keep nipping off small pieces of putty from the main lump on the rig until the rig cannot hold bottom under its own weight. When this occurs, add a small amount of snag-free putty back onto the rig to allow the rig to regain its position. You then have a perfectly balanced rig for fishing the rock.) The swim should be rested for a couple of hours before re-casting to it, assum-

ing that the river level has not dropped or fallen. After baiting the hook, allow the bait on the long tail to get pushed downstream and into the slacker water right behind the rock where the food and the barbel tend to collect.

Bites will usually be drop backs as the barbel takes the bait and turns away from the rock and downstream towards you. Strike hard, sweeping as much line over your shoulder as possible to regain the slack, and a barbel should be attached. If the barbel decides that it wants to go round the rock it must be prevented from doing so at all costs as no amount of HPPE line or Granite Juice will stop the line parting when it is being rubbed against an ancient lump of rock.

Multiple catches of barbel can be made by fishing in this manner not only because of the food trap and depression that exists behind a large rock or boulder but also because the shoal of barbel in residence will not have been fished for. Natural baits are perhaps the most successful and as always a few baitdroppers of bait introduced a couple of hours before starting to fish prime the swim up beautifully.

FEEDER FISHING

No fish responds quite as enthusiastically to a well-fished feeder as the barbel. While feeder fishing for barbel on large rivers is associated with piling in a great deal of bait to get the barbel feeding, there is also a time when only an occasional cast with the smallest of feeders will be the most effective. Nevertheless, it is the first option and the table over the page lists appropriate tackle for standard feeder fishing.

For general barbel fishing, feeders tend to fall into two categories: blockends and cage feeders. Blockend feeders tend to be more applicable to the introduction of maggots than anything else while cage feeders are superb at introducing groundbaits as well as samples of whatever bait is being fished.

Conventional cylindrical blockend feeders are impractical for a lot of river work because their cylindrical shape is all too easily rolled flat square of lead clipped to the base, which will hold bottom far more effectively in weights of up to 2oz (55g). If this is not enough then heavier clip-on leads, which can be bought separately and are known as 'dead cows', are available in weights of up to 4oz (110g) and can be so employed.

Drennan oval blockend feeders were originally designed with maggots in mind and they remain the most efficient tools in depositing maggots close to the hook bait, but their employment in barbel fishing is more diverse than that. On large rivers, especially in the winter when there is extra water and the current velocity is greater, Drennan's oval blockends will not only hold bottom better than the cylindrical varieties, but will slowly deposit a feederful of hempseed and caster into the swim as well, which with the cooler temperatures is much more to the barbel's liking than filling the swim in with bait.

around the river bed and out of position. Even by replacing the two or three swan shot or the inappropriately small clip-on leads that come as standard with a flattened bomb, they remain inferior to the oval blockends marketed by the Drennan company. These are designed with a

The bare essentials.

Cage feeders are without doubt the most valuable in the barbel angler's feeder box and their effectiveness is greater than any of the alternatives. The best suited and most versatile cage feeder for barbel fishing is made by Nisa and is constructed from wire mesh with a rectangular, bottom hugging, heavy lead of up to 2oz (55g). Cage feeders are robust, offer minimal resistance to the current and allow the swift passage of bait from the feeder into the swim. Compared with the plastic open-ended variety they are less visible in the swim, especially if the lead is coated with a suitable camouflage and the wire is painted a dull colour.

Choosing an appropriately weighted feeder is most important and barbel anglers have much to learn from match anglers in this respect. Successful match anglers will talk of critical balance in feeder fishing and it is important that the barbel angler understands this concept. All anglers require that their feeder is positioned where they want it and that it remains where they want it to. Once this has been achieved only half the job is complete; far too many anglers over-lead a feeder and anchor it to the bottom with too much lead. The more lead the angler uses above what is required to hold bottom, the less sensitive and responsive the rig will be. What match anglers are striving for when they talk of critical balance is to get the feeder teetering on the brink of shifting at the slightest disturbance to the rig from a bite, hopefully.

On large rivers this was conceived to indicate bites from small fish as well as big ones to win matches, and when this set up is being fished properly, a dace will easily move a 3oz (85g) feeder and register a drop-back bite as the feeder is dislodged. Not all barbel pull the rod in, nor are all barbel prepared to drag or bounce a heavy feeder around until the angler realizes there is a bite. With a perfectly balanced swimfeeder set-up a wary barbel can take a bait, dislodge the feeder, indicate a drop-back bite on the quivertip and be hooked before it realizes anything is untoward.

This whole approach is rendered useless if the angler does not keep casting to the same spot every cast. If the casting is somewhat wayward the angler will fail in the first objective of concentrating the bait in the same area, thereby building up a swim into one that contains a number of feeding barbel. Furthermore, if the cast is too long the feeder will be pushed out of position by the extra force that the extra line attracts from the current, and if it is too short the feeder will be over-leaded for the shorter, closer position that it is being fished.

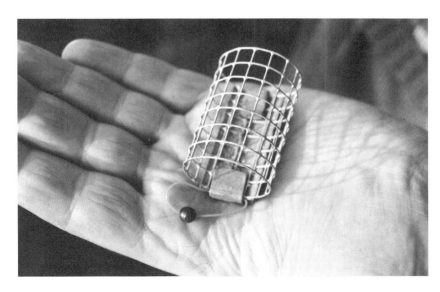

A close-up of a cage-feeder – an invaluable tool in heavy water or when you want to get rid of the bait quickly.

Accuracy over a period of time was only the beginning of the rewards here and which were to come.

Critical balance may mean that as little as two or three swan shot are all that is needed to achieve the stated objective, whereas at times weights of up to 5oz are required. It takes the same pressure to dislodge 5oz of perfectly balanced lead as it does a much smaller perfectly balanced weight, so do not fight shy of adding lead if the conditions warrant it. Such conditions as these are rare, though, and 1 to 2.5oz (30 to 70g) will usually suffice.

Achieving critical balance is an easy task; a simple cast to the desired spot will soon show whether there is sufficient lead on the feeder to hold bottom. If you find that the feeder does hold bottom, then keep subtracting lead from it by changing its weight with a lighter clip-on lead or changing to a lighter feeder altogether. After a short while a feeder will, for example, hold bottom with 1.5oz (40g) but fail to do so with 1.25oz (35g). The critical balance is some-

where between the two. The fine-tuning required is achieved with the aid of the line. By putting more pressure on the line by gradually lowering the rod tip you in turn exert more pressure on the feeder. By continuing to lower the rod tip you increase the pressure on the line and consequently on the feeder until the feeder finally dislodges. It follows that the height of the rod tip just before the feeder shifts is the point of critical balance. This is the optimum state of sensitivity and the one that should be strived for whenever possible.

On the larger barbel rivers it is the anglers who put in the work rate coupled with sustained casting to the same spot who are successful, whereas a successful angler on one of the smaller, more intimate rivers can often be effective by making no more than a few casts in each swim. The larger river approach is all about work rate; match anglers have understood this for years and in their highly competitive field they cannot afford to sit back and just wait for things to happen. Specialist barbel anglers, however, are often prepared to do just this when feeder fishing and in the process they do not do as well as they should, or indeed could. Many give up without giving things a chance and revert to casting out a lump of meat indiscriminately and going to sleep again.

While match anglers generally want to catch the biggest net of fish no matter what the species, barbel will often be the target in the appropriate rivers. The competitive methods that they have evolved should be taken on board by barbel anglers and turned to their advantage when the appropriate circumstances present themselves.

Build up a barbel swim on a big river with a feeder and a willingness to work. Once critical balance is achieved, it is time to mix up a carrier for the hookbait and attractant for the barbel. It should come as no surprise that the basis of this is hempseed. Barbel are attracted to the aroma and taste of hempseed more than they are to the seeds themselves. Swimfeeder mixes are therefore best based on crushed, grilled hempseed, which do as good a job, if not better, in attracting barbel into a swim as the seeds

themselves. Grilled hempseed that has then been crushed is more attractive to barbel than the plain crushed variety in that the grilled version exudes far more of its oily attractant into the water. A good base mix should begin with two parts of crushed and grilled hempseed and one part ordinary hempseed, the seeds having the ability to keep barbel in the swim once they have been attracted into the swim by the grilled version. The water in which the hempseed was cooked (see Chapter 6) is ideal for sponging into the groundbait mix.

Grilled or crushed hempseed and the conventional seeds do not bind sufficiently well for use in a feeder, so a binding agent becomes a necessary ingredient. This can take the form of one part of the commercially available dry groundbait mixes or a blend of any of them. Van Den Eynde and Sensas groundbaits are used by most of today's anglers. Any blend from these makes will bind the grilled hempseed base together and enable it to be cast out in the feeder.

Samples of hookbait are vitally important here and one part caster, sweetcorn or whatever else is being used on the hook should be included to get the barbel feeding, perhaps even preoccupied with it. While flavours lend themselves to being included in a swimfeeder

Feeder fishing the far bank pays off again, note tripod in background to combat high river levels.

The method and bait are obvious.

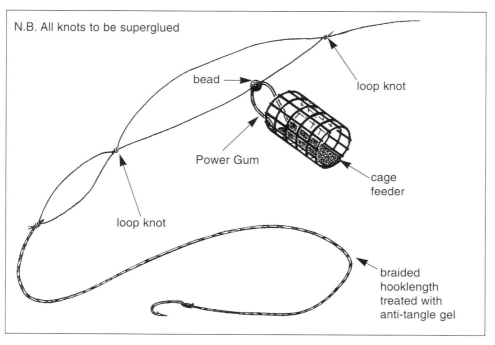

N.B. All knots to be superglued

bead

loop knot

Power Gum

cage feeder

loop knot

braided hooklength treated with anti-tangle gel

Double loop rig.

mix they should only be used when barbel become wary of this basic mix. Nothing attracts barbel into the swim quite like grilled hempseed and provided that not too much seed is introduced into the swim at the same time, the barbel will respond to the hookbait and associated free samples. A larger, deeper river requires a stiffer mix than a smaller one to get the swimfeeder, plus contents, down to the bottom intact. The importance of the accuracy required to build up a swim has already been mentioned and it is as well to choose a static object on the far bank, for instance a reflection or any form of foliage at which to aim.

With the groundbait now mixed it is time to start work. Using two rods, with one baited and cast every ten minutes to the same spot, is about right. This means that a rod is being cast and the feeder filled and the hook re-baited every five minutes. The angler is active continually but these labours can soon be rewarded. The use of two rods, not always an advantage in river fishing, can be used to bait two different lines or runs downstream. One rod may, for instance, be fished hard against a far bank run while the other can be employed to draw fish out of a near bank snag or a deep crease, depression or gully in mid current. Once one of the rods starts to produce, it really does pay to reel in the other. If you have feeding barbel on one rod, the other rod only acts as a distraction and many bites can be missed, which does nothing to prolong the stay of the barbel in the swim if they are rejecting baits before the angler has even noticed a bite. I have often found that, having caught a few barbel from the swim that initially produced the first bite, and after it has begun to die off a bit, the other line will often begin to produce a few more barbel again. The barbel move from the highly pressurized line over to the seemingly trouble-free second, bait-filled run.

When a shoal of barbel really get onto the feeder, and it usually takes an increase in levels and water colour for them to do so, they will often hit a swimfeeder rig the second it rests on the bottom. Feeder rigs are often problematical

in that the modern preference for braided hooklengths renders many braided feeder rigs nothing more than tangle machines. Even many nylon rigs are too tangle prone so it pays to stick with tried and tested ones.

The diagram opposite shows the acclaimed double loop rig. While most barbel rigs are better off with as few knots as possible, the double loop rig works for barbel because the loops themselves do not lessen the breaking strain of the main line. The second loop in the rig not only prevents those time-consuming tangles but also prevents the line being damaged by the feeder itself, provided that the second, smaller loop, is longer than the feeder. The cautious angler will dab each loop knot with a rig glue, to seal the knots and make sure that the friction between the lines does not weaken them.

Another vitally important component in a good feeder rig is the use of the bead, which joins the feeder to the main line. So much less line damaging than a swivel, a large-bore, hard plastic bead (less friction than a rubber bead) can run up and down the main line thousands of times causing no damage at all. The relatively less kind swivel eye will kink and weaken the same line far sooner; also, swivels are more tangle prone. This basic feeder rig, together with a short length of Power Gum between the bead and the feeder, is certainly the most reliable and all embracing rig there is for feeder work. The inclusion of Power Gum – 11lb b.s. works the best – acts as a shock absorber between the line and the feeder when casting. When playing a barbel, especially when heavy feeders are in operation, this shock absorption prevents any possible weakening of the hookhold.

The double loop feeder rig is far too neglected by specialist barbel anglers, and those who have used it will know what an efficient and tangle-free rig it is. While its anti-tangle construction is its greatest boon, the rig's other great strength is the ease with which extra lead can be added over and above that required for a perfectly balanced set-up. Unfortunately these days a lot of barbel are wising up on the harder fished rivers so by creating that extra bit of resistance as the barbel takes the bait and turns, the pull of the fixed feeder bolts the barbel and renders its hooking, particularly in high water conditions, a foregone conclusion.

Tangling has always been a bigger problem with feeder fishing than most advocates will admit and many rigs depicting rig tubing work better in the minds of their creators than they do in practice. The true test of any feeder rig is how consistently it performs and reacts to the high work rate so necessary to get the best out of the method. To sit and de-tangle complicated feeder rigs detracts from the concentration and discipline required to build up the swim and wastes valuable fishing time. Such rigs are often tangled and not fishing effectively while in the water after being cast out, which in turn never allow the angler to feel settled and to fish with confidence. The double loop rig, apart from its other practical applications, allows the angler to do this. There are several variations to the basic double loop rig, but for barbel fishing purposes, that shown on page 120 is perfectly adequate.

Tying a double loop in a length of line could not be easier. The diagram shows how to tie a loop knot without the feeder attached, for simplicity. Begin by taking about 18in (45cm) of line and doubling it over as shown and tie in the loop. To tie the second loop take the bottom 6in (15 cm) of the first loop and tie exactly the same knot again. The hooklength can be attached to the second loop using a normal double Grinner or Uni knot.

Unfortunately there are too many barbel that will ignore baits if they are presented on nylon line. Berkley XL will extend the life of a nylon presentation somewhat but eventually a braided hooklength braid has to enter the equation. Although braid is tangle prone this disadvantage can be overcome by applying a rig glue to the upper of the hooklength as well as yet another Kryston product to the rig, their Super Stiff Anti-Tangle Gel. This solution stiffens the braid sufficiently for it to be cast and allowed to settle before the effect of the water dissolves the solution, thereby restoring the braid to its orig-

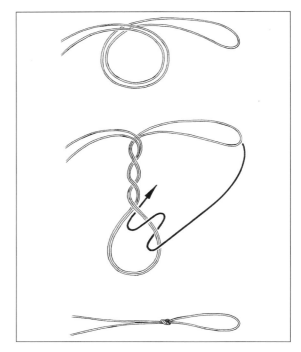

The loop knot.

inal, supple state although the glued length remains stiff. Although this is slightly time consuming for the busy feeder angler it is time well spent between casts when fishing braid for nylon-shy barbel, and the more trouble the feeder angler takes under these circumstances, the more successful the outcome.

A day's feeder fishing causes more wear and tear to tackle than any other method. The brunt of this abuse occurs to the line. Nylon line technology in the form of Berkley Trilene XT or Silver Thread is such that excessive feeder use has minimal effect upon it. The application of some Kryston Granite Juice to the line prior to beginning the swim build-up process reduces the wear and tear still further and the chances of the line weakening, or becoming damaged, are very remote. Alternatively, HPPE line is superbly effective for serious feeder work and in larger rivers is positively advantageous for the reasons already discussed in Chapter 5.

Successful feeder fishing does not have to revolve around piling in a great deal of bait and getting the barbel going. As with all forms of angling it is the angler who interprets events under the water and exploits them who is the most successful. Barbel can be hammered on the feeder for a while and they can become so preoccupied with the splash that they home in and take the hookbait before it reaches the bottom, or 'on the drop' as it is more commonly known. Under these circumstances a longer hooklength may be employed, allowing the bait to take longer to reach the bottom than with a more conventional, shorter hooklength. There are many occasions when a barbel is more inclined to take baits off the bottom than on it and feeder fishing is no exception. As time goes by, the splash of a feeder will often make the barbel disappear and the constant recasting of the feeder into the swim will only ensure that their absence is permanent. Under these circumstances the most successful angler will be the one who makes only an occasional cast and waits for the barbel to return, come across the hookbait and the feeder contents, and not associate these with the dreaded splash and depositing of bait. On other occasions barbel will only take a bait that has been inserted inside a cage feeder before casting and emerges from the feeder as it settles on the bottom.

The presence of any form of feeder in the swim might well prevent the barbel from re-entering the swim. Where a baitdropper is impractical, cast a few feeders full of bait out into the swim to prime it, then take the feeder off and wait for the barbel to return.

While it is often easy to observe these changes in the barbel's reaction to feeders in the clear, low waters of the summer, coloured water makes it impossible. Nevertheless, by adopting slightly advanced tactics over previously successful ones that are no longer as effective, the odd jigsaw piece may join up and turn a blank day into a memorable one.

A small barbel taken on the feeder contests its freedom in a shallow glide.

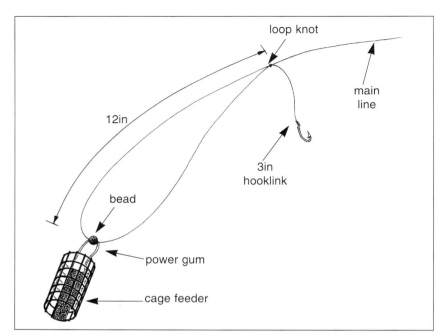

The Dink-Dink rig.

loop knot

main line

12in

3in hooklink

bead

power gum

cage feeder

One of the unlikeliest looking feeder rigs to come out of match fishing is the extremely effective Dink-Dink rig. This rig catches a lot of fish for match anglers, and under certain circumstances it does the same for barbel, which will often home in on a feeder and take loosefeed as well as the hookbait within seconds of it entering the water. This means that an awful lot of bait is taken by the barbel off the bottom. Barbel will, for reasons best known to themselves, ignore baits laying dormant or alone on the bottom and continually seek feed crashing through the surface, subsequently taking it either midwater or immediately it hits the bottom. They often appear to become preoccupied with free-falling bait. The Dink-Dink rig fishes the bait suspended off the bottom. This method works particularly well with particle baits such as maggots and casters and while the original Dink-Dink was made from Drennan Feederlinks and crammed with maggots, cage feeders work even better for barbel, especially if filled with a grilled hempseed-based mix as well as maggots or casters. The clouding effect really excites the barbel and they love to hit the bait if it is obscured by a cloud of hempseed-flavoured groundbait.

This method seems to work better for barbel if pieces of groundbait and loosefeed fall from the feeder during its descent through the water. The cage feeder, if observed at close quarters, sinks with the bait and groundbait trailing behind it, especially if the groundbait is mixed on the slightly wet, sloppy side. This is undoubtedly the way to fish the Dink-Dink for barbel.

A feature of this method is hard work, and once everything settles down on the bottom and clears the bait begins to look a trifle silly and is, not surprisingly, ignored. To make the method work a freshly filled feeder has to be cast continuously to the same spot, almost so the barbel begin to expect its arrival. Bites can come at any time, so, as the feeder hits the water, snap over the bale arm, bring the rod over your shoulder, follow the feeder down with the quivertip and do not be surprised to get a pull from a barbel the instant the feeder hits the bottom or even before!

As the rig is fixed the barbel will feel the resistance and bolt off, giving extraordinarily easy bites to hit. This type of fishing puts a lot of strain on the line and, as with the other feeder rigs, wear and tear can be reduced by coating

Feeder fishing the far bank; the session saw two doubles and a nine-pounder.

all the main line with Granite Juice as well as sealing all the knots in rig glue, which ensures that extra bit of safety.

Another great method that can loosely be described as feeder fishing is commonly known as 'The Method'. Originally designed by match anglers wishing to catch small carp in still waters, it evolved into a superb method for carp of all sizes. 'The Method' makes a smooth transfer to other fishing circumstances and is beginning to play a role in barbel fishing.

The rig involves an in-line frame-style feeder, around which is moulded a ball of stiff groundbait. Into this is inserted a hookbait tied to a short hooklength. Perhaps the most effective feeder for using 'The Method' for barbel is the FX Match In-line Feeder; the diagram overleaf shows exactly how the rig is prepared and this set-up has proved to be very effective for barbel, just as it has for carp. The original idea was that carp would come along and feed on the small amount of groundbait and take the hookbait at the same time.

This hookbait can take any form, and particle-style baits work particularly well, especially if a small number of hookbait samples are included within the ball of groundbait wrapped around the feeder.

The running water in which barbel reside has a different effect on the rig, but it is no less effective. There are a number of permutations available to the barbel angler and one particularly effective one is a groundbait ball of 50 per cent grilled hempseed and 50 per cent groundbait mix sprinkled liberally with hempseed, with hempseed on the hook. What makes this unlikely sounding method work for barbel is that the current breaks down the groundbait ball and carries the hempseed scent downstream, thus attracting the barbel upstream to the hempseed. This works exceptionally well for shy barbel, who will arrive and feed on the few

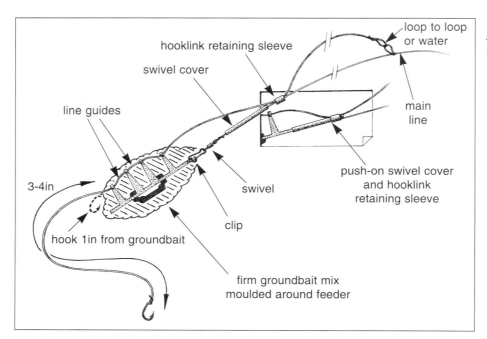

hooklink retaining sleeve

swivel cover

line guides

loop to loop
or water

main
line

3-4in

push-on swivel cover
and hooklink
retaining sleeve

swivel

hook 1in from groundbait

clip

firm groundbait mix
moulded around feeder

The Fox Match In-Line Feeder Rig (the method).

grains of hempseed that are surrounded by traces of the irresistible hempseed-based groundbait. Methods of attaching hookbaits in the form of hempseed or tares are the same as those described in Chapter 7. Any form of particle can be fished successfully using 'The Method' for barbel and, given the bait, groundbait and flavouring permutations available, the different options are numerous.

Another approach is to add The Pellet from Solar Tackle. By making a quantity of pellet powder groundbait and rolling the groundbait ball in 5mm pellets and subsequently moulding some of this groundbait around the frame feeder, the same principle as the hempseed-based rig is therefore adopted.

Liquid and powdered flavours, as previously recommended in the bait chapter, will give us that all-important edge and can be incorporated into the mix.

TARGETING BIG BARBEL

The first objective when embarking upon a big barbel quest is to make sure that the barbel you are after exists. This is an obvious statement, I know, but we need irrefutable proof that such a fish exists and precisely where. This can be done in three ways: witnessing them for yourself, being told by a trustworthy informant or, less reliably, reading about a capture in the angling press. The only way of being completely sure, however, is to see the target fish yourself.

Exactly what makes a big barbel? The answer is simple: if it is big to the angler who catches it then it is a big barbel. Some anglers' ambitions extend no further than an 8lb fish; but the majority tend to pursue the hallowed ten pounder. Beyond that we have anglers pursuing ambitions, dreams almost, of catching huge barbel, all the way up to and beyond the record, currently standing at 16lb 2oz from the River Medway in Kent. Whatever the ambition of the individual angler, targeting a big barbel requires patience, a composed temperament and confidence.

The basis of being selective is the ability of the angler to observe and assimilate the actions of the group of barbel, study precisely the movements of the largest barbel in the group and set a trap accordingly. Larger than average barbel should be watched minutely so that their comings and goings are monitored. Any angler who watches barbel grazing on loosefeed will notice how some of them will feed for a period and then melt away into the background, thus allowing other fish to move up and feed themselves. There is often a discernible pattern to this behaviour, which can take time to take shape, but your patience will eventually be rewarded as patterns begin to emerge.

A large barbel typically enters and exits using the same route each time. Often its movements become predictable with the barbel entering and re-entering the baited area every 15 to 20 minutes, for example. Once such behaviour has been witnessed we can then map out our plan of attack. If we do have a big barbel visiting the swim with at least a 15-minute gap each time, it makes no sense at all to place a bait only seconds after the fish has vacated the swim. This renders the hookbait vulnerable to attack for at least 15 minutes from unwanted, smaller barbel or the barbel angler's bane, chub.

With this in mind we need to time the placing of the hookbait so that it coincides with the imminent return of the target fish. A 15-minute pattern would, for example, require that a bait is in position as little as a minute before the return of the targeted barbel. Things can go wrong here; an early or a late return is possible but by reacting to the behaviour of the barbel as you see it and planning the tactics according to its movements you will be right more often than you are wrong.

Another vital aspect to this approach is that, as the arrival of the target fish nears, the barbel currently in the swim will be about to depart. Quite how the smooth changing of the guard is understood among the barbel is unclear, but anybody who has observed barbel closely under these circumstances for long enough will know that their behaviour is not an abstract thing, but orderly and deliberate.

Clear water is vitally important here, but so is a visible bait. Sweetcorn and prawns are two such baits and to be able to see such a bait as

these on the bottom will assist the angler greatly in trapping the prize. It is imperative that the bait is visible so that it can be twitched out of the way of an unwanted barbel that appears to be about to eat it.

Fortunately, barbel is not a species generally attracted by a bait bouncing out of feeding range – unlike chub, which appear to love catching up with a bait moved in this fashion for fear of it escaping. As we have already seen, the comings and goings of the target barbel are often predictable; further predictability can often occur when they enter the swim and begin to feed. A big barbel will always seem to feed on the baits as close to a feature or to cover as possible. This can often be nearby streamer weed, up a slope or sometimes something such as a sunken branch. If this tendency has been noticed then it makes obvious sense to position the bait on the edge of the carpet of bait as close to the cover as possible. Remember, we are targeting big barbel here and we have to load the percentage in our favour as much as possible.

The importance of the precise positioning of the bait cannot be over-emphasized, as a matter of inches out of position can sometimes mean that the bait is ignored. An understanding of our quarry is vitally important, as this is the time that our homework should begin to pay dividends, and so that we can appreciate just how tight we must be to succeed in our objective. The barbel, in particular the target fish, will usually be displaying caution and an appreciation of the circumstances it finds itself in. By entering and vacating the swim on several occasions the barbel are showing us that they are not completely settled. By feeding as close to cover as possible they are further displaying their trepidation by playing the percentage game just as we are. We know that the natural curiosity and greed of the barbel will be its eventual downfall, and that is our edge. We must appreciate that if the barbel was overly cautious, it would not be in the swim in the first place. Its mere presence gives us our optimism and hopefully the opportunity of catching it. This gives us the final ingredient of the

I watched this barbel's movements for six hours before I could confidently cast, expecting to catch it.

Intelligence gleaned after hours up a tree paid off when eventually a bait was cast to this giant.

scenario, namely confidence in ourselves and what we are doing.

Assuming, then, that we have placed our bait in position a minute or so before the expected return of the target fish and that we have positioned it in the favoured side of the bait carpet, we can allow the events to unfold before us. Deep concentration is vital and the whole of one's mind should be focused on the bait and the return of the target fish. By concentrating on the bait lying on the bottom we will be alert, so any arrival of barbel will be noticed immediately. The reactions to the bait can take many forms but we must keep our nerve and not over-react to anything other than a positive pull. If the bait disappears, it may well have done so because a barbel is sitting between you and the bait, thereby obscuring it from your view. A disappearing bait does not necessarily mean that it has been taken. If a bait disappears without any indication to the line then resist the temptation to strike, otherwise you will spook the target and undo hours of patient work.

Without any doubt touch legering is made for this type of selective fishing and if a bait is genuinely taken you will feel it. It makes no sense to count on a visible bite indication when you should be watching the bait and the barbel. This is what makes touch legering under these circumstances so effective: the bite indication is felt, not seen.

Very often a big barbel will edge its way up to a bait slowly and even inspect it before taking it. This can be a very nerve-racking period and again a cool head is needed. Unless you can see the barbel take the bait, and very clear water is required to enable you to do this, do not strike. If the barbel is over the bait, it is sometimes possible to feel the barbel rubbing against the line. This sensation is the cause of the frequently mentioned sawing sensation on the line (which often precludes a take). All that is happening is that the barbel is over the rig and sitting hard on the bottom. Over and above this the line bite is often the catalyst to disaster as the angler strikes at it, believing it to be a genuine bite. Touch legering enables the angler

This barbel's circuit through weed was established after several hours before a bait was cast.

to be fully aware of everything that is occurring in the swim as well as offering a clear, focused view of all the underwater developments. For instance, the target fish enters the swim and eventually moves up to the bait. If the barbel is at any time between you and the bait a line bite is possible. The line can quite easily catch a fin, pulling the line against the angler's indicating finger. Such an indication should be interpreted for what it is, provided that you are concentrating hard enough and understand precisely what is taking place. Consequently, lowering the rod and allowing the barbel room to manoeuvre over the bait carpet will severely reduce the chances of spooking the barbel as it feels the line pulling against its body, and allow it to move up to the bait and take it if it is so inclined. The bite will then appear as exactly what it is in the form of a pluck or pull on the line. The response is now obvious: hit the bite hard and await the fireworks.

If the barbel approaches the bait and refuses it immediately or after a period of time spent inspecting it, then all is not lost by any means.

Quite often a cautious barbel will inspect a bait on several occasions before taking it. Whenever you have a bait in the swim at the same time as your target fish, then you are in with a great chance of catching it. It is worth bearing in mind that if a bait has been rejected once and the barbel returns it may well take it after a

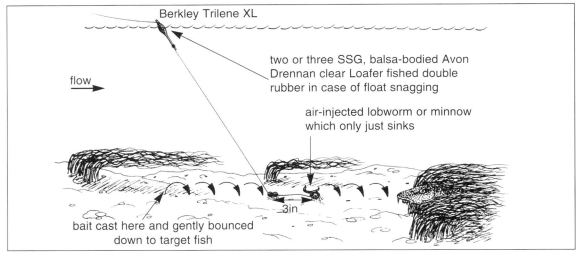

Stret-pegging stalking rig.

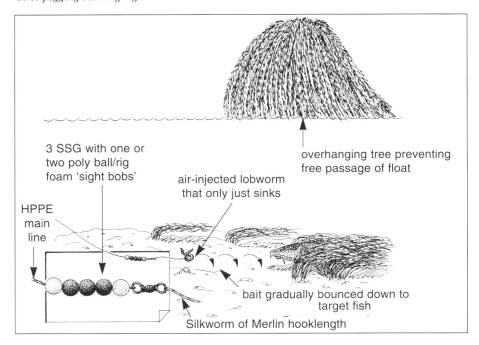

Poly ball/rig foam stalking rig.

short period of consideration. Barbel under these circumstances do not forget that the bait is there after they have rejected it and will often decide that they want it after all by swimming straight up to it and engulfing it without any further ceremony.

During the dog days of summer a shoal of barbel will often spend much of the day tightly packed together very close to or even within dense snags. Where these situations arise it can be extremely difficult to separate individual barbel from the tightly knit group. A somewhat radical approach to this problem has been developed over the last few months by a small group of barbel specialists, and this has led to the downfall of several good fish. The method is best fished using lobworm or a minnow as bait with the bait being slowly manoeuvred or even lowered right beneath the nose of the target fish. Although flying against many accepted barbel fishing principles, a barbel laying inert on the bottom can often be prompted into taking the worm or minnow out of sheer instinct. Such an approach requires that the bait is moved very slowly towards the target fish until it is within touching distance of its snout. By injecting a little air into the worm, thereby causing it to waver directly in front of the barbel, indeed on occasions virtually tickling its nose, it can often all become a little too much with the bait being taken violently. If the barbel is really not interested then it will turn away; this reaction should not, however, preclude a reeling in of the bait. Again the principle of challenging the barbel not to take the bait comes into play; while the barbel may well have disappeared for a little while, it did not choose to spend the day in that particular spot for no reason and neither did the rest of the group. That big barbel could well be back. Lobworms, minnows, and to a lesser degree caddis, are by far the best baits for presenting a bait right up against a barbel's snout, and regardless of such an approach's apparent implausibility, it works.

There are a number of ways that baits can be manoeuvred towards a tightly packed group of fish as well as individuals. One of the best

methods is with the aid of a small balsa bodied float, sufficient shot to cock it and a perfectly balanced bait. The idea is to allow the bait to settle gently on the bottom. By lifting the rod top slightly, the bait will shift and move a short distance downstream towards the barbel before settling once more a short distance downstream and therefore closer to the barbel. A bait fished on a buoyant hook works far better than a bait carrying the natural weight of the hook as it is far more buoyant and can be manoeuvred much more easily to precisely where you want it. This process can be repeated in a patient, steady manner until the bait eventually reaches the target area. This is commonly known as stret-pegging, a method more associated with the higher waters of winter than those of summer, but I have found it to be an immensely efficient method under the circumstances I have described, provided threre is sufficient current to enable the rig to operate.

A less refined but very useful alternative to the stalking, stret-pegging approach can be used where overhanging foliage, for instance, prevents a free passage for the float to travel downstream to the target fish. By dispensing with the float it is still possible to inch a bait directly down to an individual fish, but the main problem here is keeping track of the precise whereabouts of the bait now that we have dispensed with the float. While lobworms and minnows appear to be exceptionally good baits at eliciting an instinctive take from the individual barbel, they are extremely difficult baits to spot once in the water. We have two choices here: one is to change the bait to a more visible one and the other is to attach something to the line that is visible and that will indicate precisely where the bait is. One such method is the inclusion of a white polystyrene ball or a brightly coloured square of rig foam attached a little way up the line from the bait and if at all possible beside the weight. By studying the sight bob inserted on the rig at, say, 6in (15cm) up-line from the hookbait, we can then assume that, should the coloured polystyrene ball or foam square be about 1ft (30cm) from the

A huge Wye barbel stalked with a bunch of lobworms.

target fish, we have only about 6in (15cm) to go before the air-injected lobworm starts touching the barbel's snout.

This ploy was, I believe, originally devised by Terry Lampard and Tim Norman as a means of detecting minuscule barbel bites on their local rivers, the idea being that if the sight bob moved then it was a bite! While under the particular circumstances we are looking at here the sight bob can still be used for bite detection, I prefer touch legering with HPPE to indicate the bite, relying on the sight bob as a hookbait marker for manoeuvring the bait to the target fish. I have often struck as the sight bob has moved only to realize that it was a small chub or a shoal of bleak having a go at it, probably believing it to be a lump of breadflake. I have consequently spooked the target fish for some considerable time. The sight bob idea as a bait marker more than a bite indicator has put a lot of barbel on the bank for me that I would not

have otherwise caught, and I have been grateful for this little trick on many occasions.

The existence of 'non-feeding' giants is not a fanciful notion among barbel anglers who cannot catch them, as virtually all barbel anglers of my acquaintance have reluctantly confirmed their sightings of such fish. The methods I have described, in particular that of getting a 'Medusa's Head' of lobworms or even more likely a fat minnow deadbait to touch the barbel's snout, will one day bank for me one of the giants, I am convinced. But for a faulty hookhold recently I would be telling the tale of its success and not lamenting a very near miss.

BOAT FISHING AND RECONNAISSANCE

The origins of boat fishing for barbel go back a very long way, and Victorian anglers of the calibre of Francis Francis were associated with barbel fishing in the Thames from moored punts and taking massive catches of fish. Mooring a punt and barbel fishing on the navigable rivers of today is asking for trouble from all the other river users; we are much better off using boats on non-navigable rivers, preferably a small rowing boat or better still a two-seater kayak. Here we will look at their use in reconnaissance and in reaching hitherto inaccessible spots.

A lot of prejudice exists among anglers with regard to boats and much of it is unjustified. Canoeists do no damage to rivers or fish, neither do they cause pollution. They do anglers very little harm at all. Most canoeists are aware of the angler's needs and act accordingly. Both camps have their extremists with canoeing families being showered with maggots from vandals masquerading as anglers, while certain canoeists have deliberately fouled anglers' lines to spoil a day's fishing.

Both angler and canoeist should be able to enjoy their contact with the splendour of our river valleys in different ways. Canoeists do not need to see the river's inhabitants; we do! Conversely, we do not need to see miles and miles of the river; they do! This mutual understanding appears to have developed positively over the last few years and while jet skiers and cruisers will never be anything other than environmental vandals, the angler and the canoeist can be compatible. So much so that, should the angler have any form of boating access to a good barbel river and not get afloat upon it, an awful lot of superb barbel-spotting opportunities will be missed, as well as the discovery of many new swims, not all of them hidden from the bank.

While angling can offer the canoeist no advantage, the advantages of the angler becoming a competent canoeist are immense, and, by putting prejudice aside and getting into one, great strides can be made in both knowledge

A kayak session revealed a shoal of barbel so I jumped out and caught one!

and results. While many barbel stretches are not realistically viable to go canoeing on during the fishing season, time spent in the close season slowly drifting around is still an option with immense possibilities.

We have already discussed the value of observing the whereabouts of barbel from the bank in the weeks leading up to the opening of the season, but the miles of uncharted river available to us from a kayak are greater than anybody realizes. Reconnaissance from a kayak immediately gives us two major advantages over the angler who chooses to walk the bank in search of fish. First, we have a better view of the fish, especially if the kayak has both a rower and an observer and, second, a barbel is less alarmed by a disturbance in the water than on the bank. I have observed on many occasions the way that barbel react to a flotilla of canoes passing through the swim: certainly they melt away but only very briefly on most occasions, while a 'skyliner' from the bank will spook the fish for hours.

Anyone who has ever been on a river, large or small, in a small rowing vessel of any description, will be amazed at the amount of water that is unfishable and inaccessible from the bank. Even though such areas are as little as 10 yards (9m) long, it is no surprise to see barbel grouped up within the shelter of a brief line of alders or willows on both banks.

On certain other rivers these impenetrable runs can stretch for up to half a mile (800m) and more and it is in these areas that barbel will reside and flourish uncaught and unseen for their whole lives. I have drifted through areas such as these that resemble a scene from *Apocalypse Now* and the barbel have led charmed lives for decades.

This exploratory canoe work will therefore reward the angler who is prepared to make the effort and get into a boat and go searching. The effort involved in this is not only a wonderful excuse for being out and about on the rivers during the close season, it can in turn reward us by making barbel available that can quite possibly have led sheltered lives. This can quite

commonly give us a passport to enjoying sport the like of which has rarely been experienced before.

Once a shoal of barbel are found we need to plan our method of attack. Very often, owing of the nature of these swims, it can be very easy to tie up against bankside vegetation. On certain rivers there may be dense beds of sedge or bulrushes while on others branches and other foliage draping into the river make ideal characteristics upon which to moor. Anything will do, but where nothing suitable can be found we will be forced to anchor up in the slowest water to be found, yet as close to the barbel as possible. It is always advisable to moor as close to the bank as possible for two reasons: we are less

Drifting downriver revealed a shoal of barbel that were to prove ridiculously easy to catch.

conspicuous to the barbel and it is safer should an accident occur.

For this roving, boat-fishing style we need to travel as light as possible and with the minimum of tackle. First we need a life jacket, and one particularly suitable one for the angler is the Leeda Crewsaver Automatic Lifejacket, which is both light and very comfortable. Further boat-fishing attire should run to an angler's waistcoat, designed to keep all the bits and pieces of tackle in an assortment of pockets and exterior clips. The Wychwood Tackle Company makes a particularly useful waistcoat suitable for this brand of barbel fishing. Vital items of tackle that we take for granted – such as hook sharpeners, rig glue, hooks, leads and tweezers – are immediately to hand, which is so important within the constraints of the boat.

For boat fishing, we need to restrict ourselves to one rod, so this rod has to be adaptable. The Seer 10ft 6in Specialist Rover is perfectly suited to the job in question. Relatively short yet perfect for boat fishing, this rod with its hollow tip was designed with touch legering in mind, as well as quivertipping, as the rod comes with a

push-on quivertip should more sensitive bite indication be required. The rod's crisp action makes it more than suitable for trotting baits through a barbel run; indeed, its versatility is equally of benefit on the bank and in the boat.

Boat fishing previously inaccessible areas is best approached utilizing three main avenues of attack – trotting, trundling and touch legering, probably in that order. Barbel that are naive to anglers' baits are often said to require time to become educated as to what is food. This is perfectly true, of course, with sweetcorn being a prime example. To educate naive barbel onto anglers' baits is a thoroughly pointless exercise before natural baits have been fully exploited. Pre-baiting campaigns from boats in inaccessible stretches are not only a waste of time but also hard work, in that quite often the boat is required from which to do them!

The way to go about things here is to fish natural baits on the move. Trotting or trundling maggots, casters, minnows, caddis or worms through an unsuspecting shoal of barbel from a boat will bring instant results and will in all probability bear the catches spoken of earlier.

9 PLAYING, LANDING AND DESNAGGING BARBEL

PLAYING, DESNAGGING AND LANDING TECHNIQUE

One of the golden rules for beating a barbel is to make sure that you play the fish and not to let it play you. There is rarely any logic or intelligence to the way a barbel fights, just power and instinct. It is often possible to play a barbel near a snag without the barbel going anywhere near it – unlike a carp, which would make straight for it. Barbel are nevertheless adept at submerging themselves deeply into streamer weed, which appears to be their favourite way of attempting to shed the hook.

Backwinding – fishing with the anti-reverse off and backwinding the reel handle to give line – allows the barbel to get up a head of steam and charge all over the place. The best way is to play a barbel off an appropriately set, tight clutch. This allows the angler to play the fish with greater emphasis on the rod handle than the reel handle. Playing a barbel off the clutch gives the angler far more control during the fight and especially at the time of netting. With backwinding it becomes necessary to let go of the reel handle with the anti-reverse not engaged, to net the fish. The rod hand is usually attempting to apply pressure on the spool. At the same time it is trying to prevent line being given at this point; the whole scene is awkward, unwieldy, unsafe and is not what the reel was ever intended for. This manoeuvre is fraught with danger, especially if the barbel surges off at the net just as it appears to be beaten! By using the clutch as it should be used, the barbel angler is imposing the maximum control over the fish at this critical moment.

Barbel are unique in their strange gyrating form of fighting. Inexperienced anglers can sometimes be fooled into believing that the fish is snagged. This behaviour can sometimes work a hookhold loose but fortunately the barbel is blessed with a tough, fleshy mouth and once hooked usually stays hooked. If a hook does pull out of a barbel, it is usually because the fish was not hooked properly in the first place; no backwinding will improve your the chances of landing it. Playing a barbel on a stiffly set clutch is not only a hair-raising experience, but also the most effective method of doing so. It just needs a little bit of confidence and belief in the tackle.

If a barbel becomes snagged, it is best to call its bluff, completely ease off the pressure and wait. Very often a barbel will respond directly to the amount of pressure being applied while it is being played, and pull back accordingly. In other words, the harder you pull the barbel, the harder it will pull back. By slackening off completely the barbel will often do likewise and just rest to regain its strength before ambling off believing itself to be free. Often when a barbel swims into a snag it will eventually swim right out again still attached to the hook and line having de-snagged itself! You should therefore resist the temptation to pull for a break or antagonize the fish out of the snag and just be patient. The barbel swam into the snag and will therefore have to swim out again, with or without your help. The barbel becomes the means of de-snagging itself, not the angler.

The success rate of this approach is remarkably high, which is due in all probability to the placid nature of the barbel when it eventually vacates the snag. Be prepared for fireworks, however, upon tightening up to the freed barbel and resuming the fight again after the fish has had its breather. The combat starts all over again!

No coarse fish gives its all during the fight in quite the same manner as a barbel does; consequently no other species is so exhausted when it eventually arrives inside the landing net. It is difficult for many inexperienced barbel anglers fully to appreciate the extent to which a barbel that has just given them an arm-aching and aggressive fight suddenly becomes a fragile, gentle and docile creature on the bank.

The table shows the equipment that is needed after landing barbel. At this critical moment the barbel requires more care and attention than any other species, except a deeply hooked pike or perch. There are a number of strict rules that all barbel anglers must follow to ensure that the barbel eventually swims off in good condition:

> **Essential Post-Landing Equipment**
> - Steel tweezers
> - Gold Label Ulti-mat
> - Gold Label pike of barbel tunnel
> - Gold Label weigh or photography sling
> - Salter Electro Samson digital scales
> - Kryston Klin-ik or Solar Tackle Remedy fish sterilizing solution

- Try to unhook any small barbel while they are still in the water. The worst thing to do to a barbel is to take it out of the water in an exhausted state and allow it to gasp for oxygen in the dry air. On many occasions it is really not necessary to take small barbel out of the water at all. Any small fish unhooked in this way should be held with its head upstream until it is strong enough to swim off on its own accord.

'... barbel are barbel; the others are just fish!'

Giving a barbel recovery time in this fashion is vital.

• If you net a barbel, give it a few seconds of recovery time in the shallow water at the edge of the swim. Remove the barbel from the water by gripping the bottom of the mesh of the landing net and placing the fish onto an unhooking mat that has been thoroughly doused in water. Make sure that the dorsal fin does not catch on the mesh of the net. Never lift the barbel any higher than is necessary to move it from one position out of the water to another. Any barbel that is dropped, even a couple of inches, will be harmed and further distressed.

• Apply a couple of drops of Kryston Klin-ik or Solar Tackle Remedy Solution at the point of hook penetration to ensure a speedier healing process and prevent infection.

• When you return the barbel to the river, grip it by the tail 'wrist' or (for larger specimens) support its body at the pectoral fin area and between the pelvic and anal fins. Point the fish upstream and wait for it to recover sufficient strength to swim forcefully back into the main body of the river. Do not allow the fish to swim off at its first attempt, as it is usually too weak to do so. You will know when it is ready as you will not be able to hang on to it!

• When a weight check is necessary, a Gold Label weigh or photography sling is ideal for weighing the fish before it can be lowered momentarily back into the water while preparations are made. Whenever possible, hold the barbel as close as possible to the surface of the water in case it suddenly lunges out of your grip and falls. Everything must be prepared beforehand. A digital pair of scales can be zeroed so that weigh slings are deducted in advance. It takes just a couple of seconds to determine the exact weight of the fish from the digital display.

• If you need a photograph and there is

All barbel are special; take care of them and safeguard the future.

nobody to take it for you, place the fish in a Gold Label pike or barbel tunnel for the briefest possible time. Never use a carp sack, which does not allow sufficient water to pass through it in order for the barbel to revive itself. Always make sure that the barbel has sufficient strength to hold its own in the tunnel, and prepare the photographic equipment as quickly as you can.

• Never place more than one barbel inside a tunnel. They cause each other no harm when jockeying together in the current but two distressed barbel rubbing against one another in captivity will damage each another, with a loss of protective mucus, bruising and even scale loss.

• Before releasing any barbel check for any other damage, particularly earlier hook holds or parasite lesions around fin roots, that should also get the Klin-ik or Remedy treatment.

10 SUMMER AND AUTUMN FISHING

From the earlier chapters of this book I hope that the reader is fully conversant with the necessary tackle, effective baits and proven rigs. We can now marry these practicalities to an overall approach to barbel fishing.

CLOSE SEASON GROUNDWORK AND HOW TO SPOT THE QUARRY

The start of the barbel fishing season in June will often find the barbel in and around shallow, pacey water following their earlier spawning rituals. Indeed, the weeks leading up to the season's onset are really the days to be out and about as it can be quite revealing spending days watching the barbel at this time of the year. It is then that the true potential of any given stretch can be assessed for numbers of barbel present and a check made on the possibility of any big fish that may be present. It can often be quite astonishing to witness the amount of barbel that do inhabit any one stretch, and it is quite common to be surprised at just how big some of them are.

Witnessing these post-spawning barbel flashing and holding their own in the current gives an extremely accurate picture of the stocks in any given stretch. The sighting of one particularly large fish can serve as an inspiration throughout the season, and the fact that you know that many big barbel are present makes you keener, sharper and more confident, frequently a sure-fire recipe for success.

Assuming that the river is clear enough to spot fish, any available day leading up to the

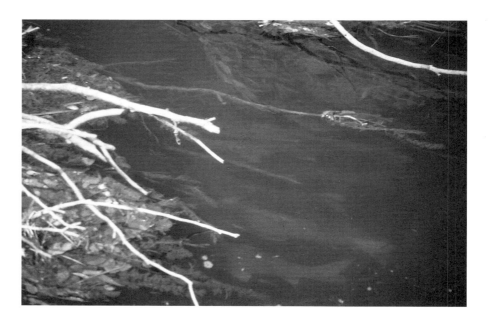

Assessing a stretch's potential!

start of the season should be spent on the bank locating and watching barbel. The knowledge and understanding of the quarry gleaned from these simple observations is invaluable, and a few minutes spent watching a shoal of barbel working a gravel bed and their associated interaction and behaviour is priceless knowledge for any barbel angler throughout the season.

Barbel can be ridiculously easy to locate at this time of the year, especially when they inhabit the shallows with their spawning instincts in overdrive. Barbel have an uncanny knack of becoming quite invisible in the water provided they remain motionless on the bottom for any length of time. On occasions such as this we need a bit of patience and a pair of good quality polarized sunglasses, with the Optix brand still the best. While barbel can initially appear to be virtually invisible, the secret of spotting them is to be aware of the little give-aways that betray their presence.

By studying for a few minutes a typical barbel run (for instance, a patch of clean gravel running between beds of *Ranunculus*) that seems to be devoid of any barbel, it is not uncommon for the pinkish colouration of a pectoral fin to be the first part of the barbel to appear gradually against the gravels. By studying this particular fin for a short while and then trying to ascertain where the tail of the barbel will be, that too will gradually come into focus. The skill is to change your field of vision to incorporate both the pectoral and the tail fins and then, and only then, will the whole of the fish begin to emerge. There is undoubtedly a knack to this and an outline of a barbel will slowly emerge. By focusing on the barbel and not on the surface of the water the eye will eventually yield to the object of your attention. Furthermore, just as one barbel manifests itself from within the water, others will, as

A virgin barbel from a virgin swim. Lobworm, predictably, was the successful bait.

if by magic, do the same. The secret is to be patient and allow the eye to adjust, just as it does in the dark. To assist this process, a baseball cap worn tight down to the polaroids helps cut out glare, and you will find that by gently swaying the head from side to side and looking slightly away from the suspected position of a barbel it will come into focus much quicker. There is undoubtedly a skill to this, and practice makes perfect.

Ever conscious of cover, barbel are very often tucked underneath *Ranunculus* during the day, and one plant can be home to several fish. When barbel pack themselves sardine-style under *Ranunculus* , their whole outlines are not going to be seen. Under these circumstances we are, however, still looking for that pectoral or tail fin to reveal itself slowly. Virtually all streamer weed, by its very nature, moves back and forth in the current. If one studies *Ranunculus* it will soon become apparent that, while it appears to move in almost rhythmic

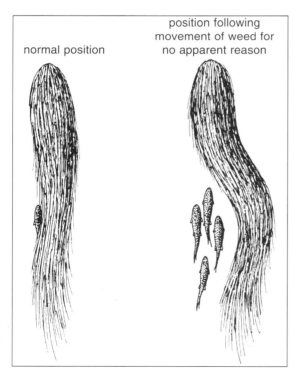

Barbel hiding beneath a Ranunculus *bed.*

unison with the current, it does occasionally do something quite out of the ordinary and move right over to one side and back again for no apparent reason. This action thus exposes the area ordinarily concealed by it for a number of seconds.

Several minutes will often elapse before this unexpected and radical change in its normally sedate swaying to and fro occurs. When it does, and if the barbel spotter has been studying hard enough and with eyes focused, then quite often several unsuspected barbel will be visible, which have been sheltering beneath the plant. With this knowledge, it can then become possible to make out the odd fin here and there among the weed. No matter if you cannot! You now know that barbel are in residence.

Another sure-fire give-away is the common flash of a barbel, and the fact that barbel regularly flash can be of immense benefit to the barbel spotter. It is a general rule that if the bottom of the river can be seen clearly then eventually the barbel will be seen as well, provided the magic eye technique is used. Where the bottom of a river cannot be seen for some reason, perhaps depth or a tinge of colour, then all is not lost. With the same pair of sunglasses and the same amount of patience, by studying the depths themselves it is often possible eventually to see a barbel flash at you. Once one flashes it is by no means uncommon for the rest of the shoal quickly to follow suit. The near-white underside of the barbel is shown for a second and not only gives away its presence but just how big it is as well. This location technique can be quite effective in relatively coloured water, and while not all barbel flash, indeed in some rivers they hardly seem to flash at all, on rivers where such behaviour is common, it is a considerable help in locating them.

It is a great misconception that some anglers have the happy knack of locating fish either by luck, instinct or a particularly deep understanding of the fish's habits and where they are at any given time. While there are some who do possess these characteristics to a degree, the main reason they locate seemingly invisible barbel is through the techniques so described, whether they care to admit it or not!

Once these skills are perfected, you will stand head and shoulders above anyone else who has not acquired them. It is not a question of having superior eyesight, indeed many experienced practitioners should have had glasses years ago!

Where it is not possible to spot barbel, perhaps because of a coloured river where the barbel are not given to flashing, or where there are deep but brisk swims or on the larger rivers that have barbel holed up in mid stream, we need to read the water. Again, reading the river is wrapped up in all sorts of mystic folklore with the impression being that it is a gift endowed to the chosen few. This is certainly not the case. For barbel fishing, the common denominators are rarely absent. What we need to look for has almost become a cliché in barbel literature but it is true nonetheless – a smooth, even glide of water running anywhere between a medium to brisk walking pace. Upon finding such a run the possibilities of it holding barbel are increased substantially if there are sufficient *Ranunculus* beds for cover, or any form of cover afforded from the bank such as overhanging trees or trailing branches. Any gradient or depression in the gravel bed is particularly attractive, as is anything that is sunken and collects food in the form of a slipstream in the current directly behind it.

THE STATIC AMBUSH APPROACH

While some barbel anglers are fortunate enough to have whole stretches available for multiple swim operations, others are not so fortunate and are forced, or indeed prefer, to stay in the same

A liver-flavoured boilie took this 'double' no fewer than twelve years ago.

The bewitching hour.

swim all day. Many well-known barbel stretches do have very limited choice, quite often because of angling pressure or even restricted access. Whatever the cause, such single swim sessions are the most common and require a different approach and philosophy.

On stretches such as these summer barbel, during most of the daylight hours, are usually congregated together somewhere. They are not always visible, but they can often be sheltering under cover and out of sight. Under these circumstances it may well become necessary to attract barbel into our swim away from their shelter to catch them. If we are prevented from either seeing the barbel or being able to fish where we believe them to be, then we will have to create a suitable feeding habitat for them in an adjacent swim of our choice.

With snaggy or inaccessible swims where we cannot attempt to fish we have to take the next best option and draw the barbel out. The same applies to barbel tucked in behind a large bed of inaccessible bulrushes or taking it easy beneath a jungle of overhanging trees, behind large sharp rocks, within gnarled, knotted, exposed tree roots, beneath vast beds of immovable *Ranunculus*, between rows of dense, mature trees on both banks or anything else you care to think of which renders the barbel inaccessible and impossible to fish for. We must bring them a realistically short distance upstream into an area that gives us a chance of catching them.

Should this be our option, then our choice of where to fish should be made bearing two things in mind. First, and most important, is it close enough to attract the sheltering and inaccessible barbel into, and second, are we fishing in a suitable area for them to feel secure and confident enough to move up and feed in? What we should be looking for in order for this to occur is ideally a clear area of gravel. A square yard is not too small, especially if it is adjacent to streamer weed or any sort of feature that will serve as potential cover to the barbel should the need arise: in other words, a confidence-boosting piece of cover for the barbel should they need it. This ambush point should be as close as possible to their natural daylight abode and certainly no more than 10 to 15 yards (9 to 14m) upstream of it.

If we find ourselves in a position where we cannot find a suitably clear feeding habitat for the barbel to move into, then we shall have to make one by removing a modest quantity of streamer weed and creating a small clearing. The beauty of creating a feeding area for the barbel is that you can locate it precisely where you want it to be. If we take this option it makes sense to use all the advantages that such a choice offers us. First we must make sure that the make-up of the river bed where we wish to create the fishing gap is hard and therefore gravel. Provided we have a gravel bottom we can create

the swim as close to the barbel as it is possible to do so. Ideally, we can ensure that it is on the near bank; a yard or so further out than the rod top is perfect. We should site the clearing if at all possible on a gradient of gravel upon which barbel love to feed, and we can construct the gap in the weed at precisely the size we want it to be.

Our simple objective is to create a small hole in which to fish, close in and where the barbel can feed in total, but mistaken confidence.

Without doubt the delicate operation of removing a couple of feet of streamer weed or 'cabbages' (submerged lilies) is best done with a small blade designed specifically for the purpose. These are available from some tackle shops or more commonly through the larger mail-order tackle outlets. Although these blades are a little on the small side, they can be attached to a landing net handle and provided they are kept very sharp they will do a splendid

A lovely barbel taken from a tiny clearing at dusk.

job. Throwing out a weed rake and dragging it back in tench fishing style is a horribly crude method of swim-clearing for barbel and should be avoided at all costs. Clearing these little areas is best done with the aid of a willing helper as streamer weed is not particularly easy to cut on one's own, as it is very difficult to get any purchase on the weed. A helper with a second landing net pole can prevent the weed constantly moving away from the blade in the water as an attempt is being made to cut it. Furthermore, another person can also save us from drowning should the need arise! Ideally, 3ft (90cm) pruned off the end of a plant will usually reveal a lovely clear piece of gravel underneath. When baited up, this becomes an extremely attractive feature that barbel find difficult not to explore.

'Cabbages' require a bit more work, not least because they often tend to be in slightly deeper water. While chopping off 2 to 3ft (60 to 90cm) of streamer weed is comparatively easy, a cabbage patch run is not. The best way of doing it is to cut them off at the stalk, garden-cabbage style, working from the edge of the bed inwards. As little as a half a dozen cabbage removals is all

that is required here and restraint is the order of the day as getting carried away and demolishing vast beds of aquatic plant life is detrimental to the river and the swim.

Virtually all this kind of swim preparation requires the angler to get in the water with either thigh boots or chest waders. As noted a number of times in this book, the value of chest waders to the barbel angler cannot be underestimated and their worth here is priceless. The added advantage of creating these little swims in the manner described is the amount of knowledge we can glean about the swim in question by the simple expedient of wading around in it. It is without doubt massively beneficial to have seen the swim at first hand, as opposed to making judgements from the bank some distance away.

Contrary to popular belief, there is no reason why the clearing cannot be fished on the day of its creation. While any barbel in the surrounding area will have been spooked by all the activity, the effect rather oddly will not be particularly profound. Whereas a careless cast or a blown bait will spook barbel for some considerable time, aquatic disturbance does not have the

Perfect barbelling territory.

same startling effect on them. I have observed several occasions where on certain rivers barbel appear quite happy to hold their position in the current yards from cattle wandering around in the adjacent shallows, but a mere smattering of sweetcorn a few yards upstream will see them all turn round and bolt off in unison.

The moment the work is complete it pays to introduce some form of attractant, usually hempseed. Our objective now is to draw the barbel from their lair and into our trap. The reactions of the barbel will almost definitely be instant. By this we should understand that the barbel will be aware of the hempseed scent at the earliest possible moment, that is to say as soon as the scent is carried down to them by the current. How the barbel choose to react is

up to them, but you can be sure that they will know it is there.

Having said all that, it is still wise to give the freshly cleared area a complete rest for the duration of the afternoon and in any case for at least three hours. What the swim architect does in the interim is a matter of choice, but one has to be mindful of the fact that these activities may not have attracted the attentions of only the barbel. Other less scrupulous barbel anglers, those external forces once again, are more than happy to witness some unfortunate soul, or two, beavering away for a couple of hours creating a perfect clearing in which to entice the resident barbel the instant you have popped down to the local for some well-earned refreshment. Sadly, it pays to be more cynical about the nature of our brothers of the angle than about the caution displayed by the barbel. The message is clear: if you are sure your labours have not been witnessed by any such parasites, then disappear and let the river take on its own peace once more. If you are in any way uneasy about it, be sure and stay to protect your investment!

It is interesting to note that the reaction of the barbel to all this disturbance is not at variance with their behaviour when bait is introduced into their underwater domain. That is to say they will still bolt as if their lives depend on it, but a 'conference' of sorts appears to take place as one of their members, often the biggest, greediest fish of the bunch is despatched to investigate events with surprising haste. Such an analogy may well appear to be somewhat flippant and if it is I apologize, but it is to my mind the clearest way of describing the reactions of barbel under such circumstances.

Having allowed our enterprise to rest awhile, we can now commence the war of nerves and wait for the barbel finally to yield to the challenge and make their move. We have already made ours, we have created the swim, we have deposited within that swim an irresistible attractant; now let the barbel fret about it. When they eventually make the decision that we always knew they were going to make, we will be ready for them.

Barbel will feed on any of these small bare areas between the Ranunculus.

We have a number of hookbait options open to us: casters, lobworms, minnows, sweetcorn, prawns, tares or wheat can all be highly effective on their day when fished over hempseed. Early in the season the combination of a lobworm, caddis or a couple of minnows, closely rivalled by casters fished over hempseed, certainly takes some beating. A 'Medusa's Head' of two or three lobworms will often be the best bait at these times. Although it is not easy to better lobworms fished in this way, it can be done by injecting both ends of one of the worms with air with the aid of a standard syringe. The untreated worms will counterbalance the buoyant one but will not prevent its head and tail wafting enticingly in the current. There is no need to introduce worm segments in with the hempseed here as the barbel will need no introduction to the worm, their favourite natural food.

Over and above the lobworm and deadbait approach we still have a number of baits that can prove, on their day, to be equally successful. Barbel are prone to preoccupation with particles in much the same way as carp. The successful barbel angler has to be aware of this and must always strive when preparing one or several swims not to overdo it with the hempseed. If too much hempseed is introduced, barbel can become deeply preoccupied and ignore any other bait. This is fine if hempseed is the intended hookbait but where it is not, or where the angler is not in a position to present hempseed successfully on the hook, then it can spell disaster.

The barbel's tendency towards preoccupation with certain particles can be exploited to the full and there is perhaps no better bait that complements hempseed quite as well as casters. Casters and hempseed are a lethally effective combination and barbel will often become preoccupied with *both* baits and exclude all other alternatives from their minds.

An early season barbel that fell to a hempseed/caster combo.

Casters are delicate baits and are much more suitable for presentations on small hooks, but, unfortunately, small hooks result in lost barbel so our presentation requires a little thought. Too large a hook will virtually break the caster in two and certainly most of the casters cast out on such a hook will break on impact with the water's surface. A compromise hook that is strong enough to land barbel and not destroy the bait is the Drennan Starpoint in size ten, or at a push twelve. These hooks are relatively thin in the wire and yet very strong. Several casters can be hooked on these and provided the angler is careful the casters will remain unbroken and not break up as they hit the surface. Alternatively, there is no reason whatsoever why casters cannot be fished in exactly the same way as the 'Medusa's Head' maggot rig or indeed the threaded maggot rig; after all, they are the same thing.

Where casters are the intended bait, it is imperative that they are included in the initial baiting process: 60 per cent caster to 40 per cent hempseed is not too much and, although casters will catch barbel without prior introduction, a liberal proportion included in the baiting process certainly improves the appeal of the hookbait.

Maggots require a rather different approach from casters. While nuisance fish will take casters, fishing with maggots can be an absolute nightmare.

There is nothing that can be done to prevent minnows, fry and everything else nibbling at the hookbait. The overall answer is to get the barbel preoccupied with the maggots in which case the nuisances are struggling! This approach requires the introduction of an awful lot of maggots, depending on the size of the river. Up to a gallon of maggots can sometimes be necessary to really get the barbel switched on. Feeder fishing is a particularly effective method of building up a barbel swim and is described in Chapter 8. The introduction of maggots into a small clearing by way of the baitdropper can be more effective because of the lesser noise and disturbance overall.

Four pints (2 litres) of maggots take 12 casts with the large baitdropper and the whole job can be done in less than five minutes. How long it takes with a large Drennan Feederlink is open to question. Again, it bears repetition that on a larger river the gradual introduction of feed over a long period of time works, but on smaller rivers the constant casting of a feeder into a small swim does nothing but spook the fish.

For a very delicate one-cast introduction, a PVA tube filled to the brim with maggots or casters is hard to beat. Christened the 'condom rig' by Tony Miles, each end of the tube is tied together with a strong PVA string and can be either lowered into the swim or attached directly to the rig in place of a feeder. This approach is particularly effective where barbel have become wary of the sight of a feeder in the swim or where the barbel are so switched on to maggots that a couple of 'condoms' full of maggots are all that is required to get them feeding.

To get the best out of introducing maggots in PVA tubing it is imperative that the maggots or casters are dry and have not sweated. Grease and moisture from the maggots will render the whole creation useless and nothing other than a gooey mess.

What we have discussed so far centres around the creation of a small clear area among streamer weed. Where such areas exist naturally the same approach applies.

As an aside and a complete reversal of the concept of clearing small areas of the river bed, we can often be confronted with stretches of river that are aquatically suitable for barbel but where the physical characteristics of the bank are not. During the summer months in stretches that do not afford any bankside cover at all, barbel can be particularly difficult in such environments and appear to have no bolt hole should they become spooked.

Under these circumstances, and provided nobody objects, it is in our own interests to help nature along a bit. By no means original, one or two willow saplings planted every 20 yards (18m) or so along a barren section of bank can, after as little as a couple of seasons, act as magnets to barbel. Willows are perhaps the most suitable with their tendency to trail their branches in the water; they are also incredibly proficient at taking root and all that is required is that a branch be cut from a mature willow in the spring, the end daubed with a bit of rooting powder and then jammed deeply into the bankside. This is a technique that has been used quite successfully in many of the open-banked upper rivers of Norfolk, as habitat creation not only for barbel, but for chub too!

Although this is a long-term strategy, chub have been seen to take up residence the following day. Barbel, however, require the new feature to be somewhat more mature before taking up residence. A lot of this kind of swim creation is initiated by using too small a branch: by hammering in one of 6ft (1.8m) or longer the desired effect will be a lot sooner in coming. When taking a branch from a mature willow for this purpose make sure it is one that overhangs the bank, not the river, as there is no point in taking existing cover away from barbel to create it on more barren stretches.

MULTIPLE SWIM FISHING

It has been said on many occasions that the art of summer barbel fishing is based on the

A day's session in a single swim produced this and several other barbel.

preparatory work done before the fishing commences. Barbel are often quite predictable fish and if we work to a system, understand precisely the ways of the barbel and believe in our approach, there is no reason why we cannot expect to catch barbel on every trip.

Barbel are so frequently very visible in the summer that, quite understandably, it can be a real wrench not to begin fishing right away. By resisting this temptation, more barbel on the bank are guaranteed.

Let us consider a hypothetical but typical roving barbel session in high summer. There is rarely a need to turn up particularly early, so at 10am we arrive, and first we need to walk the stretch and establish what swims we fancy fishing as well as spending most of the morning studying the water and locating as many barbel as we can with the aid of polarized sunglasses.

Let us say that two swims have visible barbel in them, with a couple of snaggy swims looking particularly promising. On top of this we have located half a dozen glides adjacent to some form of cover or current deflection also showing promise. We eventually decide to bait ten swims. With one of our large baitdroppers (3 to the pint or 5 to the litre) we deposit a pint of hempseed into each swim as gently and surreptitiously as possible. We may well find that this action in the swims where barbel were visible will be the cause of them vacating it. Worry not! If the hempseed has been introduced as quietly as possible then we have little to fear.

Barbel are odd fish in that it is quite common for them to respond to something that they are attracted by – such as hempseed – by high-tailing it in the opposite direction! If the stretch has not been hammered to death with hempseed, then the barbel will soon return. It almost seems as if the barbel disappear to have a 'conference' about what they have seen and then elect a member from their ranks to be the first one back to sample the goods! This can often be the largest, greediest member of the group, good news for us, although occasionally a smaller representative appears to be given the job. Whatever, the natural curiosity of all the

barbel is ordinarily too much for them. It is often the case that after a quite short period of time, larger as well as smaller barbel will gradually begin to reappear in the swim.

The 'elected taster' will uphold its responsibilities and be the first to make a cautious and jittery foray over the hempseed and begin to sniff and sample it. Eventually, more barbel will follow the lead, often taking it in turns to graze on the bait. Every time a barbel returns to the hempseed it will spend longer and longer over the bait with its confidence building up all the time. This is very often the sequence of events if one wishes to hang around and observe them, but on this occasion we have a lot more work to do and more swims to bait up in exactly the same manner as this one.

It is purely a matter of personal choice as to whether one includes a few free samples of hookbait in with the hempseed. Hookbaits should ordinarily extend only to particles and naturals in the summer – as we have already learned, these are infinitely more successful

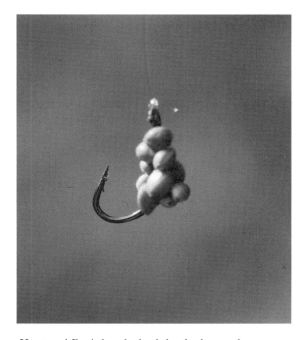

Hempseed Bogied to the hookshank about to be cast.

barbel catchers than the larger baits that work so well in winter.

Particle baits such as sweetcorn do benefit from a little bit of prior introduction but it is very easy to overdo it with sweetcorn, as barbel are often spooked by its bright colour if it appears in the swim in any great abundance before they really begin to become preoccupied with it. Taking it to extremes, as little as half a dozen grains per baitdropper is much preferable to a whole can. I find that many baits, especially naturals, are best left in the baitbox and fished on their own over the hempseed, particularly lobworms and minnows.

Hempseed enhances greatly the appeal of sweetcorn or mini boilies and natural baits and I find that little is often gained by giving barbel free samples unless their recognition of the bait as a food item is a little suspect, and we have no worries on that score regarding naturals. Exceptions to this are maggots and casters,

more of which later, as well as mini boilies, small paste baits and meat particles. Certainly with lobworms and minnows as mentioned, as well as other baits such as prawns, caddis and tares, no prior introduction is required when fished over a bed of hempseed.

Our activity may well have taken us up to lunch time, which is as good a time as any for a break. Stay well away from the whole river and allow the primed swims to develop. Let the barbel build in confidence and begin feeding in the swims: the longer we give them the greater their confidence will be.

Now we have a decision to make, given that we have spent a couple of hours on the river already and as yet have not cast a bait. We can alternatively start fishing, or, more prudently, re-bait the swims and wait for a couple of hours longer. The latter option is undoubtedly the most professional and certainly successful approach but as the afternoon draws on we

A worthy fish from a compromise swim.

should at least come to a compromise and get fishing: surely we have been patient enough! I suggest that a compromise is the order of the day here and find that re-baiting swims where the barbel were originally visible, as well as the more open runs between the streamer weed, advisable. The compromise is to spend two or three hours fishing any of the snaggy swims that do not necessarily benefit from the introduction of any more bait and yet will still manage to produce confident and settled barbel.

This compromise strategy is based on pure logic. Barbel that are resident in swims that boast better than average cover – snag swims, tree cover or even both – will feed with greater confidence because of their greater sense of security than barbel resident in the more open swims.

As the afternoon passes into late afternoon or early evening and with the snags having been fished, we can now move onto the remaining swims with terrific anticipation. Having already baited the swims twice, several hours apart, we should, barring any external forces, have at least a couple of swims with confidently feeding barbel in them. External forces may mean other anglers inadvertently moving into one of the pre-baited swims during the afternoon, or a series of erratically controlled canoes unsettling the fish who may also be slightly edgy owing to the presence of bait in the swim. With a multiple swim approach one has to take the odd set-back philosophically, and if an angler moves into one of your swims and catches some barbel then so be it, there is nothing that can be done. Nobody has the right to monopolize a whole stretch of river at the cost of other anglers wishing to fish there.

It has been suggested in the past that every pre-baited swim should be fished in turn by working up or down river and fishing each prepared swim as it comes. While this approach

This barbel was one of many to come from the open water in the background.

undoubtedly produces a lot of barbel, a bit of thought can produce even more. Not forgetting that the swims with more cover tend to house more secure-feeling barbel, the shrewd approach is to leave the more open swims containing the more vulnerable barbel until very late in the day and fish the more intermediate swims in the interim. Having given our best to the heavy cover or snag swims we should now move onto these middling swims still boasting cover, usually in the form of *Ranunculus* , rocks or other obstructions. Barbel feel very secure in *Ranunculus* , hence several fish sitting beneath it for hours on end, just as they do in the near vicinity of other large physical features.

As the day draws on we can move into each of the intermediate swims and make the first cast of the day into them. The first few minutes will soon show us how our labours are going to reward us. Provided that everything has gone according to plan and the dreaded 'external forces' have not been at work, these first minutes are the most important of the day. It is vital that we are aware of this as I have seen too many days ruined by anglers not concentrating at this crucial time. It is perfectly understandable that, after all the work of the previous hours and following that first cast into the swim, the angler pours from a flask a cup of coffee, lights a cigarette or fiddles around with an item of tackle the moment the rods are placed in the rests. How many times have we heard anglers moan that they missed the only bite of the day just as they were pouring out the coffee? It was nobody's fault but their own because they did not observe one of the basic rules of barbel fishing – the most crucial cast is the first cast and the most crucial part of that is the two or three minutes that follow. I cannot recommend strongly enough that absolutely everything that you need to do should be done before that first cast is made. The moment the bait plops into the swim you should put everything else out of your mind and concentrate on that rod top or quivertip. Too many barbel anglers have become somewhat nonchalant about rod-wrenching barbel bites and believe

that these are the only sort of bites that the barbel give, yet I have caught countless barbel, a number of them over 10lb, that gave such a delicate bite that if it had been a gudgeon I would not have been surprised.

Following our visits to the intermediate swims, we can at dusk then confidently move into the more open swims such as the bare, sloping gravels, gullies or depressions where there is relatively little cover but where barbel love to feed, particularly at dusk and into darkness. The beauty of this is that the more open swims are very much easier to fish in darkness, as well as being more productive.

To recap then, by selecting particular swims because of their physical features and characteristics and not because they are the next one up or downstream, and assessing how they are likely to fish at certain times of the day, far more barbel will be caught than by not fishing to the snag – intermediate – open swim system. Believe me, open swims where barbel are clearly visible do fish better at dusk and in the dark whereas snaggy, overgrown swims can and certainly do produce barbel for longer periods during the daylight hours.

Of course 'always' and 'never' are the two words that should never be used in angling so it does not pay to be too dogmatic in your approach as barbel can be caught well away from any form of cover in the middle of a bright sunny day. However, in order to give yourself a sizeable advantage, that all-important edge, by following my logical progression through the swims, your chances of success are genuinely greater in the long run.

This approach applies to most barbel stretches in the UK where the barbel have been caught but not unduly hammered. Exceptions to fishing each swim in a logical sequence and not as they come along as you wander down the riverbank are over-fished stretches where the barbel usually feed only in the dark and through till dawn. The other happy exception is on a river where the barbel have never seen an angler's bait before, when you can do what you like when you like; sadly these circumstances are all too rare!

A previously baited swim gave an immediate bite.

The culmination of logical swim progression.

What we have so far described may or may not fit your own personal barbel stretches, indeed many stretches may be bereft of any form of cover. Whatever the situation you have in mind for your own barbel stretches, the basic principles of fishing times still apply. On stretches where cover is scarce, much of the fishing should centre around late evening, dusk and beyond. Other stretches may well be full of overhanging trees, submerged trees, rafts and all manner of barbel-holding features, which can be fished right through the day with considerable success. The key is to be adaptable and fish according to the situation.

11 WINTER FISHING

THE RIGHT TIME TO FISH

The committed barbel angler can, if so desired, fish the season through from June to March, something that would never have been considered worthwhile until quite recently. While barbel are synonymous with summer and autumn days spent on the river, winter specialists have found them to be more predictable during the colder months. This trait, coupled with the fact that barbel weigh that bit more during the winter months, especially late in the season, has made winter fishing a very attractive option.

True winter barbel fishing does not really commence until the autumn rains have cleared the fallen leaves, the trees are bare and the first few frosts have killed off all the weed. This can often mean late November or early December before the rivers are clear of rubbish.

To be a successful winter barbel angler one is not required to sit out in all weathers waiting for the rod to hoop over. Neither is winter barbel fishing a question of putting a great deal of time in on the bank; it is waiting for the right opportunity to present itself and then exploiting the favourable conditions.

Virtually all winter specialists are agreed that temperature is everything in assessing the possibilities of a productive session, but the taking of a single water temperature is not sufficient to put the angler in a position to say one way or the other as to whether the barbel are feeding. For temperature to tell us anything at all, we need to assimilate other information and have grounds on which to base our judgement. First we require a temperature of at least 40°F (just over 4°C) or above to have any realistic chance of sport at all. As I have said, this isolated read-

A rising water temperature and lots of it. Fish at all costs!

ing does not tell the whole story but only a small part of it. We do need to know much more if we are to make an informed and worthwhile assessment of the situation.

To make any sort of value judgement it is vital to take several temperature readings over a period of time. What we are looking for is a rising temperature, and it is this rising temperature gradient that is so much more important than the temperature itself. For example, a reading of 46°F (slightly under 8°C) and rising rapidly is far more conducive to good barbel fishing than a rapidly descending 50°F (10°C). Furthermore, the speed of the temperature increase appears to be directly related to the enthusiasm and willingness with which the barbel will feed.

Such is the crucial importance of temperature and its progress up or down the scale, that if at all possible a river's temperature should be taken every day that it is possible to do so when not fishing and constantly when you are. During periods of severe cold the exercise would be pointless, but whenever possible a temperature should be taken and recorded. The moment it starts to rise is the time to fish. Some barbel anglers lucky enough to live very close to their barbel rivers keep a thermometer permanently to hand and are always in a position to know exactly what the temperature is

doing throughout the whole of the winter. Intelligence gathering to this degree is invaluable and several weeks may go by before a bait is even worth casting. For those not quite so fortunate in their location, alternatives will have to be considered. One extremely useful aid in being aware of water temperature fluctuations is to have a contact on the river who is prepared to share them with you. If you can get plugged into the temperature network that exists between barbel anglers on all the major barbel rivers, it can truly be a godsend.

If this is not possible, and for most winter barbel anglers this may well be the case, there are alternatives. For instance, a barbel angler can have a successful winter weekend fishing in a steady 50°F (10°C) on a barbel river but may be unable to return until the next weekend. As the week progresses, it is necessary to know whether fishing will be possible the following

I waited 2½ weeks before these perfect conditions presented themselves.

A wet and windy winter's day is heaven for the barbel angler.

weekend, and whether or not it is necessary to make the appropriate advance preparations. What must constantly be done during the week is to study the weather, be it local or otherwise depending on the fishing location. It is important to know whether that 50°F will remain at that level or, hope against hope, rise by a degree or two.

The Teletext weather service can play a crucial role here in enabling the angler to deduce what the water temperature is likely to be doing on the river in question. If the air temperature has remained constant for the week, at, say, something in the high fifties with no overnight frosts, then the water temperature may well have remained constant or perhaps even risen a little. Under these circumstances the barbel angler should make the decision to go fishing. Should there have been any warm rain as a result of a low-pressure weather front coming

across from the south-west, then the water temperature may well have risen noticeably, with the river having had an influx of warmer water that will also have brought colour. The NRA (National Rivers Authority) can be useful here, as a telephone call to the appropriate automatic answering service the afternoon before the trip for the area you plan to fish will reveal the river level, thus enabling you to make the correct decision as well as getting a picture in your mind of what you can expect on your arrival. While the NRA service does not unfortunately extend to water temperature readings, knowledge of the level of the river can denote the quantity of rainwater that has entered the river. This, of course, assumes you knew the NRA's reading at their gauging station on your previous trip and can make a comparison.

Like a series of water temperature readings, river-level readings only begin to tell you things when a series of readings are taken in close proximity to one another and are studied and analysed. A prior knowledge of the river level can at times determine what swim to fish, as the experience of previous level readings will have shown that, for instance, one swim is conducive to good sport when the river level is 2ft (60cm) above normal summer level while another is the better option when the river is running at 3ft (90cm) above normal summer level at the gauging station. Such conditions as we have hypothetically described here are the optimum conditions in which to go winter barbel fishing and a trip must be arranged at all costs!

Unfortunately, these ideal conditions do not present themselves as often as we would like but, under other circumstances where an influx of warm water does not occur, the key to fishing on the right days is when the water temperature is nonetheless rising. Any increase in water temperature is good news for the winter barbel angler and goes a long way to explaining why some anglers always seem to catch barbel when they turn up in the middle of winter while others do not. It is a fair bet that a combination of a thermometer, Teletext and the NRA gauging station have all been consulted.

To stretch the point but without going to extremes, it is perfectly feasible for a keen winter barbel angler with no knowledge or understanding of water temperature and river levels to turn up on a succession of weekends through maybe December, January and February, with the water temperature falling, or certainly very low, and not see a single barbel, nor have a single bite throughout those months. Believe me, I have seen it happen!

Conversely, a temperature watcher may only make a handful of carefully chosen trips and catch barbel, lots of them, every time. This occurs to a slightly lesser degree with regular monotony on several barbel rivers and can lead to a lot of frustration for the unfortunate souls who regularly blank. Remember, successful winter barbel fishing is not about putting in the rod hours, it is all about putting in an odd rod hour when it really matters.

NORMAL WINTER RIVER LEVELS

Here we shall be looking at situations and

The wake of this autumnal tree was packed with barbel, water temperature was 50°F, a mouth-watering prospect.

approaches applicable to rivers running at normal winter levels – or no more that 1ft (30cm) or so above – with a detailed look at the rather different concept of floodwater fishing later.

As we have already seen, barbel can be extremely easy to spot during low water, summer conditions but the coloured, higher waters of winter require that the river is read so that barbel are located. As is very often the case, productive summer barbel swims are rarely situated too far from snags or cover and it is not uncommon for these same swims to become very turbulent and too inhospitable for the barbel during the winter months, thereby causing them to move out and vacate the area. This is not always the case as there are swims that contain barbel twelve months of the year. Virtually all rivers boast summer swims and winter swims and the seasonal migrations of summer

barbel to their winter quarters on hard-fished rivers is often very predictable and well chronicled.

In more neglected stretches where their movements are not quite so well known, or with barbel that are slightly more nomadic than is generally supposed, we have to locate them ourselves. While the precise winter swim that winter barbel eventually choose to inhabit is not always predictable – indeed, many barbel will visit a number of these swims – the type of water and degree of current velocity that they are attracted to and are most comfortable in most definitely is. It is not uncommon for a particular stretch of river to have a low number of summer barbel swims, say two or three, whereas at the onset of winter the amount of potential barbel swims can double, sometimes even treble. This can initially be a little off-putting, but the correct approach can soon get

An incredibly mild November day saw this barbel succumb to chilli flavoured paste.

to the bottom of the barbel's exact where-abouts.

Before we look at this correct approach let us first discuss how such swims may be recognized. It is important to realize that featureless but gravel-bottomed swims, which are only 1ft (30cm) or so deep and devoid of barbel during the summer months, will often become first-rate barbel swims during the winter with the higher water levels of winter flowing over the top of them. The featureless nature of these swims will often result in the smooth, flat glides with a steady to brisk walking-pace flow rate so beloved of winter barbel. Barbel also love to move onto these new feeding grounds in winter and will often stay there for the remainder of the season, bar spells of particularly adverse conditions when they can be forced out.

During the winter months it is important to see the river as a completely different feature: it is bigger, meaner and not as amenable as its distant relative the summer river. The extra water that a river carries in the winter radically alters so many swims that one might as well be fishing a different river on many stretches.

In winter, barbel appear to be much less nervous in more open swims, quite probably because of the extra, coloured water which they inhabit. I have never found that the logical swim progression, so important in the summer, offers the angler any advantage in the winter months.

One such winter characteristic is the importance of the 'crease'. Phrases come and go in angling, but just as 'patrol routes' are forever associated with the accomplished bream angler Graham Marsden, so is the 'crease' associated with that dynamic chub and barbel duo, Trefor West and Tony Miles.

Many lesser anglers refer to a 'crease' as if they had invented the phrase and fully understand what it is, without ever explaining it. It is just a descriptive word that more than adequately describes two entirely different sections of water, travelling in roughly the same direction, but at different speeds and quite often at different angles too. The motion of the two dif-ferent bodies of water where they meet therefore forms a crease, which is easily visible on the surface of the water before it inevitably peters out as both bodies of water merge into one at some point downstream.

Good examples of a winter crease are where a normally exposed feature such as a bush has become partially submerged, causing a different flow rate to travel in its wake and alongside the faster water of the main flush. Other examples can be caused by bends, no matter how slight, where the faster water shoots round the outside causing the water to slow up a little on the inside. Often a crease, and it matters not how short the crease is, will form immediately downstream of a bend, create a food trap and become a favourite haunt for the barbel.

What is further misunderstood about a crease is that it goes all the way down to the bottom. Underwater, a crease appears almost as a wall and, as the faster water brushes against the slightly slower flow, food is deposited into the slower section where it comes to rest in an area that is a natural larder for the barbel.

There are also occasions when a crease will be visible on the surface of the water for no obvious reason; these swims also hold barbel in as great an abundance as the others and should not therefore be ignored. The cause of such creases is virtually always underwater obstructions or features, which, as we now know, make always consistently good barbel swims.

Barbel love to sit right by a crease on the more comfortable and less turbulent side. Crease swims make superb winter swims not only because of the way they collect food, but also because of the regularity with which such swims are adjacent to features, snags, obstructions, call them what you will.

The fact that barbel may inhabit more potential swims during winter than summer is of little consequence to the winter barbel angler. The only difference is that more swims have to be primed with bait during winter than summer, but a lot less bait needs to be introduced into each one. For example, a known summer barbel swim may well receive 4 pints of

A barbel river running at its normal winter level.

hempseed for a summer session, but for winter fishing this quantity of bait is quite sufficient to bait eight different swims during these cooler conditions – half a pint of hempseed, plus whatever small quantity of hookbait samples you wish to introduce, per swim.

It is not in the least bit uncommon to be confronted with long smooth glides, with a regular depth and of quite a length, in which the barbel could be sitting just about anywhere. By introducing a half a pint of hempseed every few yards or so into likely looking areas, swims within swims can be created. On many stretches of river, particularly those that are long and relatively featureless, it can quite often prove difficult to be in a position to know exactly where the hempseed was introduced several hours earlier into all the likely looking spots. While barbel are quite prepared to move up to the hempseed in winter, they are often reluc-

tant to move away from it to feed on a lone hookbait, and if a bait has been cast to land several feet away from the baited area because an angler does not know precisely where the hempseed and hookbaits have been introduced, the chances of a bite are reduced considerably.

Where stretches of river exist that boast several potential swims, all of which have been baited, together with the fact that the swims may not be visited until several hours later, it really pays to have some sort of marker and means of recording precisely what has been introduced and where. Sometimes a bush or something similar will stand out, but on occasions there will be nothing of any substance that can be used as a marker for the precise area that has been primed. It is not uncommon for barbel anglers to prime up to twenty swims in preparation for a day's barbel fishing (this includes quite often a substantial part of the night as well). It is quite easy to lose track of what has and has not been done, particularly at night.

An excellent means of recording exactly what preparatory work has been accomplished is to mark each spot with something like a tent peg, which can be driven into the ground directly opposite where the bait has been put in. These pegs are quite discreet and can remain in the bank by the swim until the angler eventually arrives to fish, or indeed to introduce more bait. On larger rivers it also pays to be in a position to know exactly where and how far out the bait is. A small notebook is invaluable here in recording such detail as well as features, if any, which can be used as markers on the opposite bank. A system of numbering each swim, and jotting down precisely where the bait is in each swim, is worth its weight in gold and it is not until this is consulted that the angler realizes just how much is forgotten about the details of the preparation undertaken in twenty or more swims. The notebook also becomes invaluable if one is of the inclination to record what, if any, barbel were caught and from exactly where, so that if a pattern does begin to emerge, the angler will be in a position to recognize it. This concept works particularly well on those long, seemingly featureless but perfectly paced runs, where there is no obvious reason why any one spot out of 200 yards (180m) or so produces fish while the rest of the run does not. Quite often an angler can enjoy a cracking day's sport in such a spot, but because of adverse or poor conditions cannot get back, and would be wasting time in returning in any case until the conditions improved again. If the improvement in weather takes a number of weeks to arrive it is often very difficult to recall precisely where the hot spot was, or more accurately is. By referring to the notebook it can be located precisely. It also pays, on coming across a hot spot among long featureless stretches, to keep the tent peg in place for future reference. Again, the angler will often be amazed that the precise location of the swim is a number of yards from where it was thought to be. The tent

Keeping a note of information helps in big swims such as this upon making a later visit.

peg and notebook system will not fail.

It is not being suggested that what makes a good spot on a featureless run one day will necessarily do so on return, but at least you will know for certain if that is the case, or better still if it is not. One final tip: should you wish to adopt this little habit, then make sure that you use a pencil, as ball point pens are not the most reliable things in sodden wet, hempseed and meat encrusted fingers scribbling away in some downpour in the middle of the night!

The introduction of hempseed and free hook samples into barbel swims is associated more with summer fishing than anything else, but if the water temperature is not too cold, say anything above 45°F (about 7.5°C), hempseed will still work its magic provided not too much is put in. As little as one dropper full – the 3 to the pint or 5 to the litre size – is often sufficient when the water temperature is between 45 and 50°F (7.5 to 10°C). Anything above that and two or three full droppers become more appropriate.

When priming winter swims it is a matter of personal choice as to whether a few bait samples are included in the dropper or not. In the long run the best approach is probably to include two or three small lumps of flavoured meat, for instance, and on returning later to re-bait the swim, repeat the meagre quantity of bait introduced so as not to overdo it. When such a swim is eventually fished, the best approach is to fish the stringer rig holding only one or two bait samples. It certainly pays to err on the side of caution until the exact situation in the swim becomes clear. For instance, a swim that produces a couple of quick barbel would probably benefit from a slight increase in bait samples, say to four or five, and a two-hour rest. Filling a winter swim in with bait if the barbel appear hungry is a mistake as you clearly do not know how many fish are feeding in the swim, nor can you be aware of exactly how little bait it would take to make them stop feeding! The concept here is to be cautious and to catch the barbel, not to feed them.

The approach of baiting multiple swims with hempseed and bait samples works well where conditions can be described as good to excellent. Although such an approach can be demanding and at times quite exhausting, this is yet another area where a positive mind and hard work reaps rewards. It can be disheartening if several such swims are fished without a touch, but we can take confidence from the fact that the approach is a series of eliminations and, as each swim is fished without incident, the swim that will eventually produce gets ever closer.

When the fishing of the long straight glides commences, the real work only then starts. A method originally brought to light in the book *Quest For Barbel* (The Crowood Press, 1991) has really taken off among winter barbel anglers. With its roots in the match fishing practice of upstreaming a perfectly balanced bait, the approach is to cast a bait upstream with a lead that will only just hold bottom and, by gently easing the bait back with the current every so often, relatively large areas of potential barbel-holding water are covered. The two main advantages of this approach are that, first, to cover as much ground as possible, only one cast to the head of the run needs to be made and, second, as the rig is eased back by the angler, it does so in a straight line and not across the current as it would if it were cast downstream and then dislodged. This approach renders a hookbait as natural as it can be to the barbel because it comes to the fish in a natural fashion as well as without the disturbance of a cast, or at the very least the cast having been made several minutes beforehand and further upstream at that.

To start with, the standard breakaway legering rig is perfectly adequate for this type of fishing. The value of being able to switch leads easily is important here until critical balance is achieved. Furthermore, the standard barbel legering rig with the Power Gum attachment system works exceptionally well and certainly outscores the more cumbersome snap or link swivel. The process of easing back baits as described is prone to odd small snags on the bottom and the breakaway capabilities of the rig ensure that the only item of tackle lost is usually the lead and not the baited hook. While no angler should be happy leaving any item of terminal tackle in the river, one lead is better than a whole rig, especially if the rig contains a baited hook. It really is amazing how often the lead snags rather than the hook and it is folly in the extreme if a barbel rig of this nature does not have the breakaway capability, as the snagging possibilities do not disappear when a barbel is hooked.

This upstream style of fishing requires a good flow rate so that the current can push back the rig towards the angler, who can search out the swim properly. On runs of a slow steady flow the method does not

Barbel like this make the winter months worthwhile.

work anywhere near as well.

The first cast, just as in virtually all barbel fishing, is vitally important. Let us take a hypothetical look at the tactical approach to, say, a prime barbel stretch. Given that twenty or so swims have been primed throughout the morning, we have thus far fished eight swims a short distance apart but with no success. The water temperature is 47°F (8.5°C), we have an extra 1ft (30cm) of water on the normal summer level and there is no prospect of a dip in temperature for the next two or three days. With these seemingly conducive conditions, the first requirement is absolute confidence that, somewhere on the journey through the baited swims, we are going to cross swords with some as yet undiscovered barbel.

We begin at the downstream end of the run and it is our intention to move gradually upstream as we enter and fish each primed swim in turn. By working upstream we never disturb or walk past a swim, the only disturbance being the casting to the head of it and then gently inching baits back through it.

A typical stay in a swim along the lengthy glide will have commenced with the location of the tent peg and reference to the notebook that denotes exactly the location of the primed area. By consulting the notebook we find that swim nine received two baitings of hempseed and a handful of curry-flavoured meat at 8am and 11.30am. The baitings were aimed at two distinct areas, one on the gradient that shelves off gradually towards the central channel and another a small run that appears to flow at a slightly quicker pace along the near bank. We arrive in the swim at 2pm and, confident in the knowledge that we are going to catch barbel but not as yet sure exactly where, we make the first cast a few yards from our downstream fishing position, ideally about 10 yards (9m) away from the area being fished. It is not uncommon by any means to be sitting directly opposite the water that was being fished during our stay the previous swim, in this case swim number eight. Having made the cast, the rod should not be placed on a rest, but held with the rod pointed upwards and the quivertip allowed to take on its natural arc as the pressure on the line pulls the whole set-up taut. We have already discussed the importance of the correct choice of weight, but the correct choice of quivertip is also not to be underestimated. Too stiff and it will not arc over, too light and it will point directly at the bait. Both positions are useless and do nothing other than obscure and mask any bite that may be forthcoming. Bites fishing in this style are rarely savage, with gentle plucks and then a steady drawing and tightening of line being the norm.

Following the initial cast it pays to give the bait a little time, say ten minutes or so, to settle down and also to allay any fears that may have been aroused in the barbel. Assuming that no bite has been forthcoming, we now lift the rod slightly and gently ease the bait back a yard or so before reeling in the slack and allowing the bait to settle once more. It is uncommon for a bite to be forthcoming as the bait is in motion, but the instant it settles on the bottom once more, a bite is likely if there are any barbel present.

There are a number of ways that bites can be detected here and the most obvious is indicated by the quivertip. The importance of achieving an arc in the quivertip is revealed now, as the most common bite is a 'drop back', which reveals itself on the quivertip as a sudden straightening and release of tension. This is the time to strike, as a barbel is usually the culprit. Other forms of bite indication manifest themselves in the form of the line falling slack and appearing to speed up. This reaction to a barbel taking a bait is indicated by the quivertip also, but watching the line as well will often show whether the barbel has merely dislodged the bait and lead and is lying inert on the bottom,

or whether it has turned and is heading downstream. All the quivertip will tell you as it springs back is that a barbel has in all probability taken the bait, but because we are upstreaming it, we need to know also what amount of slack line we have in front of us to pick up before setting the hook. If a barbel has taken the bait and moved downstream 1ft (30cm) or so then we can confidently strike immediately. Should the line be falling back at an alarming rate, then it will become necessary to take this excessive amount of slack up on the reel quickly before then driving the hook home with a firm strike.

HPPE lines are wonderful for this style of fishing for several reasons. One of the main advantages of HPPE is that, as the bait is moved very slowly back towards you, you can feel everything as it scrapes along the bottom. It really is uncanny how this line allows you to become fully conversant with the exact nature of the river bed. If it is soft and silty (and useless for barbel), the bomb will not be felt scraping or bouncing along a hard bottom but will register as a slight drawing on the line as it is pulled from the mud or silt. Should the bottom be hard and covered in gravel (ideal territory), the bomb can be felt moving over every stone and pebble on the bottom.

The main advantage of HPPE under these circumstances is the ability that it has to transmit anything that the barbel does in an amplified way up to the quivertip or better still up to the angler's fingertip. We have already looked at the positive aspects of HPPE braid in touch legering and the same principles certainly apply here. Quite often a tiny pluck can be felt on the line before a more tangible bite develops. This tiny pluck, vibration almost, gives the angler an edge by causing awareness of the bite before it registers properly. This is not the time to strike, but as the bite develops the angler's concentration will undoubtedly be total.

HPPE has the advantage that its non-stretch ability gives to the upstreaming method. Quite often, as we have seen, the barbel comes towards the angler thus increasing the amount

A lovely winter fish.

of slack line between him and the fish. A couple of quick revolutions on the reel handle will often make up the difference, but with nylon's ability to stretch, a strike can get somewhat cushioned, yet with an HPPE line the strike hits home a lot more directly and does hook a lot more fish. It has been argued by sceptics that they never miss a barbel on nylon when fishing upstream in this fashion. What they do not realize is that they are failing to see as many bites as the angler fishing an HPPE line. A nylon-only angler boasting of a 100 per cent strike rate is one thing if, say, five bites have been forthcoming to nylon, but the HPPE user may well have felt as well as seen seven or eight. Needless to say the strike rate would not be any less.

The thinner diameter of HPPE line offers less resistance to the current, therefore allowing a smaller lead to be used. This not only makes

less of a disturbance upon entering the water but also makes the physical act of striking that much easier. Remember that while the lead is imperative for this sort of fishing, at the time of the strike it only acts as a shock absorber and cushions the force of the strike from where it matters most, the hookpoint.

That aside, let us return to our session. Assuming that we are armed with an HPPE line, coupled with a flattened bomb of 2oz (55g) and a 2.5oz (70g) test-curve quivertip and have made our first cast, we need to adopt the finger position of the touch legerer, but with the rod at a 45-degree angle to the river and pointing towards the bait. It is beneficial to have a fully adjustable bank stick and a Drennan quivertip rod rest head here, which allows us to set up the rod's position and correct angle and enables us to hold the rod and feel for the bites as we lean it against the rest.

Make sure that the line has a free passage through the rod rest head so that all the tweaks and pulls on the HPPE are transmitted up to the fingertip. The rod rest acts as a stabilizer and allows the angler a better chance of feeling bites than simply holding the rod in an unsupported fashion.

Once we are facing the direction of the bait (upstream) and with a finger resting against the line, the quivertip as well as the line needs to be watched intently. After the initial cast and subsequent wait of approximately ten minutes, we can now gently ease the bait back downstream and through the swim, purposefully dislodging the rig every five minutes or even less if you are so inclined. It often pays to move a lead no more than a few inches at a time, as on occasions the movement of the bait will induce a barbel to take the second the bait comes to rest again.

It is not uncommon for barbel to ignore a static bait completely, only to take one that hops a couple of inches along the bottom and comes to rest again. This is quite likely an example of a barbel feeling confident that no other barbel is interested in the titbit, but feeling suddenly competitive and selfish the moment the bait becomes more attractive by moving slightly.

Suddenly, out of the blue, we feel a gentle pluck on the line warning us of the impending events, the quivertip then springs back and the line appears to be drifting downstream towards us. A couple of quick cranks on the reel handle and a sweeping strike over the shoulder sets the hook and after five minutes or so we have our first barbel, the weight of which is up to the reader. We now have a decision to make: do we introduce more bait and return in a couple of hours or do we cast again and await events? The prudent decision appears to be not what you

The fat shoulders of this winter barbel typify their extra weight late in the season.

would think, ie to err on the side of caution and to introduce more bait and return later. Quite frankly, to lump in a dropper full of hempseed and hookbait samples will cause more disturbance to barbel that are settled and feeding fish than another bait edged downstream towards them. Barbel, especially in the winter, appear to care not one jot that a hooked fish spends five or ten minutes charging up and down scrapping vainly for its freedom. The clump of a baitdropper depositing hempseed and hookbait samples or the sight of a badly presented bait or a bad cast right on top of them will, however, spook them, following the capture of a fish, for the rest of the day and will ruin the swim.

What we need to do now, bearing in mind that we have at last found them, is to cast to the head of the swim again, and wait the obligatory ten minutes before easing the bait back into position bit by bit. If a bite is immediately forthcoming then we will know that we have at last found a shoal of fish and not just a loner. By not getting too excited, and patiently edging baits down the swim, more barbel are a probability and not just a possibility. If bites start to dry up after a couple more fish, by all means withdraw and carry on working swims upstream in an effort to find yet more barbel, as not every barbel will be in the same swim. Swims that have produced fish during the day are best left until darkness before a return is made.

There is a groundswell of opinion that winter barbel fishing is much more productive at night, indeed, many regular winter barbel anglers only fish at night, such is their belief in the nocturnal activities of barbel. It does not pay to be quite as dogmatic as this as barbel can and do feed at any point during a twenty-four hour period. However, the angler who fishes between 4pm

This chilly winter sunset preceded a frenzied feeding spell in mid-stream.

and midnight will catch more barbel than one who fishes from 8am to 4pm. This does not apply on all rivers, but on the majority certainly it is a case of fishing and finding out on whatever river you happen to be fishing at the time. Night fishing as a subject is covered in more detail under the appropriate heading.

Some swims can be visited up to three or four times a day before a barbel is eventually caught. It does no harm after failing to catch in a swim to top it up with bait again, as the chances are that you will not spook anything while doing so.

This highly mobile, attack-minded policy can be exceptionally productive, but conditions have to be pretty good to get the best out of it, that is to say a relatively warm water temperature with the river running 1 to 2ft (30 to 60cm) above its normal winter level. Where conditions are not so favourable, which unfortunately is much of the time, our approach needs to be different. Typically, we would be looking at rivers carrying 2 to 3ft (60 to 90cm) of visibility with a steady water temperature reading somewhere between 40°F (4.5°C) and 43°F (6°C).

Once much of the colour disappears from the river and it drops back to its normal winter level, or even lower, then our approach needs to be modified. While many of the good swims available to us remain, there will be swim losses along the way because of the reduction in flow rates and levels and the alterations these changes in conditions make on the current's turgidity. This apparent downturn in conditions does not cause us any particular problem; indeed, the fewer available swims reduce the labour-intensive swim preparatory work. The large aromatic baits that are so successful under the right conditions become less so, with smaller baits, not necessarily particles, consequently picking up more fish. The complete transformation from large aromatic baits such as flavoured meat or blue cheese to particles such as casters, mini boilies or sweetcorn is one recommended by many barbel anglers. While particles, in particular maggots, are often success-

ful during average winter levels and temperatures, other effective baits are our standard flavoured meats, but in drastically reduced sizes. There is no reason why meat, paste or anything else cannot be fished particle style in winter and to do so puts a lot more barbel on the bank than would otherwise be the case.

Garlic sausage or a 'hot' flavoured Bacon Grill diced into ⅛in (3mm) squares, or the hot Pepperami cut into similar lengths, all make very durable and very effective baits for these conditions, as do pastes moulded into baits of similar size. Midi boilies fished over a small carpet of mini boilies also score well, particularly those with one of the 'hot' flavours such as curry. Remember particle baits are particle baits because of their size, not their composition. Swim preparation can follow its usual course with these baits introduced by way of a baitdropper in the usual manner. With the effectiveness of hempseed losing much of its appeal here, a small baitdropper half full of bait samples and no hempseed, introduced into each likely looking area, is all that is required. For very cautious barbel it is wise to introduce small quantities of bait not with the aid of a baitdropper but with the aid of either PVA string or a PVA bag or tube. Each swim can have a bag or tube containing small quantities of the chosen bait very gently lowered into each swim using a suitably heavy bomb to get it down to the bottom. This operation can be accomplished extraordinarily quietly with barely a ripple on the surface. Cubes of meat can also be introduced in this fashion, either on a PVA stringer or in the bag or tube. By waiting a minute or so for the PVA to dissolve, the job is done. Baitdroppers are much more suitable for the larger river or where casts have to be made to mid-river areas out from the bank. On the smaller rivers the discreet lowering of PVA bags of bait is far less obvious to the barbel. The exception to the smaller bait rule appears to be the lobworm, which continues to serve the barbel angler well through thick and thin and is no less effective here than in a flood.

During periods of low rainfall in winter,

On this winter's day only 'hot' flavoured particle meat baits would work.

which usually coincide with cold, high-pressure periods, the water temperature may well dip below 40°F (4.5°C) – time to stay at home! Barbel fishing in poor conditions and catching nothing only serves to disillusion the angler, who will be far better off roaming the river with some meat or cheese in search of chub.

The relatively recent upsurge in winter barbel fishing – after November – has indeed proved that barbel can be caught all year round in the right conditions. Indeed, successful winter carp fishing preceded winter barbel fishing by some years. This fact alone just goes to show how little we as anglers really understood about the barbel until very recently. Our learning curve is still in the ascendancy and while barbel fishing will always be associated with clear summer waters and visible fish flashing over the gravels, many serious barbel anglers do not get down to proper barbel fishing until the leaves

have long gone from the trees. Seasonal weight fluctuations among barbel compared with other riverine species such as chub and roach is quite high. I can cite a number of personal instances where barbel have been caught at well over a pound and a half over their normal summer weight during the latter weeks of the season. To see a big barbel roll on the surface after a long fight in a coloured late-February river at its optimum weight is too good an experience for a barbel angler to miss, but sadly for many of them, they do!

FLOODWATER CONDITIONS

Barbel respond more positively to a flood than any other species and hitherto difficult fish can become quite easy to catch. A flood will often herald a downturn in fishing conditions, but will certainly promote a pronounced upturn in feeding conditions, which if tackled correctly will improve results dramatically. For the purposes of this chapter floodwater fishing means a coloured river running at anything from 2 or 3ft (60 or 90cm) above its normal autumn or winter level right through to the river having burst its banks with the angler needing thigh boots to reach the swim!

Barbel love these conditions and no matter how high the level the barbel angler should be out there regardless. Floodwater fishing means autumn and winter fishing and, although the odd flood can occur in the summer months, we shall be concentrating solely on the cooler months and associated tactics.

Many anglers, confronted by the seemingly hostile conditions of a decent flood, turn round and go home, not to return until the river has subsided substantially. In doing so, they will be denying themselves the likely prospect of a very good day's barbel fishing. More and more barbel anglers are beginning to recognize this fact and are reaping their rewards. Nevertheless, flooded rivers rarely play host to more than a few anglers, and, if you relish the idea of a day's fishing with only the barbel for company, then floods are definitely the time to enjoy this. Fishing in and even approaching flooded rivers requires caution and, while many of the pitfalls are obvious, it can be easy to get caught out by not thinking enough about what may appear obvious in retrospect.

On the occasions that a river does burst its banks and flood the meadows, features such as dykes, small depressions in the ground and even on occasions livestock feeding troughs are submerged and hidden and it is quite easy to wade across a flooded plain, head down and weighed down with mountains of gear, to a well-known swim, lose your bearings slightly and step into or fall over something that you had forgotten was there. This could be a fatal mistake. Furthermore, only a fool would walk across a flooded meadow he has never seen or is unfamiliar with.

A rarer, yet no less dangerous folly, is wading to a swim across the floodplain, usually a higher piece of dry ground, and enjoying a few hours of sport on a rising river only to find oneself cut off with the river still rising and nightfall imminent. This is a more obvious and certainly more common problem on spate rivers but several well-known barbel anglers have been caught out on the relatively more benign lowland rivers in this fashion more than once!

What constitutes a good barbel fishing flood is rain, much of it and relatively warm weather – a higher temperature than the water in the river. This generally is the result of a low-pressure weather front moving over the country from the south-west and precipitating accordingly. Should the rain have been pushed in from the north-east, for instance, then it will usually be cold and not conducive to successful barbel fishing. Rain after periods of ice should be given time to flush the salt from the roads and through the rivers before any fishing is commenced. Salt from roads will kill sport. The same can be said for melted snow water, which not only brings salt with it, but such water is still extremely cold as well as very low in oxygen content. A snow-water flood gives by far the worst possible conditions in which to attempt to fish for barbel.

On a more positive note, given a warm-water flood and a belief that such conditions are first rate for barbel, it can be somewhat off-putting to discover that favourite swims are no longer fishable. The first thing to realize here is that a flooded river will often move barbel out of their regular haunts into new swims that will never see a barbel in them at any time other than during a flood. These floodwater swims are few in number; indeed, in certain rivers they can be miles apart. Do not despair: by thinking positively it should become clear that fewer swims mean a higher concentration of barbel residing within them, all willing to feed!

Finding these swims is easier than one would imagine and the best way of doing so is by elimination. During a flood the surface of the water is far more broken and volatile than it is in more normal conditions, and by this token it reveals a lot more about itself than you may think. Swirling, boiling eddies and stretches with currents that criss-cross each other and appear turbulent will not contain barbel. These areas do not possess any stability for the barbel and are virtually always full of the usual flood-borne rubbish, which also unsettles the fish. Stretches that contain ever-varying currents should also be eliminated as all the barbel is looking for is a steady and predictable current.

We are attempting to locate, through elimination, a current rate and nature not dissimilar to that in which we will find barbel during more common and less adverse conditions. What we are looking for is a flow rate of similar speed to that in any of the popular barbel swims, so often between a steady to brisk walking pace, which also appears smooth and even on the surface.

What tends to throw a lot of potential flood-water barbel anglers is the fact that such swims often appear in areas that are ordinarily shallow, completely dead looking and devoid of any barbel for most of the year.

Anglers therefore feel reluctant and lacking in confidence when contemplating fishing these normally unproductive swims, which is a big mistake. Barbel love to be able to feed in flat, brisk glides over gravels that have not been grazed since the last flood. These flat-looking glides can appear in the unlikeliest of places and be both quite sizeable and obvious as well as obscure and quite minute. These segments of water can stretch virtually from bank to bank or they can appear isolated in midstream and surrounded by a swirling mass of turgid water. No matter in what shape or size they appear they are all worth fishing. Furthermore, it will soon become obvious that the pace and nature of a good floodwater swim is in many ways very similar to the pace and nature of a summer swim. Barbel love a certain smooth, steady flow rate and will often travel great distances to find it. On locating smooth water in a flood travelling at a medium to brisk walking pace, you will often locate barbel at the same time.

Depending on the extent of colouration the river is carrying, barbel will sit in quite shallow water and feed. Barbel are extremely enthusiastic when feeding in 2ft (60cm) of water over flooded, grazed meadow land close by the main flow as well as ordinarily dry, exposed areas of gravel and unkempt banksides of weed and bushes.

The reaction of barbel to a river flooding is quite logical. When a river floods, areas of the bank become submerged that are exposed for most of the year. These areas are rich in food and the high water enables barbel to move onto these areas and feed in virgin, unexploited terrain. Indeed, the increase in levels allows the barbel much more scope to explore and discover rich new sources of food. Compounded by the fact that barbel are seeking out displaced food sources such as lobworms and minnows, it is little wonder that this is the time that barbel see fit to gorge themselves. In the natural world it is either exploit or die, and this instinct is no less suppressed in barbel than in anything else.

One of the best floodwater swims there is consists of one or a number of sizeable trees or bushes that, because of the flood, are partially submerged causing a slower, flatter current to trail in their wake. The leaves of the bushes all help to slow and calm down quite turbulent, inhospitable water into the type of water that barbel prefer. These swims are particularly effective as autumn floodwater swims because of, principally, the leaves, more than the branches, slowing down the current. Once the leaves fall from the tree the amount of resistance caused by the foliage to the current is reduced substantially, which can cause the swim to become too turbulent for the barbel once more. This is not always the case, but very often the barbel will move out after leaf fall and take up residence in another, less turbulent swim.

Bankside vegetation is only one factor in the creation of good floodwater swims. The lee of a sharp bend can slow or brake water sufficiently to create the smooth water so beloved of barbel, as can large boulders, bulrush beds, bridge supports or anything else that has the ability to slow and calm water down sufficiently.

Quite often the water you are looking for is

A flat wake behind a shrub. The barbel will be sitting immediately on the crease, not in the slack.

closest to the bank. Steep or even banks that drop straight down to the river in the form of miniature cliff-faces will cause a slowing down of the current. Furthermore, if any form of undercut exists beneath such a bank then barbel will no doubt be in residence. Do not worry if you are fishing an area that you may have sat in and fished during the summer or watched cattle wade in and drink; the barbel certainly will not.

The steep or near-vertical banks being scoured by floodwater may appear on the face of it a little too brisk, but the current speed will be substantially less near the bottom than the top, thus being more to the barbel's liking than it initially appears. Banks that are being continually scoured and undercut by floodwater currents are prolific food sources for the barbel, particularly in the form of lobworms, and such swims are far too often overlooked, as many is

the time that a large shoal of barbel are feeding immediately beneath the sceptical angler's feet.

Fishing the near bank is a very simple process as the velocity of the current will push the hookbait exactly where it would end up naturally, which in turn is where the barbel will be lying. To achieve this, it becomes necessary to fly in the face of convention and fish a relatively light rig and throw the tackle to the mercy of the current. A light bomb rig is often the ideal set-up to allow the rig to get pushed right under the near bank and under the noses of the barbel. It is a case of flicking out the bait into midstream and allowing it to bounce down and around before settling hard against the near bank. Do not be in the least bit surprised if the rod buckles over as a barbel takes the bait the instant the bait settles.

Most advocates of general river fishing say that the time to fish a river is as it subsides after

Letting the tackle push into the nearside bank.

a flood. This doctrine is erroneous, and should be ignored; the first hint of colour from the oncoming flood will often trigger barbel into a prolonged feeding spell. While many of these advocates will further state that it is a waste of time fishing a rising river, they again prove themselves wrong. Barbel love feeding in rising rivers provided the influx of floodwater is of a higher temperature than that already in the river, so do not believe anything to the contrary.

The prospective flood fisher must make a check on certain factors before it is possible to fish with absolute confidence. We have already discussed the negative influences of snow, salt and cold rain. When a river begins to colour up and its levels slowly begin to rise we must be aware of the temperature of the incoming water, and if at all possible the temperature of the river prior to the flood. This knowledge can determine our entire approach and may even

decide whether we fish or not. If the temperature of the river is being increased substantially by the incoming floodwater, then we can safely expect the barbel to be feeding heavily in the swims we have earmarked as floodwater holding spots.

While barbel are very active during periods of flooding they rely almost exclusively on their sense of smell in their search for food. It therefore follows that baits for floodwater fishing should have some sort of aroma or label that the barbel will detect and consequently recognize as food. It is at times such as these that flavoured meats, cheese, pastes and boilies really start to score, with lobworms being almost as effective. Strong-smelling garlic sausage or Bacon Grill flavoured with any of the flavours mentioned in the bait section are made for flood-water fishing and will now come into their own. The correct choice of bait is less

An even floodwater flow, always attractive to barbel.

important in a flood than at any other time in the barbel fishing calendar; provided that the barbel recognize the particular bait in use at the time as a food item, and provided that the bait is large and smelly, it will usually catch as barbel throw caution to the wind and feed with a vengeance.

At times of flooding, fishing conditions deteriorate while feeding conditions improve. Although a flood drastically improves sport, the mechanics of fishing are made much more difficult. One of the worse aspects can be to differentiate between false bites and real ones because of flood debris catching the line and pulling the quivertip round. At times there can be barely any rubbish coming down, while on other occasions there will be enough to move the bait out of position every few minutes or so. This all too regular occurrence is irritating and detracts from a successful bait presentation. Should this be the case there are two alterna-

tives: the first is to work out a way of getting the line out of the main current and yet continuing to fish that important flat run of water. This can sometimes be achieved by switching over to the opposite bank or putting the rods on the highest setting of the Leeda Rods High Tripod and attempting to get the line to run over the rubbish-strewn main current and enter the water in the flat, slower run that is being fished. When fishing a near bank run, it may be possible on occasions to position the rod top several feet under the surface in an effort to avoid the flood-borne debris and rubbish. Another trick is to allow the line a little bit of slack so that the current pushes it hard against the near bank, causing it to miss the dead leaves and weed that can play havoc with a day's barbel fishing at times of flood.

Another solution is to use the rubbish to your advantage. By casting upstream, and provided not too much rubbish is coming down, it is sometimes possible to allow it to collect on the line. After a period of at least five minutes, preferably ten to fifteen, the accumulated rubbish will shift the tackle back downstream towards you a few feet. As the tackle shifts, part of the rubbish will become detached from the line, especially if it is twitched by the angler as it does so. This then enables the process to begin again. By allowing this to occur you are searching the swim to a degree and although this is not the best option of floodwater fishing at your disposal, it certainly beats packing up early because of the current-borne rubbish rendering the river seemingly unfishable.

Fishing at these times is never easy and false bites will be struck and missed on several occasions throughout the day, but there is no mistaking that lunge of the rod when a barbel does eventually appear out of the coloured, angry depths. It is easy to become a little disgruntled if all that you are striking at is leaves, plastic bags and twigs but, as with so much barbel fishing, a positive, confident approach will almost certainly succeed in the end.

Because of the fact that barbel feed by smell more than anything else in floods, they do not respond at all well to baits that are constantly being moved out of position or trundled through the swim. By far the best approach is to fish a static bait and let the barbel find the bait itself. Providing that one of the smelly baits already mentioned is out there, they almost certainly will do so, given that the barbel are in the swim. It does no harm upon arriving at the stretch to introduce a baitdropper full of hookbaits into each swim that you intend fishing, prior to setting up. Half a dozen balls of paste, boilies, some chopped lobworms or a flavoured meat dropped into each 'flat' goes some way to priming each swim for your return with a baited hook!

Under these circumstances it is not uncommon to have a bite from a barbel within seconds of the bait settling on the bottom, and in most cases certainly within 15 minutes in small swims. If a bait has been cast into a larger swim and no bite has been forthcoming after 30 min-

utes, it is unlikely to be forthcoming at all. A maximum of 45 minutes spent in any swim will decide whether a barbel is to be caught, and if no action has been forthcoming it is best to move on.

Barbel are extremely reluctant to move from one floodwater swim to another during a flood, so it makes logical sense that if one swim fails to produce another is more likely to do so. On some stretches of river, more floodwater swims exist than on others; this usually means that the barbel have more choice as to where they reside during the flood and it therefore follows that more swims equal fewer barbel per swim. This can be an advantage to the barbel angler who can fish each swim in turn, with luck taking a couple of fish before moving on to the remaining swims and doing the same in any number of them. The angler can then return and fish them through again until each of the swims has been thoroughly exhausted.

Floodwater swims that are few in number on a particular stretch generally hold more fish and on occasions can produce large numbers of barbel, but will unfortunately often tail off with several barbel still in residence. These circumstances require that the swim be rested for a couple of hours or so and if there is an alternative swim to try, do so, even if it is some distance away. It is a pointless exercise fishing for spooked barbel when a move can put you back on hungry, eager fish again. It matters not how far one travels between floodwater swims in a day, and if it means having to get in the car and drive a few miles then do so; you will rarely be disappointed.

Floodwater fishing is all about choosing the right swim and an appropriately aromatic bait. Tackle and rigs take second place to location and bait but, nevertheless, correct tackle choice can often be pivotal to success. Experienced floodwater barbel anglers will always say that one has to fish the river and not for the fish in a flood. By this they mean that the most important aspect of floodwater fishing is to let the river choose the appropriate tackle that will enable you to fish the particular spot you have chosen. In other words, the choice of tackle and rigs is dictated by the conditions and not the barbel. If it takes 4oz (110g) or even more of flattened lead to hold bottom in a mid-river 'flat' then put it on; the barbel will take care of the rest. The prime objective here is to get that bait to where the barbel are present, and await events.

The basic barbel rigs are perfectly adequate for floodwater fishing and, on the many occasions that position cannot be held, the option of the ultra-thin HPPE lines is there as opposed to the much thicker, current-catching nylon.

WINTER NIGHT FISHING

With the possible exception of the bream, the barbel is our most nocturnally active species and, whether in June or January, it can be caught at any hour between dusk and dawn. While summer night fishing for barbel is simply an extension of the daylight fishing, winter night fishing requires a completely different mental approach and, as we will see, the habits of winter barbel at night are at variance with those of summer and require a wholly different strategy and understanding. The barbel's natural night feeding habits are often compounded by angling pressure during the daylight hours and barbel are quick to respond to common lulls in angling pressure, such as late at night, and feed with greater confidence accordingly.

Let us consider this brief summary of developments that have occurred on one or two particularly hard-fished stretches, to illustrate this particular point. On these certain stretches of river, daytime barbel fishing in winter has become very difficult with the barbel not beginning to feed until nightfall at the very earliest. Anglers have recognized this and fished successfully until as late as midnight, which appears to be a natural cut-off point for some would-be night owls. Where angling pressure during the hours leading up to midnight has become particularly heavy, barbel have changed their habits once again, only to feed in

the early hours of the morning and right up until dawn, whereupon they cease. In instances where anglers have again recognized precisely what is going on, these few dedicated souls have fished from midnight until dawn and continued to catch several very big barbel.

Where this nocturnal activity has been overdone, daytime angling has become fruitful again. This is not exactly common and applies to only a very few highly pressurized stretches, but what it teaches us about barbel is very illuminating. What is generally underestimated about winter barbel is the propensity with which they will feed during the hours of darkness, with far greater enthusiasm and less caution than during daylight. To be as successful as we would like, we will have to be prepared to spend time on the riverbank at night in the middle of winter, even just an hour or so in the dark. Should we do so, our results will usually improve quite dramatically. Even where there has been little or no angling pressure on certain stretches, or even on whole rivers, barbel can still be caught in greater numbers at night, especially during the winter by the angler who believes.

During the winter months, as we have seen, the feeding habits of the barbel are dictated to more by the temperature than anything else. When barbel are triggered into feeding they will often do so at any time of the day or night. In winter a barbel will happily feed at 11pm, for instance, not having fed much during the day for no other reason than it did not wish to do so. When winter conditions are less than perfect, for example where the water temperature is 41°F (5°C) and not rising, perhaps very gradually falling, the barbel will only feed for short periods of time regardless of the time of day. There is no reason whatsoever why a barbel angler cannot arrive at a stretch of river in complete darkness, fish for several hours and pack up in complete darkness, in an effort to catch them when they begin to feed.

Many barbel anglers make a habit of fishing, say, two evenings a week throughout the summer and autumn and stop abruptly when

Ultraspice flavoured meat in mid-winter is always a reliable choice.

the nights draw in and as winter arrives, which prevents them reaching the river before dark. This is a grave error: the darkness should be treated as a minor disadvantage in aesthetic and comfort terms and only that, as winter nights spent at home by the fire do not catch barbel.

Staying on in the dark after a daytime fishing session is a simple matter of packing away as much tackle as possible for the sake of tidiness, and to reduce the chances of leaving something valuable behind. All that needs to be left out are bits and pieces such as scissors, rig glue and tweezers (for easy access) and a small pencil torch for re-baiting that can clip onto a pocket flap.

The key to having quick and easy access to items of tackle is to lay out the essentials in the same position, whenever possible, every time we are out barbel fishing at night. A simple but effective means of keeping small items of equipment close to hand, and to prevent the chance of loss in the dark, is to keep all the items of active fishing, be they anything from hair-rig needles to PVA string as well as the items already mentioned, in a small groundbait mixing bowl placed within easy reach. Begin by placing a reasonably powerful but light-coloured torch, which is more visible at night, beside the bowl for emergencies – anything from netting a big fish to checking that strange noise from a nearby bush. The landing net should have two powerful Isotopes whipped to the tip of each arm and should be placed in exactly the same position during every session. By this token, the mechanics of night fishing for barbel during long periods of darkness will soon become second nature and reaching for items of tackle will be instinctive.

Turning up during darkness, which in mid-winter can be as early as 4pm, presents different problems but the same positional system still applies. To turn up in darkness and to get the best from a swim, the angler must be conversant with the contours and physical characteristics of the swim as well as the bank. To arrive at a barely known swim in darkness not only invites trouble, but reduces the angler to having to fish blind and should be avoided at all costs. It also makes a great deal of sense to set up the rods at home, or at least during daylight prior to any arrival in darkness, as apart from terminal tackle being tied more reliably at home in daylight, it is also much, much easier. Tackle companies such as Wychwood, Kevin Nash and Rod Hutchinson all market rod holdalls (made for the carp fishing fraternity but ideal also for barbel anglers) that can take made-up rods, and I suggest that you never turn up in darkness without the rods already set

up. Although it is never possible to determine what weight of lead will be required for a winter session, I tend to leave the lead off the rig until my arrival when I can slip on whatever is required by way of the knotted Power Gum attachment.

It is too easy when night fishing to make the assumption that the cardinal sins of standing on the skyline, stamping around the riverbank, crude rig presentations and clumsy use of the baitdropper are no longer relevant with the cloak of darkness apparently stifling and nullifying such carelessness. This is by no means the case, and barbel can quite easily be spooked by an angler standing on the skyline on nights illuminated by only a crescent moon. Indeed, all the good habits of daytime fishing must be observed at night too, because barbel, with their increased nocturnal activities, are just as aware and alert at night, if not more so given

This barbel fed just as the Beatalites began to glow.

their increased activity.

The secret here is to think daylight, and an arrival at the river in darkness should in no way preclude the baiting of a number of swims, just as you would in the day, and fishing your way through them accordingly. There are many nights that are sufficiently well lit by the moon to inspire confidence in fishing the mobile approach, and after a few hours of fishing at night your eyesight in the dark becomes surprisingly good. Only use a light out of absolute necessity: this includes rebaiting, introducing bait or the playing or landing of any barbel. With a little practice all these tasks can be accomplished in darkness. An extremely simple yet effective tip is on occasions where tight and accurate casting is required at night and is difficult to achieve because of the darkness, is to dip the lead in the river and then into some flour, which will render the lead surprisingly visible without scaring the fish. This is a marvellous idea for use where edgy barbel can be easily spooked by light from the bank or clumsy, inaccurate casts. Needless to say the flour quickly disappears when the tackle comes to rest. Unfortunately tangles and hair-rigging baits do require some sort of artificial light and the best method of masking the white light from the small pencil torch is to cover the glass with a red filter or, better still, buy a Mag-lite torch with ready-made red and yellow filters (sometimes available in tackle shops). The diffused red light is much softer on the eye and does not impair the angler's night vision anything like white light does. Furthermore, a small red light does not spook barbel if shone accidentally onto the river.

Lights that can be placed on the head with an elasticated strap should be avoided at all costs while fishing – looking up momentarily and shining the light into the river will spook the barbel. These items are best employed when walking to and from the river.

Another essential is a mobile telephone. This offers several advantages, not least in case of emergency. Anglers' cars are not safe and can be stolen or vandalized by people believing the car

to be abandoned owing to the lateness of the hour. A barbel angler several miles from home, in the middle of nowhere, on a filthy winter's night with no car, is put in a very undesirable situation if there is no way of contacting anybody. Another great advantage is that a mobile telephone takes the pressure off having to get home on time if the barbel begin feeding rather late. There is nothing more galling than having to pack up to fulfil a promise to return home at a certain time just as the barbel are switching on!

It is not until a lengthy night session that the value of two Isotopes on one quivertip is fully appreciated, and once used they are never dispensed with. One major difference with night fishing is the fact that a second rod, an increasingly popular daytime habit among barbel anglers, often causes more problems than any advantages it might offer. Playing a barbel at night can often be a little chaotic as their surging runs will often leave the angler wondering exactly where the fish is. Having another line in the water only complicates the situation and acts as another potential snag. This need not be the case for an experienced barbel angler, but the greatest advantage of fishing only one rod at night is that it allows the angler to touch leger as well. Without doubt the double Isotope, quivertip method of bite indication is an excellent one for night fishing, but by resting a finger, touch-legering style, against the line, those little flicks and small pulls that look like possible bites on the Isotopes will be confirmed as genuine bites, or not, on the fingertip, especially when using an HPPE line.

Another invaluable aid to night fishing is the preparation of rigs at home prior to the session. By tying up a dozen or so hooklengths to swivels and two or three different hook sizes and mounting them on a little rig board or placing them in a rig wallet, a lot of time spent fiddling around on the bank in torchlight is saved, and there is no doubt that knots tied and glued up at home are more reliable than those hastily done on the bank in the dark with cold, impatient fingers.

To conclude, winter night fishing requires

organization; things that we take for granted during the day require thought at night, hence always placing the gear in the same place every time you go fishing so you know precisely where it is. Rigs tied at home save a great deal of trouble, and provided our winter clothing is of the highest quality, we will remain comfortable. If the nocturnal winter barbel angler is neither organized nor comfortable then the session can degenerate into farce.

Never underestimate just how active winter barbel can be at night. This is confirmed week in week out in the angling press with countless big barbel being photographed at night. No angler catches a big barbel during the day and waits until nightfall before photographing it. Conversely, most of the winter barbel that appear to have been photographed in daylight are also caught at night, and how can you tell? Just look at the state of some of the anglers holding them – they have obviously been up all night!

USEFUL ADDRESSES

Anglers Co-operative Association
23 Castlegate
Grantham
Lincolnshire
NG31 6SW

Penge Angling (mail order)
309 Beckenham Road
Beckenham
Kent
BR3 4RL

The Barbel Society
c/o Steve Pope
1 Matchingfield
Kelvedon Common
Brentwood
Essex
CM15 0XB

Bennetts of Sheffield Ltd (mail order)
Stanley Street
Sheffield
S3 8JP

Carrilon UK Ltd (neoprene mittens and
socks)
23 Raglan Road
Retford
Nottingham
DN22 6LN

Dave Swallow Centrepins
Bridge Farm
Iford Bridge
Ringwood
Hampshire

Drennan International
Bocardo Court
Temple Road
Oxford OX4 2EX

Fox International
Fowler Road
Hainault Industrial Estate
Hainault
Essex
IG6 3UT

Graham Phillips Onstream Specialist Rods
(custom built barbel rods)
Unit 4
Lon Dewi Sant
Nefyn
Gwynedd
LL53 6NY

The Harris Angling Company (mail order)
Blacksmith House
Church Road
East Ruston
Norfolk NR12 9HL

Ian Kilgour (second-hand book dealer)
3 Hall Farm Road
Thurcaston
Leicester
LE7 7JF

Korda Developments (Carp Leads)
8A Elm Parade
Elm Park
Essex
RM12 4QG

Kryston Products
Bolton Enterprise Centre
Washington Centre
Bolton BL3 5EY

Leslie's of Luton (mail order)
89–93 Park Street
Luton
Bedfordshire
LU1 3HG

Nisa Swimfeeders
64 Lowestoft Road
Carlton Colville
Lowestoft
Suffolk

Paul Morgan
Coch-y-Bondhu Books
Penegoes
Machynlleth
Powys
Wales

Nutrabaits
Units C1–2
Canklow Meadows Industrial Estate
West Bawtry Road
Rotherham
S60 2XL

Philip Hopper (second-hand book dealer)
119 Grove Road
Chadwell Heath
Essex
RM6 4PE

Salter Abbey (digital weighing scales)
St Botolphs Lane
Bury St Edmunds
Suffolk
IP33 2AX

Seer Rods (custom built barbel rods and digital thermometers)
PO Box 88
Bromyard
Herefordshire
HR7 4DP

Shimano UK Ltd
Unit B2
Lakeside Technology Park
Phoenix Way
Llansamlet
Swansea
SA7 9EH

Solar Tackle
PO Box 22
Orpington
Kent
BR6 7XF

Specialist Tackle (Classic Centrepins)
93 Chase Cross Road
Collier Row
Romford
Essex

Streamselect Ltd (Richworth)
Island Farm Avenue
West Molesey
Surrey
KT8 0U

Walkers of Trowell (mail order)
Nottingham Road
Trowell
Nottingham
NG9 3PA

Wiggly Worms (mail order worms)
Lower Blakemere Farm
Lower Blakemere
Herefordshire

FURTHER READING

There are countless hints, pointers and thought-provoking ideas described in many of the old angling books about barbel, and I have included a number of these books in the list below. While many have been out of print for years, it is worth trying to find copies and read them. I have also included many more recent books, which contain varying degrees of information, stimulation and inspiration within their pages. The list is not intended to be exhaustive – that would be virtually impossible – but these recommendations are all from my bookshelves and should contain items of interest to all those who love barbel.

A few books on carp fishing are included. They contain valuable insights into understanding assorted rigs and their specific applications, and are a mine of information concerning bait ingredients and flavours, which all barbel anglers need to understand if they are to develop their own fishing.

Arbery, Len, *The Complete Book of River Fishing*, David & Charles, 1993.

Bailey, John, *From Water to Net*, Crowood, 1991.

Bailey, John, *In Visible Waters*, Crowood, 1984.

Bailey, John, *In Wild Waters*, Crowood, 1989.

Bailey, John, *The Fishing Detective*, HarperCollins, 1995.

Bailey, John, *The Great Anglers*, David & Charles, 1990.

Barnes, Tag, *The Exploring Angler*, Eyre & Spottiswoode, 1945.

'BB', *The Fisherman's Bedside Book*, Eyre & Spottiswoode, 1945.

Braddock, Archie, *Fantastic Feeder Fishing*, Pisces, 1992.

Chalmers, Patrick, *At the Tail of the Weir*, Philip Allan, 1932.

Cholmondeley-Pennell, H., *Fishing: Pike and Other Coarse Fish*, Longmans, Green & Co, 1885.

Cholmondeley-Pennell, H., *The Modern Practical Angler*, Routledge, 1870.

Clegg, John, *The Freshwater Life of the British Isles*, Warne, 1952

Cope, Ken, *Barbel, Catch More Series*, Wolfe, 1974.

Crouch, Fred, *Understanding Barbel*, Pelham, 1986.

Cundiff, Julian, *Practical Carp Fishing*, Crowood, 1993.

Dyson, Colin (ed.), *The Haig Whisky Guide to Coarse Fishing in Britain*, Collins Willow, 1985.

'Faddist', *Coarse Fish Briefs*, Gilbertson & Page, 1951.

'Faddist', *Memorable Coarse Fish*, Burlington, 1953.

'Faddist', *Baits and Groundbaits*, Gilbertson & Page, 1950.

Falkus, Hugh and Fred Buller, *Freshwater Fishing*, MacDonald & Janes, 1975; reprinted in 1994 by Grange Books.

Forbes, David Carl, *Catch a Big Fish*, Newnes, 1967.

Francis, Francis, *A Book on Angling*, Herbert Jenkins, 1920.

Francis, Francis, *Angling*, Horace Cox, 1883.

Frost, Peter, B*arbel Fishing, Step-by-Step Series*, Cassell, 1976.

Gammon, Clive, *The Fisherman's Fireside Book*, Heinemann, 1961

Gibbinson, Jim, *Modern Specimen Hunting*, Beekay, 1983.

Graham, Colin, *The New Encyclopaedia of Coarse Fishing Baits*, MacDonald & Janes, 1976.

Guttfield, Frank (ed.), *The Big Fish Scene*, Ernest Benn, 1978.

Haines, Alan, *The Complete Book of Float Fishing*, David & Charles, 1989.

Harper, Steve, *Angling Afloat*, Crowood, 1989.

Harper, Steve, *A Line on the Water*, Creel, 1991.

Hayes, Matt, *Coarse Fishing*, Crowood, 1995.

Head, Len, *River Fishing*, Crowood, 1985.

Housby, Trevor (ed.), *Specimen Hunter's Handbook*, Blandford, 1987.

Housby, Trevor, *The Art of Angling*, Evans, 1965.

Howcroft, Ian, *Barbel*, Osprey Anglers Series, 1975.

Howes, William, *The Quest for Barbel*, Thorsons, 1960.

Lamb, Ted, *The Bait Book*, David & Charles, 1979.

Lane, Billy, *The New Encyclopaedia of Float Fishing*, Pelham, 1987.

Lees, Ron, *Perfect Your Legering*, Crowood, 1993.

Maddocks, Kevin, *Carp Fever*, 10th edition, Beekay, 1990.

Mansfield, Kenneth (ed), *The Art of Angling*, Caxton, 1957.

Miles, Tony and West, Trefor, *Quest for Barbel*, Crowood, 1991.

Miles, Tony, *Big Fish Angling*, Crowood, 1990.

Norman, John (ed.), *Coarse Fishing with the Experts*, Allen & Unwin, 1956.

Orme, Andy, *Barbel Mania*, Crowood, 1990.

Orme, Andy, *Roving for Barbel*, Seer, 1994.

Parker, Captain L.A., *This Fishing; or Angling Arts and Artifices*, Bennett, 1948 (reprinted in 1960 by Cleaver-Hume).

Pearson, Alan, *Hempseed Fishing*, EMAP, 1962

Plummer, Dave, *Tales of a Coarse Angler*, Oxford Illustrated, 1988.

Raversdale, Tom, *Understanding Coarse Fishes*, Crifford, 1973.

Ransome, Arthur, *Rod and Line*, Jonathan Cape, 1929.

Rickards, Barrie, *Angling, Fundamental Principles*, Boydell, 1986.

Roberts, Bob, *The Complete Book of Legering*, David & Charles, 1993.

Rogers, Pete (ed.), *Red Letter Days*, Crowood, 1994.

Rogers, Pete and Burke, Steve (eds.), *The Book of the Perch*, Oxford Illustrated Press, 1990.

Shephard, Michael, *Come and Fish*, Museum Press, 1952.

Sheringham, H.T., *Coarse Fishing*, A & C Black, 1912.

Stone, Peter, *Bream and Barbel*, EMAP, 1963.

Stone, Peter, *Come Fishing with Me*, Pelham, 1973.

Stone, S. Donald, *Barbel, How to Catch Them Series*, Herbert Jenkins, 1955.

Taylor, Fred J., *Angling in Earnest*, MacGibbon & Kee, 1958.

Taylor, Fred J., *Favourite Swims*, MacGibbon & Kee, 1961.

'Trent Otter', *Barbel & Chub Fishing*, The Angler, 1896.

'Trent Otter', *Coarse Fish Angling*, W, Brendon & Son, 1908.

'Trent Otter', *My Fishing Days and Fishing Ways*, W, Brendon & Son, 1908.

'Trent Otter', *The Trent Otter's Little Book on Angling*, Simkin, Kent & Co, 1910.

Turnbull, Chris (ed.), *Big Fish from Famous Waters*, David & Charles, 1990.

Various, *The First Angling Times Book*, EMAP, 1955.

Various, *The Fourth Angling Times Book*, EMAP 1965.

Various, *The Second Angling Times Book*, EMAP, 1962.

Various, *The Third Angling Times Book*, EMAP, 1963.

Vaughan, Bruce (ed.), *Top Ten*, Beekay, 1983.

Venables, Bernard, *Freshwater Fishing*, Herbert Jenkins, 1967.

Venables, Bernard, *Mr Crabtree goes Fishing*, Daily Mirror, 1949.

Walker, Richard, *Catching Fish, Knowing their Feeding Habits,* David & Charles, 1981.

Walker, Richard, *Dick Walker's Angling,* David & Charles, 1979.

Walker, Richard, *How Fish Feed,* Angling Times Publication, 1958.

Walker, Richard, *No Need to Lie,* EMAP, 1964.

Walker, Richard, *The Shell Book of Angling,* David & Charles., 1979.

Watson, Bill, *Floatmakers Manual,* Ernest Benn, 1978.

Wheat, Peter (ed.), *The Angler's Year No. 1,* Pelham, 1970.

Wheat, Peter (ed.), *The Angler's Year No. 2,* Pelham, 1971.

Wheat, Peter, *Fishing as we Find It,* Warne, 1967.

Wheat, Peter, *Improve Your Coarse Angling,* Davies, 1967.

Wheat, Peter, *The Fighting Barbel,* Ernest Benn, 1967.

Wheat, Peter, *The Pelham Manual of River Coarse Fishing,* Pelham, 1978.

Williams, Tom, *A River for all Seasons,* Cassell, 1980.

Willock, Colin, *Coarse Fishing,* Faber & Faber, 1955.

Wrangles, Alan, *Coarse Fishing,* Newnes, 1966.

Yates, Chris, James, Bob & Miles, Hugh, *A Passion for Angling,* Merlin Unwin/BBC, 1993.

Yates, Chris, *The Deepening Pool,* Unwin Hyman, 1990.

The following bait and tackle catalogues are available from tackle shops:

Gold Label
Korda
Nutrabaits
Richworth
Rod Hutchinson
Solar Tackle

These magazines are good reading for contemporary developments:

Anglers' Mail,
Kings Reach Tower,
Stamford Street,
London
SE1 9LS.

Carpworld,
1 Grosvenor Square,
Sheffield
S2 4MS.

Coarse Fisherman,
67 Tyrrell Street,
Leicester
LE3 5SB.

Improve Your Coarse Fishing,
Bretton Court,
Bretton,
Peterborough
PE3 8DZ.

INDEX

BACK WHERE WE BELONG

STORY OF THE SEASON 18/19

WORDS: TIM SPIERS   DESIGN: SIMON HILL

Express & Star

IT WAS
THE
BEST
SEASON
OF MY
CAREER

FOREWORD: CONOR COADY CAPTAIN

WHAT AN ABSOLUTELY PHENOMENAL SEASON FOR THIS BRILLIANT FOOTBALL CLUB. AS PLAYERS WE DREAMED OF PLAYING IN THE PREMIER LEAGUE – NOT ONLY DID THAT DREAM BECOME A REALITY, BUT WE MANAGED TO FINISH IN SEVENTH PLACE, A WONDERFUL ACHIEVEMENT.

To come into the league as a newly-promoted team, finish that high in the table and qualify for Europe is absolutely exceptional. We stuck to our principles and played the way we wanted to play, home and away.

The boys and the staff all stepped up in the best league in the world and we made some memories to last a lifetime. Wins over Chelsea and Spurs were amazing, the victory at Everton was arguably the perfect away performance and being 3-0 up at half-time at home to Arsenal was absolutely fantastic.

The FA Cup quarter-final win over Manchester United, though, topped the lot. It was the best game of my career – we made history that night and the noise from the stands was incredible, I couldn't hear a thing out there.

How this club has evolved in two years has been sensational. We all want to work hard for each other and it's without doubt the best changing room I've been involved in, especially in terms of players going that extra mile for their team-mates.

We listened intently to the manager's instructions and took it week by week, game by game, which stood us in good stead.

From a personal point of view I was honoured to play every single minute of the season in league and cup. I don't tend to score goals or get assists! So to achieve that statistic makes me very proud and to captain the team throughout has been a massive privilege. It was the best season of my career.

We've all seen the excitement building around the city as the club has grown and if we all keep learning and working hard we'll do our best to continue making those fans happy. They've been a huge help in pushing us on week after week – it's always appreciated.

We'll look back on 2018/19 with very fond memories.

Now we want to make some more.

THE NEXT THREE YEARS ARE NOW ABOUT HOW TO CHALLENGE THE TOP GUYS

JEFF SHI EXECUTIVE CHAIRMAN OF WOLVERHAMPTON WANDERERS FC

FOSUN'S WOLVES SUPREMO JEFF SHI SAT DOWN WITH TIM SPIERS FOR AN EXCLUSIVE INTERVIEW TO GIVE US HIS INSIDE TAKE ON ANOTHER UNFORGETTABLE SEASON AT MOLINEUX.

He's the man who's helped spearhead Wolves' stunning transformation from a mid-table Championship team to one riding high in the top echelons of the Premier League – and now the Europa League, too. The likeable Shi, who in contrast to many men in his position is quiet, methodical and unassuming, has a clear plan of where he wants Wolves to be. Given what's happened in the past two years, you'd back him, Fosun and Wolves to deliver.

WHAT ARE YOUR REFLECTIONS ON THE SEASON?

It's been a great season. At the beginning on the year, personally I thought to finish in the top 10 would be amazing. To stay in the league would be the first thing we should do, but the top 10 would have been unbelievable.

Now we've over-performed from that. That's good, but in general it's a long road; year one, year two, year three.

Now is the time to think forward. Two or three years ago we were trying to be promoted to the top flight but now it's another challenge – we're trying to challenge the top six and the top four.

For promotion, it's difficult because you have limitations in how much you can spend, so you have to outperform others by making the right signings, etc.

For the future, when you're battling with the big guys in the Premier League, it's not just about making the right signings but also having unique strengths overall as a club, from the coach, to the pitch, the academy, the management, the fans. Every bit of edge you can have will help you.

You can't spend as much as Manchester City or Manchester United. So the only way is when you're building a squad that's unique and has the support from the fans.

Even if other clubs are spending more they can't copy some special things that we have – so we can use those special things as a weapon. We're still thinking about what the strengths are and how we can build it in our way.

In general I'm so happy and Nuno and all the players are doing a very good job. It's given us a very good base for the next few years.

If you look at the past three years, the pathway from League One to the Premier League, we've built an established squad. The next three years are now about how to challenge the top guys.

THE CLUB IS AHEAD OF ITS STATED SCHEDULE – DOES THIS MEAN RESETTING TARGETS FOR THE SEASONS AHEAD?

We're ahead of where we want to be but it's just one year earlier. There's still a long way to go. We are talking about 10 years – or actually maybe Fosun will run the club for 20, 30, 40 years, you never know. I think if you are aiming to get something within the 10 years – we're in the fourth year now – we're thinking about what to do in the future.

THE CLUB'S RECRUITMENT HAS BEEN EXTREMELY GOOD – IS THAT THE KEY FACTOR BEHIND THE TEAM'S SUCCESS FOR THE PAST TWO SEASONS?

Yes, I think in the first season maybe we were not doing things right in recruitment, but in the past two seasons it's gone well. In the Championship,

or when you're trying to survive in the Premier League, recruitment is maybe 80 per cent of the job, if you make the right calls you'll do well.

When you're fighting with the big clubs it's different. Recruitment still needs to be right but it's not only about that. It's about the philosophy of the head coach, about how smart the management can be to create an atmosphere and the right mix, or also how to break down the defences of the small teams – that's a headache for us now.

NUNO'S TITLE IS 'HEAD COACH' BUT HE CLEARLY PLAYS A BIG ROLE IN THE CLUB'S RECRUITMENT.

We are having a very good chemistry between the head coach, between Kevin Thelwell and us. I think now we are trying to find a good balance. Nuno has the final say on every signing for the first team, but he's the head coach, not a scout.

We are trying to do something. We have a very good scouting network to find the right players and we understand Nuno very well, so we can propose players to him. The chemistry is important, so we can find the right signings.

NUNO'S JOB IS TO BUILD THE TEAM. MY JOB IS HOW TO BUILD THE CLUB, TO BE READY TO BATTLE FOR A LONG TIME

I feel at other clubs that they can have a top head coach but if the team behind the coach don't know him well, or the head coach is too arrogant and wants to control everything, it doesn't work.

HOW HAVE YOU ENJOYED THE PREMIER LEAGUE EXPERIENCE?

I've enjoyed being in the Premier League but I enjoy going to every game. For example, even now we're in the Premier League I still go to League One and Championship games. I want to experience more about the culture here and we have many players loaned to other clubs. I've seen a lot of football in the last three years – I've driven a lot. In the last three years I've driven more than the total miles I've driven in China!

WHAT LESSONS HAVE YOU LEARNED ABOUT FOOTBALL ALONG THE WAY?

The most important thing is you have a close-knit team and also there is a certain chemistry behind that. Sometimes you can have good coaches, good players, but if you haven't built it properly –

it can work maybe for a while, but not in the long term. We're always aiming for the long term.

Maybe next season will be worse than this season, maybe we'll face a lot of struggles, but if you have a team here you can go through that. For example, Nuno's job is to build the team. My job is how to build the club, to be ready to battle for a long time.

ARE THERE ANY PARTICULAR STAND-OUT MATCHES FROM THE SEASON YOU'VE ENJOYED?

Actually my favourite game was the under-23s winning at Manchester United, we scored three goals in the last 10 minutes and it was very dramatic, I think it was my favourite. For the first team, maybe the 4-3 game over Leicester City. It was absolutely amazing.

THE ATMOSPHERE THAT DAY WAS FANTASTIC AND IT'S BEEN THE SAME ALL SEASON – HAS THAT PLAYED A KEY ROLE TOO?

I think the fans are very good. The home atmosphere maybe can be a bit better but the

away support was fantastic. If the home can be the same as away, that would be perfect.

In nature, football is still about entertainment, so I'm watching the habits of English fans, they like to go to the pub, drink and talk a lot. If we can provide more things for them to do for the whole day it will be a day out and they can look forward to it every week and spend the whole day with the club. The light show, the DJ, maybe in future more food, music, a fan park, more things like that.

THE FA CUP SEMI-FINAL DEFEAT WAS OBVIOUSLY A CRUSHING BLOW, BUT THERE MUST BE PRIDE IN THE TAKING THE CLUB THAT FAR IN THE COMPETITION FOR THE FIRST TIME SINCE 1998?

It was a great run. Personally I didn't think we would do well in the FA Cup because the Premier League was our priority. I'm always fearful that cup games will distract focus from the league – you can see the example of Watford, they tailed off at the end of the season after the semi-final.

Our players managed to do very well in both competitions. They didn't let the FA Cup impact on their league form. That's the kind of ability we should have because next season we may have the league, the FA Cup, the EFL Cup, the Europa League, so how to have a squad who will make efforts for every tournament is a challenge.

WHICH PLAYER DO YOU MOST ENJOY WATCHING AT MOLINEUX?

I like Diogo Jota, he's fantastic. I truly believe he will be a top player in the world. His style is so direct, he works very hard and is like a bull. He's still young – I think he's the most improved player throughout the season.

AFTER FINISHING SEVENTH AND REACHING THE FA CUP SEMI-FINALS, WHERE DO YOU GO FROM HERE?

It's hard to set a target for next season, I'm always reluctant to say that. I'm keen to say we

want to be the best in the league in the long term, but for next season it's hard to say.

Of course, the higher the better and we will try to improve the team. But you never know. I don't want to give the team too much pressure, talking about the top six or the top four. Maybe it will take more years to achieve that – if you rush to get the job done it may cause some problems and you go backwards.

The only thing we must do is try to improve the team. If we manage that, sooner or later the results will come. We could stay seventh next season but earn more points, which is still good enough.

WHAT'S GOING TO BE THE KEY TO BRIDGING THE GAP TO THE TOP SIX – IS INVESTMENT THE OVERRIDING FACTOR?

You have to invest. You have to make the recruitment right and have a good academy, to produce top young players. Also I think you have to be very consistent on what you are doing.

EUROPE GIVES US MORE OF A CHALLENGE BUT IT WILL SPEED UP THE GROWTH OF THE CLUB

It's important to keep a high quality of work and a consistent strategy for 10 years. Your opponent may do something fantastic for one or two years but it's hard to keep doing the right thing for a long time. It's a marathon. Eventually, the more consistent and excellent management teams will triumph, that's my view.

HAS WOLVES' SUCCESS BEEN REFLECTED IN THE CLUB'S ADDED IMPORTANCE WITH FOSUN?

Chairman Guo is now a super-fan! Three years ago before we bought the club he didn't know much about football. Now he is a super-fan.

I watched the Liverpool game on the last day of the season sitting next to him – I felt he was more excited than me! It's a good sign when your boss is really buying into the club. He will, of course, try his best to support us.

Also, in the meantime, he's a successful entrepreneur so he knows how to find the right people to run the club. I'm very pleased to work with him.

Investment levels will not slow down. Financial fair play is still there and you cannot bypass that, but under the line we will try our best to improve our club.

HAS THE CLUB'S FANBASE SIGNIFICANTLY GROWN IN CHINA?

We already have many more fans in China than one year ago and we are opening a megastore in a very good location in Shanghai, it's very good.

This season we beat the majority of the top six, which is big news for the fans there. Eventually, if we want to achieve a really big fanbase in China, we have to win something. It still depends largely on the performance of the first team.

If you can win the Premier League, play in the Champions League, or win the FA Cup, the fans will welcome us more quickly. But you have to compete with the top six equally.

We'll work hard to increase the fanbase but you have to have a better squad to compete.

WOLVES HAVE QUALIFIED FOR EUROPEAN FOOTBALL FOR THE FIRST TIME IN 38 YEARS – DOES IT COME TOO SOON, OR IS IT A NATURAL PROGRESSION FOR THE CLUB?

It's a natural progression. The players in the squad are more keen than me to play in Europe! You can see the pedigrees of them, like Joao Moutinho, Raul Jimenez, they've played in the Champions League for many seasons.

If you want to attract more top players to come you need to give them a big stage. If they're keen, they're the players, so we can see it's natural to progress to there. I'm quite happy. We'll stay with a small squad, that's the identity of Nuno.

The challenge is to have a top squad of 18 and then the young players ready to do something when we need them. The only thing is if you go into Europe you have to be ready – about the squad, the academy, everything.

It gives us more of a challenge but it will speed up the growth of the club.

TIM SPIERS

THE EXPRESS & STAR'S WOLVES CORRESPONDENT TIM SPIERS GIVES HIS TAKE ON THE CLUB'S RAPID RISE TOWARDS THE TOP ECHELONS OF ENGLISH FOOTBALL.

From playing at Stevenage in front of 4,600 people in 2014, to losing at Burton and flirting with another return to League One in 2017, to beating Manchester United (twice), Arsenal, Chelsea and Spurs, reaching an FA Cup semi-final and qualifying for Europe in 2018/19 – the upsurge has been as magnificent as it has been meteoric.

This was the season the wolf howled at the top table of English football once more, some four decades since Wolves were last a major force in the domestic game. Victories over the league's big boys were exhilarating, producing memories that will last for decades, but just as impressive was the manner in which Wolves – a delectable combination of elegance, energy, eagerness and effrontery – swaggered into the nation's consciousness. They carried momentum and a feelgood factor generated from last season throughout the campaign with only one real blip of five defeats in six – ended against Chelsea during the first of many wild nights at Molineux when Nuno Espirito Santo's team (via arguably the season's pivotal moment when Ryan Bennett tackled Willian at 1-0 down) crash-bang-walloped their way to a fabulous 2-1 comeback victory.

That was one of several blockbuster wins, the best of which was undoubtedly the night this Wolves team came of age, beating Manchester United 2-1 in the FA Cup quarter-finals. The head-splitting roar for Diogo Jota's folkloric winner could have shattered glass or taken off a layer of skin. Molineux's foundations were rocked to their very core that night – a night of genuine emotion when grown men openly wept. Yes, it means that much.

At the Express & Star we've followed Wolves' progress – mostly in awe – every step of the way. As a paper we've covered Wolves since the

19th Century, chronicling the club's glory days of the Stan Cullis era to the depths of despair of the 1980s. Personally, it is a true privilege and honour to carry the baton of 'Wolves correspondent' during what is one of the most enthralling periods to follow the club.

Our coverage has changed beyond recognition over the years, from staid match reports and a short story or two buried in the sports pages, to a large number of daily articles, videos, podcasts, features, interviews, press conferences, web-chats and 24/7 news and views on Twitter. But the essence of the job remains the same – forming that crucial link between the club and its supporters; reporting news accurately and contemporaneously while reflecting the opinions of a deeply passionate fanbase in a one-club city which has a thunderous beating heart of gold and black.

We delved into uncharted territory this year by taking the E&S Wolves Podcast on the road

with two very nerve wracking, but equally very fun, live shows, with my colleague Nathan Judah whose inimitable character was made for the stage. Joe Edwards made a fine addition to our reporting team and during a long campaign the highs strongly outnumbered the lows, with jaunts to Switzerland and Wembley among the many highlights. Along the way it's been a pleasure to meet so many ardent supporters. In pubs, bars, shops and on every street in the city they just want to talk about one thing – Wolverhampton Wanderers.

Wolves are always the talk of the town, but there's a tangible buzz around the place that this grand old club is embarking on only the start of a wondrous journey. The years in the wilderness – of lower league football, of a crumbling stadium, of play-off anguish, of apathy, of Bolton, Palace, Norwich and the Albion, of successive relegations, of overspending, of underachieving – are over. **Wolves are back where they belong.**

PREPARATIONS

Rarely could anticipation ahead of a Wolves season have been so palpable. A year earlier they were going into the unknown with a new boss, new players, new formation and new philosophy. Twelve months of fantasy football and thrilling success later, there was giddy excitement amongst a throbbing and bullish fanbase about what may lie ahead in the coming nine months.

Before a ball was even kicked there was a feeling that Wolves already belonged in the Premier League – and for once that wasn't just because of their rich history, big stadium or large, passionate supporter base. Nuno Espirito Santo's team were well versed in playing 'Premier League' football when they stormed to the Championship title – and possessed a young and burgeoning squad full of players ready to make a name for themselves on the big stage.

"We're looking at doing more than surviving," managing director Laurie Dalrymple said. "The strategy we've had has been about building a squad and a structure we think is going to be viable to take further, beyond promotion. We've got a really strong nucleus of people that can do that. We want to be excited about the fact we're going to Chelsea, Man City, Liverpool etc, but not overawed by that. We want to go with the mindset of we're going to play a match we think we have a right to win, just as much as they do. That will come from self confidence but also a strategy in terms of developing the squad and the club that can stand up and compete."

Nuno added: "In year two we know the challenge is even more difficult, but we have something that we hold on to – we have our own identity. The players know how we play, they know and understand our game. We have to hold on to it, further develop the performance of some players, getting them to a higher level, and at the same time we will increase the quality. When you speak about increasing the quality, of course the squad is going to change."

Change wasn't restricted to just the playing squad. For starters the kit underwent a revamp, moving to

a lighter shade of gold, harking back to the club's glory days, as well as the return of the traditional white away kit, both produced by Adidas as part of a new multi-million pound deal.

Molineux and Compton Park also underwent facelifts to prepare for Premier League life. The training ground underwent a seven-figure revamp with new high-tech warm-up equipment, pitches which mirrored the surface at Molineux, media and press conference facilities, offices,

canteen (plus a new chef) and a head-tennis court complete with wolf graffiti and inspiring slogans.

At Molineux a brand new state-of-the-art dressing room included a pitch mosaic on the floor, while the manager's office, referee's room, players' lounge, broadcast interview and press conference rooms were all updated to comply with Premier League regulations and the stadium's floodlights were improved to cater for super slow-motion replays.

There was also a new statue or Sir Jack Hayward overlooking the golden palace, stood by the stand which bears his name and situated by an overhauled subway with gold and black graphics and pictures, depicting both Wolves' glorious history and exciting future.

Appropriately, Sir Jack's pose was a beaming smile with his thumbs up. He'd certainly have approved of Wolves' phenomenal rise to the top table.

SIGNINGS

The remit for Wolves' summer business was clear – evolution, not revolution. Nuno already had quality, youth and pace in his ranks but a bit of experience and top-level proven quality was lacking, so the Wolves recruitment team set about plugging the gaps. It's safe to say they managed it.

First off, last year's loan stars were snapped up on permanent deals. Diogo Jota (£13m), Willy Boly (£10m), Leo Bonatini (£5m) and Ruben Vinagre (£2m) penned long-term deals, but there was a shock departure in Benik Afobe who left for Stoke City just 11 days after completing a £10m move.

Mexican striker Raul Jimenez arrived with international pedigree when he joined on a season-long loan from Benfica (for a £3m fee). Then Wolves went 'next level' with the capture of Euro 2016-winning Portugal goalkeeper Rui Patricio on a 'free' transfer, which after protracted negotiations became a £16m deal.

If the signing of Patricio turned heads, a £5m deal to bring his multi-title-winning compatriot Joao Moutinho to Wolverhampton from Monaco was a genuine jaw-dropper. "I'm very excited, I want to help the team and the players in the club to progress," the wily Moutinho said. "I hope to help the club achieve their objectives – it's a very good project and that excited me."

Barry Douglas made a surprising exit to Leeds United, with Spaniard Jonny Castro Otto his replacement, before Wolves went big in the final days of the window to snap up arguably the Championship's most exciting player in Adama Traore, whose £18m move from Middlesbrough smashed the club's transfer record yet again. Defender/midfielder Leander Dendoncker completed the summer business with a late loan move from Anderlecht.

The total transfer outlay was a whopping £69m. Wolves definitely weren't planning on just making up the numbers – they planned to make a big splash in the big time.

JUNE 1 WILLY BOLY (PORTO, £10M)

JUNE 1 DIOGO JOTA (ATLETICO, £13M)

JUNE 12 RAUL JIMENEZ (BENFICA, LOAN)

JUNE 18 RUI PATRICIO (SPORTING, £16M)

JUNE 30 LEO BONATINI (AL-HILAL, £5M)

JUNE 30 RUBEN VINAGRE (MONACO, £2M)

JULY 24 JOAO MOUTINHO (MONACO, £5M)

JULY 25 JONNY CASTRO OTTO (ATLETICO, LOAN)

AUGUST 8 ADAMA TRAORE (MIDDLESBROUGH, £18M)

AUGUST 9 LEANDER DENDONCKER (ANDERLECHT, LOAN)

PRE-SEASON

Wolves prepared for Premier League life by pitting themselves against high-quality European opposition during their pre-season campaign.

Basel, Young Boys and Ajax were all on the verge of playing Champions League qualifiers when they faced Nuno Espirito Santo's team – and Wolves beat both Swiss sides while claiming a creditable draw against Ajax. Conor Coady and Danny Batth lifted the giant Uhrencup during a productive week in Switzerland, with the players enjoying the luxurious surroundings of picturesque Montreux, overlooking Lake Geneva, before

returning to England to take on Ajax at Walsall's Banks's Stadium and then Championship opposition in Derby County and Stoke City.

Results were mixed, but Nuno repeatedly stated the irrelevance of friendly victories. Instead the weeks were about integrating new signings Joao Moutinho, Raul Jimenez, Rui Patricio and Jonny Castro Otto into the group and building up fitness ahead of the big kick-off. An experiment with Romain Saiss at centre-half was also trialled, while arguably the standout performer of pre-season was young left wing-back Ryan Giles who, in the initial absence of

Otto and Ruben Vinagre (who was away on international duty), impressed with a string of attacking displays.

The pre-season campaign ended with a comeback victory over La Liga outfit Villarreal at Molineux, where new-boy Jimenez netted a confidence-boosting winner in front of the South Bank. "I hope it is the first goal of many," Jimenez stated. Captain Coady felt the players were ready for the huge challenge ahead: "The quality opposition have been there all pre-season, even Stoke and Derby are really good sides. We had Young Boys, Basel and Ajax and we've got to

get used to that sort of opposition. We can't wait for the season to start, we feel good and ready. You see the calibre of players coming in, and you add that to last season as well, it's really, really exciting for the football club."

Ahead of the curtain-raiser at home to Everton, Nuno shared Coady's excitement and confidence. He said: "We wanted the base of the squad to be the same as last season – we have a very good group of players. We cannot control expectations, there is no aim or target position. We're ready and highly motivated."

JULY 7, PORT-VALAIS, SWITZERLAND
NEUCHATEL XAMAXV 1-1 WOLVES (HAUSE 70)

JULY 10, BIEL, SWITZERLAND
BASEL 1-2 WOLVES (MIR 17, JOTA 51)
Wolves first half (3-4-3): Ruddy; Batth (c), Hause, John; Rasmussen, Goncalves, Watt, Giles; Mir, Benny-Seal, Cavaleiro.
Wolves second half (3-4-3): Norris; Bennett, Coady (c), Boly; Doherty, Neves, Gibbs-White, Douglas; Costa, Bonatini, Jota.

JULY 14, BERN, SWITZERLAND
YOUNG BOYS 0-4 WOLVES
(CAVALEIRO 26, COSTA 30, BONATINI 54, MIR 89)
Wolves (3-4-3): Ruddy (Norris 45) (Sondergaard 83); Bennett, Coady (c), Boly (Hause 63); Doherty (Batth 63), Neves (Goncalves 63), Gibbs-White (Watt 63), Giles (John 63); Costa (Mir 63), Bonatini (Ashley-Seal 63), Cavaleiro (Enobakhare 45).

JULY 19, BANKS'S STADIUM, WALSALL
AJAX 1-1 WOLVES (NEVES PEN 74)
Wolves (3-4-3): Norris (Ruddy 45); Bennett (Saiss 71), Coady (c) (Batth 84), Boly (Hause 84); Doherty, Neves (Watt 84), Gibbs-White (Goncalves 71), Giles (John 84); Cavaleiro (Ashley-Seal 71), Jota (Mir 84), Costa (Enobakhare 84).

JULY 22, BOCHUM, GERMANY
BOCHUM 0-0 WOLVES (5-4 ON PENS)
Wolves (3-4-3): Patricio; Bennett, Coady (c), Hause; Rasmussen, Goncalves, Neves, Giles; Enobakhare, Jimenez, Jota.

JULY 22, BOCHUM, GERMANY
REAL BETIS 0-0 WOLVES
Wolves (3-4-3): Ruddy; Saiss, Batth (c), Boly; Doherty, Gibbs-White, Watt, John; Costa, Ashley-Seal, Cavaleiro.

JULY 25, BET365 STADIUM
STOKE CITY 0-0 WOLVES
Wolves (3-4-3): Ruddy (Patricio 45); Bennett (Saiss 45), Coady (c) (Batth 64), Hause; Doherty (Rasmussen 64), Neves (Watt 64), Gibbs-White (Goncalves 45), Giles (John 64); Costa (Ashley-Seal 64), Jimenez (Bonatini 45), Jota (Cavaleiro 32) (Enobakhare 64). Subs not used: Norris, Otto.

JULY 28, PRIDE PARK
DERBY COUNTY 2-1 WOLVES (JOTA 67)
Wolves (3-4-3): Patricio (Norris 61); Saiss (Bennett 61), Coady (c), Boly; Doherty, Neves, Moutinho (Gibbs-White 45), Otto (Giles 61); Costa, Bonatini (Jimenez 45), Jota (Enobakhare 73). Subs not used: Batth, Hause, Rasmussen, Goncalves, Ashley-Seal.

AUGUST 4, MOLINEUX
WOLVES 2-1 VILLARREAL (BOLY 49, JIMENEZ 55)
Wolves (3-4-3): Patricio; Saiss (Bennett 45), Coady (c), Boly; Doherty, Neves, Moutinho (Gibbs-White 72), Otto; Costa, Jimenez (Bonatini 72), Jota (Cavaleiro 77). Subs not used: Ruddy, Norris, Batth, Hause, Vinagre, Enobakhare.

GAME BY GAME

Premier League SEASON 18/19

WOLVES ARRIVED IN THE PREMIER LEAGUE BRISTLING WITH HOPE AND EXPECTATION. NINE MONTHS LATER THEY HAD FINISHED SEVENTH, QUALIFIED FOR EUROPE AND REACHED THE FA CUP SEMI-FINALS, CREATING A HOST OF INDELIBLE MEMORIES ALONG THE WAY. WHAT FOLLOWS IS MATCH REPORTS, ANALYSIS, QUOTES, STATS, RATINGS AND FAN VERDICTS FOR ALL 46 OF WOLVES' LEAGUE AND CUP GAMES IN 2018/19 AS THEY WERE REPORTED AT THE TIME. THIS IS THE STORY OF SEASON – AS TOLD BY THE EXPRESS & STAR.

WOLVES
(NEVES 44, JIMENEZ 80)

EVERTON
(RICHARLISON 17, 67)

2

2

MOLINEUX STADIUM, 5.30PM
AUGUST 11, 2018 ATTENDANCE: **31,231** (2,970 AWAY)

Wolves (3-4-3): *Patricio; Bennett, Coady (c), Boly; Doherty, Neves, Moutinho (Gibbs-White 85), Otto (Vinagre 76); Costa (Bonatini 71), Jimenez, Jota. Subs not used: Ruddy, Hause, Saiss, Enobakhare.*

Everton (4-3-3): *Pickford; Coleman, Jagielka (c), Keane, Baines; Gueye, Schneiderlin, Sigurdsson (Holgate 43); Walcott, Tosun (Niasse 81), Richarlison (Digne 86). Subs not used: Stekelenburg, Davies, Ramirez, Calvert-Lewin.*

Reality; noun – the state of things as they actually exist, as opposed to an idealistic or notional idea of them.

This opening-day fixture promised to offer an ideal litmus test for what Wolves' limitations might be this season. It ended up being both a reality check – and an encouraging afternoon. We learned that Wolves' fighting spirit, which earned them so many points on their way to the title last year, is in fine fettle. We also learned of some rarely seen weaknesses (the defence were fragile with Willy Boly and Conor Coady making uncharacteristic errors, while there was a lack of spark from the usually-electric Diogo Jota and Helder Costa) and some new strengths (the incredibly hard-working Raul Jimenez looks like he could make an impact in the top flight and Jonny Castro Otto was sound defensively).

Some things change, some things stay the same and the latter can apply to the continued brilliance of Ruben Neves who starred with a goal (from outside the box, of course) and an assist. His stock could be about to soar in front of the watching world. In front of Molineux's biggest crowd since 1981 of 31,231 it was a special occasion and the game lived up to its billing with two quality teams going toe to toe, although Wolves needed the helping hand of a Phil Jagielka red card to really get going.

The step up in quality from the Championship was there for all to see (Everton were streets ahead of any team Wolves played in the second tier) and the fact Wolves had to dig so deep for a point against 10 men shows you the task they face in the next nine months.

For Wolves' first Premier League match for six years the atmosphere at a packed Molineux – complete with a gold and black sea of flags – was absolutely stunning. But after a confident start from nerveless Wolves in which they got on the front foot and sprayed it around nicely, it soon went flat at Molineux as an early reality check took hold with £50m man Richarlison, making his Everton debut, netting from close range.

Neves and Joao Moutinho were seeing plenty of the ball, but there was a lack of incisiveness in the final third. Then five minutes before half-time came the game's pivotal moment – and Wolves were handed a lifeline that they grabbed with both hands. Phil Jagielka's heavy touch saw the ball roll towards Jota just outside the box – he slid in on the Portuguese forward with the studs up on his right boot and took out Jota. Referee Craig Pawson awarded what looked like a harsh red card, but Wolves weren't complaining.

They took full advantage in some style. With one swing of his right boot, the mercurial Neves took the roof off an ecstatic Molineux with a perfect 20-yard free-kick into the top corner. It was his seventh goal in a Wolves shirt...and they've all come from outside the box.

As the heavens opened at the start of the second half, 10-man Everton continued with a positive approach which paid off when the excellent Richarlison made it 2-1 with a fine curling effort. The Toffees retreated and dug their trench just outside the penalty area. It was attack versus defence with Wolves searching desperately for that one golden chance – and when it came Jimenez made no mistake. Neves looked up

and sent a perfect cross into the corridor of uncertainty where the Mexican peeled off his man to head home. Wolves pressed for a winner, but a killer final pass was lacking and despite a frenetic finish it ended 2-2.

A heartily-earned point against a very decent Everton team after falling behind twice is to be commended. Neves was the undoubted star of this show. While a few of his team-mates struggled to instantly make the big step up in class the Premier League requires, Neves did so with the panache and assurance we have come to expect from him. The maturity this man shows belies his 21 years. Does anything faze him? You could ask him to walk a tightrope at 10,000 ft and he'd slide across in slippers while puffing on a cigar. The midfield maestro defines class – and here he announced himself on one of the biggest stages of all with a star performance.

Jimenez also clearly has something about him. He is a workhorse, which is an important attribute in that 'linking' role Nuno likes – his touch is good, his passing is accurate and he's full of running. Lost causes were chased down all evening. Crucially though he comes alive in the box and looks to have a few goals in his locker.

A victory would have topped off a perfect day, but for Wolves to be disappointed with a point shows their mentality. This opener didn't offer a conclusion that Wolves will be a top-half side this year, but it suggested they are ready to compete. And that's a pretty good start.

NUNO

It was a tough game, but a game we were always chasing, so that requires a lot of energy. Sometimes you make the mistake of thinking playing against 10 men is easier – it is not. You control the game but space is not there and you have to defend. We have to find solutions, knowing if a chance might come, you must keep the balance in defence. It was a fantastic atmosphere at Molineux. I knew it was going to be like that, the sound of the people was incredible. My players always take lessons from the game – positive and negative lessons. This is the process of growing and building the team.

FAN VERDICT – CHRIS HUGHES

Welcome back! After six years in what Sky described as 'the wilderness' many Wolves fans will have spent Friday night like excited children on Christmas Eve, awaiting the gift from Nuno Espirito Santo Claus of a return to Premier League football. Testament to our character, we continued to play brand Nuno football even after we fell behind. Overall there was a lot to be encouraged about and some clear areas that need to be worked on, but enough to feel that we'll be able to compete over the 38 games. The stand-out player was Neves. While not quite dominating, he racked up the most completed passes of anyone on the pitch, plus a goal and an assist.

POSSESSION: **57% / 43%** | SHOTS: **11 / 8** | SHOTS ON TARGET: **4 / 5** | CORNERS: **3 / 6** | FOULS: **8 / 7** | BOOKINGS: **0 / 1** | REDS: **0 / 1**

STAR MAN - RUBEN NEVES

You know when your first-born child goes to school for the first time, you're upset and apprehensive, but you needn't worry because they have a great day and show everyone how amazing they are? Ruben Neves' Premier League debut couldn't have gone any better and there were thousands of very proud Wolves fans delighted that their little star showed the world how good he is. His stunning goal and perfect assist announced himself on the Premier League stage. His piercing passes weren't as prevalent owing to a lack of space but that'll come. Oh and he really, really hates shooting from inside the box doesn't he?

TWEET OF THE GAME

 Tim Spiers ✔
@tim_spiers_Star

Things Ruben Neves doesn't need...

1) The penalty area

That is all.

 11 Aug 2018

TABLE

	TEAM	P	GD	PTS
5	MAN UTD	1	1	3
6	TOTTENHAM	1	1	3
7	EVERTON	1	0	1
8	WOLVES	1	0	1
9	ARSENAL	0	0	0
10	BURNLEY	0	0	0
11	LIVERPOOL	0	0	0

LEICESTER CITY
(DOHERTY OG 29, MADDISON 45)

 2

WOLVES

 0

KING POWER STADIUM, 3PM
AUGUST 18, 2018 ATTENDANCE: 32,043 (3,305 AWAY)

Leicester City (4-2-3-1): Schmeichel (c); Pereira, Evans, Maguire, Chilwell; Mendy, Ndidi; Albrighton (Amartey 60), Maddison (Iheanacho 82), Gray (Silva 82); Vardy. Subs not used: Ward, Morgan, Fuchs, Ghezzal.

Wolves (3-4-3): Patricio; Bennett, Coady (c), Boly; Doherty (Gibbs-White 69), Moutinho, Neves, Otto; Costa (Bonatini 45), Jimenez, Jota (Traore 45). Subs not used: Ruddy, Hause, Saiss, Vinagre.

Wolves must have smashed the mirrors in the King Power dressing rooms, walked under 25 ladders and been despot medieval tyrants in previous incarnations to deserve this result.

Welcome to the Premier League. Nuno Espirito Santo's team could have been 3-0 up after 21 minutes – instead they were 2-0 down at half-time. Yes, Wolves made a few mistakes; yes, they should have scored when they were on top; and yes, strictly speaking they can only blame themselves for losing this game. They were profligate up front and naive in defence.

But come on. Hitting the woodwork once is unlucky. Twice? That's black cat levels. And Leicester's two goals come from an own goal and a deflection? Misfortune in the extreme. You can point to mistakes, tactical flaws, defensive naivety and a couple of poor individual performances all you like, the fact is that Wolves were damned unlucky not to win this football match, let alone not even earn a point.

They took the game to the Foxes, who didn't know how to cope with their pace and mobility in the early stages when Wolves regularly got joy in the final third. Overall it was a good performance. They were punished, though, for a slack period 15 minutes before half-time. For the goals, Diogo Jota gave the ball away twice and Wolves didn't close Marc Albrighton (who crossed for the first goal) and James Maddison (who scored the second) down quickly enough.

But Nuno's team will play worse than this and win this season. They had the better of the match, amassed 11 shots to Leicester's four (only one on target for the Foxes), looked potent in attack and controlled possession for long spells.

Try as they might in what was an attack-versus-defence training drill, they couldn't force Kasper Schmeichel into a meaningful save. Hitting the post and bar on two occasions is mightily unlucky but bleating won't get far in the harsh reality of the Premier League. Nuno wants Wolves to impose their ideas, their football, their philosophies on the opposition.

The boss named an unchanged team but there was a new face on the bench in the form of Adama Traore, the club's £18m record signing. Wolves, sporting their new white away kit, had by their own admission been anxious on the opening day – but they were nerveless at the King Power and should have been 2-0 up inside four minutes. They attacked Leicester with pace and purpose from the off with Helder Costa and Diogo Jota rampaging down the flanks and Raul Jimenez regularly finding space in behind the backline. The Mexican crossed towards Matt Doherty, who kept the ball alive and it came for Joao Moutinho, who crashed a superb 18-yard effort off the crossbar.

If that was unlucky, there was no misfortune a minute later when Doherty somehow spurned a wonderful opportunity – Jimenez brilliantly kept it alive and Doherty had half an open goal to aim at from six yards, but shot straight at a defender. It was an open, entertaining game with both teams committed to attacking – and leaving gaps to exploit. Like the team in general, Jonny Castro Otto was showing more attacking intent than last week and he skipped past a challenge to set

up the lively Jimenez – he span and shot from 20 yards and it cannoned off the post.

It had been an excellent showing from Nuno's team – but their bad luck and poor finishing was to be punished in the most ruthless of fashions. On 29 minutes, the Foxes took the lead when Albrighton's cross flashed over the head of Conor Coady and it diverted off Doherty's forehead and past Rui Patricio. Wolves couldn't get going again... and by half-time they were 2-0 down. The increasingly-influential Maddison was allowed to shoot from 20 yards – it hit Coady and deflected past a wrong-footed Patricio.

Traore's introduction at half-time reenergised Wolves. The winger soon clicked into gear and embarked on a couple of full-throttle bursts down the flank, ghosting past players like they didn't exist. Jamie Vardy's red card for a no-holds-barred and dangerous foul on Doherty handed Wolves a further boost. Traore, an express train in a hurry, switched to the right wing now and made Jonny Evans look like he was walking through treacle with a Zimmer frame before teeing up Leo Bonatini, who wasted a great chance from 12 yards. There were more decent opportunities, but defensive-minded Leicester saw it out with ease.

A hard luck story? Absolutely. But Wolves need to become as streetwise as their last two opponents if they're to start turning possession and shots into points. At least they've got a nice easy home game next week... Welcome to the Premier League indeed.

NUNO

Last week we drew, this week we lost, but we are playing the way we want. The team has a lot of things to improve, this is our job. I am proud of the boys because this is the way we want to be ourselves in every pitch. It was evident that luck wasn't with us, everybody saw that. We will look for that last touch of quality. We need to be more ruthless, clinical, but at the same time relentless to keep on doing the same things because this is how we work, this is how we train and this is how we want to control the game, manage the possession of the ball and create chances. The way we played makes me proud but I am not happy with the result.

FAN VERDICT – ROB CARTWRIGHT

Very, very unlucky Wolves. We took the game to Leicester and really went for it in the first half hour. If we'd been 3-0 up it would not have flattered us. Moutinho hit the bar, Jimenez hit the post and, maybe, Doherty had the easiest chance from the six yard line where he should have buried it. It's not an exaggeration to say we were all over them and would have gone on to win if it wasn't for two cruel twists of fate. For the second week running, we couldn't really make the most of an additional man. The challenge by Vardy was a disgrace and unnecessary at that time and place on the pitch. On to Man City, which I consider a "free hit".

POSSESSION: 43% / 57% | SHOTS: 6 / 11 | SHOTS ON TARGET: 2 / 3 | CORNERS: 1 / 9 | FOULS: 10 / 8 | BOOKINGS: 2 / 1 | REDS: 1 / 0

STAR MAN – ADAMA TRAORE

Ever seen a train drive through a field of weepy trees, destroying everything in its path? Nor me, until yesterday. Adama Traore is a force of nature and boy is he going to get Wolves fans on their feet. Time and again he ran past players like their boots were glued to the turf. A couple of times he picked the wrong pass, but he sent a decent cross to Jimenez and teed up Bonatini on two occasions for presentable opportunities. A special talent who will surely start next week? Hold on to your hats.

TWEET OF THE GAME

Tim Spiers ✔
@tim_spiers_Star

Full-time, 2-0 Leicester. Wolves hit the woodwork three times but spurned some good opportunities and couldn't find a way through despite having a man advantage. Lessons need to be learned - but they'll play worse than this and win #wwfc

                     18 Aug 2018

TABLE

	TEAM	P	GD	PTS
11	BURNLEY	1	0	1
12	NEWCASTLE	2	-1	1
13	SOUTHAMPTON	2	-1	1
14	WOLVES	2	-2	1
15	CARDIFF	2	-2	1
16	BRIGHTON	1	-2	0
17	ARSENAL	2	-3	0

WOLVES
(BOLY 57)

1

MANCHESTER CITY
(LAPORTE 69)

1

MOLINEUX STADIUM, 12.30PM
AUGUST 25, 2018 ATTENDANCE: **31,322** (2,970 AWAY)

Wolves (3-4-3): Patricio; Bennett, Coady (c), Boly; Doherty, Moutinho, Neves, Otto (Vinagre 85); Costa (Traore 72), Jimenez, Jota. Subs not used: Ruddy, Hause, Saiss, Gibbs-White, Bonatini.

Manchester City (4-3-3): Ederson; Walker, Kompany (c), Laporte, Mendy; Bernardo Silva (Jesus 62), Fernandinho, Gundogan (Sane 77); Sterling (Mahrez 85), Aguero, David Silva. Subs not used: Muric, Stones, Otamendi, Delph.

Most managers would have come up with a different approach, parked the bus, or perhaps sacrificed their principles, when faced with the prospect of trying to stop one of the world's best teams. Most managers aren't Nuno Espirito Santo.

Not only did Nuno stick with the same formation and the same bold approach despite the standard of opposition – he also stuck with the same team that had been beaten 2-0 at Leicester. In doing so he resisted the temptation to start with Adama Traore – who had done more in 45 minutes at the King Power Stadium than Helder Costa and Diogo Jota had managed between them in the opening two matches. He also chose not to bring in the defensive protection of Romain Saiss, despite having conceded four goals in two games. All his decisions were wholly vindicated.

Yes Wolves rode their luck – City hit the woodwork three times and Wolves' goal was wrong twice in being a handball from an offside position – but they earned it. Swapping Costa for Traore would have been an easy – and logical – switch to make but Nuno trusted Costa to harrass and harry the City back line, as did Jota and Raul Jimenez in what was a key part of the game-plan, to stop City building from the back with aggressive, non-stop defending.

Aggression was a key characteristic of their attacks too. They broke at pace and in big numbers, neutralising Benjamin Mendy and Kyle Walker and isolating a vulnerable Vincent Kompany whenever possible. It was a bold and whole-hearted approach which paid off.

A full-throttle first half full of positive intent from the home side saw their whole-hearted approach cause City more than a few problems. They gave as good as they got and earned the goalless scoreline at half-time. City's threats came from all over the pitch with left-back Mendy as effective as world class striker Sergio Aguero. But a tried and tested back three of Ryan Bennett, Conor Coady and Willy Boly kept City at bay with a herculean effort of disciplined positioning, smart covering and last-ditch tackles.

Wolves were also indebted to Rui Patricio for a quite breathtaking fingertip save to push Raheem Sterling's 25-yard half volley on to the woodwork, channelling his inner Mr Tickle with a save he'll have to go some way to topping this season. That was the third heart-stopping moment in three minutes as the game came to life from the 20-minute mark. The tireless workhorse Jimenez – who displayed more energy than the Duracell bunny – had the ball in the net from Jota's cross in a two-on-two but was correctly flagged offside and then Aguero placed against the base of the post just seconds later.

Patricio had earlier saved from Ilkay Gundogan who incorrectly chose to shoot towards the near post when well placed, in what was City's other big sight of goal.

It was Costa's moment of magic that changed the face of the match when he scampered clear of both Kompany and Aymeric Laporte to race through on goal – he should have scored but tried to round Ederson who blocked his shot. However, from the resulting corner Wolves took a

shock lead. Joao Moutinho's whipped cross was skimmed by Matt Doherty and bundled over the line by Boly via his hand. It was the slice of luck Wolves needed – but their lead didn't last long.

Neves tripped Sterling just outside the box and Gundogan curled the free-kick on to the head of Laporte whose bullet header was too good for Patricio. It looked like the game was then petering out – but substitute Traore injected life with a couple of barnstorming runs, riding challenges and delivering crosses from the right. One was half volleyed just over by Jota and the other was desperately cleared by Kompany. It typified Wolves' bold approach, which more than earned them a hard-fought point that was loudly cheered at full-time.

To place the draw into context, Wolves were massive 12/1 outsiders to win this game, they had 11 shots (only three teams managed at least that many against City last season), while City only failed to win six of their 38 games in 2017/18. Their line-up cost an eye-watering £402m to assemble – with a further £207m on the subs' bench to total £609m. Wolves' 18 cost £86m – a huge amount by their own standards but nothing compared to City. And the luck Wolves rode here made up for last weekend when they were on the end of some rotten misfortune at Leicester.

They may not have won, but this felt like Wolves arriving in the big time. Kudos to Nuno for that. While Neves & Co are announcing themselves on the Premier League stage, so too is Wolves' brilliant head coach.

NUNO

I think it was a good performance overall. We have to be cautious knowing what you have with the opponent – the best team, the champions of the Premier League – we have to stick together, cover, and reduce the space. When you have the ball, we create chances, we play good football. If there is a 'but', and there is always a but, after we score, we should manage better this couple of minutes. It is a growing process. One more game, one more tool to work on it and improve for next week. We want to create a team and build something that is able to adapt. People in the club, the city of Wolverhampton, must be engaged with the team, trying to create something.

FAN VERDICT – NATALIE WOOD

Going toe-to-toe with the Premier League champions, a team really looking like they are starting to gel and Rui Patricio showing what he can really do – hello near-perfect Saturday! For the game to finish 1-1 was a great result, thank God for the crossbar. Our performance was a warning sign to the rest of the league that we are a team to take seriously. There were signs of the side we could become – we looked confident, organised and exciting to watch. Man of the match would be Willy Boly, but Helder Costa also stood out. I think this game will be a defining moment of our season.

POSSESSION: 29% / 71% | **SHOTS: 11 / 18** | **SHOTS ON TARGET: 2 / 6** | **CORNERS: 5 / 9** | **FOULS: 13 / 8** | **BOOKINGS: 1 / 2**

STAR MAN – JOAO MOUTINHO

Like a very fine bottle of vintage Malbec, Moutinho is full bodied, distinctive, expressionist, sultry, improves with age and should be enjoyed on a Saturday afternoon. The guy exudes class and on days like this his experience counts for so much...when you've won Euro 2016, four domestic titles and a Europa League, a game at home to Manchester City is a bit 'meh'. Exerted his influence from the off and was often the catalyst for a Wolves attack with a piercing ball into the City half. On paper Wolves don't have much bite in midfield but Moutinho belied that notion with his intelligent movement and positioning to offer great protection in front of the back three/five. Whipped in a great cross for Boly's goal too. Could be the fulcrum around which a successful season is built – he's up to match sharpness now and has adapted quickly to the Premier League.

TWEET OF THE GAME

 Tim Spiers ✔
@tim_spiers_Star

Love the approach - it's wholehearted and it's positive. No bus parking here.

 25 Aug 2018

TABLE

	TEAM	P	GD	PTS
10	CRYSTAL PALACE	2	0	3
11	ARSENAL	3	-1	3
12	BRIGHTON	3	-2	3
13	WOLVES	3	-2	2
14	CARDIFF	3	-2	2
15	NEWCASTLE	2	-1	1
16	SOUTHAMPTON	3	-2	1

 **SHEFFIELD WEDNESDAY** **0**

 WOLVES **2**
(BONATINI 53, COSTA PEN 85)

HILLSBOROUGH, 7.45PM
AUGUST 28, 2018 ATTENDANCE: **13,597** (2,945 AWAY)

 SECOND ROUND

Sheffield Wednesday (3-5-2): *Wildsmith; Jones (Kirby 86), Fox, Preston (Nuhiu 72); Lee, Nielsen, Baker, Hutchinson, Boyd; Fletcher (c) (Stobbs 72), Forestieri. Subs not used: Dawson, Palmer, O'Grady, Hunt.*
Wolves (3-4-3): *Ruddy; Dendoncker, Coady (c), Hause; Doherty, Watt (Goncalves 62), Saiss, Vinagre; Gibbs-White (Costa 72), Bonatini (Ashley-Seal 80), Traore. Subs not used: Norris, Bennett, Giles, Otto.*

Ah, the Championship, we remember you well. This game was reminiscent of last season in so many ways – some good, some bad. For a start Wolves won and kept a clean sheet, as they did here in 2017/18. Then there was the fact Wolves received some downright rough treatment from their limited opponents, John Ruddy had barely anything to do (bar one stunning save in the second half) and Leo Bonatini scored a goal. Yes, remember that notion? Bonatini finding the net? It had been eight months and 24 days since he managed it last, away at Blues in December.

That was a wait of 27 appearances. In terms of minutes on the pitch it was precisely 23 hours and 59 minutes before his drought ended. Only Jack Bauer defusing a nuclear bomb could have timed it better. Bonatini scored it but much of the credit went to Adama Traore, who made it with a now-trademark lightning-fast searing run down the right wing, seconds after he'd left two defenders seeing stars when teeing up Morgan Gibbs-White, who would later hit the post with a great shot from range.

Only two players – Conor Coady and Matt Doherty – remained from the team that drew 1-1 with Manchester City on Saturday. Belgian international Leander Dendoncker was handed a debut at centre-half while Scottish youngster Elliot Watt made a senior bow in central midfield. However, there was no room in the squad for club captain Danny Batth, whose future at the club would appear in doubt.

Championship mid-table outfit Sheffield Wednesday made a wholesale 11 changes from their 2-1 win over Ipswich, but still fielded a few familiar names in Fernando Forestieri and ex-Wolves players Steven Fletcher and David Jones. What followed, perhaps unsurprisingly for two cobbled-together line-ups, was a dog of a first half with precious little quality or excitement on show.

Wolves looked threatening whenever Gibbs-White and Traore, playing either side of Bonatini, had space to run into but in general their passing game was off. The best chance of the half fell to Gibbs-White, who was roaming to Bonatini's left and cutting inside to allow Ruben Vinagre space to bomb forward. Bonatini slipped the ball to the teenager, who moved towards the box having peeled off his man, but he dragged his 15-yard left-footed shot just across goal.

Traore tried to spark Wolves into life with a couple of his express train runs down the right wing, but Wednesday had two men on him to snuff out any meaningful end product.

At the other end, Ruddy was redundant and Dendoncker didn't have a huge amount to do defensively. He did impress when moving the ball out from the back though, in a composed and authoritative manner. Fellow debutant Watt enjoyed a tidy first 45 minutes as a senior pro, coming deep to pick the ball up from the back three and recycling possession quickly and sensibly.

No doubt after a few stern pointers at half-time Wolves came out looking much more like themselves after the break – and soon took charge. It was inspired by Traore who almost set up a goal in the 52nd minute, brilliantly turning one player and beating another before slotting to Gibbs-White who should have done better from just inside the box. Seconds later he repeated the trick – and this time Wolves finished it off. Traore hared to the byline and cut back for Bonatini, who ended his achingly-long wait for a goal with a smart sidefooted finish from 15 yards.

The relief was etched all over the likeable Brazilian's face. With their tails up, Wolves were inches from making it 2-0 six minutes later when Gibbs-White let fly from 25 yards and it smacked off the post. Then the Owls almost levelled things up from nowhere – Fletcher cleverly looped a shot goalwards with his back to goal and Ruddy had to pull off a stupendous save. Wolves looked the more likely scorers – and so it proved when they wrapped things up five minutes from time. Helder Costa raced past his man and was hauled down in the box for a clear penalty, which he took himself and beat Joe Wildsmith to make it 2-0 and ensure Wolves' passage into the second round.

There were plenty of positives to take, with four debutants (Pedro Goncalves and Benny Ashley-Seal came off the bench) all making their mark, Traore was outstanding, Costa made an impact and also scored, Gibbs-White was impressive and, of course, Bonatini scored. The result also extended Wolves' record of not conceding a goal in this competition for 489 minutes. A successful evening, then.

NUNO

We're all satisfied – there are a lot of positives; a starting XI with youth, players playing for the first time, good answers. The main thing is the team competed well and went through. The Carabao Cup, the FA Cup, they're all important to us because they're games and we take positives and negatives from every game we play. It's very good for Bonatini, it gives confidence to the player, but he has my confidence – that is more important. You know me... goal, important yes, he did a good job but it goes much further than that. It's about the team. Every time a player wears the shirt of Wolves he knows what he has to do, he's inside of the shape and works very hard.

FAN VERDICT – CLIVE SMITH

A tedious first half was forgotten as the second half was a joy to watch. Half-time words of encouragement from Nuno worked wonders as we came out and raised our game. Watt did not look out of place, MGW had boundless energy and movement while Vinagre was the star performer. He was better than I remember him being last season, full of confidence and playing like a winger in a 4-4-2. Traore was both unplayable and wasteful. The £18m fee is based on a lot of potential. His pace and balance for the goal was impressive - the first of many assists hopefully.

POSSESSION: **39% / 61%** | SHOTS: **6 / 12** | SHOTS ON TARGET: **2 / 5** | CORNERS: **6 / 2** | FOULS: **10 / 13** | BOOKINGS: **2 / 0**

STAR MAN – ADAMA TRAORE

You know when you're having a nightmare that you are a matador and a massive bull is running towards you and there's no time to get out the way? Facing Adama Traore must feel like that. That's three Wolves appearances for the 22-year-old and three star turns from a man who is rapidly becoming one of the most exciting players to pull on a gold shirt in recent years. Morgan Fox can join Leicester's Jonny Evans and Manchester City's Benjamin Mendy as defenders who just will never quite be the same again after being tormented by the human express train. Endured a frustrating first half with Wednesday hacking him down at every opportunity but in the 53rd minute he turned the game in Wolves' favour with a superb run and cross down the right flank to tee up Bonatini. Seconds earlier he'd literally run a ring around one player and skipped past another before setting up Gibbs-White for what should have been the first goal. You're not supposed to stand up and cheer in the press box but Traore makes you want to do just that.

TWEET OF THE GAME

Tim Spiers ✔
@tim_spiers_Star

Bonatini hadn't scored for 23 HOURS AND 59 MINUTES

Only Jack Bauer defusing a nuclear bomb could have timed that better

28 Aug 2018

 **WEST HAM UNITED** **0**

 **WOLVES** **1**
(TRAORE 90+3)

LONDON STADIUM, 3PM
SEPTEMBER 1, 2018 ATTENDANCE: **56,947** (3,000 AWAY)

 Premier League

West Ham United (4-4-2): *Fabianski; Fredericks, Diop, Balbuena, Cresswell; Snodgrass (Yarmolenko 45), Sanchez, Wilshere (Obiang 64), Antonio (Hernandez 75); Anderson, Arnautovic (c). Subs not used: Adrian, Zabaleta, Rice, Noble.*

Wolves (3-4-3): *Patricio; Bennett, Coady (c), Boly; Doherty, Moutinho, Neves, Otto; Costa (Bonatini 72), Jimenez (Vinagre 87), Jota (Traore 62). Subs not used: Ruddy, Hause, Saiss, Gibbs-White.*

On the big London Stadium stage Wolves didn't freeze. Only one of these two teams was enacting a coherent game-plan, only one team looked confident and assured in themselves, only one team looked like they'd been in the top flight for the past six years and only one team still believed they could win this game when the clock ticked over to 93 minutes.

West Ham spent £100m on improving a team that finished 13th last season and in Manuel Pellegrini they have a manager who's won the Premier League. But, while opportunities in front of goal were fairly evenly split, Wolves were the better team.

And of the money they spent in the summer, £18m for Adama Traore already looks like money well spent. For the third game in a row the Spaniard came off the bench and for the third time he changed the face of the football match. It looked for all the world like Wolves would pay for missed opportunities yet again, but then Traore took fellow sub Leo Bonatini's pass and drove it emphatically past the keeper to send thousands of sun-kissed Wolves fans into ecstasy. It was exactly what Nuno's team deserved for a performance of attacking intent – even in injury time they were still going for it with their incessant pressing in West Ham's half and they were handed a just reward of three points.

West Ham came into the game on the back of three defeats from their opening trio of fixtures. In theory they were there for the taking – and that was reflected in a first half that Wolves certainly had the better of. As against Leicester two weeks ago, an unchanged Wolves side attacked from the

off and looked to get that all-important first goal by committing big numbers into the West Ham third. They repeatedly won the ball back in the Hammers' third of the field with Joao Moutinho and Ruben Neves doing a sterling job of closing down Jack Wilshere & Co. Matt Doherty and Jonny Castro Otto were effectively playing as wingers, while Diogo Jota and Helder Costa looked to dribble from deep and cause problems for what looked like a fragile backline.

Their tactics, as at the King Power Stadium, were working a treat, but as in the East Midlands the away team were just lacking that clinical final touch in front of goal. Half-chances came to Raul Jimenez on two occasions, with the Mexican firing wide from 20 yards. Doherty was getting plenty of joy down the right flank and he forced a smart save from Lukasz Fabianski with a fiercely-struck drive from the edge of the area that was top-corner bound, after being teed up by Costa.

The best opportunity of the half fell to Jota, who stormed in at the back post to meet a lofted Moutinho cross, but sent his header over the bar from six yards. The London Stadium was quiet and the home fans impatient – when they roused themselves to make a noise, it was usually to deride a misplaced pass or chastise a player for not closing a Wolves man down.

Nuno's message will have been for more of the same, but West Ham increased their tempo at the start of the second half and put Wolves on the back foot, forcing Rui Patricio into action. Back came Wolves and Jimenez was presented with a free header of his own from Moutinho's free-kick, but placed it straight at Fabianski.

Traore and Bonatini were sent on, then, on 79 minutes, came the chance Wolves had been patiently searching to fashion all afternoon. Neves sprayed to Doherty in loads of space down the right, he ventured inside and placed a low cross on the proverbial plate for Jimenez, who peeled off his man and was all alone, six yards out, keeper to beat... and could it against himself and fell over. It was a comical miss, but no-one in gold was laughing... and two minutes later they were nearly punished in the most ruthless manner possible when Conor Coady was roasted by Marko Arnautovic, who skipped into a fantastic shooting position, only for his shot to hit Patricio in the face.

The game was heading for a goalless stalemate, but Wolves continued to press – and won it in perfect circumstances in the dying seconds. Bonatini fed the rampaging express train Traore and he struck the ball low and true to beat Fabianski and give Wolves a fantastic victory – and their first three points of the season. The boisterous celebrations in the London sunshine after both the goal and the full-time whistle reflected the importance of getting that first 'W' on the board, especially after two good performances in the previous two games yielded only a point.

This should give Wolves the confidence to really kick on – and with appetising fixtures to follow in the coming weeks Nuno's boys could be about to realise the potential we all know they have.

NUNO

The win was special because we didn't change since day one – and for us, day one was last season. We play the same way and do the same things. We deserved the win but you have to look and think that there were moments in the game where either team could have won it. The belief we have is a perfect example (in helping us to get the win) but I think the organisation is the most important part of the game. Adama came late to the club like everybody knows. He still has things to do, to adapt himself and the team has to know and recognise him better, knowing what he can give us.

FAN VERDICT – GULRAJ KULAR

There is no better feeling as a football fan than a late winner, miles away from home. Wolves thankfully were able to provide us all with that feeling. It was a relief. I sat there at half-time shaking my head. Had we come away? Why were we so comfortable? West Ham were there for the taking. Their negativity gave us encouragement that we probably wouldn't have expected. I know the Hammers have had a bad start to the season, but they were more like the Pickaxes. Tentative, vulnerable and just plain scared for the first half. I'd have been seething if we didn't leave Stratford with three points but we pulled through. Bring on the next challenge.

POSSESSION: 48% / 52% | **SHOTS: 13 / 15** | **SHOTS ON TARGET: 3 / 6** | **CORNERS: 4 / 4** | **FOULS: 10 / 11** | **BOOKINGS: 2 / 1**

STAR MAN – JOAO MOUTINHO

Metronomically consistent, occasionally flamboyant, incessantly hard-working – and an all-round class act. Yet another one of those 'can you believe this guy plays for Wolves?' players. Moutinho is the real deal, he's making Wolves tick and displaying all the class and experience that Wolves knew they'd be getting when they forked out just £5m for him. A pass accuracy of 92.4 per cent tells a story but the most impressive aspect of Moutinho's performance was his constant haranguing of West Ham's midfielders as he repeatedly won the ball back in the Hammers half. Whipped in a great free-kick which Jimenez could have scored from, too and put a cross on Jota's head for a big first half chance. Exudes ingenuity.

TWEET OF THE GAME

Tim Spiers ✓
@tim_spiers_Star

They absolutely deserved that. Fantastic attitude, kept attacking, kept searching and got their rewards. Traore is a GAME CHANGER

1 Sep 2018

TABLE

	TEAM	P	GD	PTS
6	BOURNEMOUTH	4	1	7
7	EVERTON	4	1	6
8	LEICESTER	4	1	6
9	WOLVES	4	-1	5
10	SOUTHAMPTON	4	0	4
11	FULHAM	4	-2	4
12	BRIGHTON	4	-2	4

ANALYSIS

They had to wait 2,401 days – but it was worth it for the feeling at 4.50pm. Yes, Wolves last won a Premier League game on February 4, 2012. At the time if you'd told the club's supporters they'd have to wait that long to witness their beloved team win a top-flight match – six-and-a-half barren years – they'd have been devastated. It's been an inexorably long wait – but Nuno's Wolves look set to make up for lost time.

That 2012 victory also came in London, at Queens Park Rangers, but that's where the similarities between the two victories immediately end. The Mick McCarthy era ended a week after the Loftus Road win, when Wolves were a club plummeting headfirst for oblivion and successive relegations to League One. There was no plan for Wolves' future 2,401 days ago. The opposite is true now. Wolves' previous four seasons in the Premier League were all spent looking over their

shoulder. Yes, there were some great days, some unforgettable memories, but each season was a relegation dogfight. They weren't a team to be feared, opposition fans expected to see them defeated. Again, the opposite is true now.

The insipid Hammers looked there for the taking and indeed they were, it's just that Wolves left it extremely late, which made it all the more sweet for their travelling supporters. Nuno's team proved in terms of quality on the ball, control of possession, organisation, shape and creating chances they have what it takes to compete in the Premier League. It seemed they'd be kicking themselves – literally in Raul Jimenez's case – for spurning chances, before Adama Traore's timely intervention for a win they richly deserved.

They fully earned their victory for a wholehearted and positive approach that will win them many fans this season. Their mentality, their drive, their

hunger, their determination and sheer will to win is deeply impressive. It all comes from Nuno. How many managers of a newly-promoted team would have settled for a point at 80 minutes? Not Nuno. He made a tactical switch on 87 minutes, replacing Raul Jimenez with Ruben Vinagre, who stretched play down the left and allowed Leo Bonatini to be in a perfect central position to receive Joao Moutinho's pass and set up that man Traore for a glorious winner. The goal was borne out of another of Nuno's tactical successes – pressing West Ham's midfield time and again with Jonny Castro Otto, Moutinho and Ruben Neves harassing Jack Wilshere and Carlos Sanchez.

> ## "I'M SO HAPPY, NOT ONLY FOR THE GOAL BUT THE PERFORMANCE OF THE TEAM. WE'RE WORKING SO HARD, I'M HAPPY FOR THE FIRST WIN AND I WANT TO KEEP GOING"
> ADAMA TRAORE

The latter had his pocket picked by Neves in the build-up to the winner. Moutinho and Neves combined brilliantly for the goal and enjoyed another productive afternoon as their burgeoning partnership takes shape. Plenty, this correspondent included, thought

Wolves wouldn't have enough bite in midfield with the two Portuguese players not exactly known for putting their foot in. Well, there's a piece of humble pie being delivered to E&S HQ. Time and again the pair won possession and got Wolves back on the attack. They held their positioning, both registered a pass accuracy of higher than 90 per cent and dictated the tempo of the match. A word too for Ryan Bennett, whose consistent form is one of the stories of Wolves' season so far, while Matt Doherty enjoyed a superb game to complete an impressive turnaround since that off-day at Leicester.

After an iffy opening two games it's starting to come together. Wolves are earning points to back up the plaudits. Welcome back to the Premier League, Wolves. You might hang around a bit longer this time, I reckon.

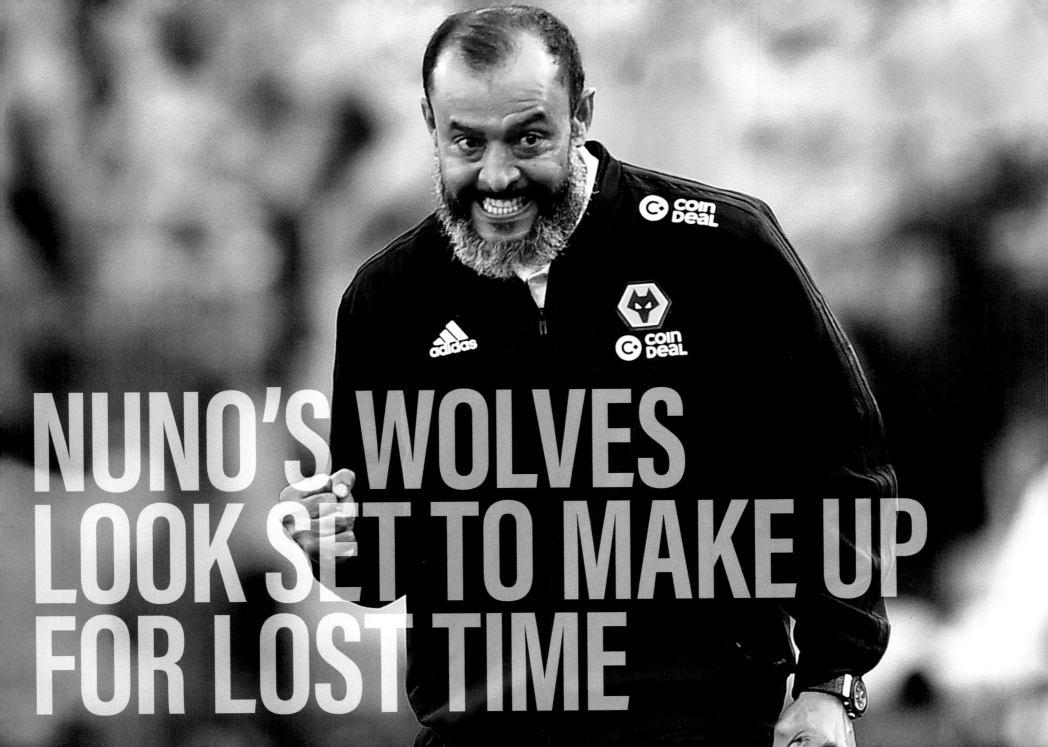

NUNO'S WOLVES LOOK SET TO MAKE UP FOR LOST TIME

WOLVES
(JIMENEZ 61)

BURNLEY

1

0

Wolves (3-4-3): *Patricio; Bennett, Coady (c), Boly; Doherty, Neves, Moutinho, Otto; Costa (Traore 66), Jimenez (Bonatini 76), Jota (Gibbs-White 88). Subs not used: Ruddy, Hause, Saiss, Vinagre.*

Burnley (4-4-2): *Hart; Bardsley, Tarkowski, Mee (c), Taylor; Lennon, Hendrick (Westwood 79), Cork, Gudmundsson; Vokes (Wood 70), Barnes (Vydra 56). Subs not used: Heaton, Lowton, Ward, Long.*

The history books wil suggest that Wolverhampton Wanderers edged past Burnley in a tight encounter on September 16, 2018. However, everyone in the stadium – including even the most diehard Burnley supporters – knew this was a 1-0 thrashing. An obliteration. An annihilation. Wolves absolutely hammered the visitors 1-0, with the scoreline doing absolutely nothing to reveal the sheer dominance enjoyed by the home team.

Chance after chance came and went, with Wolves almost wholly responsible for making this a far edgier finale than it needed to be. Joe Hart made a couple of inspired saves, too, while some heroic Burnley defending (they cleared three off the line) also helped keep the scoreline down amid a melee of 30 (THIRTY) attempts at goal from hungry Wolves. The post-match message from Nuno will inevitably therefore, as after the victory over West Ham, centre around Wolves' need to be more clinical in front of goal. While that's absolutely true, they should be nothing but lauded for an utterly dominant, all-encompassing performance against an established Premier League side that finished seventh last season.

Wolves were comfortable at the back, they controlled play in midfield and they created an almost endless number of presentable opportunities. They should have won by a bigger margin, but goodness me do they look like they belong at this level. This was a fantastic performance of attacking intent, of movement, of pace, of swagger and of high quality. The fine tuning will come. For now, their supporters can marvel at the fact that their team are showing

so many signs that they can make a big impact in this division, as we all suspected they could. Five games, two wins, only one defeat and a point against the champions. Pretty good start, Wolves. Pretty good.

Nuno named the same XI for the fifth league game of five this season – becoming only the second Premier League team to do so at the start of a campaign in the past 10 years. The Clarets were playing their 11th game of the season already owing to Europa League commitments – more than a quarter of the matches they'd played during the whole of 2017/18 – and it showed in a first half that Wolves dominated. Nuno's team were on the front foot from the off and Hart somehow kept out a fierce drive from Raul Jimenez, although the striker should have scored from 10 yards. The same player headed the rebound goalwards, but it was cleared off the line by James Tarkowski and then 30 seconds later a Jonny Castro Otto effort was also blocked on the goal-line as Wolves ramped up the pressure.

The only thing Wolves hadn't done in the first half was create a glaring 'must score' opportunity in front of goal, but they did that within 30 seconds of the restart. A dreadful Phil Bardsley back-pass saw Diogo Jota race towards goal down the left – he squared to Jimenez for practically an open goal, but the ball wasn't quite in his path and the striker fired over the bar from 18 yards. And then, finally, came the reward they had been searching for. Matt Doherty played a lovely give-and-go with Helder Costa, raced into the box and picked out Jimenez, who guided his side-footed shot in off the far post for his second Wolves goal.

Doherty then scuffed wide from a great position in what was Wolves' 21st shot on the afternoon, compared to Burnley's five. Leo Bonatini replaced Jimenez and tried to get in on the act with a shot on the turn, which became their third effort of the game cleared off the line with Tarkowski again defending heroically. Bonatini should have made it 2-0 in stoppage time when he scuffed wide from Adama Traore's pass with Wolves' 30th attempt, but they had to settle for 1-0.

The wing-backs were the stars of the show but Jimenez is beginning to look the real deal. Link-up play? Check. Work rate? Check. Good in the air? Check. A match-winning goal? Check. He unlocks the doors for others and if Wolves keep creating chances he'll reach double figures at least this season.

Some will have been rubbing their eyes in disbelief at the one-sided nature of the contest. Indeed, one gleeful elderly fan told me when leaving the ground that he hadn't seen as commanding a performance as that since the 1950s (although Wolves would have scored 15 goals back then instead of the one they managed this time, he remarked).

Yes they should have scored more, but let's all just marvel at how unequivocally excellent Wolves were. For a newly-promoted team to outshine any opposition in every single area of the pitch, from numbers one to 11 (or rather two to 37) is an impressive feat by any standards. They were better than Burnley, they were better than West Ham and they deservedly held Everton and Manchester City. Whatever way you look at it they belong in the Premier League.

NUNO

I am very, very satisfied with the win. We played good football, we stayed organised and created chances. I think we should be more clinical - and we keep insisting on that. But to produce the chances we did against Burnley makes me very proud of the way we played. We scored one goal and that is the most important. We kept a clean sheet which is important for us. The talent of the players is there so things will come naturally. We have to improve like we always do and we are going to work very hard together – work on finding this final touch that puts the ball inside.

FAN VERDICT – ADAM VIRGO

Back-to-back wins, first home victory of the season, another clean sheet and a fantastic performance. The only thing that was missing was more goals. Having 30 attempts to Burnley's seven shows how much we dominated the game. I thought everyone played their part and on another day, the game could have been at least 5-0. Doherty has proved to a lot of people in his last few performances that he is good enough for the Premier League. Moutinho and Neves really are a dream partnership. I'm still in awe at the fact we have both of them playing for us. If we put in a similar performance next weekend at Old Trafford there's no reason we can't get a result.

POSSESSION: 59% / 41% | **SHOTS: 30 / 7** | **SHOTS ON TARGET: 7 / 2** | **CORNERS: 8 / 2** | **FOULS: 10 / 9** | **BOOKINGS: 2 / 4**

STAR MAN – JONNY CASTRO OTTO

A constant positive presence buzzing up and down that left flank. This was exactly the type of all-action display you'd want from your wing-back, full of effective runs, smart link-up play and defensive solidity. Aaron Lennon barely saw the byline all afternoon. It seemed Otto was being brought in as a steady defensive addition but his game is about so much more than that. Mirrored Matt Doherty's excellence and could have got himself on the scoresheet a couple of times too. Very, very good.

TWEET OF THE GAME

Tim Spiers ✔
@tim_spiers_Star

Just the 30 (THIRTY) shots for Wolves today. They belong in the Premier League, there is no doubt.

16 Sep 2018

TABLE

	TEAM	P	GD	PTS
6	TOTTENHAM	5	4	9
7	ARSENAL	5	1	9
8	MAN UTD	5	0	9
9	WOLVES	5	0	8
10	EVERTON	5	-1	6
11	LEICESTER	5	-1	6
12	CRYSTAL PALACE	5	-2	6

MANCHESTER UNITED ①
(FRED 18)

WOLVES ①
(MOUTINHO 53)

OLD TRAFFORD, 3PM
SEPTEMBER 22, 2018 ATTENDANCE: **74,489** (3,129 AWAY)

Manchester United (4-3-3): De Gea; Valencia (c), Lindelof, Smalling, Shaw; Fred (Martial 63), Fellaini, Pogba; Lingard (Pereira 75), Lukaku, Sanchez (Mata 63). Subs not used: Romero, Bailly, Young, McTominay.

Wolves (3-4-3): Patricio; Bennett, Coady (c), Boly; Doherty, Neves, Moutinho (Saiss 80), Otto; Costa (Traore 75), Jimenez, Jota (Gibbs-White 87). Subs not used: Ruddy, Hause, Vinagre, Bonatini.

A result and performance that was unbelievable – and yet entirely believable at the same time. Unbelievable because it still feels surreal to see little old Wolves taking on the big boys at their own game or on their own ground, no matter how grand the stage. It also made total sense to see Wolves play attractive football against Manchester United and earn a deserved point, because anyone who has followed them since Nuno Espirito Santo walked through the door in June 2017 knows that Wolves don't lie down for anyone. They unleash their own indomitable style, whoever the opposition. Jose Mourinho wanted the headlines, but it was his compatriot Joao Moutinho who nabbed them here – and deservedly so.

The stats will tell you that United had more shots and more possession. But Wolves were excellent value for their well-earned point at the home of one of the biggest clubs on the planet. They approached the game, as we all knew they would, with positivity and attacking intent. Promoted teams just don't play this way. Their technique, their quality in possession, their threats up front, their defensive rigidity – it was almost as good in every area as Manchester United had to offer. And boy was their heart, their determination and their courage there too – courage not just to attack one of the best teams in Europe on their own turf, but to come from behind and then battle during a very difficult last 15 minutes to win a point. United threw everything they had at Wolves in the closing stages and we saw the rare sight of Wolves sitting deep, throwing bodies at the ball and whacking it clear. They can do that too.

The match was billed as 'pupil versus master' with Nuno taking on his old Porto boss Jose Mourinho, but in the opening 17 minutes is was the pupil who saw his team dominate. Wolves took the game to their illustrious hosts. They created three opportunities in the early stages and attacked with positive intent with their eager wing-backs bombing forward.

The impressive Raul Jimenez had the first opportunity of the game when his smart shot on the turn was saved by David De Gea with his feet. Two corners created further chances – the first was powerfully headed just over by Ryan Bennett and the second was met forcefully by a diving Willy Boly, drawing an impressive reflex stop from De Gea. Nuno's team were in the ascendancy – but just a minute later their enthusiasm was punctured by a United opener against the run of play. Conor Coady headed a cross clear to Paul Pogba, who slipped a short pass to Fred and he, in the blink of an eye, side-footed into the bottom corner with a finish that screamed precision and quality. They were indebted to Rui Patricio for keeping the score at 1-0 at the break – on the stroke of half-time the goalkeeper clambered across his line to keep out a curling Fred free-kick that had brilliantly bent around the wall. It was a pivotal moment in the game.

Early in the second half Helder Costa's low cross was controlled by Jimenez, who could have had a shot on the turn, but cleverly looked back and teed up Moutinho, who slotted a curling shot into the top corner from the edge of the box. De Gea didn't even move. Nuno continued to send his team on the charge – Costa and Diogo Jota were

both close to wriggling free in the box and Jota forced a save from De Gea at his near post.

At the other end, Patricio tipped a Jesse Lingard pile-driver over the bar. In the closing minutes, it was one-way traffic as Wolves struggled to get out of their own half, although substitute Adama Traore fashioned a couple of opportunities on the break. The defending became last-ditch and was desperate stuff at times – but Wolves' solid shape and superb discipline meant Patricio didn't have to make another save.

Not since almost 40 years ago have Wolves been able to match the biggest clubs in the land. Almost exactly two years ago, they were losing 2-1 at Wigan Athletic on a miserable, wet Tuesday night. They had 34 per cent possession and when boss Walter Zenga looked for inspiration from the bench he found Paul Gladon and Ola John. Two very quick years later and things couldn't be more different. Wolves are already making a big impact in this division and you wouldn't bet against them taking a few prize scalps in the months to come.

A few thousand travelling fans sang their hearts out all afternoon, their voices echoing around an otherwise-silent stadium. Their repertoire included "Mourinho's right, your fans are s***e" as the home fans started leaving on 80 minutes and "Nuno's the special one". He certainly is.

NUNO

I'm proud of the character that we showed after we conceded and proud of the way that we played. I'm proud of the way that we defended, stayed organised, put bodies in front of the ball and the way we created our chances. We played the way we wanted to play. I thought Willy Boly played well, but everybody made their tasks. It is not easy to come to Old Trafford, it is a fantastic club with fantastic players and a fantastic manager. But we did it, so let's get better so we can play every week like this, this is the goal that we want to achieve. I'm watching my players' mentalities grow.

FAN VERDICT – RUSS EVERS

Looking good ay it! The last four games have yielded eight points – a fantastic return despite two away games at arguably the world's biggest club (Manchester United), the Premier League's biggest spenders (West Ham) and home games against the reigning champions (Manchester City) and a team who qualified for Europe last year (Burnley). Not bad, eh? It was almost a case of two points dropped as we matched and at times outplayed the Red Devils. We deserved a little more than a draw. Everyone played their part with the defence outstanding, while Joao Moutinho outshone Paul Pogba who was easily their best player.

POSSESSION: **65% / 35%** | SHOTS: **15 / 11** | SHOTS ON TARGET: **6 / 8** | CORNERS: **5 / 4** | FOULS: **5 / 17** | BOOKINGS: **1 / 1**

STAR MAN – HELDER COSTA

There's a reason why the club's £18m record signing can't get in the team – and that reason is Helder Costa. Improving week by week and this was his best display so far. Produced a number of darting runs into the heart of the United half with that trademark close control. Looks to be growing in confidence too – he sent Lindelof to Altrincham with one particularly zippy turn of pace. Defended brilliantly from the front, pressed the United back line and played his part in the goal with good persistence to work an angle for a cross. Excellent.

TWEET OF THE GAME

Tim Spiers ✓
@tim_spiers_Star

**Wolves 1-1 Manchester City
Manchester United 1-1 Wolves**

They've taken on two of Europe's best teams and matched them, home and away. Magnificent!

22 Sep 2018

TABLE

	TEAM	P	GD	PTS
7	BOURNEMOUTH	6	-1	10
8	LEICESTER	6	1	9
9	ARSENAL	5	1	9
10	WOLVES	6	0	9
11	CRYSTAL PALACE	6	-2	7
12	EVERTON	5	-1	6
13	BRIGHTON	6	-3	5

 **WOLVES** **0**

 LEICESTER CITY **0** (1-3 ON PENS)

Wolves (3-4-3): Ruddy; Dendoncker, Coady (c), Hause; Otto (Bennett 75), Gibbs-White, Saiss, Vinagre; Traore, Bonatini (Ashley-Seal 83), Cavaleiro (Jota 57). Subs not used: Norris, Giles, Watt, Goncalves.

Leicester City (4-2-3-1): Ward; Pereira, Morgan (c), Evans, Fuchs; Iborra, Silva (Choudhury 84); Ghezzal, Okazaki (Gray 60), Albrighton; Vardy (Iheanacho 60). Subs not used: Jakupovic, Soyuncu, Amartey, Diabate.

Wolves have played six matches in the Carabao Cup under Nuno Espirito Santo – and they've yet to concede a single goal. However, they've now been dumped out of the competition on penalties after a 0-0 draw for the second year in a row.

It's been a remarkable run of six matches and 600 minutes. Last year's defeat to Manchester City felt oh-so cruel after Wolves put on a heroic display at the Etihad, but in truth Leicester were fair victors in this one. Nuno's team enjoyed more of the ball (60 per cent) but it was the Foxes, who selected a strong team that included Jamie Vardy, who fashioned the night's better opportunities in front of an impressive attendance of 21,562.

For a while it felt like a dazzling pre-match lights show, plus the usual fireworks and fire, would be the most interesting thing to happen all night, but this cup tie slowly warmed up at a chilly Molineux with both teams motivated to progress to round four. Wolves had enjoyed a comfortable win with a similar XI against Sheffield Wednesday in the last round but they found Leicester a far tougher nut to crack and the Foxes should have had the game won twice over as we headed nearer to a rare Molineux penalty shoot-out – the first at the stadium since an FA Cup defeat to Fulham in January 2015.

Wolves were indebted to a superb John Ruddy save and a poor Marc Albrighton miss, while at the other end – reflecting their league form – they just couldn't find that clinical spark. It's a crying shame for the likes of Ruddy, Kortney

Hause, Ruben Vinagre and Romain Saiss that they will find game-time hard to come by now until the FA Cup starts in January. But Wolves' priority is very much the Premier League – even more so after this defeat.

Ivan Cavaleiro made his first appearance of the season after recovering from a back injury, while Leander Dendoncker made his Molineux debut in defence. Only Conor Coady and Jonny Castro Otto remained in the team that drew 1-1 at Old Trafford on Saturday. There was a decent atmosphere in the opening stages with the South Bank full, the North Bank practically full and Leicester bringing around 2,000 with them from the East Midlands. It was the Foxes who had the better of the opening stages with Vincente Iborra whistling one wide from 20 yards and then dropping a header just over the bar as Wolves began on the back foot.

Wolves fashioned their first opportunity when Otto lashed over after a nice header into his path from Cavaleiro. And then Vinagre took matters by the scruff of the neck, driving past two defenders and sprinting into the box where his shot from a tight angle was pushed over by Danny Ward. Adama Traore and Cavaleiro were doing their best to get Wolves going with a couple of purposeful runs from deep, although the latter was understandably short of match sharpness.

Otherwise though Wolves were lacking inspiration and control, with the absence of Ruben Neves and/or Joao Moutinho keenly felt. Leicester edged the half and could have gone ahead when Rachid Ghezzal headed

goalwards, only for Coady to clear off the line for what felt like the 149th occasion in a Wolves shirt.

Leicester continued to have the better of it after the break, fashioning another couple of half chances. Wolves were full of endeavour but not enough quality and Leicester almost took advantage when a left-wing cross was allowed to bounce across goal and Albrighton met it at the back post – but Ruddy produced a wonderful stop from point-blank range to keep it goalless.

Traore burst to life and raced from deep with Wolves four on three – he slipped in Morgan Gibbs-White but his 20-yarder was too close to keeper Ward in what was Wolves' clearest opportunity for some time. Ryan Bennett headed a Gibbs-White free-kick just over the bar in the dying seconds as Wolves piled on some belated pressure in injury time, before Demarai Gray was stretchered off injured in the final few seconds with what looked like a serious injury. It went all the way to penalties – and Ward made himself a hero for Leicester with three excellent saves. Youngster Benny Ashley-Seal confidently netted but Ward saved from Saiss, Diogo Jota and Traore as Leicester won 3-1 at a disappointed Molineux.

NUNO

I'm sad we didn't win, but proud of the way we worked. The game was the proof and evidence that we have a good squad, all the options are good. And the most important thing is the way the boys wait for their chance, the way they work on a daily basis knowing that maybe sometimes they are not an option, but knowing when the chances come, good answers must be given. And they gave a good answer. I think well done with our organisation and with our shape. Changes don't mean anything for us, we keep the same style, we keep the same ideas and philosophy and game by game, it doesn't matter what competition, we wanted to win.

FAN VERDICT – ADAM VIRGO

Losing on penalties is something I've been used to with Wolves, but if we had won I don't think it would have been deserved. Leicester were the better side over the 90 minutes and had the better chances. Getting a clean sheet was a positive to take out of the game, mainly thanks to some top drawer saves from Ruddy who kept us in it at times. Not conceding a goal in the Carabao Cup under Nuno is good going. To say we made nine changes from Saturday, on paper we had a good team and it shows how far we have come. Our strength in depth will only keep improving over time.

POSSESSION: 48% / 52% | **SHOTS: 8 / 16** | **SHOTS ON TARGET: 2 / 3** | **CORNERS: 6 / 4** | **FOULS: 8 / 12** | **BOOKINGS: 1 / 2**

STAR MAN – JOHN RUDDY

A second successive clean sheet in the Carabao Cup but this is likely to be his last appearance until January. A solid performance between the sticks, the highlight of which was a superb save from Albrighton in the second half. Didn't have a huge amount to do, with Leicester registering only three shots on target, but dealt with all that was thrown his way.

TWEET OF THE GAME

PENALTIES

LEICESTER PEN 1	FUCHS MISSES *(HITS WOODWORK)*
WOLVES PEN 1	SAISS MISSES *(SAVED)*
LEICESTER PEN 2	GHEZZAL SCORES
WOLVES PEN 2	JOTA MISSES *(SAVED)*
LEICESTER PEN 3	CHOUDHURY MISSES *(SAVED)*
WOLVES PEN 3	ASHLEY-SEAL SCORES
LEICESTER PEN 4	IBORRA SCORES
WOLVES PEN 4	TRAORE MISSES *(HITS WOODWORK)*
LEICESTER PEN 5	IHEANACHO SCORES

WOLVES
(CAVALEIRO 79, OTTO 87)

SOUTHAMPTON

2

0

MOLINEUX STADIUM, 3PM
SEPTEMBER 29, 2018 ATTENDANCE: 31,147 (2,970 AWAY)

Wolves (3-4-3): Patricio; Bennett, Coady (c), Boly; Doherty, Neves, Moutinho, Otto; Costa (Traore 52), Jimenez (Bonatini 90+1), Jota (Cavaleiro 77). Subs not used: Ruddy, Hause, Saiss, Vinagre.

Southampton (4-4-2): McCarthy; Soares, Hoedt, Vestergaard, Bertrand (c); Redmond, Hojbjerg, Lemina, Elyounoussi (Armstrong 71); Austin (Gabbiadini 77), Ings. Subs not used: Gunn, Yoshida, Targett, Romeu, Davis.

Wolves' only real weakness in the opening weeks of the season has been a lack of composure in front of goal. Step forward Ivan Cavaleiro. Ice-cool, deft touches from the Portuguese forward have been sorely missed so far this season despite Wolves' impressive start. And here he took just 90 seconds – and one touch – to make the desired impact on what had looked for so long like being a frustrating afternoon.

Wolves required patience and persistence to break down a stubborn Southampton outfit, who were doing a very effective job of quelling their usual free-flowing passing game. The physical Saints tackled, fouled and intercepted Wolves all over the park, while rarely threatening Rui Patricio's goal. It looked like a dead cert for being last on Match of the Day...but their super-subs Cavaleiro and Adama Traore changed all that, before Jonny Castro Otto sealed the points after great work from the impressive Matt Doherty.

Wolves will come up against all sorts of different methods and tactics in this league of wildly-contrasting styles. So far they're answering almost all the questions posed of them – and very much look at home in the Premier League. For a club that's only spent four years of the past 34 in the top flight, that's quite something.

It was no surprise to see Nuno name the same team for a seventh consecutive league game. There was one alteration on the bench though with Cavaleiro named in a league squad for the first time this season. Despite their Premier League new-boy status, Wolves

were big favourites going into the game (you could get 4/1 on a Southampton win) and the home team set about trying to dominate from the off. The first 15 minutes were played out almost exclusively in Southampton's half, with the visitors resorting to regularly fouling Diogo Jota and Helder Costa in a bid to stop them breaking free.

After 10 minutes came the first real chance for the hosts. A well-worked move saw Costa skip past Wesley Hoedt and feed Doherty – his low cross fell to Otto whose shot from 15 yards was pushed wide by keeper Alex McCarthy. But then Southampton began to find a foothold and create a few opportunities of their own in what was a one-sided spell of about 10 minutes.

Wolves weathered the storm and ended the half on top. A gorgeous Ruben Neves 50-yard rake to Doherty saw the Irishman cross low for Raul Jimenez whose snap-shot on the turn was saved by McCarthy. It was a pretty even first half, but Wolves were nowhere near their best – they lacked their usual tempo and aggression in the final third and the ball just wasn't sticking up top often enough. Southampton were doing a good job of disrupting their flow with a physical – and smart – defensive display.

The second half continued in the same manner and the game had that feeling of a Southampton late winner about it – but from nowhere Traore sparked Wolves into life and then into the lead. He buoyantly raced down the right flank, beat his man and crossed low for Jimenez who – just like at Old Trafford last week – collected and teed up a team-mate, this time

Cavaleiro who smashed past McCarthy from 12 yards to send Molineux potty.

The place was transformed – and so were Wolves, who nearly doubled their lead when Jimenez flicked on Joao Moutinho's cross with a great header, only to be denied by a superb McCarthy save. It was all Wolves now and they deservedly doubled their lead when Doherty showed great persistence to get to the byline and played to Otto, who fired low past McCarthy for his first goal for the club.

Since 1973, Wolves have only finished in the top half of the top flight on one solitary occasion (in 1980). They'll never have had a better chance to do so again. Accomplished, efficient, cohesive and hard-working – Wolves have a team in every sense of the word and have found their feet at Premier League level after just a few weeks.

Ten points clear of relegation before the end of September, three points off the Champions League places, five games unbeaten, an unchanged team for seven matches in a row, only two goals conceded since the second game of the season (both to the big Manchester clubs) – Wolves are making the impact we all knew they could and, boy, are they doing it with style. They're daring to dream all over again – and, as we all know, Nuno loves making dreams a reality.

NUNO

(With Cavaleiro) this is what we want, when a player comes in, either in the starting XI or coming from the bench, he must do his task and help the team. He did well. I think we are happy with our start, knowing that it is only the start. There is a long way to go, knowing that we have to improve. It was a difficult game. Southampton created us problems. I think we also managed to create chances. We passed tough moments in the match, Southampton really put us against the ropes, but we hung on. Tough moments will arrive and we have to be ready for it.

FAN VERDICT – CHRIS HUGHES

How good is it to finally have a team that can put in a 'below-par' performance and still win a Premier League game? For years at this level we turned up for games knowing we'd have to be absolutely at 100 per cent to have a chance of getting anything and even then it was often not enough. In a game where our standards slipped slightly, it was the back three who stepped up to the plate and prevented Southampton from turning the lion's share of possession into meaningful chances to trouble Patricio. Barring a couple of miskicks each Boly and Bennett were outstanding, while Coady continued to press his claims to be given an England chance by marshalling the line superbly.

POSSESSION: 49% / 51% | SHOTS: 14 / 17 | SHOTS ON TARGET: 6 / 6 | CORNERS: 8 / 6 | FOULS: 11 / 7 | BOOKINGS: 3 / 1

STAR MAN – MATT DOHERTY

On September 29, 2015, Matt Doherty couldn't even get in the team when Wolves beat Fulham 3-0 in the Championship. Three years later the Irishman is one of the stand-out wing-backs in the Premier League – and arguably in the best form of his career. He's always been consistent, but in the past five matches he's performed to an incredibly high standard. Here he constantly offered an outlet down that right flank and set up Wolves' best two chances before their late show of goals with low crosses for Jonny Castro Otto and Raul Jimenez. His persistence earned Wolves a second goal when he set up Otto. Delivering end product and quality on a weekly basis too. Martin O'Neill doesn't think he gets to the byline enough...as a fellow glasses wearer I would respectively suggest you get yourself down to Specsavers, Martin.

TWEET OF THE GAME

 Tim Spiers ✔
@tim_spiers_Star

Wolves just look so comfortable at this level. For a club that's only spent four of the past 34 years in the top flight, that's quite something.

29 Sep 2018

TABLE

	TEAM	P	GD	PTS
5	ARSENAL	7	5	15
6	WATFORD	7	3	13
7	LEICESTER	7	3	12
8	WOLVES	7	2	12
9	BOURNEMOUTH	6	-1	10
10	MAN UTD	7	-2	10
11	EVERTON	7	0	9

CRYSTAL PALACE

 0

WOLVES

(DOHERTY 56)

1

SELHURST PARK, 3PM
OCTOBER 6, 2018 ATTENDANCE: 25,715 (3,027 AWAY)

Crystal Palace (4-3-3): *Hennessey; Wan-Bissaka, Tomkins, Sakho, Van Aanholt; McArthur (Meyer 63), Milivojevic (c), Schlupp (Sorloth 82); Townsend, Ayew (Kouyate 72), Zaha. Subs not used: Guaita, Ward, Kelly, Puncheon.*

Wolves (3-4-3): *Patricio; Bennett, Coady (c), Boly; Doherty, Moutinho, Neves, Otto; Costa (Saiss 84), Jimenez (Cavaleiro 75), Jota (Traore 87). Subs: Ruddy, Hause, Gibbs-White, Bonatini.*

We associate Wolves with class, grace, elegance and entertainment. They usually resemble the Royal Philharmonic Orchestra – but at Selhurst Park they showed they could do some coarse, rough-and-ready Rage Against the Machine funk metal too. There are many ways to skin a cat and Wolves are proving adept at a few different methods already.

Do you think they may have got the hang of this Premier League lark? Six games unbeaten, successive wins and clean sheets, only two goals conceded in six (to the Manchester clubs) and up to seventh in the table. As against Southampton last week, Wolves weren't at their fluent best. But this team just knows how to grind out a result – irrespective of the venue, the opposition or the league. They've been doing it for more than a year now – and they're showing no signs of slowing up. West Ham, Burnley, Southampton, Crystal Palace – all beaten since the start of September. And they all failed to score.

These are the type of teams that will have aspirations of finishing in mid-table or higher – and Wolves now look completely capable of doing just that. They worked incredibly hard for this victory and there was some heroic, last-ditch defending (the ball was even, wait for it, hoofed clear on a couple of occasions). It bucketed down with rain all afternoon in London – not a problem for a weathered Irishman like Matt Doherty – and the match-winner was absolutely superb again here as he continued the rich form of his football life. It doesn't get much better than what Doherty's doing right now – and you could say the same for Wolves.

Nuno named the same XI for the eighth league game in a row, with Helder Costa having recovered from the knock that saw him hobble off against Southampton last weekend. Ex-Wolves keeper Wayne Hennessey started against the club for the first time since leaving in 2014. Wolves came into the game in form and on a five-game unbeaten league run – but they actually contrived to produce their worst half of the season. The visitors just couldn't get going – they had just 30 per cent possession of the ball and lacked control and tempo. Nuno will have hated it.

That said, they still created the best chance of the half when Diogo Jota played in Raul Jimenez, who beat the offside line and was in a great position just 10 yards out, but Hennessey made an excellent save to block his shot. Jimenez later returned the favour when played to Jota inside the box but the Portuguese forward crashed his shot high and wide in a moment indicative of his lack of confidence in what was an off-colour display. At the other end, Jeffrey Schlupp had Palace's best opportunity when an uncharacteristic Rui Patricio fumble from a corner presented him with the ball 12 yards from goal, but he smashed it just over the bar. Wolves lacked cohesion and composure and made a succession of sloppy errors, with Joao Moutinho and Ruben Neves overcrowded in midfield.

However, at the start of the second half they found renewed purpose and vigour. The game opened up with Neves firing a 20-yard rasper of a half-volley over the bar. And then came the magic moment Wolves had been lacking all afternoon – and it was man-of-the-moment

Doherty who produced it. He drove inside from the right flank with purpose, played a one-two with Jimenez and struck the ball low and true to beat Hennessey at his near post. Palace came back strong – Jordan Ayew headed a corner over and then Patricio pulled off an excellent double save to deny Max Meyer and then Schlupp's follow-up with a brave block. Willy Boly produced a goal-saving block as Nuno's team desperately tried to weather the Palace storm but they almost sealed it at the other end when substitute Ivan Cavaleiro's half-volley flicked off the crossbar.

The dying minutes saw Wolves revert to 'backs to the wall' mode and there was some defending of the last-ditch variety with bodies thrown on the line and the ball hoofed clear. But Patricio didn't have another save to make and Wolves saw it through. The celebrations at full-time showed just what this meant to the players, the head coach and his adoring public. Nuno took the acclaim of the 3,000 travelling fans, who must still be pinching themselves.

In just 14 months they've seen their team completely transformed, from one that ended 2016/17 in turmoil, to one that's on a six-game unbeaten run in the Premier League, taking on and beating teams that have aspirations of qualifying for Europe. Fitness and form permitting, this could now very much be Wolves' goal. On the evidence we've seen so far, they're good enough to reach it. Another special season is unfolding.

NUNO

The game was not easy but I am really pleased because Selhurst Park is a tough stadium to come to. With this pitch we know the ball is very fast but we did good. I think we didn't start so good but when you look at all the game, we were the better team. We controlled the second half and while Crystal Palace were breaking against us, we had the better chances and I am really pleased with the result. The supporters made us feel like we are at Molineux. Let us do it again because together we are stronger. Our points tally is good. I think the standards are high; we want to repeat them and improve on them.

FAN VERDICT – CLIVE SMITH

Even a wet and rainy day could not dampen the Nuno dream. We were not full of expansive football but ground out a good result with a resolute defence and swift counter attacks. The defending started with our front three never giving Palace time on the ball. We closed down swiftly, while picking our moments to hunt in a pack to gain possession. Palace did the same to us. With the greater onus on them to attack, it always looked like a breakaway would provide a goal. We have seen the Doc get in similar positions several times since the 3-4-3 formation arrived. He is well placed to score quite a few goals at this level.

POSSESSION: 67% / 33% | **SHOTS: 11 / 7** | **SHOTS ON TARGET: 4 / 2** | **CORNERS: 6 / 3** | **FOULS: 11 / 13** | **BOOKINGS: 3 / 4**

STAR MAN – WILLY BOLY

The wall is back! At his imperious best with a dominant display. Given a tough test by Zaha in the early stages, who ghosted past him at one stage, but soon recovered his composure and he defended with brute force and yet elegance at the same time, like a poetry-reciting prison guard. One goal-saving block was particularly important. Superb.

TWEET OF THE GAME

Tim Spiers ✔
@tim_spiers_Star

- Unbeaten in 6
- 3 clean sheets in 4
- Successive wins
- Up to 7th

Wolves are pretty good aren't they

                                      6 Oct 2018

TABLE

	TEAM	P	GD	PTS
4	CHELSEA	7	10	17
5	BOURNEMOUTH	8	4	16
6	ARSENAL	7	5	15
7	WOLVES	8	3	15
8	MAN UTD	8	-1	13
9	WATFORD	8	-1	13
10	LEICESTER	8	2	12

 **WOLVES**

 **WATFORD**
(CAPOUE 20, PEREYRA 21)

 0

 2

MOLINEUX STADIUM, 3PM
OCTOBER 20, 2018 ATTENDANCE: 31,133 (2,731 AWAY)

 **Premier League**

Wolves (3-4-3): Patricio; Bennett, Coady (c), Boly; Doherty (Traore 72), Neves, Moutinho, Otto (Vinagre 45); Costa, Jimenez (Cavaleiro 60), Jota. Subs not used: Ruddy, Hause, Saiss, Bonatini.

Watford (4-4-2): Foster; Femenia, Mariappa (c), Cathcart, Masina; Hughes, Doucoure, Capoue, Pereyra; Success (Prodl 75) (Wilmot 88), Deulofeu (Gray 69). Subs not used: Gomes, Sema, Quina, Navarro.

There were fears that the international break may have arrived at a bad time for Wolves – and those worries were realised. This was comfortably the worst display of the campaign from Nuno Espirito Santo's charges. They lacked their usual speed and flair as they fell to their first defeat of the season at Molineux, courtesy of two quickfire Watford goals within a minute. The real difference-maker for the Hornets was how quickly they got up the pitch, particularly for the second goal scored by Roberto Pereyra, who linked up with Isaac Success and Gerard Deulofeu to great effect. Wolves just could not match that. They did not carry a genuine goal threat.

Raul Jimenez cut an isolated figure before going off on the hour mark. The story of the season continued for Diogo Jota and Helder Costa – both worked hard but were not anywhere near their best. Jonny Castro Otto was hauled off at half-time after a sluggish performance at left-wing-back, while Matt Doherty was kept quiet on the other side. Ruben Neves and Joao Moutinho lost the midfield battle against first goalscorer Etienne Capoue and Abdoulaye Doucoure, too. It was the same starting line-up for the ninth game in succession and some of the players seemed tired. Watford looked a yard or two quicker, they were very quick to pounce on any loose balls. Ruben Vinagre, Ivan Cavaleiro and Adama Traore came off the bench and teenager Vinagre was Wolves' best performer. They perhaps would have got away with switching off as they did here in the Championship. In the top flight, though, you have to be bang at it from the first whistle right up until the last.

There was one change to the Wolves bench from the Crystal Palace victory as Vinagre came in for Morgan Gibbs-White. The Hornets were without talisman Troy Deeney – but did not miss him at all. Deulofeu and Success led the line and caused the hosts all sorts of problems with their pace and trickery. Nuno's men began well enough. Neves's free-kick caused Adam Masina to nod the ball over for a corner and Moutinho's inswinger found Ryan Bennett, whose header was tipped over the crossbar by Ben Foster. Nothing came from the second corner, though, and with each passing minute, well-drilled Watford grew in confidence.

Capoue sprayed the ball around confidently and broke forward to put the visitors ahead. Unmarked, on the edge of the box, his low drive flew through the legs of Conor Coady and left the unsighted Rui Patricio rooted to the spot – Doucoure the provider. And the Hornets swiftly doubled their advantage. Wolves were caught napping – Pereyra timed his run to perfection before coolly lobbing Patricio again. They say you are at your most vulnerable when you have just conceded – and this was a clear example. The Hornets were really in the mood while Wolves, frankly, were at sixes and sevens. A fair few groans, understandably, started to ring around Molineux. Neves lunged in on Will Hughes and was booked. Pereyra, Doucoure and Kiko Femenia all had efforts for Watford, while at the other end, Jimenez dragged a shot wide prior to the welcome interval for Wolves.

Nuno made a switch for the start of the second period. Vinagre replaced Otto, who was not up to his usual standards after his exploits with Spain. Wolves looked brighter after the change, as the crowd did their utmost to rally the troops. Vinagre was keen to get up the pitch and support the attackers but Wolves just could not find a way through. Willy Boly's back-heel was gathered by Foster, and Jota, just as he was about to pull the trigger, was tackled inside the area. Substitute Ivan Cavaleiro and Costa tried their utmost to salvage something, but each of their attempts flew off target as Watford saw out a deserved victory. The manager of the month curse struck.

Nuno is yet to suffer back-to-back league defeats as Wolves chief. Last season's 2-0 home loss to Nottingham Forest at Molineux – which panned out very similarly to the Watford encounter, with two quick-fire first-half goals – was followed up by three triumphs on the spin. A repeat of that is a huge ask with games against Brighton (a), Tottenham (h) and Arsenal (a) coming up. Realistically, most fans would probably be happy with a return of four points from those three matches. One loss does not call for wholesale changes, but having two or three different faces in the starting line-up at Brighton next weekend would not go amiss. This was a harsh lesson for Nuno's men on the ruthlessness of the Premier League. Hopefully, it is one they learn from quickly.

NUNO

We didn't play good, we didn't play well, we didn't perform. So when you don't perform, you don't get the result. It was a disappointing day. When you concede, you must control the situation knowing that there is a lot of the game to go. You cannot immediately make another mistake that unbalances and creates the second goal of Watford, very bad first half, very bad. Everything changed in one minute. In the second half I think we showed some character and we tried until the end. Even when we lose, how we lose is important. If you lose, you must lose with dignity. Watford deserved the win.

FAN VERDICT – ROB CARTWRIGHT

Watford had an excellent game plan to reduce our creative threat. They were first to loose balls in midfield and doubled up on our wing-backs to stifle their ventures. Capoue, Hughes and Doucoure, in particular, were too strong and fast for Neves and Moutinho, thus cutting off the source of most of our attacks. There were only 58 seconds between the Watford goals and both were assisted by man of the match Doucoure. A killer blow on the day. It wasn't always like that though – Wolves shaded the first 20 minutes and were starting to build momentum. I was confident we would go on to win the game comfortably...!

POSSESSION: 45% / 55% | **SHOTS: 10 / 9** | **SHOTS ON TARGET: 1 / 3** | **CORNERS: 8 / 2** | **FOULS: 23 / 13** | **BOOKINGS: 3 / 1**

STAR MAN - RUBEN NEVES

Picked up his third booking of the campaign, out of frustration, and it is a worry that he is being cautioned at such a regular rate. However, Neves was arguably Wolves' best player, with little help from those around him. Later denied Watford what may well have been a third goal with a perfectly-timed challenge on Doucoure.

TWEET OF THE GAME

Nathan Judah ✓
@njudah_star

Manager of month curse
Ref was terrible
Players tired after internationals
Subs were strange
Tim was off

Credit to Watford, no team has nullified the midfield like that all season - well organised and deserved 3pts.

#wwfc will be back at Brighton and they'll be hungry! 🐆🐾🐆

20 Oct 2018

TABLE

	TEAM	P	GD	PTS
5	ARSENAL	8	9	18
6	BOURNEMOUTH	9	4	17
7	WATFORD	9	1	16
8	WOLVES	9	1	15
9	MAN UTD	9	-1	14
10	LEICESTER	8	2	12
11	EVERTON	8	1	12

BRIGHTON
(MURRAY 48)

WOLVES

1

0

AMEX STADIUM, 3PM
OCTOBER 27, 2018 ATTENDANCE: 30,654 (2,992 AWAY)

Premier League

Brighton (4-4-1-1): Ryan; Bruno (c), Duffy, Dunk, Bong; Jahanbakhsh, Stephens, Kayal, Izquierdo (Knockaert 81); March (Bissouma 71); Murray. Subs not used: Steele, Bernardo, Balogun, Andone, Locadia.

Wolves (3-4-3): Patricio; Bennett, Coady (c), Boly; Doherty, Moutinho, Neves, Otto (Bonatini 84); Costa, Jimenez (Cavaleiro 60), Traore (Jota 60). Subs not used: Ruddy, Dendoncker, Vinagre, Gibbs-White.

Wolves' lack of goals this season has been nothing more than a slight annoyance – up until about a week ago. When they were only scoring once against West Ham, Burnley and Crystal Palace, it didn't matter at all as they were keeping a clean sheet on each occasion. But after two games in seven days in which they've failed to score – and lost both games against teams they'll have fancied their chances against – it's becoming a problem.

Glenn Murray showed them how it should be done. Nuno Espirito Santo's team managed to conjure up almost four times as many shots as the Seagulls (25 to seven). Many of those were blocked long-range efforts from outside the box, but there's no doubt whatsoever Wolves created better opportunities than the hosts and, on the balance of play, deserved at least a draw. Due to a combination of poor finishing, some bad luck and a couple of inspired saves from keeper Mat Ryan, they instead drew a blank for a second week in a row. It leaves their goal tally at nine, from 10 matches, which is beginning to become a recurring theme and an ongoing problem. Murray only needed one attempt at goal – it was pretty much the only thing he did all afternoon.

Build-up play, control of possession and tempo, defensive rigidity, it was all there again at the Amex. But in front of goal Wolves' attacking talents, as has been the case for most of the campaign so far, lacked a clinical touch. On paper the Seagulls look ordinary but they're incredibly well-drilled and resolute – once that first goal went in Wolves' task became pretty damn difficult. That's a recurring theme too –

when Wolves take the lead under Nuno, they tend to keep hold of it. Indeed, they've yet to lose when scoring first since he took charge at the start of last season.

After naming the same league XI for the opening nine games of the season, Nuno finally made a change and it was little surprise to see Diogo Jota on the bench. Adama Traore got the nod over Ivan Cavaleiro to make his first league start for Wolves.

Nuno asked for an improved performance after Watford – and in the first half he certainly got one. Where they'd been shackled in midfield by the Hornets and lacked ideas and creativity, here they were buzzing around the Brighton half and put the Seagulls on the back foot almost from the off. In freezing cold weather they didn't take long to warm up. Conor Coady and Willy Boly were sending piercing balls to the flanks, Joao Moutinho and Ruben Neves exerted control in midfield and Traore was a livewire on the left, making a couple of Brighton defenders look foolish.

However, the standout man, as he has been on a couple of occasions already this season, was Matt Doherty. The Irishman channelled his inner Stanley Matthews with a succession of darts to the right byline, regularly getting in behind left-back Gaetan Bong who looked like he was counting down the seconds to 4.50pm. He was involved in the three key moments of the half from a Wolves perspective – flashing the ball across goal, crashing a shot into the box from which Nuno was convinced Wolves should have had a penalty, for a Jose Izquierdo handball and

then engineering the chance of the half when he side-footed inches wide after a one-two with Raul Jimenez. At the other end Wolves were rarely troubled but Shane Duffy somehow sent a free header past the post from about three yards.

Nuno would have hoped for more of the same after the break. Instead Brighton took the lead. Just a couple of minutes had passed when Bruno drilled the ball low into the box and Murray, suspiciously quiet in the first half, was left all alone to turn it past Rui Patricio with a smart finish. Wolves probed, but organised and resilient Brighton were a tough nut to crack. Wolves' main source of creating a chance came from out wide. That nearly worked when Cavaleiro hung a cross to the back stick for Doherty, who side-footed into the side netting. That man Doherty was involved again when he smacked one from range that Ryan pushed wide as Wolves started to hammer at the Brighton door.

The closing stages were one-way traffic and everyone thought they'd nabbed an injury time equaliser when Ryan Bennett's shot headed for the corner – but keeper Ryan somehow pulled off a stunning save to deny Wolves a point. They could feel hard done by, but in the same breath they only had themselves to blame. Wolves' supporters have been spoiled under Nuno and this is a rare mini blip. Improvements needed? Yes. Would you back Nuno to engineer them? Yes.

NUNO

It's disappointing. I feel we deserved more – we played better than last week, better than our opponents. We created a lot of chances and I'm disappointed we conceded in the only moment when Brighton had a really clear shot. Tough game, tough day but a good reaction from the boys. It was not the same as last week. We played better, deserved more, so we have to improve and make it next week. The result was not what we expect and not what the boys worked for, but the performance was good. Everybody saw it was a clear handball (by Izquierdo), the referee didn't see it and sometimes that is football.

FAN VERDICT – RUSS EVERS

We had 60 per cent possession, 25 shots to their seven and our keeper was required to make zero saves against theirs who made seven – yet we still lost. Quite how, no-one is sure, but the bogey team tag sticks. Our best two chances fell to Doherty but neither was converted and we were punished by a striker on top goal-scoring form earning his wages. The way the entire Brighton team engulfed their keeper at the final whistle speaks volumes but this is an unforgiving league and we need to start scoring to maintain the feel-good factor. A good performance but a poor result.

POSSESSION: **40% / 60%** | SHOTS: **7 / 25** | SHOTS ON TARGET: **1 / 7** | CORNERS: **1 / 10** | FOULS: **11 / 8** | BOOKINGS: **3 / 0**

STAR MAN – MATT DOHERTY

Maintained his excellent form with another stand-out display. Was at the heart of almost everything positive that Wolves did in the final third – constantly made himself an outlet and regularly got to the byline, in behind Gaeten Bong who had an afternoon to forget. By his own admission he should have scored when he side-footed just past the post. Also placed a shot into the side netting and saw a long-range effort well saved. Absolutely full to the brim of confidence and his attacking intentions were incessant. A player at the top of his game.

TWEET OF THE GAME

TABLE

	TEAM	P	GD	PTS
6	BOURNEMOUTH	10	7	20
7	WATFORD	10	4	19
8	EVERTON	9	3	15
9	WOLVES	10	0	15
10	MAN UTD	9	-1	14
11	BRIGHTON	10	-2	14
12	LEICESTER	10	0	13

WOLVES 2
(NEVES PEN 68, JIMENEZ PEN 79)

TOTTENHAM HOTSPUR 3
(LAMELA 27, LUCAS 30, KANE 61)

MOLINEUX STADIUM, 7.45PM
NOVEMBER 3, 2018 ATTENDANCE: **31,185** (2,938 AWAY)

Wolves (3-4-3): Patricio; Bennett, Coady (c), Boly; Doherty, Moutinho (Gibbs-White 62), Neves, Otto; Costa (Traore 84), Jimenez, Cavaleiro (Bonatini 62). Subs not used: Ruddy, Dendoncker, Hause, Vinagre.

Tottenham Hotspur (4-3-3): Lloris (c); Trippier, Alderweireld, Foyth, Davies; Sissoko, Dembele (Son 7) (Eriksen 59), Winks; Lamela, Kane, Lucas (Sanchez 79). Subs not used: Gazzaniga, Aurier, Skipp, Llorente.

There was a seven-minute spell during this thrilling and fascinating encounter when Wolves supporters were probably feeling as despondent as they have since Nuno Espirito Santo took charge. Harry Kane had put Spurs 3-0 up, taking advantage of yet more slack defending as the visitors showed Wolves the way to goal. Wolves had wasted several chances and been punished for lapses of concentration at the back. They were heading for a third consecutive deflating defeat and a third blank in front of goal.

What followed, from 68 minutes onwards, restored any lost faith. This is why we love watching Nuno's Wolves. Yes, they still lost this rollercoaster match, which was reminiscent of the 3-3 classic these teams served up in 2011. But they showed heart, determination and fight in those closing stages and almost earned the unlikeliest of points. Their consolation goals were from penalties but Wolves had fully merited them with a vibrant and buoyant approach, one which they had shown for long spells of this game even when they were being outclassed in front of goal by Spurs. That approach was typified by Morgan Gibbs-White, whose stellar contribution drove the team on when they were flagging. The teenager inspired his more senior colleagues. Their response at 3-0 wasn't to fold.

Ivan Cavaleiro was handed his first league start as Nuno made one alteration to the team that lost 1-0 at Brighton. This was the third game for Spurs in a sequence of four in eight days, giving Wolves hope they'd caught Mauricio Pochettino's team at a good moment. Amid a fantastic Molineux atmosphere for a rare

Saturday night game Wolves were vibrant in the early stages – and then came the deja vu. Erik Lamela was given far too much space in-between Willy Boly and Jonny Castro Otto to make it 1-0 with a smart finish. Then Lucas Moura sent a free header past Rui Patricio despite there being seven Wolves defenders in the box. Two goals in quick succession, just like against Watford. Wolves were all over the place but responded before the break and should have got back into the game when Raul Jimenez took Matt Doherty's header after brilliant work from the Irishman and Joao Moutinho and beat Hugo Lloris from close range. Doherty, though, was incorrectly flagged offside.

That front-foot approach continued after the restart with Wolves creating three opportunities in quick succession, but somehow not scoring, with the revitalised Helder Costa at the heart of their good moments and Lloris making a superb save from Ruben Neves. As has often been the case this season, Wolves were just lacking a predatory touch – and that was hammered home when Kane displayed just that to score a third with a smart finish. At a downcast Molineux that looked like game over, but Wolves pulled a goal back with 23 minutes to go. Juan Foyth tripped Jimenez in the box and Neves coolly sent Lloris the wrong way from the spot to reduce the deficit.

Substitute Gibbs-White then carved out the opportunity Wolves craved, playing a perfect through ball to Costa who beat the offside trap and was through on goal – but prodded agonisingly wide. It was a golden chance. However, a few minutes later they were awarded another penalty when Foyth fouled Otto after

good work from Leo Bonatini. This time Jimenez stepped up instead of Neves – and he too sent Lloris the wrong way. Molineux was absolutely bouncing now; from nowhere Wolves were back in it and chasing an unlikely point. Sadly, a third goal was too much to ask. Spurs defended resolutely and saw it through.

Given the chances they'd created and Doherty's offside goal, Wolves would have won this on another day. They fought back valiantly and were deservedly cheered off at full-time by their encouraged supporters, who also sang Gibbs-White's name. What a future he has. The Stafford-born midfielder was handed his big chance by Nuno, with 28 minutes to impress rather than five, and boy did he do just that. The teenager took the game by the scruff of the neck and galvanised Molineux with a performance of gumption, positivity, character and vibrancy. This was like the Gibbs-White of last season – he got his head up, he looked to make things happen, he played incisive passes and he ran at defenders.

A third consecutive defeat, yes, but Wolves played with real quality and attacking intent against quality Champions League opposition and arguably deserved a point. They've got a few problems in both boxes that need ironing out but there's absolutely nothing wrong with Wolves' fighting spirit. Some perspective, if needed...two years ago they were 19th in the Championship and without a manager.

NUNO

We could have drawn, we could have won. It was a very good game of football, a very emotional game. We started good but then we conceded – and then conceded again to make it 2-0. Then the reaction was good. Even in the first half, we were able to have a go. You knew that one goal could change the dynamic. With the heart of the team, the character of the team, we took more risks. We played good football up until the end. Sometimes you get rewarded, sometimes you don't. Keeping a clean sheet is always the first goal a team must have.

FAN VERDICT – CHRIS HUGHES

Another frustrating night. For 25 minutes we controlled the game and restricted an average-looking Spurs team to one chance but then, for the second successive home game, we conceded a quick-fire double to give ourselves another mountain to climb. Overall there were signs of encouragement but we still had the chronic failure to convert good play into good chances in the final third and made more basic defensive errors. Still, just over a quarter of the way into the season, and not having yet played anyone among the division's current bottom four, we can be happy to sit nestled in mid-table. Gibbs-White was very impressive and outshone England international Winks in midfield.

STAR MAN – MORGAN GIBBS-WHITE

He has arrived. Handed his big chance by Nuno, with 28 minutes to impress rather than five, and boy did he do just that. Took the game by the scruff of the neck and inspired his more senior colleagues with a performance of gumption, positivity, character and vibrancy. This was like the Gibbs-White of last season – he got his head up, he looked to make things happen, he played incisive passes and he ran at defenders. What a pass for that Costa chance too. The South Bank sang his name as the teams left the field. A superstar in the making and offers Wolves something different and unpredictable in midfield.

TWEET OF THE GAME

 Tim Spiers ✓
@tim_spiers_Star

Yes it's disappointing etc but before everyone completely loses the plot and starts typing in angry capital letters, just a reminder that Wolves are 11th in the Premier League.

Two years ago they were 19th in the Championship and without a manager.

3 Nov 2018

TABLE

	TEAM	P	GD	PTS
8	WATFORD	11	3	19
9	EVERTON	11	4	18
10	LEICESTER	11	1	16
11	WOLVES	11	-1	15
12	BRIGHTON	11	-4	14
13	WEST HAM	11	-4	11
14	CRYSTAL PALACE	10	-6	8

ARSENAL
(MKHITARYAN 86)

WOLVES
(CAVALEIRO 13)

1

1

EMIRATES STADIUM, 4.30PM
NOVEMBER 11, 2018 ATTENDANCE: 60,030 (3,003 AWAY)

Arsenal (4-3-3): Leno; Bellerin, Mustafi, Holding, Kolasinac (Mkhitaryan 76); Torreira, Xhaka, Ozil (c) (Ramsey 75); Iwobi (Guendouzi 45), Lacazette, Aubameyang. Subs not used: Cech, Sokratis, Maitland-Niles, Nketiah.

Wolves (3-4-3): Patricio; Bennett, Coady (c), Boly; Doherty, Moutinho, Neves, Otto; Costa (Traore 75), Jimenez (Gibbs-White 85), Cavaleiro (Jota 61). Subs not used: Ruddy, Dendoncker, Vinagre, Saiss.

This wasn't supposed to happen. Wolves had lost three in a row, Arsenal were unbeaten in 14 – there was only expected to be one winner. As it was, Wolves could have won 4-3, they could have lost 4-1, but somehow this game ended up as just about the most thrilling, tension-filled, frenetic 1-1 draw you'll see.

Wolves played their part in a fabulous encounter which had goals, quality, chances, near misses and late, late drama. That drama wasn't just restricted to Arsenal's heartbreaking equaliser, only four minutes from the end of the 90. Twice in injury time Wolves could, perhaps should, have won it but substitutes Adama Traore and Morgan Gibbs-White were denied by Bernd Leno and the crossbar.

Arsenal had piled on almost insurmountable amounts of pressure in the second half, but the Gunners couldn't have complained had Wolves won it. Nuno's intrepid team gave a performance of heart, commitment, soul, team spirit and plenty of quality. This was about more than earning a point in a game of football. This was about restoring a bit of belief after three consecutive defeats and proving, not that Wolves necessarily needed to, that they are a team to be reckoned with this season. Four times they've taken on the big boys, four times they've matched them.

Nuno showed faith with the same XI that had lost 3-2 to Spurs last weekend – and he was rewarded with an almost perfect first half. Wolves sat deep, defended resolutely and created several chances on the counter-attack. Arsenal began as they meant to go on by dominating possession in the early stages, but

Ruben Neves and Joao Moutinho were regularly winning it back in midfield and Wolves were getting joy down the flanks, too. After just 13 minutes, their passive-aggressive approach paid early dividends. Granit Xhaka inexplicably allowed the ball to run across him in midfield and Ivan Cavaleiro picked it up and headed straight for the box. He played right to Raul Jimenez, who instantly returned the favour for Cavaleiro to side-foot home from six yards. It was a clinical goal with Wolves taking full advantage of an opposition error, not something that's happened too often this season. It was also a fifth assist of the campaign for the unselfish Jimenez.

Arsenal began to pile the pressure on but Wolves' determination just grew stronger. It was blood and guts defending of the unsubtle variety – and Ryan Bennett and Conor Coady in particular excelled. Coady made a stupendous block when he threw himself at the ball to deny Alexandre Lacazette, who looked set to fire home from six yards, before later executing a perfect sliding tackle in the box. The tenacious Bennett also stopped a certain goal when he put his head in the way of a powerful Hector Bellerin strike which was bound for the top corner. Wolves' granite-like backline meant Rui Patricio didn't have a thing to do in terms of saves, while their counter-attacking was lightning quick, particularly via the sprightly and direct Helder Costa.

Arsenal ramped it up after the break and Patricio was almost at full stretch to tip a Lucas Torreira dipper from 20 yards over the bar. The Gunners were a whisker away from an

equaliser when Bellerin flashed a left-footed effort inches over. It was one-way traffic now and the Gunners went closer still when Pierre-Emerick Aubameyang, anonymous to this point, side-footed against the post from just six yards. Every tackle and every clearance was being cheered heartily by a tense away end.

It could and should have been 2-0 with just a few minutes left when Jimenez broke down the right and played across goal where substitute Diogo Jota's shot was blocked at point-blank range. The tension was unbearable – and then Arsenal broke Wolves' hearts. An inswinging Henrikh Mkhitaryan cross from a short corner went over Coady's head and dropped into the bottom corner, beating everyone. It was a devastating moment but Wolves regrouped and went back on the attack – Traore bounded forward, beat Rob Holding and was in on goal, but Bernd Leno made the block. It was a huge opportunity for an injury-time winner – and then Wolves created another. Again Traore was involved, he raced down the right and teed up Gibbs-White whose fabulously-struck curling 20-yard effort smacked off the underside of the bar and somehow stayed out. It was a breathtaking end to a fabulous, nerve-shredding encounter.

Many teams would undoubtedly have rolled over against an Arsenal team of rich quality and on an unbeaten 14-game run but Wolves went the other way – they took the game to the Gunners on the counter. For their ballsy approach, their desire and their quality, they deserved to come away from North London with a memorable victory. That they didn't should take nothing away from this most heartening of performances.

NUNO

I'm very proud, so let's work more to try to make this moment again – the joy and happiness. I was thinking, wanting and wishing Morgan's strike to go in. I almost prayed for it to go in. He came on and brought energy. The subs changed the dynamic of the game. We were looking for more speed because Arsenal were really high. There was space for us to explore – and we almost did it. If there was more time, maybe we still have another chance. In that moment, what enabled us to get those chances was the way we were defending. We didn't allow Arsenal to play.

FAN VERDICT – NATALIE WOOD

Imagine two years ago thinking one day we'd be leaving the Emirates deflated and disappointed we only had a point. Box-to-box we were superb, one of the best away performances I have seen in years. We really did look something special again, defensively we were a step above Arsenal at times. Man of the match would either be Otto or Costa. We didn't look like an underdog putting in an exceptional performance – we looked like Arsenal's equal. My only slight concern is the amount of chances we missed...our finishing is still a big issue and we need to start taking these opportunities. But I'm looking at the positives and there were plenty of those.

POSSESSION: **72% / 28%** | SHOTS: **10 / 13** | SHOTS ON TARGET: **3 / 5** | CORNERS: **11 / 2** | FOULS: **9 / 16** | BOOKINGS: **2 / 2**

STAR MAN – RYAN BENNETT

Oh yes Ryan Bennett, that's more like it. Occasionally sluggish against Spurs but here came arguably his best performance in a Wolves shirt. Outstanding. This was a proper defender's game... Wolves don't have many of those but Bennett excelled with some monumental blocks, including when he saved a certain goal from Bellerin. More clearances (six) than anyone on the pitch. He and Doherty nullified Aubameyang's threat from that left flank.

TWEET OF THE GAME

TABLE

	TEAM	P	GD	PTS
8	MAN UTD	12	-1	20
9	EVERTON	12	4	19
10	LEICESTER	12	1	17
11	WOLVES	12	-1	16
12	BRIGHTON	12	-5	14
13	WEST HAM	12	-4	12
14	NEWCASTLE	12	-6	9

 **WOLVES** **0**

 **HUDDERSFIELD TOWN** **2**

(MOOY 6, 74)

 Premier League

MOLINEUX STADIUM, 4PM
NOVEMBER 25, 2018 ATTENDANCE: **30,130** (1,838 AWAY)

Wolves (3-4-3): Patricio; Bennett, Coady (c), Boly; Doherty, Moutinho (Gibbs-White 45), Neves, Vinagre; Costa (Jota, 75), Jimenez, Cavaleiro (Traore 45). Subs not used: Ruddy, Saiss, Dendoncker, Bonatini.

Huddersfield Town (3-5-2): Lossl; Smith (c), Kongolo, Schindler; Hadergjonaj, Mooy, Hogg (Mbenza 90+3), Billing (Williams 90+3), Durm; Pritchard (Stankovic 90+3), Mounie. Subs not used: Hamer, Kachunga, Sobhi, Depoitre.

Wolves contrived to produce yet another insipid display after an international break, mirroring the performance and result against Watford last month. Make no mistake, Wolves deserved absolutely nothing from this game. For a team that possesses such rich quality and energy, they were remarkably poor.

What must be noted is with the scoreline at 1-0, they did at least make a resurgent start to the second half and looked to have equalised when Raul Jimenez met Adama Traore's cross with a simple header towards goal – it looked in, but Philip Billing's tremendous clearance kept 1.8cm – yes, 1.8cm – of the ball on the wrong side of the line. Who knows what may have happened had that gone in, but what did transpire was a most un-Wolves-like surrender as impressive Huddersfield, shortly after Jimenez fluffed his lines when through on goal, began attacking again and soon made it 2-0.

Nuno made one change from the team that drew 1-1 at Arsenal two weeks ago and it was entirely as expected, with Ruben Vinagre making his first league start for 11 months in place of Jonny Castro Otto, injured while on international duty with Spain. The usual spectacular pre-match fireworks at a darkening Molineux set the stage perfectly for Wolves to do their thing – but what followed was, by a distance, their worst 45-minute display of the season. Wolves were sluggish in possession, short of ideas, sloppy at the back and outthought and outfought by their opponents. The players seemed a yard off the pace – never more so than for Huddersfield's surprise early opening goal with their first meaningful attack. As Matt Doherty jogged back down the touchline, Erik Durm raced

by him and Ryan Bennett before crossing low for Aaron Mooy to sidefoot home with an impressive finish. Rui Patricio had no chance. After Mooy's strike they only threatened Jonas Lossl's goal on one occasion during the rest of the half, when Ivan Cavaleiro was nicely fed by Jimenez in the box, only to be denied by a superb last-ditch tackle. That was as good as it got for Cavaleiro who, to put it generously, endured a stinker of a first half, continuously and maddeningly giving the ball away.

Ruben Neves and Joao Moutinho were jumped on every time they had the ball at their feet by Huddersfield's committed midfielders, while the Terriers also carried a more potent attacking threat and were led by the inspirational Mooy. The one good thing from a Wolves perspective was they were only 1-0 down at the break. Other than a wonderful, old school crunching tackle from Conor Coady on Florent Hadergjonaj, which really got the fans going, there was a lack of passion too and Wolves were duly booed off at half-time for what must be the first occasion in Nuno's reign.

It was no surprise to see Cavaleiro and Moutinho taken off at half-time, with Traore and Morgan Gibbs-White sent on to transform Wolves' fortunes. Traore almost did that within 10 minutes when he delicately lifted a cross to the back post where Jimenez headed goalwards – but the athletic Billing brilliantly and acrobatically cleared off the line. There was definitely more urgency about Wolves' play, but resilient Huddersfield were making it difficult for them. Then Jimenez was presented with a golden opportunity. Terence Kongolo was down injured near the corner flag so Jimenez was onside, despite being beyond the Huddersfield backline, and

clean through on goal. Bizarrely, he elected to cut inside a recovering Huddersfield defender and then the chance went begging, to the huge frustration of the Molineux masses. It turned out to be a pivotal moment, as Huddersfield embarked on their first attacking spell of the half and within a few minutes they doubled their lead. Mooy produced another technically excellent finish to curl a 20-yard free-kick past Patricio at his near post, but strangely and criminally there was a huge hole between Neves and Helder Costa at the end of the wall, which Mooy duly put the ball through. Thereafter the game died a death, with Wolves humiliated as Huddersfield sprayed the ball around to cries of "ole" from the away fans.

The Terriers were everything Wolves should have been – they were vibrant, positive and confident. They also had a game plan which they enacted perfectly, nullifying the threat of Neves and Moutinho in what's becoming a concerning recurring theme. Not one player – except Coady, who produced a couple of inspiring sliding tackles – did himself justice here. Cavaleiro had a big off-day, Doherty didn't look himself (especially for Huddersfield's first goal), there was barely anything decent in the final third and not even Gibbs-White could produce some inspiration from the bench as in recent weeks. It was turgid, dire stuff. It's not time to panic – only two weeks ago they outplayed Arsenal – but Nuno has to ask some serious questions of his players and himself to stop this becoming an alarming rut and an inevitable slide down the table.

STAR MAN – CONOR COADY

A couple of slack passes, but otherwise Coady was superb, he really was. A crunching sliding tackle on Pritchard in the first half was magnificent – and should have been the catalyst for the team to improve. Produced another in the second half too. Sets standards in terms of performance and mentality that his team mates should aspire to.

TWEET OF THE GAME

TABLE

	TEAM	P	GD	PTS
8	BOURNEMOUTH	13	4	20
9	WATFORD	13	0	20
10	LEICESTER	13	1	18
11	WOLVES	13	-3	16
12	BRIGHTON	13	-5	15
13	WEST HAM	13	-8	12
14	HUDDERSFIELD	13	-14	10

 **CARDIFF CITY**
(GUNNARSSON 65, HOILETT 77)

 **WOLVES**
(DOHERTY 18)

 2

 1

Cardiff City (3-1-4-2): Etheridge; Ecuele Manga, Morrison (c), Bamba; Gunnarsson; Camarasa, Arter (Harris 76), Ralls, Hoilett; Murphy (Reid 66), Paterson. Subs not used: Smithies, Peltier, Bennett, Ward, Mendez-Laing.

Wolves (3-4-3): Patricio; Saiss, Coady (c), Boly; Doherty, Neves, Moutinho, Vinagre (Cavaleiro 82); Traore (Gibbs-White 72), Jimenez, Costa (Jota 66). Subs not used: Ruddy, Bennett, Giles, Bonatini.

Wolves have fond memories of their last trip here – their memories of this Friday night, though, will be nothing but miserable. Five defeats in six, edging towards the relegation strugglers, a team bereft of confidence – this is getting serious now. Wolves had never lost under Nuno Espirito Santo after taking the lead. They'd never failed to win on a Friday night under him either. Yep, it's unknown territory for Wolves under the man fans have worshipped like a demigod for 15 months.

It was all going so well when Matt Doherty gave them an early lead. Nuno had enlisted a back-to-basics approach in order to generate a much-needed result and it was working, Cardiff were frustrated. But their downfall, as it has been time and again this season, came in front of goal.

As well as Ryan Bennett, Ivan Cavaleiro was also axed with Adama Traore making his second Wolves start as Nuno pulled out a bold selection. At a soaking Cardiff City Stadium there was a big-game atmosphere in the build-up, reminiscent of that effective title decider back in April – and indeed the first half felt like a Championship match. Whereas a few teams have matched Wolves' three-at-the-back formation this season to try and counter them (yes, including Cardiff), it was Nuno's team who took a leaf out of their opponent's book, to great effect. They were physical, raw, kept it simple and yes, hoofed the ball clear on several occasions, an act that would probably normally lead to a two-week wage fine under Nuno. With the team in need of a result they were happy to sacrifice their usual style.

Romain Saiss, Conor Coady and Willy Boly were all impressive in the first half, especially the former who slotted seamlessly into the back three. In front of them, Ruben Neves and Joao Moutinho were tight and compact and the wing-backs rarely ventured forward. An issue was up front where the ball just wasn't sticking. Wolves often looked for Traore with a long ball over the top to utilise his pace, but neither he, Raul Jimenez or Helder Costa seemed to keep possession for more than two touches, much to Nuno's clear frustration.

It meant Wolves couldn't build up any momentum and the ball kept coming back at them. But it was a successful half in terms of scoring first and earning that all-important lead, which came to them via the rare source of a set-piece, with Jimenez's near-post header from Moutinho's outswinger well saved, but Doherty lashed home the rebound into the roof of the net. Cardiff were within a whisker of equalising when Harry Arter's fabulous hit smacked the post after Wolves failed to clear a corner, before having a penalty shout turned down after Ruben Vinagre clashed with Callum Paterson, whose thick, bushy moustache made him look like his surname should be Carolgees. Other than that the half was bereft of chances and also quality.

It was a slow, fairly turgid start to the second half with the two sides regularly giving possession away. Neves was booked for a late trip, his fifth yellow of the season, meaning he'll miss Wednesday's game against Chelsea, but that blow paled into insignificance when, minutes later, Cardiff equalised. Seconds after Arter

flashed a fabulous volley inches wide via a Coady deflection, Wolves miserably failed to deal with a high hoof into the box from a cleared corner. Sean Morrison was all alone to head to Aron Gunnarsson who had the time to take a touch and volley home from six yards, past a flailing Patricio who neither stayed nor went to collect the high ball. It was statuesque defending from the whole defence. Cardiff had the momentum and, with a passionate home crowd now fully behind them, they took the lead with 13 minutes to go in stunning fashion when Junior Hoilett curled a majestic 20-yarder into the net via the bottom of the bar. Wolves threw everything at the hosts in the closing stages but couldn't repeat any late Cardiff heroics and slipped to a miserable defeat.

As at Arsenal three weeks ago, they needed to find that killer second goal. An elusive clinical touch was so sorely lacking. Nuno's selection of Saiss at centre-half raised eyebrows aplenty but Saiss played well, he wasn't the issue. It was up front, where the ball just didn't stick all game and Wolves couldn't create or find a goal when it mattered. It's been their bugbear all season long. Traore, Costa, Diogo Jota and Cavaleiro cost £48m in total but have contributed three goals and no assists between them all season. It's not good enough – and at this rate it will cost Wolves a successful season. Solutions are required – and fast.

NUNO

We knew Cardiff were a very physical team and for almost all of the game, we were able to equal that physical intensity. But there was one moment where we could not – the moment we conceded. Until then, I think, in the first half, we were in control. We equalled that intensity – trying to play and create situations. After the equaliser the game became difficult. That was the moment where we lost a little bit of control. There's nothing to say in terms of hard work, on how we stick together as a team. But, individually, we have to raise our standards in certain moments that can define games. Some teams adapt to our formation, and they had success.

FAN VERDICT – CLIVE SMITH

A solitary three-hour drive home allowed for plenty of time for reflection. It was not enough time to come up with much positivity I am afraid. A changed line-up brought only a marginally improved overall performance – even the luxury of an early lead failed to energise us. Too many long passes were over hit while shorter passes frequently failed to find their man. We were constantly beaten to the second ball while being out-muscled. We give away cheap fouls while getting brushed aside easily. Our front three rarely linked up together. Frankly we were second best again.

POSSESSION: 48% / 52% | **SHOTS: 17 / 15** | **SHOTS ON TARGET: 3 / 4** | **CORNERS: 7 / 6** | **FOULS: 3 / 12** | **BOOKINGS: 1 / 2**

STAR MAN - WILLY BOLY

Just the 15 headers won (most on the pitch) and 15 clearances (most on the pitch) from Boly who didn't deserve to be on the losing side. Seemed to have a magnet in his forehead attracting the ball to it. Again, wasn't the best at bringing it out, but defensively he was superb.

TWEET OF THE GAME

Tim Spiers ✔
@tim_spiers_Star

A few of you won't thank me for saying it and yes tonight was devastating and the run is dreadful, but Wolves are still 11th in the Premier League and will be no lower than 12th tomorrow. They're where they want to be. Big improvements needed but this isn't a crisis.

30 Nov 2018

TABLE

	TEAM	P	GD	PTS
8	BOURNEMOUTH	13	4	20
9	WATFORD	13	0	20
10	LEICESTER	13	1	18
11	WOLVES	14	-4	16
12	BRIGHTON	13	-5	15
13	NEWCASTLE	13	-5	12
14	WEST HAM	13	-8	12

WOLVES
(JIMENEZ 59, JOTA 63)

CHELSEA
(LOFTUS-CHEEK 18)

2

1

MOLINEUX STADIUM, 7.45PM
DECEMBER 5, 2018 ATTENDANCE: 31,300 (2,967 AWAY)

Wolves (3-5-2): *Patricio; Saiss, Coady (c), Boly; Doherty, Dendoncker, Neves, Moutinho, Otto; Jimenez (Traore 89), Jota (Gibbs-White 81). Subs not used: Ruddy, Kilman, Vinagre, Costa, Cavaleiro.*

Chelsea (4-3-3): *Kepa; Azpilicueta (c), Rudiger, Luiz, Emerson; Kante, Jorginho (Willian 72), Kovacic (Loftus-Cheek 57); Pedro (Hudson-Odoi 62), Higuain, Hazard. Subs not used: Caballero, Christensen, Barkley, Giroud.*

After 39 minutes of this exhilarating encounter, Wolves were staring down the barrel of a sixth defeat in seven matches. With Chelsea already 1-0 up, Eden Hazard set Willian racing through on goal and, with only Rui Patricio to beat, it was surely 2-0 and probably game over. Then, out of the corner of this correspondent's eye, Ryan Bennett (dropped at Cardiff last time out) came as if from nowhere, caught the Brazilian and walloped into a booming sliding tackle of perfection, both in time and execution. It was a breathtaking moment for which the word 'pivotal' should have been invented.

Twenty minutes of football later Wolves were 2-1 up having completed an invigorating comeback which was as unanticipated as it was extraordinary.

Every Wolves player raised his game in what was a barnstorming, committed, whole-hearted and dogged performance against a team that had only lost once in the Premier League. Their woeful struggles against Huddersfield and Cardiff were instantly forgotten during a night that may yet count as one of the most important of the season. It was invigorating fare amid a rasping atmosphere under the Molineux lights.

Nuno Espirito Santo went rogue, making a series of hitherto unseen changes that worked to devastating effect. Morgan Gibbs-White played an inspirational role in midfield on his full Premier League debut in a newfangled 3-5-2 formation. There were long throws, new tactics and even the sight of Leander Dendoncker in a Wolves shirt, while Diogo Jota and Bennett were restored to the XI and would play crucial roles in this wonderful win.

Wolves came into the game on by far their worst run under Nuno of five defeats in six matches, but they've performed well against the big teams this season, earning points against Manchester City, Arsenal and Manchester United. And they weren't shirking the challenge in what was a confident start to the game, typified by Gibbs-White as he looked to make an impression on the big stage. The teenager rode one challenge as he broke into Wolves' half before brilliantly sliding past Antonio Rudiger with a skilful switch to his left.

However, their early optimism was punctured by an unfortunate opening goal. Ruben Loftus-Cheek sent what looked a fairly harmless shot goalwards and it deflected off Conor Coady's head into the bottom corner past a helpless Rui Patricio. The crowd instantly began to applaud in a bid to rouse their team – and despite a lack of chances Wolves did respond well for the rest of the half.

In a theme of the first 45 minutes, Romain Saiss – restored to his traditional midfield role – showed Wolves' dogged approach by regularly winning the ball back. The problem came after that – they struggled to keep possession (32 per cent) and couldn't muster a shot on target.

Jota was looking to make the most of his opportunity and he dug out a cross for Raul Jimenez, who headed over, before Gibbs-White was denied a free shot from 15 yards by a superb last-ditch Cesc Fabregas tackle. Talking of last-ditch tackles, Bennett then produced one of the best you'll see anywhere all season. Willian raced through on goal and was about to pull the trigger before Bennett arrived from nowhere to wipe out man and ball.

Chelsea sporadically threatened and Patricio had to be at full stretch to tip a Willian free-kick over, but generally Wolves competed well and the scoreline was a fair reflection of the half. For the first 10 minutes of the second period, Wolves were chasing shadows – they needed a spark from somewhere and it was the academy youngster Gibbs-White who provided it. He dropped a shoulder and broke from midfield before playing a perfect through-ball for Jimenez, who struck low and through keeper Kepa Arrizabalaga from 10 yards to send Molineux potty.

The momentum was with Wolves and just four minutes later they completed a stunning and scarcely-believable turnaround to take the lead. Joao Moutinho played wide to Matt Doherty, whose low ball across the face was placed absolutely perfectly for Jota to slam home his first goal of the season. A giddy Molineux was the loudest it's been all year.

Gibbs-White was afforded a rapturous standing ovation when he was replaced by Helder Costa with 18 minutes to play and then Dendoncker replaced Jimenez to signal a change of tack as Wolves went defensive. Nuno wildly flailed his arms to try and raise the volume at an increasingly nervous Molineux, as Chelsea controlled the ball with Wolves sat deeper – but five minutes of stoppage time passed by without a chance for the visitors as Wolves held on for a stirring victory.

NUNO

Playing against Chelsea and coming from behind, it's great. I think it was a good performance, even in the first half. We were behind, but we stayed organised and compact. Chelsea have enormous quality – their players and Sarri's possession of the ball is hard to deal with. It requires effort and running. The boys did that. They stayed in the game. When we got the equaliser, I think not only me but Molineux felt we were back in the game. Credit to the boys for the way they believed and the way they worked, and for the fans – how they became so noisy and pushed the team.

FAN VERDICT - ROB CARTWRIGHT

What crisis? Nuno was spot on with his team selection and his tactical substitutions. Chelsea play quick, slick football and are good at keeping the ball. Wolves never gave them a second. Our midfield and wing-backs were definitely more at it than we have seen recently; breaking up their patterns of play and winning the second balls. It's hard to understand the difference between this performance and the last two games. Everyone stepped up. My head says Bennett for man of the match, but my heart awards it to Gibbs-White. To start this game was a massive step up for him and a show of faith that Nuno has in him. He played forward and caused problems for Chelsea.

POSSESSION: 30% / 70% | SHOTS: 6 / 17 | SHOTS ON TARGET: 2 / 3 | CORNERS: 1 / 5 | FOULS: 18 / 10 | BOOKINGS: 4 / 4

STAR MAN – MORGAN GIBBS-WHITE

Became the youngest player to set up a Premier League goal against Chelsea since Francis Jeffers for Everton in 1999. Gibbs-White wasn't even born then. A huge responsibility was on his shoulders, playing in a new role against such quality opposition, but the 18-year-old played with the carefree nature of a kid down the local park. His enthusiasm, positivity and energy are all infectious but it's the serious quality Gibbs-White is now showing that's really impressing. Only 27 touches but boy did he make them count. This kid can be a star.

TWEET OF THE GAME

 Tim Spiers ✔
@tim_spiers_Star

- A fabulous comeback victory
- A Jota goal
- Gibbs-White announcing himself
- Long throws
- A new formation
- Leander Dendoncker

What a night at Molineux. What a night.

5 Dec 2018

TABLE

	TEAM	P	GD	PTS
9	LEICESTER	15	3	22
10	BRIGHTON	15	-2	21
11	WATFORD	15	-3	20
12	WOLVES	15	-3	19
13	WEST HAM	15	-3	18
14	NEWCASTLE	15	-8	13
15	CRYSTAL PALACE	15	-9	12

ANALYSIS

When Morgan Gibbs-White made his league debut 18 months ago, he did little of note and was replaced after 54 minutes. On his full Premier League debut, he took on the might of Chelsea and produced a match-changing moment that inspired a famous Wolves win. The boy has become a man.

After weeks of the same old story, the same tactics, the same formation and pretty much the same players – all yielding pretty much the same result – this was maverick Nuno's Sgt Pepper. The Wolves boss changed his spots and went experimental. A new formation? Yep, Gibbs-White in the '10' in a 3-5-2. Plan B? Sure, long-throws from Ryan Bennett of course (!). Leander Dendoncker? Sorry, who? Ah yes, he came on for his Premier League debut. Nuno has come across as stubborn in these last few weeks, but this was a marked departure from his usual thinking – and boy did it work.

Recalling Bennett and Diogo Jota to the line-up may have seemed a little more obvious but the two players would contribute immeasurably to this vital victory.

Bennett had been dropped at Cardiff but responded to his instant recall with a superb performance and a game-changing moment, when he raced back quicker than Usain Bolt desperate for the toilet to catch Willian and deny him a free shot at goal with a thunderous and perfectly-timed sliding tackle that took man and ball. It was a brave and exceptional challenge.

Wolves' answer to Tessa Sanderson also came

up with, completely out of the blue, a series of looping long throws as Wolves enlisted a new tactic for an alternative route to goal, coincidentally or not just a few days after being troubled by Cardiff's same approach.

Bennett wasn't just floating them in either – they had dip and bend and caused Chelsea problems.

As for Jota, not only did he finally net his first goal since April, arriving in familiar fashion at the back post to slam home Matt Doherty's low cross and generating unadulterated carnage in the stands, but he also caused Chelsea numerous problems with a galvanising attacking performance.

Jota, who has struggled for form and fitness all season so far, gave absolutely everything to the cause and epitomised the 'never give up' approach Nuno had called for.

> ## "IT WAS A PLEASURE TO PLAY – WE HAVE A GOOD TEAM AND IT WAS A GREAT ATMOSPHERE."
> LEANDER DENDONCKER

Romain Saiss also excelled in midfield, the back three were absolutely outstanding, Joao Moutinho rediscovered his mojo and Gibbs-White showed confidence and pizazz, as well as his enormous potential, when producing the moment that changed that match, teeing up Raul Jimenez for the equaliser before Jota's big moment.

It's been a few weeks, but Wolves are back in some style. Just when you think they're struggling, they go and produce one of the best nights this stadium has seen in recent decades. Nuno, we never doubted you.

THIS WAS MAVERICK NUNO'S SGT PEPPER

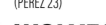

NEWCASTLE UNITED **1**

(PEREZ 23)

 WOLVES **2**

(JOTA 17, DOHERTY 90+4)

Newcastle United (3-5-2): Dubravka; Lascelles (c), Fernandez (Manquillo 46), Clark; Yedlin, Diame, Ki, Atsu (Kenedy 89), Ritchie; Perez, Rondon (Joselu 86). Subs not used: Woodman, Dummett, Muto, Longstaff.

Wolves (3-4-3): Patricio; Bennett, Coady (c), Boly; Doherty, Saiss (Gibbs-White 60), Neves, Vinagre; Costa (Moutinho 76), Traore (Jimenez 60), Jota. Subs not used: Ruddy, Cavaleiro, Dendoncker, Bonatini.

The Wolves we know and love are very much back. And so is Diogo Jota. Two games, six points and two very dramatic victories that have seen them soar back into the top half of the table.

It looked for all the world that this would be an afternoon of frustration for Nuno Espirito Santo's side. They had been 1-0 up and then a man up – but also toiled for long spells in a game low on quality. Then, with just seconds left, that never-say-die attitude came to the fore once again as they struck their second last-minute winner of the season via the head of the tireless Matt Doherty.

What a moment – and it was Jota who created it, channelling his inner Maradona with a jinking run from deep. Jota's earlier goal, superbly well taken, was his second in two games and the Portuguese forward looks to have finally rediscovered his elusive confidence. This was a rank game at times but there are so many positives for Wolves to take. After selecting the same XI for so long at the start of the season, a horses for courses approach may now benefit them going forward. Either way, it's great to have the collective smile back on the face of this club. What a difference a week makes.

Nuno surprisingly made three changes from the team that had so brilliantly beaten Chelsea 2-1 on Wednesday. He reverted to his tried and trusted 3-4-3 formation and left out Joao Moutinho and Raul Jimenez for the first time this season, with Morgan Gibbs-White joining them on the bench. In came Adama Traore, Helder Costa and the suspension-free Ruben Neves. The hope

was that Wolves would take confidence and momentum from that Chelsea win into the game – and they certainly did in the opening stages.

Nuno's team looked assured in possession and were full of attacking intent. The front three were combining to great effort with Traore, in particular, making a great start to the game. After a few early corners and plenty of Wolves pressure, they took the lead after 17 minutes with a seriously classy goal. Costa drifted inside from the right, looked up and delivered a perfect cross towards Jota, who had time to chest the ball down and coolly beat keeper Martin Dubravka from close range. It was a long-awaited first assist of the season from Costa and a second goal in two games for Jota, who previously hadn't netted since April.

Wolves were full of beans and in complete control – but then the whole dynamic of the game changed when Newcastle equalised against the run of play. Salomon Rondon struck a wicked 20-yard free kick which cannoned off the underside of the bar. Wolves didn't clear their lines or push out of the box and when Rondon swung the ball back in, Ayoze Perez stole a march on Conor Coady to flick an impressive header past a helpless Rui Patricio.

Thereafter Wolves' quality on the ball and threat up top both vanished. They sat deeper, continuously gave the ball away with Traore and an off-colour Neves guilty more than most, and also gave away a succession of silly free-kicks. Nuno repeatedly and ruefully shook his head as he watched his team's control disintegrate. A dull game reignited on the hour mark when Jota

nicked the ball off a hesitant DeAndre Yedlin, who cynically pulled the forward back as he hared towards the box. Jamaal Lascelles was covering nearby but referee Mike Dean had no hesitation in showing the American a red card.

On came Gibbs-White and Jimenez for Romain Saiss and Traore as Wolves looked to take full advantage, but they didn't create a single chance in the next 15 minutes. Then Jimenez smacked a piledriver against the underside of the bar, before Doherty's left-footed curler was brilliantly tipped wide by Dubravka. The three points were there for the taking – and with just seconds to go Wolves took them. Jota embarked on a jinking run from deep and saw his shot saved by Dubravka but Doherty, who sprinted fully 50 yards in the dying seconds, headed home the rebound to spark ecstatic scenes on the pitch, on the sidelines and in the stands.

They left it very, very late, but the result was all that mattered. Nuno, the man who strives for the perfection he can never achieve, will have been disappointed with the manner in which his team went from being a dominant, composed and attacking team in the early stages to a side that couldn't string two passes together. Ultimately, did it matter? No. Many would have taken a point here and Wolves gleefully gobbled up all three in exhilarating fashion.

NUNO

We know how difficult it is to achieve back-to-back wins in the Premier League, so I must be happy, of course. Getting a goal in the last minute, you cannot disguise it. You have to be happy (but) the performance, we are going to analyse. It was not, for moments, one of the best ones. But it was consistent enough for me to say that we stayed on the game. We stayed in shape. It's very difficult to play against 10 men, credit to Newcastle, they didn't sit down. They created problems. It was a very tough game. St James' Park is a very, very difficult place to come and compete like we did, so well done to the boys. All my respect goes to Rafa as I really admire him as a coach.

FAN VERDICT – ADAM VIRGO

Nothing beats a last minute winner. This was nowhere near our best performance but there's been plenty of times this season where we've drawn or lost when we should have had a better result. It was an interesting team selection but I can only imagine he rested a few key players ahead of a busy schedule. It's not always easy to break down 10 men as we found out against Everton in the opening game of the season but thankfully we got a breakthrough – for Doherty to run 50 yards or so up the pitch at that time and head in a rebound just goes to show the effort he puts in.

POSSESSION: **50% / 50%** | SHOTS: **12 / 13** | SHOTS ON TARGET: **4 / 6** | CORNERS: **4 / 6** | FOULS: **10 / 17** | BOOKINGS: **2 / 5** | REDS: **1 / 0**

STAR MAN – DIOGO JOTA

Diogo Jota is well and truly back. Two games, two goals, one assist – that's what you call end product. Classy finish for the opener and a jinking, teasing run for the winner. Also caused the Yedlin red card when he nipped in and won possession, with some classic Jota pressing and attacking intent. We all know how good this guy is and he's starting to bring his game to the big stage.

TWEET OF THE GAME

 Tim Spiers ✔
@tim_spiers_Star

Jota WHAT A RUN it's Maradona 86 they can;t get ball off him shot saved and DOHERTY HEADS IN THE REBOUND

                          9 Dec 2018

TABLE

	TEAM	P	GD	PTS
7	EVERTON	15	4	23
8	BOURNEMOUTH	16	-1	23
9	LEICESTER	16	1	22
10	WOLVES	16	-2	22
11	WEST HAM	16	-2	21
12	BRIGHTON	16	-3	21
13	WATFORD	15	-3	20

WOLVES
(JIMENEZ 12, CAVALEIRO 90+4)

 BOURNEMOUTH

2

0

 **Premier League**

MOLINEUX STADIUM, 3PM
DECEMBER 15, 2018 ATTENDANCE: 30,997 (1,785 AWAY)

Wolves (3-4-1-2): Patricio; Bennett, Coady (c), Boly; Doherty, Neves, Moutinho, Otto; Gibbs-White (Saiss 75); Jimenez (Cavaleiro 89), Jota (Costa 46). Subs not used: Ruddy, Dendoncker, Vinagre, Traore.

Bournemouth (3-4-2-1): Begovic; Cook, Ake, Mings (Rico 36); Ibe (Wilson 58), Surman (c), Lerma, Daniels; Stanislas (Mousset 80), Fraser; King. Subs not used: Boruc, Pugh, Brooks, Defoe.

Wolves had played 304 games in English football's top flight since they last won three in a row, when beating Coventry 3-1 in March 1980. John Richards scored a brace that day and, while Raul Jimenez is extremely unlikely to get anywhere King John's phenomenal Wolves goalscoring tally, boy is he making a big impact for them this season. That's five goals and five assists for the Mexican before we've even reached the halfway point of the campaign. If he gets to 10 goals and 10 assists then that £30m option fee next summer won't sound too outlandish at all. In that 1979/80 campaign Wolves finished sixth – they're now up to seventh and the way they're progressing as a team you wouldn't bet against Nuno Espirito Santo's boys finishing in the upper echelons of the division.

A top-half finish should certainly now be their minimum aim, given the position they're in and the quality they possess. As at Newcastle they weren't at their best, but defended well to keep a first clean sheet since early October. They're playing different formations, utilising different players and finding different ways to win football matches. For the teams around them, that's ominous.

Nuno made four changes to the team that beat Newcastle last weekend. In came Morgan Gibbs-White, Jimenez, Joao Moutinho and the returning Jonny Castro Otto, back two weeks earlier than expected from a knee injury. The unfortunate Ruben Vinagre and Romain Saiss both dropped to the bench, as did Adama Traore and Helder Costa, as Nuno rejigged his formation back to the 3-4-1-2 he enlisted against

Chelsea. There was a boost for Wolves with Bournemouth unable to field new England striker Callum Wilson from the start owing to injury, but the Cherries didn't look too weakened by the absence of their star striker, producing some enterprising football in an even first half.

Wolves soon began to settle into their stride and it was the in-form Diogo Jota who inspired their opening goal on 12 minutes. The Portuguese forward intercepted a slack Bournemouth pass and dribbled towards the box, taking on Jordan Ibe before his cross-shot was turned in by Jimenez at the back post. That warmed the fans up inside a freezing Molineux and might have been the signal for Wolves to take control, but it remained an even game with Bournemouth attacking at pace and finding gaps in the Wolves third. Junior Stanislas ballooned over the bar from a good position and then Ryan Fraser used his electrifying pace to get the better of Conor Coady, but his low cross was unrewarded.

On the stroke of half-time came a big moment in the game. Jimenez released Jota through on goal with a gorgeous curved pass – Jota was vying with Steve Cook who forcefully shoulder-barged him to the floor just outside the penalty area. That was the end of the afternoon for Jota who hobbled off, having arguably been Wolves' best player in the first half. The good news was Wolves were ahead at the break for only the second time this season.

The rain worsened at the start of the second half with the swirling wind generating atrocious conditions. Ruben Neves hit a deflected shot wide, Jimenez had a promising effort blocked

and ex-Wolves man Andrew Surman sent a low effort past the post as the two sides continued to trade blows. Then the lively Gibbs-White released Costa with a perfect pass down the right – he raced inside and into the box but slashed a right-footed shot horribly wide at the near post, to the loud frustration of all those inside Molineux as several players put their head in their hands. Junior Stanislas bent a vicious 20-yard free-kick onto the top of the crossbar, before Rui Patricio did well to get behind a powerfully-struck Jefferson Lerma shot from range. It was a nervy end to the game – but in added time Wolves sealed the win when substitute Ivan Cavaleiro broke, exchanged passes with Costa, homed in on goal and beat the keeper with aplomb.

As Nuno would say, a 'tough, tough game'. But Wolves prevailed and what will have pleased the boss more than anything is a rare clean sheet and, for all Bournemouth's play in the final third, few clear-cut chances conceded. Five years ago Wolves were losing 2-0 at home to MK Dons in League One. These days they're seventh in the Premier League and, tantalisingly, have plenty of room for improvement. Several of their players aren't at the top of their game yet – if they can find their top form (and Jota and Jimenez are warming up nicely) who knows what this team can achieve in the coming months.

NUNO

I'm very proud of the boys because they made it possible – they achieved it through their hard work. I'm happy for our fans because we achieved something together that is very special. It's the most difficult competition in the world. We were versatile enough to see the game was about being compact. It was about being robust, balanced and defending – waiting for the right moments to try to achieve what we did. The clean sheet was very, very important. It was cold, wasn't it? Credit to everybody – the fans and especially for the players. It was hard to play football for both teams. Whoever loves football loves these types of games.

FAN VERDICT – GULRAJ KULAR

Three wins in a row in the top flight. What is this giddy feeling I'm getting? It's addictive. Truth be told – none of the last three performances have been vintage Nuno – and how satisfying it has been to see us take nine points. Raul Jimenez, the centre of much talk this week regarding his price tag, showed exactly why he may be valued so highly. A man who combines technique with tenacity in such a way that it's hard to compare to any other striker I've seen in recent years. Think Kevin Doyle, but with an awareness that makes him a much more potent force to be reckoned with.

POSSESSION: 38% / 62% | SHOTS: 10 / 13 | SHOTS ON TARGET: 4 / 3 | CORNERS: 5 / 3 | FOULS: 15 / 7 | BOOKINGS: 1 / 2

STAR MAN – RAUL JIMENEZ

The best thing to come out of Mexico since fully loaded nachos. What a fantastic signing this guy has been. Only £3m for the season on loan and he's more than repaid that already with five goals and five assists. If he continues that ratio and reaches 10 goals and 10 assists by the end of the campaign he'll also be worth the £30m option Wolves have for him. Yes, he's that good. Obviously it's not just about the stats with this guy – his work ethic and his link play is absolutely imperative to Wolves' success in the final third of the pitch. Also sent Jota through with a beautiful curved pass. More than anything, though, he manfully defended from the front (which towards the end of the game meant being as deep as 30 yards from his own goal).

TWEET OF THE GAME

Tim Spiers ✔
@tim_spiers_Star

Christmas party for the players tonight. I reckon they might enjoy themselves after that.

                     15 Dec 2018

TABLE

	TEAM	P	GD	PTS
4	CHELSEA	16	20	34
5	ARSENAL	16	15	34
6	MAN UTD	16	2	26
7	WOLVES	17	0	25
8	EVERTON	17	2	24
9	WEST HAM	17	0	24
10	WATFORD	17	-2	24

 **WOLVES**

 **LIVERPOOL**
(SALAH 18, VAN DIJK 68)

 0

 2

MOLINEUX STADIUM, 8PM
DECEMBER 21, 2018 ATTENDANCE: **31,358** (2,970 AWAY)

 **Premier League**

Wolves (3-4-1-2): *Patricio; Bennett, Coady (c), Boly; Doherty, Saiss, Neves, Otto (Vinagre 81); Moutinho (Gibbs-White 63); Traore (Cavaleiro 63), Jimenez. Subs not used: Ruddy, Dendoncker, Costa, Bonatini*
Liverpool (4-3-3): *Alisson; Milner, Van Dijk, Lovren, Robertson; Fabinho, Keita (Lallana 58), Henderson (c); Mane (Clyne 87), Firmino (Wijnaldum 76), Salah. Subs not used: Mignolet, Shaqiri, Sturridge, Origi.*

There's a right way to lose and a wrong way to lose a football match. This was the right way. Wolves gave everything against the Premier League leaders, who showed them a deep level of respect. Gone are the days when they big boys would rest a couple of star players when they came to Molineux, or took the home team lightly. Liverpool went full strength and knew they'd be in for a hell of a contest. It certainly proved that way in the first half when Wolves were arguably the better side.

They certainly created more chances and were pegging the unbeaten – and uncomfortable – Reds back, mustering a succession of decent opportunities through their daring attacking ventures. After Liverpool looked to kill the game at 2-0 Wolves still piled forward and should have scored twice. In fact the greatest compliment you can pay Nuno's team is that the only glaring difference between these two sides was in the opposition box, where Liverpool capitalised on Wolves' minor lapses in concentration and not vice versa.

As Nuno revealed on Thursday, Diogo Jota wasn't fit enough to play after suffering a hamstring injury. Adama Traore got the nod to replace him, while Romain Saiss replaced Morgan Gibbs-White in a midfield that looked set up to try and frustrate the league leaders and exploit Traore's pace on the counter attack. Liverpool brought in James Milner and Jordan Henderson as they looked to extend their lead over Manchester City at the top of the table. After a breathtaking music and lights show before kick-off which felt more suited to Ibiza than Whitmore Reans, complete with

enough fireworks to bring down the Houses of Parliament, the stage was set for the biggest occasion of Wolves' season so far – and an entertaining first half didn't disappoint.

Wolves had clearly done their homework and pressed Liverpool high early doors. It wasn't a tactic the Reds looked comfortable against. That was typified when Joao Moutinho intercepted a slack pass and played to Traore, who lashed a shot wide. Traore was the main outlet for Wolves in the first half, with Raul Jimenez the key to unlocking that door. The Mexican set the Spaniard flying towards the box after great hold-up play and this time Traore drilled across goal and wide, before Saiss also went close.

A team with as much quality and confidence as Liverpool were never going to stay mute for long and it would be Jurgen Klopp's side who opened the scoring. A momentary lapse of concentration saw Fabinho get in behind Willy Boly and Ruben Neves – he got to the byline and picked out Mo Salah, who was half a yard ahead of Conor Coady and produced a clinical low finish. Liverpool were now in their stride and Milner cut inside Moutinho and fired ominously from 20 yards, but Rui Patricio was behind it.

After finding their feet again it was Wolves who ended the half the stronger side. Matt Doherty brilliantly barged inside, played a one-two with Moutinho and passed to Jimenez who was open, but he delayed his shot and it was blocked. Then Doherty was picked out on the right and he fired one goalwards which Alisson pawed away at his near post – it was a rousing end to the half from determined Wolves, who were duly loudly

applauded from the field at half-time at a soaking wet Molineux.

Liverpool began to show off their table-topping pedigree after the break, creating a number of half chances before killing the game off with a second goal. Salah chipped the ball into the box, Ryan Bennett couldn't get anything on it and defender Virgil van Dijk guided home from close range. A defiant South Bank were still singing as they looked to rouse their team – and within two minutes Wolves should have pulled one back when Doherty headed a cross back into a crowd of players and the ball dropped perfectly for Saiss, but his snap-shot from only 12 yards was straight at Alisson. Thereafter the game died a death, but in the closing minutes Wolves again should have reduced the deficit. A cross hit Andy Robertson's heel and Gibbs-White should have netted from six yards, but could only find the side netting. It just wasn't Wolves' night.

There is, of course, no shame whatsoever losing to a team of this calibre. Liverpool were the best side Wolves have faced so far – in Salah they had a magician who danced by challenges at will and the only way Wolves would have got any change out of the imperious Van Dijk was if he pulled a couple of 10p coins out his pocket. If they approach their next fixture, away at lowly Fulham, with the same professionalism, fearlessness and daring, they'll soon be back in the points.

POSSESSION: 38% / 62% | SHOTS: 11 / 15 | SHOTS ON TARGET: 5 / 6 | CORNERS: 1 / 10 | FOULS: 7 / 3 | BOOKINGS: 0 / 0

STAR MAN - ROMAIN SAISS

Surely making a case for himself to be a regular starter now? He's been superb in his past few appearances and, after being brought back into the XI here to add some defensive steel, he was arguably Wolves' best player. Bit of an all-action display – he should have scored just after Van Dijk's goal but he kept several attacks going with his persistence and commitment. Five interceptions was the most of the pitch. Very impressive.

TWEET OF THE GAME

 Tim Spiers ✔
@tim_spiers_Star

Full-time, 0-2. Wolves gave a great account of themselves. No shame in losing to this team and the biggest compliment I can pay Wolves is that the only glaring difference in the teams was in the opposition box. Liverpool took advantage of Wolves' mistakes, but not vice versa.

                     21 Dec 2018

TABLE

	TEAM	P	GD	PTS
4	CHELSEA	17	21	37
5	ARSENAL	17	14	34
6	MAN UTD	17	0	26
7	WOLVES	18	-2	25
8	EVERTON	17	2	24
9	WEST HAM	17	0	24
10	WATFORD	17	-2	24

FULHAM
(SESSEGNON 74)

WOLVES
(SAISS 85)

1
1

Fulham (5-2-3): Rico; Christie, Odoi, Mawson, Ream, Bryan; Seri (McDonald 82), Chambers; Kamara (Cairney 73), Mitrovic (c), Schurrle (Sessegnon 67). Subs not used: Bettinelli, Le Marchand, Vietto, Ayite.

Wolves (3-4-1-2): Patricio; Bennett, Coady (c), Boly; Doherty, Moutinho, Saiss, Otto (Vinagre 82); Gibbs-White (Costa 63); Jimenez, Traore (Cavaleiro 45). Subs not used: Ruddy, Kilman, Neves, Bonatini.

Romain Saiss doesn't score too many goals – but in early Boxing Day kick-offs played in the depths of London, he absolutely loves to. For two years in a row, Wolves have set their alarm clocks for a maddeningly early hour on December 26 ahead of a testing away day. Last year it was Millwall, this year it was Fulham. On both occasions, a Saiss goal has earned them a point and on both occasions Wolves have been grateful for that point. The Moroccan barely featured at the start of the campaign but has become a key cog in this evolving team, making a positive impact in each game he's played since his first start of the season on November 30.

Nuno dropped Ruben Neves for the first time in his Wolves career, with Morgan Gibbs-White restored to the XI in the only change from the side that lost 2-0 to Liverpool on Friday night. Nuno highlighted pre-match the danger of Aleksandar Mitrovic, who had caused Wolves no end of problems in their 2-0 defeat here in February. Those warnings weren't heeded during a first half in which the Serb ran them ragged at times, while in return Wolves mustered only three shots at goal in an off-colour display. The ball didn't stick up top, Gibbs-White struggled to find space, the midfield weren't great on the ball and the three centre-halves all looked flustered and panicked against Mitrovic, who led the line superbly.

The only positive at the break for Nuno's team is that it somehow remained goalless. That was despite a decent opening few minutes in which Raul Jimenez almost scored a wonder-goal when he brilliantly chested the ball with his back to goal and acrobatically volleyed over

from 10 yards. Wolves initially handled Mitrovic well, with Conor Coady denying a barging run with a perfect sliding tackle, but thereafter he began to become influential, heading wide from a good position and seeing a couple of goal-bound efforts blocked. He then fired over from 15 yards before starting and ending a brisk counter-attack, with Rui Patricio saving his header. Andre Schurrle played a one-two with the former Newcastle striker and fired at Patricio and then Mitrovic created the chance of the half, picking up Coady's header and slaloming past both Willy Boly and Coady before Patricio saved the day, coming off his line to block from point-blank range.

Nuno reacted at half-time, withdrawing the anonymous Adama Traore and sending on Ivan Cavaleiro and the change made an instant difference with Cavaleiro combining with Jonny Castro Otto down the left. Wolves were finally playing on the front foot and using their width to good effect. Jimenez headed just wide from Otto's cross and the Mexican then curled one at keeper Sergio Rico as Wolves dominated the first 15 minutes of the half. They were attempting piercing, probing passes and Gibbs-White was more effective in an advanced position, while at the other end Saiss was sitting deeper to try and combat the Mitrovic threat. Substitute Ryan Sessegnon made an instant impact at the other end, haring past Ryan Bennett and crossing low for Aboubakar Kamara to tap home – but Boly got in a crucial touch to divert it clear.

That seemed to give Fulham some belief – and a couple of minutes later they took the lead through that man Sessegnon. Wolves' struggles

with defending set pieces were evident again as Patricio, under pressure, shanked a punch straight to Sessegnon, whose right-footed volley crossed the line before Coady could clear it. Nuno's team had enjoyed 77 per cent of the ball in the second half up to this point, but with no end product they were always vulnerable to a sucker punch and that's how it proved. With time quickly running out the head coach sent on Ruben Vinagre for Otto as Wolves probed for that killer pass... and it was Cavaleiro who provided it with only five minutes left. He sent a vicious ball across the face of goal – Jimenez missed it, Helder Costa couldn't reach it, but after the ball bounced off a defender Saiss couldn't miss from a yard out. Wolves searched for a winner, but from a simple long kick forward from Rico they nearly lost it in injury time – Mitrovic beat a flailing Bennett to the ball and send it trickling towards the goal, but Coady charged back to make an heroic goal-line clearance just in the nick of time. Saiss sent a 30-yarder only inches past the post in a frantic end to an entertaining game.

Those closing minutes resembled two knackered boxers slugging at each other in the 12th round – Wolves could easily have won it or lost it. In the circumstances, then, they'll take a point. But big improvements are needed at Wembley on Saturday if they're not to go on another winless run. Whatever happens there, the issue of them struggling against sides that try and stop them playing won't go away.

NUNO

As the season goes on, these kind of games will be more and more likely because the results mean so much to the teams. When they scored I really felt it was unfair because we had so much of the ball. I think we were rewarded when we scored, but it was tough, a tough game. The football is not so open and well played. I'm very happy with the second half performance, but first half I think we didn't quite get in the game. We had a lot of the ball and moved the ball around, but Fulham were so organised and there was no space. It was so tight, so compact, which made it difficult.

FAN VERDICT – RUSS EVERS

A better result than we managed at Craven Cottage last season and an away point is always welcome. However, I just get the feeling that this type of result will not be tolerated next season and beyond. We certainly seemed to have more about us than Fulham without especially doing much with all the possession we had. Cavaleiro made a huge difference when introduced from the bench and we deserved at least the point we earned, courtesy of the very hard-working Saiss. Hopefully, we have left something in the tank for Saturday's big trip to Wembley but we may need a little more against Spurs to gain a point or more.

POSSESSION: 30% / 70% | **SHOTS: 11 / 14** | **SHOTS ON TARGET: 5 / 5** | **CORNERS: 2 / 0** | **FOULS: 9 / 6** | **BOOKINGS: 2 / 1**

STAR MAN – JOAO MOUTINHO

He'll have had pheasant for his Christmas Day lunch. And some sort of fancy red wine-infused gravy - the guy is too classy for turkey and Bisto. After a below-par few weeks this was Moutinho at his dominant best. Well, it was in the second half at least. Drove Wolves on with some piercing and probing passes, but also won no fewer than eight tackles, the highest number produced by a Wolves player this season (the next highest was seven by, yes, Moutinho at Leicester and also Otto at West Ham). Played his part in the equaliser when he slipped Cavaleiro in. Other than that he did find it difficult to thread the needle, but it wasn't for a lack of trying.

TWEET OF THE GAME

Tim Spiers ✔
@tim_spiers_Star

After a really poor first half Wolves did improve markedly after the break in terms of probing with possession, albeit without creating much. Cavaleiro and Moutinho both impressed. Last five minutes were carnage.

26 Dec 2018

TABLE

	TEAM	P	GD	PTS
7	LEICESTER	19	2	28
8	EVERTON	19	2	27
9	WATFORD	19	-1	27
10	WOLVES	19	-2	26
11	BOURNEMOUTH	19	-6	26
12	WEST HAM	18	-2	24
13	BRIGHTON	19	-6	22

TOTTENHAM HOTSPUR 1
(KANE 22)

WOLVES 3
(BOLY 72, JIMENEZ 83, COSTA 87)

WEMBLEY, 3PM
DECEMBER 29, 2018 ATTENDANCE: 46,356 (3,158 AWAY)

Tottenham (4-2-3-1): Lloris (c); Trippier, Sanchez, Alderweireld, Davies; Winks, Sissoko; Son, Eriksen, Alli (Moura, 68); Kane. Subs not used: Gazzaniga, Walker-Peters, Foyth, Rose, Skipp, Nkoudou.

Wolves (3-4-3): Patricio; Bennett, Coady (c), Boly; Doherty, Dendoncker (Moutinho 68), Neves, Otto; Traore (Costa 59), Jimenez, Cavaleiro (Gibbs-White 85). Subs not used: Ruddy, Vinagre, Saiss, Bonatini.

As the clocked passed 90 minutes the Wolves supporters sang "we want four". Away at Spurs. At Wembley. This was a phenomenal victory. Spurs had thrashed Everton 6-2 and annihilated Bournemouth 5-0 in their previous two games. Wonderful Wolves – who the bookies had down as huge 9/1 outsiders to win – reduced them to a total of precisely zero shots at goal in the entirety of the second half. On their first trip to Wembley since 1988, they proved yet again that in 2018/19 they 1) love the big occasion and 2) should never, ever, be written off.

Nuno, not for the first time in recent weeks, sprang a surprise with his team selection. Leander Dendoncker was handed his full Premier League debut and Ruben Neves was restored to the XI, with both Joao Moutinho and Romain Saiss dropping to the bench. Spurs selected about as strong a side as possible with the injury-free Dele Alli joining Harry Kane, Christian Eriksen and Son Heung-Min in an attacking and perhaps daunting line-up, given the fact Mauricio Pochettino's side had scored 11 goals in their past two matches.

It was no surprise the hosts had the better of the first half. They enjoyed 67 per cent possession and produced 10 shots to Wolves' three. However, most of the attempts from the home side were from long range, with Wolves defending well as a unit and restricting the influence of Eriksen. It was just a shame that one of those long-range shots found the corner, via the thunderous left boot of Kane, who picked the ball up from Son, cut in from the right and send a piledriver past Rui Patricio,

who got a hand to the ball but couldn't stop it going in. In the build-up to the goal Willy Boly had fed Ivan Cavaleiro with a strong pass and the Portuguese player's touch was heavy, but he was also blocked off by Harry Winks. Referee Stuart Attwell gave no foul.

That wasn't the only controversial Attwell decision – he had earlier turned Wolves down for a penalty when Ben Davies appeared to block Adama Traore's cross with his hand, albeit from point-blank range. Most of Wolves' attacks came via the very lively Traore, who was enjoying running at Davies from deep and caused his fair share of problems. One scintillating run saw him run a ring around Eriksen, while he also fed Raul Jimenez with a couple of nice passes and floated a cross towards Cavaleiro who looked set to nod home, but the ball was just taken off his head. Wolves also looked to trouble Spurs from set-pieces, with Ryan Bennett sending a header over from a decent position.

Make no mistake, though, the hosts were dominant for the most part. Alli curled one over, Son drilled an effort just past the post, Conor Coady had to make a perfect sliding tackle in the box to deny the same player and then Patricio had to be at his very best to tip a curling Eriksen shot over the bar with a magnificent save. It was a satisfactory first period for Nuno's boys, who were very much still in the game.

Traore got Wolves moving early in the second half, but again Cavaleiro couldn't quite get on the end of his teasing cross. And the same combination again nearly yielded something for Wolves a minute later – Traore

exploded forward from midfield and almost found Cavaleiro with a through-ball, however Hugo Lloris had raced out his box to clear. Wolves suffered a blow when Traore departed appearing to clutch his hamstring – he slowly trudged off to be placed by Helder Costa. The visitors were seeing plenty of possession and Moutinho replaced a tiring Dendoncker on 67 minutes and helped up the tempo.

Wolves were continuously winning the ball back from the hosts, who could barely get out their own half. It was constant pressure – and then came their reward. Moutinho floated a perfect outswinging corner on to the head of Boly, who planted a booming header past Lloris to send 3,000 fans absolutely wild in the far corner at Wembley. But that was just the start of it. Wolves continued to attack and nine minutes later Cavaleiro danced forward before feeding Jimenez, who cutely sidefooted through Toby Alderweireld's legs and into the bottom corner past Lloris.

There was absolute bedlam in the away end – but hungry Wolves weren't done yet. Matt Doherty pushed forward and fed substitute Costa, who raced clear of the defence and coolly finished past a despairing Lloris dive. It was a scarcely believable scoreline – but Wolves fully merited their lead. Spurs hadn't had a shot all half. The Wolves fans sang "we want four" as their team sprayed it around the Wembley turf with the home supporters leaving in their droves. What a sight, what a day, what a win, what a team.

POSSESSION: 61% / 39% | **SHOTS: 10 / 11** | **SHOTS ON TARGET: 3 / 4** | **CORNERS: 6 / 7** | **FOULS: 7 / 7** | **BOOKINGS: 3 / 2**

STAR MAN – ADAMA TRAORE

The express train has returned to the station. It's been a while, but Traore being played in his preferred position yielded, lo and behold, a Traore-like performance. Picked the ball up from deep and ran at defenders in that madcap, slightly unhinged style of his that recalls memories of Jonah Lomu at the 1995 Rugby World Cup. Spurs' defence didn't know whether to laugh or cry, so they mostly tried to foul him. Floated over a couple of really nice crosses and slipped in a few teasing through balls that on another day would have yielded an assist or two. Most of all, though, he set the tone for what was to follow after his unfortunate departure with a tight hamstring.

TWEET OF THE GAME

Tim Spiers ✔
@tim_spiers_Star

Doherty on the break, slips a pass through to the RAMPAGING HELDER COSTA who so so COOLLY BEATS LLORIS FOR HIS FIRST GOAL OF THE SEASON AND WOLVES' THIRD OF THE DAY CAN YOU BELIEVE WHAT YOU'RE WITNESSING

29 Dec 2018

TABLE

	TEAM	P	GD	PTS
4	CHELSEA	19	21	40
5	ARSENAL	20	12	38
6	MAN UTD	19	6	32
7	WOLVES	20	0	29
8	LEICESTER	20	1	28
9	WATFORD	20	-1	28
10	EVERTON	20	1	27

ANALYSIS

Sometimes in life, you don't get what you deserve. This wasn't one of those days. Wolves enacted the perfect game plan, soaking up the Spurs pressure in the first half, restricting them to long shots. Then in the second half, they played. And my, did they play. In what was the exact opposite of smash and grab they dominated possession, pushed Spurs deeper and deeper and controlled play – and after 15 minutes of piling on the pressure they got exactly what they deserved with an equaliser. But they didn't stop there. They surged forward, they showed adventure, they showed audacity – and Spurs couldn't handle them. They played in the manner of a top six side. It was indicative of Nuno's Wolves – they don't sit back, they don't try and spoil games. They play to win – and in an increasingly special season, this day will be hard to beat.

Wolves took on a title contender on their 'own' vast turf – and for 45 minutes they completely outplayed them. Tottenham Hotspur had scored 11 goals in two matches. They were being talked up as title contenders. Yet in the second half they couldn't muster a single shot at goal. That wasn't due to tiredness – a feeble excuse offered by Mauricio Pochettino – and to suggest complacency doesn't explain it either. Both of those reasons would do Wolves a disservice and also fail to illustrate why they had been so dominant in the first half, peppering Rui Patricio's goal with long shots albeit without slicing Wolves open.

No, the reason Spurs wilted in the second period was because brilliant and commanding Wolves beat them into submission. After a first half in which they looked to counter Spurs and did well to stay in the game at 1-0, they upped the tempo after the break, pushed the hosts deeper, were tenacious at winning the ball back and played some sublime football. There was one five-minute spell when Spurs couldn't even get out their own half. The point is, this was no smash and grab. Wolves played like the quality side they are, they moved the ball wisely, they stretched Spurs, they prised them apart and they scored three goals to deservedly triumph in glorious circumstances. At the other end, Patricio could have worn slippers and mittens. It was quite something to witness.

The introduction of Joao Moutinho added a sprinkle of gold dust when Wolves were lacking a clinical and killer pass in the final third. Moutinho's set pieces often haven't hit the spot this season, but his beautifully-floated corner dropped on Willy Boly's head for the equaliser – and Wolves never looked back. It was a brave call from Nuno to leave Moutinho out after his virtuoso second-half display at Craven Cottage. And Romain Saiss could also count himself unfortunate to be dropped after barely putting a foot wrong in his previous few performances. But Nuno, who selected the same XI for the first nine matches this season, is now making good use of his squad – and Wolves look better for it. The back three were immense. Harry Kane didn't touch the ball inside the Wolves box on a single occasion, thanks largely to a true captain's performance from Conor Coady. Willy Boly was majestic at times, while Ryan Bennett was his usual solid self and even produced an outrageous back-heel flick down the line which was totally out of character, akin to Principal Skinner embarking on an LSD trip.

> ## "IN TERMS OF HOW WE PLAYED IT'S ONE OF THE BEST GAMES OF MY CAREER. IT WAS THOROUGHLY ENJOYABLE."
> **MATT DOHERTY**

With 20 games gone Wolves sit pretty in seventh and there is no reason why this team cannot finish in the position they currently sit. It wasn't just the fact they beat Spurs 3-1 on their own patch, it was the manner in which they achieved it. How many teams would have been tempted to shut up shop and play for 0-0, given the attacking class Spurs possess? That's not Nuno's way. Sure they've got the quality in their ranks to play that way, but Wolves deserve as much credit for their courage as their football ability. We are witnessing something special.

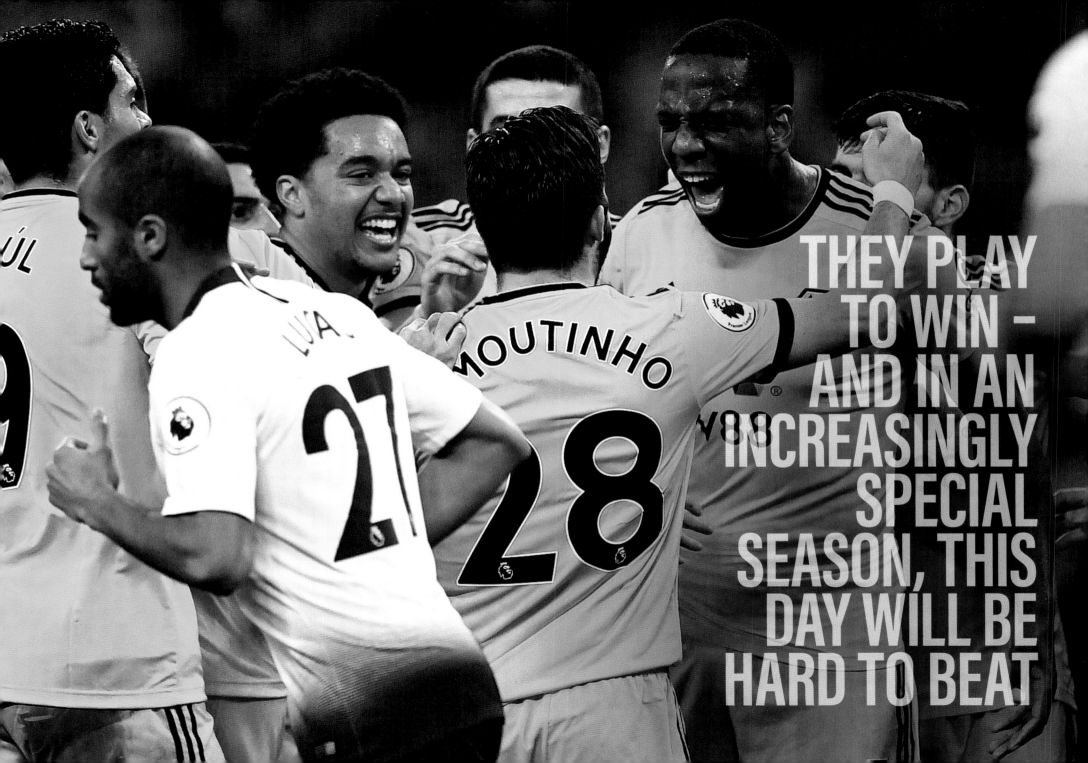

THEY PLAY TO WIN – AND IN AN INCREASINGLY SPECIAL SEASON, THIS DAY WILL BE HARD TO BEAT

 **WOLVES** **0**

 CRYSTAL PALACE **2**
(AYEW 83, MILIVOJEVIC PEN 90+5)

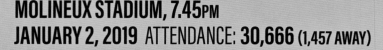 
Wolves (3-4-3): Patricio; Bennett, Coady (c), Boly; Doherty, Saiss (Neves 73), Moutinho, Otto; Costa (Gibbs-White 64), Jimenez, Cavaleiro (Traore 84). Subs not used: Ruddy, Dendoncker, Vinagre, Bonatini.
Crystal Palace (4-3-3): Guaita; Wan-Bissaka, Tomkins, Sakho, Van Aanholt; Milivojevic (c), Kouyate, McArthur; Townsend, Zaha, Ayew (Wickham 88). Subs not used: Hennessey, Ward, Kelly, Riedewald, Schlupp, Meyer.

At half-time in this game they showed a lengthy highlights reel of goals from what's been a great season for Wolves so far. It's safe to say nothing from this encounter will be added to the compilation.

Wolves' bugbear of failing to produce their big-game heroics against 'lesser' opposition came back to haunt them yet again as Crystal Palace nicked all three points from a tight and instantly forgettable encounter. At Wembley on Saturday Wolves were bold, brave, heroic and dripping with quality. They got exactly what they deserved. At Molineux last night they were none of those things – and got exactly what they deserved yet again. There was no tempo, little creativity, a lack of urgency and, importantly, no answers to the questions posed at them by a resolute and organised Palace side who always carried a threat on the break.

Nuno made three changes from his victorious Wembley team. For the seventh game in a row he changed his midfield, with Romain Saiss and Joao Moutinho coming in for Ruben Neves and Leander Dendoncker, who dropped to the bench. Helder Costa, who netted his first goal of the season at Wembley, replaced Adama Traore in the starting XI, with the Spaniard having picked up a tight hamstring. Crystal Palace came into the game six places and 10 points behind Wolves. But having beaten Manchester City just before Christmas, it was clear they were a team not to be underestimated.

Ahead of the game Nuno had called for his team to improve their home record. He'll have wanted pace, urgency, tempo and creativity from his team in the first half – he got absolutely none of that. At a quiet and freezing cold Molineux, Wolves were sluggish, careless in possession and created barely any chances of note. Yes, organised Palace sat deep and tried to frustrate the hosts. But Roy Hodgson's side were far more assured in possession and looked more threatening going forward. Rui Patricio had to tip over the bar from Luka Milivojevic's 18-yard effort after Willy Boly gifted the ball to Andros Townsend, while Townsend himself later fired over and Boly had to block from James McArthur after a mistake by Matt Doherty. At the other end Raul Jimenez sent a decent 30-yard piledriver not too far over, but otherwise Wolves created barely anything in open play. Moutinho couldn't generate much from midfield, while Costa and Ivan Cavaleiro struggled to isolate their full-backs. Cavaleiro did set up the chance of the half, though, when his inswinging corner from the left was straight to Boly, dead central seven yards out having lost his marker. Boly sent it bouncing wide as if his head was a 50p coin and then Doherty couldn't divert it in from close range. Wolves, then, didn't muster a shot on target in the first half.

There was more hurry and haste in their play at the start of the second period as the atmosphere improved too. Their passing improved – one 50-yard Conor Coady ping had the Molineux crowd purring like George Galloway at a saucer of milk – and they pushed Palace back.

With 13 minutes to go an even encounter was up for grabs, but you wouldn't exactly say it was on a knife edge, such was the rather drab and uninspiring fare on offer. Palace sensed three points and advanced further forward. Ryan Bennett had to perfectly time a sliding tackle on Wilfried Zaha in the box and the same player was alert to clear near his goal line after some scrappy pinball in the Wolves box. Palace ramped up the pressure – and seven minutes from time they took the lead. Patrick van Aanholt's shot was heading wide before it hit Jorden Ayew six yards out, he controlled and prodded past Patricio before Boly or Coady could react in time. Nuno called for Traore in place of Cavaleiro but Wolves were struggling to create an attack in response, let alone find an equaliser. Palace then sealed the win with the last kick of the game when Milivojevic netted from the spot after Bennett had brought down Zaha.

Several players were below par, the home fans were quiet and it ended up being a nothing game – until Palace grew in stature and won the match late on. It meant Wolves lost their first match of a calendar year for the first time since 2013 when their opponents were, yes, Crystal Palace. But more importantly than that, the issue of underperforming against teams below them in the table won't go away. Wolves may be trying to sign a prolific striker, but their problems here lay in creating chances. Just when you think they can establish themselves at a top-half side, as at Fulham, they play nowhere near their best. Yes it may be being over-critical, but Wolves have set extremely high standards. Unless they meet them, they'll fall short of their lofty target this season.

NUNO

I'm very disappointed. Everybody in the stadium was disappointed, naturally. But we have to look at it. The first half was very tight, the second half we started better, but all the game we didn't perform well enough. Let's be honest, Palace had one day less to recover than us, but my players were arriving late to the actions. The standard of the team was not there. That is the reality. We didn't create enough in wide areas.

FAN VERDICT – ROB CARTWRIGHT

Just typical! The highs of Wembley on Saturday, followed by a horror story at Molineux. As good as we were four days ago, this was inept. We can go away to Palace and win, but at Molineux we can hardly muster a shot on target. The plan for home games is not working. Teams set up to stifle the midfield and stop our wing-backs getting forward. Almost the reverse of Saturday, no one in a Wolves shirt could raise their game to anything near average. We are certainly missing the mobility of Jota with his ability to run with the ball. The defence looked solid, Bennett was probably our best player. The rollercoaster continues. Work in progress, but still much to be pleased with. It is clear that we need different tactics for home games. This is Nuno's biggest challenge now.

POSSESSION: **52% / 48%** | SHOTS: **9 / 17** | SHOTS ON TARGET: **1 / 4** | CORNERS: **3 / 10** | FOULS: **9 / 7** | BOOKINGS: **4 / 1**

STAR MAN - RYAN BENNETT

Had a really good night quelling the threat of Zaha, producing two fine sliding tackles to stop the flying winger and an important clearing header in the nick of time. Also made a crucial block just ahead of his own goal line. No complaints for the penalty in the final seconds, when Zaha finally got past him. He was lucky to avoid picking up a second booking of the night for that foul.

TWEET OF THE GAME

 Tim Spiers ✓
@tim_spiers_Star

No time to restart, full-time Wolves 0 Palace 2.

Nuno's team got exactly what they deserved at Wembley and you can say the same about tonight. A really underwhelming performance.

2 Jan 2019

TABLE

	TEAM	P	GD	PTS
6	MAN UTD	21	11	38
7	LEICESTER	21	2	31
8	WATFORD	21	-1	29
9	WOLVES	21	-2	29
10	WEST HAM	21	-3	28
11	EVERTON	21	0	27
12	BOURNEMOUTH	21	-9	27

WOLVES
(JIMENEZ 38, NEVES 55)

LIVERPOOL
(ORIGI 51)

 2

 1

MOLINEUX STADIUM, 7.45PM
JANUARY 7, 2019 ATTENDANCE: **25,849** (4,774 AWAY)

THIRD ROUND PROPER

Wolves (3-5-2): *Ruddy; Bennett, Coady (c), Boly; Otto (Doherty 75), Neves, Dendoncker, Moutinho, Vinagre; Jimenez (Costa 83), Jota (Cavaleiro 52). Subs not used: Norris, Saiss, Gibbs-White, Traore.*

Liverpool (4-4-2): *Mignolet; Camacho, Fabinho, Lovren (Hoever 6), Moreno; Shaqiri, Keita, Milner (c), Jones (Salah 70); Sturridge (Firmino 70), Origi. Subs not used: Kelleher, Alexander-Arnold, Christie-Davies, Mane.*

Bill Slater was the last man to lift the FA Cup for Wolves, some 59 years ago. On a night that Wolves paid tribute to their late legend, who died last month, you wonder if the current crop have one of the best opportunities in recent years to make a big impact in this famous old competition.

After all, Wolves are one of the top 10 teams in England – the league table says so. But given their penchant for beating sides from the 'big six' (league wins over Chelsea and Spurs and now a cup win over, it must be said, a severely weakened and unmotivated Liverpool) they will rightly rank as one of the favourites for the tournament. It's cup football, it's unpredictable, anything can happen and the draw may be unfavourable, but at least Nuno Espirito Santo is taking it seriously, unlike a host of Premier League managers.

Wolves may have started the game with less tempo than a group of tired grannies doing the Macarena but, after Raul Jimenez, the scorer of seven goals this season, broke the deadlock, they looked something like their normal selves in what was certainly a marked improvement on the non-performance against Palace. Two players who haven't contributed in exactly the manner they'd have hoped this season were crucial to this victory. Diogo Jota (you wonder how many more points Wolves would have earned over Christmas if he'd been fit) was sprightly and set up the opener, while match-winner Ruben Neves looked every bit the midfield maestro.

Matt Doherty and Rui Patricio were rested but other than that it was as strong an XI as possible which included a shuffle in midfield, with Leander Dendoncker and Neves joining Joao Moutinho. Liverpool, on the other hand, made nine changes and included two teenage debutants in Curtis Jones and Rafael Camacho. Divock Origi, who Wolves courted last summer, was up front, with Mo Salah, Roberto Firmino and Sadio Mane all on the bench. The game was certainly a highly-anticipated one – but a really poor first half didn't do the pre-match billing any justice. It was a dire, turgid, almost actionless 45 minutes in which both teams were well below their best. Moutinho and Neves both had shots from range but their efforts went more into orbit than a NASA spacecraft, while a succession of Ryan Bennett long throws yielded no chances of note. Then the face of the tie changed completely seven minutes before the break – and Wolves scored with the first shot on target from either side. Jota nipped in to win the ball after James Milner accidentally stood on it – he played to Raul Jimenez who raced into the penalty area and, with Jota cleverly blocking Milner's attempts to get back, had time to beat Simon Mignolet with a smart finish.

It was inevitable Liverpool would improve in the second half (they couldn't get any worse) but Wolves had only themselves to blame for letting Jurgen Klopp's team back into the game on 51 minutes. Conor Coady dithered over a clearance, the ball fell to Origi who worked an angle and fired a superb effort past John Ruddy from 18 yards. Any fears that Liverpool would take control, though, were banished just four minutes later. Neves' long shots have been well below his high standards in recent weeks but this time the midfield maestro caught his 25-yard shot sweetly

– it skipped off the turf and bounced past Simon Mignolet at his near post. Jimenez almost took advantage of poor defending from Ki-Jara Hoever but couldn't convert from a tight angle – and then Ruddy pulled off a wonderful save to tip Xherdan Shaqiri's cornerbound long-range free-kick on to the post. Klopp called for the cavalry with Salah and Firmino sent on. There were a couple of hairy moments and Mignolet came up for two set-pieces in injury time – but Wolves saw it through to reach the fourth round.

Wolves are in no danger of being relegated this season. Their target is finishing in the top 10... can they do that while maintaining a cup run, even with a small squad by Premier League standards? We may be about to find out. After all, Wolves are already sixth favourites to end their 59-year wait and lift the FA Cup (that's before either Man United or Arsenal get knocked out in round four). One thing's for sure, the club's passionate supporters would need absolutely no excuse to fully embrace a run in the competition. If Nuno continues to take it seriously and if Wolves can get a favourable couple of draws, who knows how far they can go. Up for the Cup? You bet they are.

NUNO

We are very happy for Ruben, it was such a beautiful goal. It's something we encourage him to do. Last season, we saw it pretty often. We know he has this talent. It was an important moment for us and for the fans. Molineux came alive again and from there on, we were always in control of the game against a tough team, so I'm very proud. We won the game and we did it well. It was a good performance, a tough game. We were compact, organised and we had good counter-attacks. In general, I think it was a very good game.

FAN VERDICT – GULRAJ KULAR

Let's be clear - this wasn't a slaying of a dragon or killing of a giant. When those lineups were announced I was in no doubt who had the better side. We started a little tentatively as if we were expecting a bit more from Liverpool, but as soon as we settled into our pattern we sensed blood. We harassed them at every opportunity and had it not been for some untidy interplay between the forwards could have been further ahead at half-time. This was a fully-deserved victory not only for Liverpool's clear disdain for the fixture but because on the day we were simply better than them. It took away some feeling of an upset or a momentous victory, but we go into the next round full of beans.

POSSESSION: 39% / 61% | **SHOTS: 8 / 8** | **SHOTS ON TARGET: 3 / 2** | **CORNERS: 3 / 3** | **FOULS: 10 / 2** | **BOOKINGS: 0 / 1**

STAR MAN – RUBEN NEVES

Like an expert sniper he much prefers shooting from range – that's now eight of nine Wolves goals to have come from outside the box (the other being a peno against Spurs). Since being dropped at Fulham he's responded in exactly the right way with a number of improved performances, culminating in his best display of the season here. More touches (67) than any Wolves player and his pass accuracy was a whopping 92 per cent. Did some important work defensively too. Ruben Neves is back.

TWEET OF THE GAME

 Tim Spiers ✔
@tim_spiers_Star

His long shots have been rubbish for weeks but Neves gets this one right sending a 25-yarder bouncing past Mignolet at his near post SUPERB HIT HE'S BACK IT'S 2-1

That's our Ruben

7 Jan 2019

MANCHESTER CITY
(JESUS 10, PEN 39, COADY OG 78)

3

WOLVES

0

ETIHAD STADIUM, 8PM
JANUARY 14, 2019 ATTENDANCE: 54,171 (3,000 AWAY)

Manchester City (4-3-3): *Ederson; Walker, Stones, Laporte, Danilo; Fernandinho, B Silva, D Silva (c) (De Bruyne 61); Sterling, Jesus (Aguero 76), Sane (Gundogan 74). Subs not used: Muric, Otamendi, Delph, Mahrez.*

Wolves (3-5-2): *Patricio; Bennett, Coady (c), Boly; Doherty, Moutinho (Gibbs-White 72), Neves, Dendoncker, Otto; Jimenez (Traore 46), Jota (Saiss 58). Subs not used: Ruddy, Vinagre, Caveleiro, Costa.*

Wolves have pulled off some phenomenal results so far in 2018/19, but this never looked like being one of them. If you're going to win at Manchester City you need to play out of your skin, hope the hosts have an off-day and, most importantly, you need a slice of luck. Wolves definitely didn't have the latter.

City benefited from a red card, a questionable penalty and an own goal. It bordered on taking the mickey, which is exactly what the reigning champions did in the closing stages as even their goalkeeper toyed with Wolves when playing a couple of passes near the halfway line. You can argue all day whether Willy Boly should have seen red, or whether Raheem Sterling should have stayed on his feet for the penalty, but City knew how to earn both decisions, surrounding the ref and, in Sterling's case, going to ground in a convincing manner. In that respect it's a lesson in the dark arts learned for Wolves – and that's just about all they can take from this night, which is one to chalk off to experience.

City left Sergio Aguero and Kevin De Bruyne on the bench, with Aguero suffering with illness and De Bruyne still building up his fitness after injury. But looking at their XI, that was the only good news for Wolves. The hosts had netted a remarkable 16 goals in their previous two home games, albeit against Championship and League One opposition. It was a daunting task and the last thing Wolves needed was to concede an early goal – but that's exactly what happened. Aymeric Laporte played Leroy Sane in down the left with Matt Doherty caught flatfooted – Sane sent the ball into the six-yard box where Gabriel

Jesus easily got there in front of the centre halves and Rui Patricio to fire home.

At 1-0 down Wolves were well in the game, but their task became mountainous on 19 minutes when Boly lunged into a tackle on Bernardo Silva. The Frenchman won the ball but referee Craig Pawson deemed the challenge to be dangerous and sent him off. It was a contentious decision, but what couldn't be argued is that Boly was needlessly excessive with the ball only near halfway. Leander Dendoncker went into central defence in what was now a 5-2-2 formation, with Raul Jimenez and Diogo Jota cutting in from out wide.

City were enjoying 80 per cent possession in what was very much attack versus defence. However, seven minutes before the break Wolves were able to carve out a golden chance to equalise. Jimenez barged forward on the break and passed to Jonny Castro Otto on the left of the box – he looked to find the bottom far corner but couldn't wrap his foot around the ball with his effort flying wide as Jota slid in.

Just two minutes later Wolves were made to pay for spurning a very rare opportunity with what looked like the game's killer goal. Sterling wriggled his way into the box and was given the slightest of touches from Ryan Bennett's knee – the England man needed no excuse to go down and duly did. Jesus despatched the penalty for his seventh goal in just three games and Wolves' night went from mission improbable to mission impossible.

Nuno called for Adama Traore at half-time, with Jimenez replaced, and the Spaniard made a

positive impact with a couple of searching runs, using his pace and strength to good effect to trouble Laporte down Wolves' right. At the other end, City were peppering Wolves' goal with shots from Kyle Walker and Fernandinho, while Sane shanked one wide from a good position. The away fans weren't being given much to cheer so resorted to gallows humour, cheering "ole" as Wolves enjoyed a very rare spell of possession. There would have been a wry smile from many of them when City sent on one of the world's best midfielders, De Bruyne, on the hour mark and the Belgian whistled a bullet half-volley over shortly after. With 12 left on the clock City added a third when De Bruyne whipped in a cross from the left which deflected off Conor Coady and nestled in the bottom corner The closing stages were summed up when Ederson came out of his goal to intercept a pass and then stayed near the halfway line to receive a couple of passes. It topped off a night to forget.

Wolves can take heart from their attitude and spirit and the fact they only conceded three goals (City mustered 24 shots to Wolves' three) and there were a couple of bright individual performances including from Traore who attempted to take on City on his own in the second half. Nuno was also able to substitute Jimenez, Jota and Joao Moutinho early on, with one eye on next weekend when Leicester City visit Molineux. It's games like that which will define whether Wolves achieve their aims for this season.

NUNO

It's clear, isn't it? It's a red card. We are sad, disappointed, but, at the same time we have to look at the game, knowing what happened. We started well, and then we conceded in a way we shouldn't concede, then the red card. The speed Man City have with the ball is not the speed we usually have to cope with. I think the only positive is that it was an experience for us. With one man less, we have to know that there is still something to do. At that point, we have to improve, but we knew it was tough – and it became harder. But the hard work of the boys was something that was there until the last minute.

FAN VERDICT – CLIVE SMITH

What a huge disappointment. The red card meant we could not see how competitive we could be. Already a goal down and lacking possession, it would otherwise have been a good insight. The pace of City, in so many of their players, overwhelmed us right from the start. Usually, a line of five at the back would have been sufficient to manage a front two or three, but City had four players running at pace and they found gaps easily. Had we kept 11 men, or if Jota and Otto had a yard more pace, then who knows. Thankfully there will be better days ahead. However, this was a thoroughly miserable experience.

STAR MAN – RUI PATRICIO

Predictably experienced one of his busiest nights of the campaign – and helped keep the score down. A couple of good saves from David Silva and Kevin De Bruyne and also rushed out to deny Raheem Sterling at his feet. Should arguably be intercepting Leroy Sane's pass to Gabriel Jesus for the opener, but he was given no help by his defenders for that one.

TWEET OF THE GAME

Tim Spiers ✓
@tim_spiers_Star

Full-time 3-0 City. You need luck on nights like these and Wolves had absolutely none. Chalk it off and move on.

14 Jan 2019

TABLE

	TEAM	P	GD	PTS
8	LEICESTER	22	1	31
9	WEST HAM	22	-2	31
10	EVERTON	22	2	30
11	WOLVES	22	-5	29
12	BOURNEMOUTH	22	-11	27
13	BRIGHTON	22	-6	26
14	CRYSTAL PALACE	22	-8	22

WOLVES
(JOTA 4, 64, 90+2, BENNETT 12)

LEICESTER CITY
(GRAY 49, COADY OG 53, MORGAN 87)

 4

 3

MOLINEUX STADIUM, 12.30PM
JANUARY 19, 2019 ATTENDANCE: 31,278 (2,970 AWAY)

 Premier League

Wolves (3-5-2): Patricio; Bennett, Coady (c), Saiss; Otto, Dendoncker, Moutinho (Gibbs-White, 80), Neves, Vinagre (Doherty, 73); Jimenez, Jota. Subs not used: Ruddy, Giles, Traore, Costa, Cavaleiro.

Leicester City (3-4-3): Schmeichel; Simpson (Iheanacho 83), Morgan (c), Maguire (Evans 48); Pereira, Mendy, Ndidi, Chilwell; Gray, Vardy, Barnes (Maddison 73). Subs not used: Ward, Fuchs, Choudhury, Albrighton.

And they say lightning never strikes twice. There was no comeback this time, as there was in 2003, but the drama was just as awe-inspiring, as Wolves beat Leicester 4-3 at Molineux yet again. Wolves have made unforgettable memories this season and, for all their victories against the league's big boys, a last-gasp winner from Diogo Jota in front of a disbelieving South Bank may be the best yet. It's fair enough to say that 12.30pm games tend to produce drab, fairly lifeless encounters, but this was the total opposite.

Before Jota's dramatic winner, how you viewed this game from a Wolves perspective depended on your disposition. The positive will have enjoyed a fabulous feast of attacking football – an enthralling goal-fest with chances, shots and incidents galore. You'll have been marvelling at Wolves scoring three goals at Molineux for the first time since March last year (against Burton) and purring at the performances of Ruben Neves and Jota. The glass-half-empty-minded would have been fuming at Wolves' at-times comical defending, straight out of the 'Some Mothers Do Ave Em' school, which contributed to Leicester coming from 2-0 and 3-2 down to level. After a game like that, though, you've just got to marvel at the drama and entertainment on show. It was utterly breathtaking.

Neves set the tone early on with a rasping 30-yarder that Kasper Schmeichel magnificently tipped over at full stretch. Just a minute later, rampant Wolves were ahead with their earliest goal of the season – Leander Dendoncker won possession in midfield, Raul Jimenez played wide right to Joao Moutinho and

his come-and-get-me cross was met by Jota, who finished from close range.

It was just what Wolves needed but they almost gifted Leicester an instant equaliser when Rui Patricio inexplicably started dawdling in possession on his six-yard line – Jamie Vardy nipped in but the keeper just recovered in time. It was end-to-end and Wolves doubled their lead after just 12 minutes when Moutinho's teasing corner was met by Ryan Bennett who powered a header past Schmeichel, netting his first goal since that last-gasp winner at Bristol City many moons ago.

The undeterred visitors continued to attack and Wolves were all over the shop at the back, but still causing Leicester problems at the other end and Jota should have made it 3-0 when he headed straight at the keeper after wonderful work from Jimenez down the right, the 13th shot of the match after just 30 breathless minutes. Leicester could perhaps feel hard-done-by with the 2-0 scoreline – but they made amends with a goal immediately after half-time. Bennett mistimed a header and Vardy played to the onrushing Damarai Gray, who took on the despairing dive of Romain Saiss and drilled low past Patricio.

Shortly afterwards it was 2-2. Jonny Castro Otto gifted the ball to Harvey Barnes, who fired his shot through Conor Coady from 15 yards for Leicester's second inside four minutes as the game was turned on its head.

It was the 51st minute and most inside Molineux were wondering when Wolves were going to come out for the second half. Neves

inspired them into life – nonchalantly pinging a 60-yarder into the path of Jota, who bounded into the box and confidently lashed into the net for his second of the afternoon.

Wolves had looked shell-shocked after that Leicester comeback, but now they were thriving, with almost everything Neves touching turning to gold. Leicester weren't done yet, though. With just three minutes remaining, a free-kick saw Wes Morgan get ahead of Dendoncker and beat Patricio, who was rooted to his line.

It looked set to finish 3-3, but Wolves had other ideas – Neves sprayed to Jimenez and, with seconds left on the clock, he played into Jota's path and he side-footed home to send Molineux absolutely delirious. Nuno sprinted down the touchline to celebrate and was sent off by the pernickety ref – but absolutely no-one cared when he blew his full-time whistle to end a fabulous, elating encounter.

In attacking terms, they have laid down a marker. Jota netted more than once in a game for the first time since September 2017, Neves looked back to his Championship best, Dendoncker was excellent and Moutinho and Jimenez inspirational. The problems came at the back, with Willy Boly's absence felt as he missed his first meaningful league game for 18 months. But on a madcap day like this – when Wolves suggested again they have the credentials to finish seventh – the analysis can wait for another day.

What a day, what a winner, what a match – and what a team.

NUNO

Jota showed he is back. He was injured, but he's come back and he's getting back to his best moments. The work ethic of the boys goes beyond scoring. I think all the team, offensively, did very well. In every offensive part of the game, we are very happy. When we score four goals, it means we have produced a lot of chances. Defensively? No. The set pieces, the goals we concede, but this is the game. If there were no mistakes, there would be no goals. It was a fantastic game for the people at Molineux, especially for our fans. It is difficult to contain your emotions – I am no exception.

FAN VERDICT – RUSS EVERS

Getting boring these home games v Leicester. Always the same, goals, excitement, dodgy decisions and ultimately three points. Ruben Neves and Diogo Jota showed why they need to be the rocks around which we build. Both of them on fire and a pleasure to watch as the Nuno bandwagon moves on. To be a part of this is a privilege and makes up for the years of drivel and false dawns. Every one of the team played their part and from all at Hatherton Wolves thank you for the pride, skill, passion, belief and the desire you all have and have reintegrated into a waiting public. And this is just the second step. Glorious.

STAR MAN – DIOGO JOTA

Four shots, three goals and a day that Diogo José Teixeira da Silva will never, ever forget. Neither will the 31,000 people who watched Jota tear Leicester apart with Wolves' first top-flight hat-trick for 42 years. Cleverly gets ahead of his man for the first goal, bounds forward with grace and confidence to fire home the second and then stays cooler than a cucumber on holiday to the South Pole for the winner with just seconds to go. Had his troubles at the start of the season but he could be the star of the second half of the campaign. He's got the talent, he's got the work rate and goodness me has he got the attitude.

TWEET OF THE GAME

Tim Spiers ✔
@tim_spiers_Star

That man Neves oh my days perfect pass wide to Jimenez, low ball across goal where DIOGO JOTA sidefoots home everyone's gone absolutely bonkers Nuno's down the touchline press box on its knees fans going mad bedlam at Molineux INCREDIBLE

19 Jan 2019

TABLE

	TEAM	P	GD	PTS
5	ARSENAL	23	16	44
6	MAN UTD	23	13	44
7	WATFORD	23	0	33
8	WOLVES	23	-4	32
9	LEICESTER	23	0	31
10	WEST HAM	23	-4	31
11	EVERTON	23	1	30

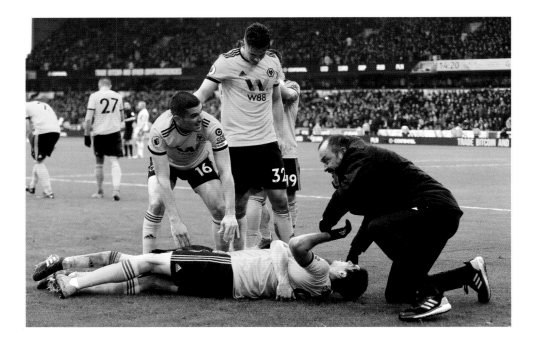

ANALYSIS

Games like this don't come around very often. The 'we score, you score' basketball-style, end-to-end madness with a late winner, euphoric victors, inconsolable losers, or two punch drunk boxers after a dead-heat draw – they're a rare beast. Wolves' most recent in this genre was probably the 4-4 against Fulham in last 2017 when Molineux lost its collective head thinking Dave Edwards had scored a 90th-minute winner – only for Fulham to kill the party with a 94th-minute equaliser. Before that? The 4-3 win over Leeds in 2015 when Wolves were chasing a play-off spot (Edwards' winner stayed a winner that time) and of course a year earlier was the ultimate goal-fest when Rotherham were beaten 6-4 amid a Nouha Dicko hat-trick, giddy delirium and pitch invasions galore.

> **"IT HAS NOT BEEN AN EASY SEASON FOR ME BUT THIS WAS ONE OF THE GREATEST DAYS OF MY LIFE."**
> DIOGO JOTA

The difference with this latest bonkers thriller was that it was played out on a global stage – a televised Premier League match that had the nation fawning and Jamie Carragher saying it was a true pleasure to be there (it still wasn't first on Match of the Day, though). The scenes after Diogo Jota's winner, with supporters losing their minds and Nuno running on the pitch, will remain in the memory bank for a long, long time.

It's a season of increasingly magical memories – outplaying and beating Spurs at Wembley, coming from behind to beat Chelsea, winning in the last minute at West Ham and Newcastle and downing Liverpool in the FA Cup – but this one might top the lot. And you'd expect there to be a few more before the season is out.

When analysing the performance, there's a clear dividing line between the attackers and the defenders. Going forward, Wolves set the standard they should aspire to for the rest of the campaign. They were decisive, creative and, as often hasn't been the case this season, they were clinical. Yes, Leicester's defending was as generous as Mother Teresa at Christmas, but

Wolves took full advantage to score more than two goals at Molineux for the first time since March 2018 (3-1 against Burton).

Defensively it was a different story. Rui Patricio set the tone early on with a couple of careless mistakes that would have made Bumblebee Man from the Simpsons blush. And then for each of Leicester's goals you can point out individual mistakes. Goal 1 – Ryan Bennett mis-times his jump, Romain Saiss is beaten all ends up by Damarai Gray. Goal 2 – Jonny Castro Otto (although perhaps impeded) presents the ball to Harvey Barnes, Conor Coady allows the ball through his legs. Goal 3 – Otto gives away a free-kick, Patricio's rooted to his line and Leander Dendoncker is outmuscled by Wes Morgan.

When the post-match elation had died down, the talk from Nuno, Coady and Jota was of improving their defensive stability. Of course, Wolves sorely missed Willy Boly. His replacement Saiss had an uncomfortable afternoon and Wolves looked better balanced with Otto at left wing-back and Matt Doherty on the opposite flank, with Ruben Vinagre not convincing either, although none of the wing-backs performed to their highest standards.

Wolves had many heroes during their Championship title success but the two players you really thought were far too good for that level – and surely destined for super-stardom – were Ruben Neves and Jota. For one reason or another, neither player had truly announced himself on the Premier League stage, with Neves perhaps struggling to adapt to his different role this season and Jota short of fitness and form from pre-season onwards. For both players, the penny seems to have dropped. Neves has begun to dominate games and Jota has started adding goals and assists with his confidence having returned. On Saturday we saw near perfection from both – and it lifted Wolves to heights they haven't achieved before now this season.

THE SCENES AFTER JOTA'S WINNER... WILL REMAIN IN THE MEMORY BANK FOR A LONG, LONG TIME

SHREWSBURY TOWN **2**
(DOCHERTY 47, WATERFALL 71)

 # WOLVES **2**
(JIMENEZ 75, DOHERTY 90+3)

MONTGOMERY WATERS MEADOW, 3PM
JANUARY 26, 2019 ATTENDANCE: **9,503** (1,641 AWAY)

FOURTH ROUND PROPER

Shrewsbury (3-4-3): *Arnold; Beckles, Waterfall, Sadler (c); Bolton, Norburn (Vincelot 87), Grant, Haynes; Docherty (Amadi-Holloway 90+6), Okenabirhie (Whally 81), Laurent. Subs not used: Charles-Cook, Angol, Eisa, Sears.*

Wolves (3-4-1-2): *Ruddy; Bennett, Coady (c), Saiss; Doherty, Neves, Dendoncker (Jimenez 59), Giles (Cavaleiro 73); Gibbs-White (Moutinho 79); Traore, Costa. Subs not used: Norris, Kilman, Otto, Vinagre.*

This was a wasted opportunity to head straight into the FA Cup fifth round – but it could have been so much worse. Nuno Espirito Santo selected a team more than good enough to win this troublesome tie on paper. Sure the pitch wasn't great, sure it was windy, sure there wasn't the usual room for Wolves to play their preferred game – but none of these are excuses for Wolves being held by League One opposition and so very nearly losing. Both Nuno and John Ruddy said beforehand that Wolves' attitude, desire, application and motivation needed to match Shrewsbury's – and then their quality should shine through. Well, it didn't in the first half, when they were lacklustre, banal and short of ideas.

Nuno handed a Wolves debut to academy product Ryan Giles at left wing-back on his 19th birthday, with his introduction one of six changes as the head coach rotated his matchday 18. It was cold, wet and windy in Shropshire and on a bobbly pitch Wolves were in unusual territory compared to their usual Premier League surroundings. In the first half, it showed. A fabulous atmosphere in the stands, with two loud Shrewsbury sections and a noisy away end, wasn't matched on the pitch where there were few chances created and precious little quality on show. Conor Coady pinged countless balls to the flanks where Matt Doherty and Giles had little joy, while a series of long balls to Adama Traore and Helder Costa unsurprisingly yielded minimal success.

Traore was involved for the best chance of the half when Doherty skipped past a couple of challenges to the byline and pulled the ball back for the Spaniard, who ballooned over the bar from 12 yards. Doherty and Morgan Gibbs-White fired half chances into the stands – and that was pretty much it from Wolves. Ruben Neves tried to pull the strings but the runs ahead of him weren't good enough against an organised back line. At the other end midfielder Greg Docherty tested Ruddy from range with a decent effort, but the keeper blocked it and then Coady cleared the danger. It was a drab first half of few highlights.

All that changed at the start of the second half – but not in the manner Wolves wanted. Neves misjudged a loose ball and suddenly Fejiri Okenabirhie was racing towards the Wolves box – he played in Docherty who lashed goalwards from a tight angle, it took a deflection off Romain Saiss and flew past Ruddy into the net. It should have been 1-1 a few minutes later but Costa sent his free six-yard header too close to keeper Steve Arnold from Doherty's floated cross.

Wolves had been sparked into life in what was now a cracking cup tie. Newly-introduced substitute Raul Jimenez had a golden opportunity with his first touch – but shanked wide from 12 yards after good work from Giles. If the home fans were noisy before, they were almost deafening now in what was an increasingly frantic encounter. Jimenez was denied by a brilliant Mat Sadler tackle after taking Doherty's pass – it was all Wolves. But Shrewsbury were still looking dangerous from set-pieces, and it was via one that they doubled their lead. A corner was sent into the six-yard box where Luke Waterfall powered home a header past a statuesque Ruddy to take the roof off the Meadow.

Nuno immediately sent on Ivan Cavaleiro for Giles – and within three minutes panicked Wolves had pulled one back. Cavaleiro twisted and turned near the corner flag on the right and whipped a wicked ball across the face where the menacing Jimenez turned it in for his eighth goal of the season. They threw everything at Shrewsbury in the final minutes via a succession of crosses and corners. And that golden chance finally arrived in the 93rd minute – Doherty powered home a header from Traore's cross to salvage a dramatic late draw that Wolves just about deserved. It wasn't pretty, but Wolves are just about in the draw for the fifth round. In a competition where they have a big opportunity to progress deep into it, that's ultimately all that matters. But they'll have to play a hell of a lot better on Tuesday week.

It was the flacid first 45-minute performance that irked more than going 2-0 down in the second half. Wolves could have put the tie to bed if they'd been at their usual levels, but they were sorely lacking in intensity. It was a dramatic end to an absolutely cracking second half – and there was nothing wrong with Wolves' fighting spirit. Boy, did they want to avoid an exit in those closing stages.

NUNO

The effort of the boys in the last minutes was amazing, to allow us to stay in the Cup. It's part of our character. This is the Cup, you need to be committed to it although we don't want late goals! We try to avoid these situations. It's a very tight schedule for us now. We knew it would be tough, the pitch, a well organised, intense and aggressive team. It was a good game of football. The way we conceded, we should look at that. Everything was different after Shrewsbury's goal, they became very aggressive and compact. Jimenez brought energy, Traore did well, Ryan did good, he's one of our back-ups. Let's try to finish it at Molineux.

FAN VERDICT – ADAM VIRGO

From the position we found ourselves in being 2-0 down, getting a draw showed great belief and character. However, being 2-0 down in itself against League One opposition isn't good enough. No one can really blame Nuno for the changes he made and personally I think the team he sent out was more than strong enough to win, with Doherty our best player. All to play for in the replay and with the likes of West Ham, Arsenal and Everton all going out, we've got a huge chance of getting further providing we beat Shrewsbury and get a favourable draw. At home we should overcome them but it's never quite as simple as that.

STAR MAN - MATT DOHERTY

Mr Dependable was Wolves' best player on the pitch. Some familiar searching runs to the byline – on a number of occasions – including when he teed up Traore for an excellent first-half chance. Five key passes was three more than anyone on the field. And there he is in the 93rd minute popping up with his second injury time goal this season, a forceful header which earned Wolves a replay.

TWEET OF THE GAME

Tim Spiers ✔
@tim_spiers_Star

Absolutely cracking cup tie in that second half by the way. Wolves deserved their replay. Spirited comeback, showed plenty of desire. Jimenez and Cavaleiro made big impacts. Will have to play a lot better in the replay, mind. But ultimately being in the hat is all that matters

26 Jan 2019

WOLVES
(SAISS 66, JIMENEZ 80, 86)

3

WEST HAM UNITED

0

MOLINEUX STADIUM, 7.45PM
JANUARY 29, 2019 ATTENDANCE: 31,122 (2,877 AWAY)

Wolves (3-5-2): Patricio; Bennett, Coady (c), Saiss; Doherty, Moutinho (Gibbs-White 88), Neves, Dendoncker, Otto (Vinagre 90); Jimenez, Jota (Cavaleiro 88). Subs not used: Ruddy, Kilman, Costa, Traore

West Ham United (4-2-3-1): Fabianski; Zabaleta, Diop, Ogbonna, Masuaku; Noble (c) (Carroll 68), Rice; Snodgrass (Obiang 68), Anderson, Antonio; Arnautovic (Hernandez 77). Subs not used: Adrian, Fredericks, Coventry, Diangana.

You'd have to go a long way to find a more dominant Wolves performance than this. Nuno Espirito Santo's team were, in every aspect, supremely better than West Ham United, a team who came into the game just a point below them.

It eclipsed the 1-0 shellacking of Burnley back in September for two reasons; 1) West Ham represent, in theory, far superior opposition and 2) they turned their dominance into goals, three of them – and it could have been so many more. They toyed with West Ham, they humiliated them. It was wonderful to witness. Their passing was slick, their movement rapid, their persistence relentless and their defending, well, perfect. Rui Patricio could have spent the night counting how many people were in the crowd.

The team showed one change from the XI that beat Leicester City 4-3 in the Premier League, with Matt Doherty coming in for the benched Ruben Vinagre. The Hammers came into the game on the back of a chastening FA Cup exit to AFC Wimbledon and their boss Manuel Pellegrini had called for a reaction from his team – but in a first half dominated by Wolves he certainly didn't get one. Nuno's team have endured a few sluggish first halves in this campaign, scoring precious few goals, but there was (almost) absolutely nothing wrong with the first 45 minutes they produced against the Hammers. After settling early on, Wolves began to prise the visitors open in the final third and could feel aggrieved not to be ahead by the break.

Raul Jimenez was at his play-linking best, Diogo Jota was an incessantly positive presence, the two wing-backs provided attacking vigour, Leander

Dendoncker regularly popped up in the box and Joao Moutinho and Ruben Neves pulled the strings. Eleven shots to two told a story, but there was also a very strong penalty appeal rejected after Doherty had tangled legs with Arthur Masuaku who appeared to bring him down. They also had the ball in the net via Dendoncker's rebound after Jimenez turned a Jonny Castro Otto cross on to the bar, but the Mexican was correctly flagged offside. The best chances came via a rampaging Doherty – whose effort from a tight angle was blocked by Lukasz Fabianski – Dendoncker, whose free close-range shot from Doherty's cross wasn't forceful enough and Otto, whose diving header from a perfect Jimenez centre whistled past the post with Fabianski motionless. The lively Jota, full of confidence, also tested Fabianski with a low 20-yarder. His link-up play with Jimenez was a joy to watch at times. At the other end Patricio had barely a thing to do and basically Wolves did everything right except score.

Backed by a vociferous home crowd who sang "Nuno Santo's barmy army" for the first 15 minutes of the second half, they probed away at the Hammers with Neves at the heart of almost everything. Wolves were in complete control and West Ham were offering absolutely nothing going forward, but with 65 minutes gone it remained goalless. Otto again went close to breaking the deadlock, taking Jota's pass and forcing a fingertip save from Fabianski. It was an increasingly frustrating night in front of goal – but then, finally, from the resulting corner Wolves took the lead. Moutinho swung in a perfect in-swinging corner and Romain Saiss edged ahead of his man to place a well controlled header into the corner. He didn't even have to jump.

Wolves continued to attack and on 80 minutes came the goal their vast superiority merited. Again it came via a Moutinho set piece, with an inswinging free-kick turned in by Jimenez who marked an exceptional display with his ninth goal of the campaign in all competitions. There was time for a third goal to cap it all off. Jimenez took Jota's pass and sublimely chipped over Fabianski to seal a magnificent individual display and put the icing on the delicious Wolves cake.

Wolves have only ever been plucky underdogs in the Premier League, battling against survival. Now they have, when in full flow, a Rolls Royce of a team, beautiful to watch but with the substance to back up their style. They were quite sensational, enchanting, captivating and stunning. Everyone played their part here, from the string-pulling midfielders to the rampaging wing-backs and the creative and harassing front-men. West Ham's defenders will have nightmares about the trickery of Jota and the, well, peerless Jimenez who gave a forward masterclass by creating a hatful of chances and scoring two goals to take his tally to 10 for the season. What a combination he and Jota are. They're Wolves' lethal weapon. Wolves came into their three-game period against Leicester, the Hammers and Everton hoping to put down a marker for seventh place. Two games in, they've done just that. And with high hopes of an FA Cup run, there's every chance this could end up as a quite unforgettable campaign. January transfer window? Who needs it.

NUNO

Raul is doing a fantastic job because we want the goals that he scores, the way he plays and the way he works. He doesn't stop. He's always giving us the first moment of reaction to loss of the balls. He has to keep on going, and these decisions (about signing him permanently) will be made when they have to be made. In the first half, we didn't score but created a lot of chances. In the second half, we kept our composure and didn't get nervous. One of the things we wanted to improve was our defence and a clean sheet is very important. Achieving such beautiful goals is well played.

FAN VERDICT - NATALIE WOOD

This was by far the most convincing performance I've seen by a Wolves team in the Premier League – a joy to watch. We looked so confident going forward and were in complete control. Doherty was causing absolute mayhem down the wing and Neves played dazzling cross-field passes. Jimenez and Jota are really becoming a powerful strike-force and their link-up play was superb all game. A very well deserved three points. This run of games was always going to be vital in the success of our season. So far, after two wins from two, I think it's safe to say we are in a great position in our mini league. Bring on Everton!

POSSESSION: 55% / 45% | SHOTS: 20 / 4 | SHOTS ON TARGET: 9 / 0 | CORNERS: 5 / 1 | FOULS: 8 / 10 | BOOKINGS: 4 / 1

STAR MAN – RAUL JIMENEZ

Mexico's greatest exports have previously been thought to be fully loaded nachos, sombreros, Speedy Gonzales and the new series of Narcos. Not anymore. Jumping to number one on the list is Raúl Alonso Jiménez Rodríguez, one of the finest strikers to have adorned the gold and black in the past 40 years. He shoots, he passes, he crosses, he comes deep to help dictate play, he's good in the air, he defends from the front, he works incredibly hard and his touch and technique are superb. His burgeoning partnership with Diogo Jota threatens to make them the most prolific duo since Robson and Jerome made two number one albums in a year. His first goal was clinical and he took his second with aplomb. Also teed up chances for Otto and Doherty and then fed Jota for a big penalty shout. Oh and he's now scored 10 goals and laid on six assists before we've hit February. Three words – Sign. Him. Up.

TWEET OF THE GAME

TABLE

	TEAM	P	GD	PTS
4	CHELSEA	23	21	47
5	ARSENAL	24	17	47
6	MAN UTD	24	13	45
7	WOLVES	24	-1	35
8	EVERTON	24	2	33
9	WATFORD	23	0	33
10	LEICESTER	23	0	31

EVERTON
(GOMES 27)

WOLVES
(NEVES PEN 7, JIMENEZ 45, DENDONCKER 66)

1

3

Everton (4-2-3-1): *Pickford; Coleman (Calvert-Lewin 73), Keane, Zouma, Baines (c) (Kenny 37); Gomes, Davies; Walcott (Lookman 59), Sigurdsson, Richarlison; Tosun. Subs not used: Stekelenburg, McCarthy, Schneiderlin, Bernard.*

Wolves (3-5-2): *Patricio; Bennett, Coady (c), Boly; Doherty, Moutinho, Neves (Saiss 49), Dendoncker, Otto; Jimenez (Traore 89), Jota (Costa 77). Subs not used: Ruddy, John, Gibbs-White, Cavaleiro.*

When these teams met on the opening day, Wolves battled to a 2-2 draw and began to find their Premier League feet. Six months later, they showed just how far they've come with – on the day a pitch-invading cat interrupted play for two minutes – a second successive purr-fect performance.

There was nothing paw in their play whatsoever – and they were feline fine for an easy final 20 minutes when Nuno's furmidable team cruised to victory. Okay that's the cat puns done. Indeed, the only thing reminiscent of that August clash was the manner of their first two goals – a dead-ball strike from Ruben Neves and a superb Raul Jimenez header from a floated free-kick. Otherwise, Wolves belied the fact that there was just one place separating these teams at the start of play. They outclassed Everton in every single department, from front to back. They were solid defensively, adventurous in attack, tenacious in midfield and wholly committed down the flanks. They wanted it more – and they took it.

Wolves, who had the suspension-free Willy Boly back in the side at the expense of Romain Saiss, quickly settled into the game with Joao Moutinho at the heart of everything. The midfield maestro almost sent Diogo Jota clear with a sumptuous pass with the outside of his boot in the opening minutes. Then with only seven minutes on the clock, Wolves took the lead. In a textbook Matt Doherty move, the wing-back drove inside, edged past his man and, just like on Tuesday night, drew a foul via a tangle of legs. This one was given, though, with Leighton Baines the guilty party. Up stepped Neves to send Jordan Pickford the wrong way.

Their next chance came soon after when Jota won the ball off Tom Davies and played to Jimenez, who worked the ball to the overlapping Leander Dendoncker – he should have doubled Wolves' lead from 10 yards, but shot too close to Pickford. One team was oozing with confidence, playing on a wavelength with intelligent movement, attacking with menace and looking threatening. The other was Everton.

But the Toffees were bound to wake up sooner or later – and that they did. After Rui Patricio rushed from his line to make a great block from Theo Walcott – the first save he'd had to make since Leicester at home – his next action was to pick the ball out the net. Andre Gomes wasn't tracked from midfield and he edged into the box before sending a stunning, rasping rocket into the roof of the net past a helpless keeper.

However, before half-time Wolves were deservedly back in front. Everton had conceded a series of needless and petty fouls and it was via one from Will Keane, who pulled Jota to the floor when the forward was never getting near the ball, that Wolves retook the lead. Moutinho floated an absolutely gorgeous free-kick on to the head of Jimenez, who guided his header into the corner past a despairing Pickford dive.

After the break Wolves frustrated Everton with relative ease, sporadically breaking when they could – and still looking like the more likely scorers. To that end, it was no surprise when they made it 3-1 to take complete control. Jimenez played to Jota, who twisted and turned in the box, firing at goal – only to be denied by a brilliant Kurt Zouma block. The ball looped up

in the air and Dendoncker captured it perfectly with a left-footed volley which flew past Pickford. It was a thronker from Dendoncker. Play was then stopped in bizarre fashion for two-to-three minutes when an intrepid black cat invaded the pitch, trotting along Patricio's goal-line, evading Ryan Bennett and making it all the way to the other end of the pitch. That was Everton's best entertainment all afternoon – and pretty much the only thing that evaded the Wolves defence. The closing 20-odd minutes, a brilliant Boly block and a free Dominic Calvert-Lewin header straight at Patricio aside, they offered nothing as Wolves cruised to victory at a half-empty Goodison Park. Wolves' supporters sang their hearts out as they toasted another memorable day in an increasingly awe-inspiring campaign.

This sets a new Wolves standard for how to perform away from home – four days after doing exactly the same thing at Molineux when fixing the bar pretty damn high in a 3-0 demolition of West Ham United. The most striking thing about this win – Wolves' first at Goodison Park since September 1979, when Andy Gray was on the scoresheet in a 3-2 victory – was just how unflappable Wolves were. You never really sensed, even at 1-1 after previously lousy Everton woke from their slumber to equalise against the run of play, that they wouldn't exert their authority and win the match. They're maturing into a team that doesn't just belong at this level, but is adding plenty to the Premier League party.

NUNO

The team that played at Everton, 70 per cent of them were with us in the Championship. And we don't forget where we came from. We achieved a good performance that allowed us to play against a good team in a very tough stadium. We were compact and didn't let Everton have too many chances. We were in control of the game, better in the first half than the second, missing some things, but, in general, it was very well done. I'm very happy for Leander because he's working very, very hard. He really helped the team.

FAN VERDICT – CHRIS HUGHES

Nuno, Nuno, Nuno, he's taking us to Europe, to Europe, to Europe, and that's the way we like it, we like it, we like it...well, you know the rest! Talk at the start of the season of us gatecrashing the top seven seemed far-fetched yet here we are, 13 games from the finish line, sitting comfortably in seventh place and seeing off established top flight sides with little fuss. We were so good in this game that Goodison was two-thirds empty by full-time. Even the appearance of a local black cat couldn't give Everton enough luck to overcome Nuno's wizardry. It was another excellent team performance where everyone contributed. Doherty was exceptional, Raul and Diogo were terrific up top and ran the Everton centre backs ragged.

POSSESSION: 64% / 36% | SHOTS: 13 / 8 | SHOTS ON TARGET: 4 / 4 | CORNERS: 3 / 1 | FOULS: 12 / 14 | BOOKINGS: 3 / 1

STAR MAN - LEANDER DENDONCKER

Cast your minds back to December 28, 2018. Marko Arnautovic's Mandarin lessons are beginning in earnest, hopes are high for the upcoming England cricket tour of the West Indies – and Leander Dendoncker has yet to make his first league start for Wolves. Fast forward five weeks and it's no exaggeration to say he has become a vital, perhaps indispensable cog in this rapidly improving Wolves team. Not only has 'The Donck', a cult hero in the making, been individually superb, adding a physical, box-to-box presence to a side that lacked one, he's also freed up Neves and Moutinho to thrive alongside him. Scored a fine goal and won eight tackles too.

TWEET OF THE GAME

 Tim Spiers ✔
@tim_spiers_Star

Two utterly dominant, stylish and one-sided performances against very decent sides in West Ham and Everton. We're witnessing what could be the infancy of something very special. As a Wolves follower of many years, it's still not easy to get your head around #wwfc

 2 Feb 2019

TABLE

	TEAM	P	GD	PTS
4	CHELSEA	25	22	50
5	ARSENAL	24	17	47
6	MAN UTD	24	13	45
7	WOLVES	25	1	38
8	WATFORD	25	-1	34
9	EVERTON	25	0	33
10	BOURNEMOUTH	25	-7	33

ANALYSIS

Wolves began a trio of games against Leicester (then eighth), West Ham (ninth) and Everton (10th) in 11th place, looking to make their mark in the race for seventh. My oh my, have they done just that. They bared their attacking teeth against the Foxes and made a breakthrough in terms of finding their feet in front of goal. They kept a rare clean sheet against the Hammers and were sumptuous going forward. And here they produced a near faultless away performance, restricting Everton's chances and creating a hatful of their own, scoring three. In doing so they've set down a marker for the last three months of the season which, at this rate, could be very, very special indeed. Their first XI is set in stone, their formation is working a treat and they have players improving by the week, especially Raul Jimenez and Leander Dendoncker. But whatever happens in the coming weeks, Wolves have announced themselves as a stylish Premier League force to be reckoned with. How good does that sound?

The stats showed that Everton enjoyed 64 per cent possession and had 13 shots to Wolves' eight. Rarely can numbers have failed as miserably to accurately tell the story of a match. Wolves could and probably should have been 3-0 ahead by the time Everton equalised through a stunning Andre Gomes strike. The Toffees enjoyed plenty of the ball, particularly in the second half, but at 2-1 up Nuno's team sat deeper and comfortably repelled anything thrown their way. Indeed, the first 15 minutes after the break were a non-event with Wolves quelling Everton's threat via their discipline and rigid organisation (with the excellent and extremely noisy Conor Coady at the heart of this), sporadically breaking when they could.

We've seen it time and again during Nuno's tenure – Wolves are incredibly adept at soaking up pressure, with three centre-halves, two defensive midfielders and a couple of deep-lying wing-backs, then cantering forward on the counter with their pace, movement and mobility. They've also mastered pressing high and winning the ball in the opposition half. Dendoncker, Diogo Jota, Jimenez, Joao Moutinho, Jonny Castro Otto – they were all at it on Saturday. Traps were set in midfield and once the ball had been won there was lightning movement from Jota and Jimenez in particular. This led to two of their three goals, with Jimenez (in the build-up to Jota winning a free-kick) and Otto to thank.

Since they last played Everton we've seen this team evolve in terms of their tactics, formation and personnel. A minor but crucial tweak to 3-5-2 has overcome the big problem they had in October/November when teams were overcrowding them in midfield. Several individuals have notably improved or matured, particularly Coady, Moutinho (who seems to have forged a wavelength with each of his team-mates), Neves, Matt Doherty, Jota (who failed to produce a single goal or assist in his first 14 appearances and now has five goals and two assists in his last eight) and the wondrous Jimenez, whose all-round game has few, if any, weaknesses. The Mexican is already enjoying the most prolific season of his European career (since moving to Atletico from Mexico in 2014) and just gets better by the week. They've all made strides though, individually and collectively, and the first XI is now set in stone.

All of which places Wolves in seventh place with some daylight ahead of the chasing pack. Fans are dreaming of a European tour – and why not? Wolves must now show consistency – and avoid complacency – in facing four teams below them in Newcastle, Bournemouth, Huddersfield and Cardiff. The foundations are in place and the stage is set for an unforgettable final three months of the campaign. Can Wolves deliver?

> **"I THINK WE'VE SET THE STANDARD. THE BOYS WERE OUTSTANDING."**
> **CONOR COADY**

FANS ARE DREAMING OF A EUROPEAN TOUR – AND WHY NOT?

WOLVES
(DOHERTY 2, 45+6, CAVALEIRO 62)

3

SHREWSBURY TOWN
(BOLTON 11, LAURENT 39)

2

MOLINEUX STADIUM, 7.45PM
FEBRUARY 5, 2019 ATTENDANCE: 28,844 (3,131 AWAY)

FOURTH ROUND PROPER (REPLAY)

Wolves (3-4-3): Ruddy; Bennett, Coady (c), Boly; Doherty, Gibbs-White, Saiss, Otto; Traore (Jimenez 77), Cavaleiro (Ennis 88), Costa (Moutinho 69). Subs not used: Norris, Dendoncker, Giles, Neves.

Shrewsbury (3-4-3): Arnold; Vincelot (Sears 38), Waterfall, Beckles; Bolton, Norburn (c), Laurent, Haynes; Doherty, Okenabirhie (Amadi-Holloway 78), Gilliead (Whalley 66). Subs not used: Charles-Cook, Ward, Edwards, Rowland.

Wolves have beaten Chelsea, Liverpool and Spurs this season, they've been the better team at Old Trafford and the Emirates and brushed aside West Ham and Everton. But few have troubled them as much as Shrewsbury Town.

Nuno Espirito Santo's team needed an injury-time equaliser from Matt Doherty to make it 2-2 in the first tie – here they needed an injury-time goal from the same player to make it 2-2 at the break. Indeed, with three goals and one assist over the two games, Wolves have a lot to thank the indomitable little Irishman for. Ahead of the tie, Nuno called for total focus from his players – in the first half he certainly didn't get it, with Wolves conceding two sloppy goals on a night John Ruddy will want to forget for allowing one to slip through his fingers. Wolves' fringe players did their first-team prospects little good. Adama Traore frightened the life out of the Shrewsbury defenders at times but he, Helder Costa and Ivan Cavaleiro didn't look like Premier League players against League One defenders, for the most part. Cavaleiro did make some amends with a fabulous finish for the winner.

To that end you wonder how strong Nuno will go in the fifth round against a resurgent and promotion-chasing Bristol City. Wolves are two wins from reaching only a second semi-final in this competition since 1981 – if he and Wolves seriously want to win this competition, can he leave anything to chance? We'll find out a week on Sunday, but the sell-out Molineux crowd who've got Cup fever will only give you one answer.

As for the first tie, Nuno made six changes to his XI. He kept the same back three and wing-backs, but changed the goalkeeper, the midfield, the forwards and also the formation, switching to 3-4-3 with Ruddy, Romain Saiss, Morgan Gibbs-White, Traore, Cavaleiro and Costa coming in. Wolves came into the game on the back of two wholly convincing and impressive victories over West Ham and Everton – and despite the changes to the XI that confidence was apparent when they took the lead inside just 80 seconds. It was pretty regulation stuff – Gibbs-White's corner wasn't cleared, it dropped at Doherty's feet and he finished into the corner.

In theory, Shrewsbury's game plan was out the window. But within nine minutes they were level when a Greg Docherty corner was met by James Bolton in the heart of the six-yard box and he headed home. Yet again it was static and poor defending – a theme of the half for both sides. Wolves actually showed a big improvement in the following minutes – Traore revved up his engine and took on defenders at will, rousing the sizeable home crowd. Traore was the go-to man, but his end product was poor, as was the case for Costa and Cavaleiro, too. That meant for all Wolves' 72 per cent possession, they created few chances. Corners were Wolves' biggest threat – from open play they were lucklustre, with little in the way of creativity or incisiveness coming from midfield.

Then came a moment which took Molineux's breath away – but not in a good way. Josh Laurent tried his luck from 20 yards, a tepid and fairly harmless shot, but the wet ball slipped through Ruddy's hands and bounced

apologetically over the line in what was an horrendous clanger, pure and simple. However, by half-time they were level again. This time, Shrewsbury's keeper made an error, with Steve Arnold dropping a cross and Doherty slamming home from close range for his third goal of the tie. The cheer inside Molineux was muted – as was statuesque Nuno's celebration.

Wolves knew they hadn't played well enough and at the start of the second half they set about putting that right. They controlled possession and dominated play in the Shrewsbury third but again, corners aside, they carried little threat. At a quiet Molineux, Wolves needed inspiring and Cavaleiro was the man to do it. Traore and Doherty played their part, with the former winning the ball and the latter playing it towards the Portuguese forward, but this was all about Cavaleiro who showed strength to shrug off his man and then arrogance and sublime skill to roll his foot over the ball, sublimely swaying inside and beating the keeper for his fourth goal of the campaign. The visitors threw everything forward in the closing stages but despite a couple of dangerous set pieces Wolves saw it through with relative ease. Nuno's team were below par here, but hey, this is FA Cup football, the game of Shrewsbury's lives and Wolves got through. In the FA Cup, that's all that matters. Some 28,844 watched it – as opposed to 4,226 who watched League One side Oldham at Molineux in the Cup in 2014. The dream lives on.

NUNO

I'm happy because we got to the fifth round. Perhaps we have to look at the game and see it was not one of the best performances, we're aware of that – everybody is aware. But it's job done. The boys came from behind. You have to show character and we go through so I'm happy for our fans. We have a moment to focus on the Premier League and then we focus on the fifth round against Bristol. Credit to Shrewsbury's fans also, it was a fantastic atmosphere. The clubs are so close to each other – it was a good game for the Midlands.

FAN VERDICT – CLIVE SMITH

Well, you've got to be in it to win it, and we are. It was not as plain sailing as you would expect, but I never really thought Nuno's Wolves were going to lose. Yet again we had a soaking wet pitch, which made footwork tricky at times and the ball over the top just skidded on too far. Our passing game looked stylish at times as we made Shrewsbury work hard without the ball. The changed line-up meant our front five were not as slick as in recent league games. After the third goal we defended set pieces more diligently for the rest of the game and that was enough to seal the win.

POSSESSION: 72% / 28% | SHOTS: 11 / 9 | SHOTS ON TARGET: 4 / 2 | CORNERS: 12 / 2 | FOULS: 6 / 6 | BOOKINGS: 0 / 1

STAR MAN - MATT DOHERTY

The indomitable Matthew James Doherty. Three goals in the tie including a stoppage time equaliser at the Meadow and another injury time leveller here – in its own way just as important as Wolves crucially went in level at the break – plus an assist for the winning goal to boot. It feels like he's single-handedly dragged Wolves into the FA Cup fifth round. He's now netted six goals this season in all competitions, more than any other Premier League defender has managed. Plus a further five assists. Having the season of his life and he's doing so in the top flight of English football.

TWEET OF THE GAME

Tim Spiers ✓
@tim_spiers_Star

Molineux FA Cup attendances against League One opposition

2014 (Wolves v Oldham) - 4,226
2019 (Wolves v Shrewsbury) - 28,844

5 Feb 2019

 **WOLVES** **1**
(BOLY 90+5)

 NEWCASTLE UNITED **1**
(HAYDEN 56)

 **Premier League**

MOLINEUX STADIUM, 8PM
FEBRUARY 11, 2019 ATTENDANCE: **30,687** (2,402 AWAY)

Wolves (3-5-2): Patricio; Bennett, Coady (c), Boly; Doherty (Traore 81), Moutinho, Neves, Dendoncker (Costa 68), Otto; Jimenez, Jota (Cavaleiro 68). Subs not used: Ruddy, Vinagre, Saiss, Gibbs-White

Newcastle (5-4-1): Dubravka; Yedlin, Schar, Lascelles (c), Lejeune, Ritchie; Perez (Manquillo 90), Hayden (Diame 85), Longstaff, Atsu (Almiron 72); Rondon. Subs not used: Woodman, Fernandez, Kenedy, Joselu.

Last year Wolves returned from a week-long jaunt to Marbella to produce a season-defining three-game winning streak that got their title charge back on track. This year... not so much. But amid a below-par display they somehow salvaged a point in the fifth minute of four added on at a stunned Molineux.

Wolves have been a lot of things this season – adventurous, attacking, inventive, organised and courageous. They've earned plaudits galore for the football they've played and the results they've pulled off – and rightly so. Perhaps more than anything, though, they are wonderfully spirited. A point wasn't the result they were looking for, but not many teams in this league would have earned it. What you certainly couldn't put the offish performance down to was lethargy or a lack of effort or attacking endeavour. Indeed they created enough opportunities to win two matches, but spurned a glut of decent chances with Raul Jimenez, so prolific in recent weeks, forgetting his shooting boots. Matt Doherty, having the season of his life in front of goal, also missed from just a couple of yards (albeit under pressure from the impressive Sean Longstaff). In the end they had to settle for a point – but it felt like a win.

Nuno's team news was entirely predictable – he named the same XI that beat Everton 3-1 at Goodison Park nine days ago, with Diogo Jota having recovered from the knock he picked up in that game. Wolves came into the clash with the fifth best defensive record in the league and Newcastle the sixth. That certainly showed in a first half in which defences were mostly on top, although both sides will feel they should have

scored. The hosts fashioned the first opportunity when Jonny Castro Otto rolled the ball fractionally ahead of the lurking Jimenez in the six-yard box. Jimenez was involved once more when Doherty picked him out with a precise low ball from the right – in his current form you'd have backed him to score, but the Mexican lashed wildly over from 12 yards. The striker was at it yet again when he took a delicious Ruben Neves pass, took on DeAndre Yedlin and found an angle from the left to test keeper Martin Dubravka, who palmed clear.

Wolves were going through the gears, but instead of making their dominance count they took their foot off the throat and it was Newcastle who ended the half stronger. The visitors went close through the dangerous Salomon Rondon, who took on Conor Coady to fire goalwards in the box – but Coady got a crucial toe on the ball to deflect it wide. Sloppiness crept into Wolves' play with several misplaced passes and a few dodgy clearances (Willy Boly was guilty of both) and the half-time whistle came at a good juncture for the hosts. They made a positive start to the second half and should have taken the lead when an outswinging Joao Moutinho corner was flicked on by Jota towards Doherty, who, under pressure from Longstaff, headed the ball over from just a couple of yards with the goal gaping.

The miss proved oh-so costly just a couple of minutes later when Newcastle took the lead via the softest of goals. Rui Patricio misplaced a pass out of play and from the resulting throw the Magpies worked the ball to Aaron Hayden, who got half a yard on Boly and then beat Patricio at his near post with the keeper only able to help

it into the net. Wolves responded well – Jota fired one at the keeper from 18 yards and then a Jimenez cross was met by Leander Dendoncker, whose header was well saved. Nuno called for the summer 2016 vintage of Ivan Cavaleiro and Helder Costa, with Dendoncker and the limping Jota departing as Wolves went 3-4-3. With 15 minutes to go, their play was becoming more rushed and frenetic, but with organised Newcastle now happy to sit deep there were few gaps to exploit.

On came Adama Traore as Nuno went for broke and the Spaniard's first touch was a shot from a deep Cavaleiro cross – it was blocked and the ball fell perfectly for Jimenez who got his angles all wrong and headed miles wide. It looked like it wasn't going to be Wolves' day, especially when the clock ticked past 94 with only four minutes added. But in the last seconds a deep Traore cross was missed by Dubravka and Boly couldn't miss from a yard out. It was the second goalkeeping error of the night – and it earned Wolves a deserved point at a grateful Molineux. They've now scored six goals in the 90th minute or later (two against Newcastle) and 14 in the 80th minute or later. Yes, 14. It highlights their battling qualities, their never-say-die attitude and their character. In a theme instilled by Nuno that's carried on from last season, they don't know when they're beaten.

NUNO

We have fighting spirit right until the last minute, until the last second, until the referee whistles for the finish. This is one of the things we must keep on doing – that character, that belief. It was not only us but the fans right until the end believed that moment could arrive. It came and I think it brings some justice. We've had a lot of late moments like this, sometimes it gets you the win, sometimes it doesn't, but we cannot look only for that moment of the game. The game was about much more things. The final touch was not there, so we have to be clinical against a team who were compact.

FAN VERDICT – RUSS EVERS

Another late goal which underlines the never-say-die attitude and the belief of this team, despite a performance that seemed to lack the spark and final touch which has been with us for most of the season. We created a few more-than decent chances but the finish was not there. The corner tally of 14-1 tells a story in itself. The goals will not be fondly remembered by either keeper but Newcastle keeper Martin Dubravka seemed to be in the right place for 94 minutes whilst Rui Patricio was largely unemployed. Let's hope the running through treacle effect is over as the biggest game of the season thus far – in my eyes anyway – approaches.

POSSESSION: **60% / 40%** | SHOTS: **22 / 9** | SHOTS ON TARGET: **6 / 3** | CORNERS: **13 / 1** | FOULS: **7 / 9** | BOOKINGS: **1 / 3**

STAR MAN – JOAO MOUTINHO

"If I cannot do great things, I can do small things in a great way," the words of Martin Luther King seem apt when describing the little genius that is Joao Moutinho. He doesn't unleash pinpoint 60-yard rakes or fire in long-range thunderbolts like his younger compatriot Mr Neves, but he does the simple things exceedingly well. With the grace of a ballet dancer playing the harp sat on a cloud, Moutinho is class personified and was the standout player for Nuno's team. Four key passes was more than anyone on the pitch and five tackles was second only to the excellent Sean Longstaff. Kept the tempo high and the passes crisp. A privilege to watch this guy at work in a Wolves shirt.

TWEET OF THE GAME

 Tim Spiers ✔
@tim_spiers_Star

Full-time no idea how Wolves have managed that! Unbeaten in six now. Molineux is stunned.

11 Feb 2019

TABLE

	TEAM	P	GD	PTS
4	MAN UTD	26	17	51
5	ARSENAL	26	16	50
6	CHELSEA	26	16	50
7	WOLVES	26	1	39
8	WATFORD	26	0	37
9	EVERTON	27	-3	33
10	WEST HAM	26	-7	33

BRISTOL CITY

0

WOLVES

1

(CAVALEIRO 28)

Bristol City (4-5-1): Fielding; Wright (c), Kalas, Webster, Dasilva; Eliasson (Taylor 46), Brownhill, Morrell (Pack 46), Palmer (Paterson 66), O'Dowda; Diedhiou. Subs not used: O'Leary, Baker, Kelly, Watkins.

Wolves (3-5-2): Ruddy; Bennett, Coady (c), Boly; Doherty (Neves 81), Moutinho, Saiss, Dendoncker, Otto; Jimenez (Traore 90+2), Cavaleiro (Gibbs-White 70). Subs not used: Norris, Vinagre, Costa, Ennis.

Two trips to Ashton Gate in 14 months – two potential season-defining wins. This one had less of the drama of January 30, 2017, but it may carry just as much importance.

Nuno Espirito Santo's team are now just two victories away from reaching their first FA Cup final for 59 years – and given the momentum they've generated and their success against the league's big boys, even a home draw against Manchester United won't dim their hopes of doing just that. In the third round Wolves produced a fabulous performance in beating Liverpool and were reliant on late drama in edging past Shrewsbury via a replay in the fourth round. At Ashton Gate, they were professional in the first half and then needed a solid rearguard after the break as they withstood some serious Bristol City pressure.

It wasn't particularly pretty, but it was effective. There were some crucial blocks and clearances and, after making a couple of glaring mistakes against Salop, John Ruddy was solid between the sticks, even saving from his opposite number during a frantic finale. It had been the proverbial game of two halves, with Wolves controlling the first period with minimal fuss.

Their team showed three changes with Ruddy in goal, Diogo Jota not risked and Romain Saiss adding steel in midfield in place of Ruben Neves. The hosts came into the game on a phenomenal run of nine consecutive victories, as well as 15 unbeaten in all competitions, with their last home defeat coming in November. However, you wouldn't have guessed those stats judging on the opening 45 minutes. There actually wasn't a single shot from either team in the first 20 minutes, but it wasn't exactly dull, with both sides looking to get a foothold in the game and Wolves mostly playing the better stuff. Matt Doherty was being afforded plenty of space down the right flank and that was Wolves' main outlet, with Conor Coady finding his new contract partner on numerous occasions with a textbook Wolves link-up.

They took a deserved lead on 28 minutes and it was that Coady-Doherty combination that paid dividends. After a patient build-up of several passes, the wing-back took Coady's pass, showed persistence to get beyond his man and pulled back a perfect pass for Ivan Cavaleiro, who coolly finished with his right foot from 12 yards. It was Cavaleiro's fifth goal in 21 games this season – an impressive return considering 13 of those appearances have come from the bench. Shortly afterwards it was nearly 2-0. That man Doherty was again at the heart of it, playing a delightful one-two with Raul Jimenez with the Mexican flicking a return pass inside the box where Doherty, via a deflection, smacked a shot off the inside of the post. Confident Wolves were purring now and they carved the Robins open again when Ryan Bennett played forward to Jimenez – he turned a perfect pass to the onrushing Leander Dendoncker, whose first-time shot was pushed wide by Frank Fielding.

The home side were sent out several minutes early at the end of the break and made a double change with Matty Taylor and Marlon Pack on. Sure enough, there was a big improvement from Lee Johnson's team, who tested Wolves via a series of corners and crosses. Callum O'Dowda twice got in behind Jonny Castro Otto and on the second occasion picked out Jay Dasilva for a free shot from 18 yards, which was ballooned over. It was a let-off. The first 25 minutes of the second half were almost all Bristol City's, but time and again they failed to test Ruddy. Wolves just couldn't make it stick up top. They were being pegged back in their own half and the hosts were dominating possession, albeit without stretching Wolves too hard.

There was respite at the other end when Joao Moutinho came close to doubling Wolves' lead with a superb curling free-kick, which Fielding tipped over. But it was back to normal within a couple of minutes as the hosts retook the initiative. Doherty had to clear a shot just ahead of the goal-line and then Pack put an 18-yard effort too close to Ruddy as the pressure was ramped up again.

After Morgan Gibbs-White spurned a one-on-one Ruddy brilliantly tipped Taylor's looping header over the bar and then Pack somehow bundled over from close range. In five minutes of stoppage time, the kitchen sink was thrown at Ruddy's goal. Keeper Fielding came up for a corner and even had a shot, but Ruddy and Moutinho made crucial blocks as resilient Wolves saw it through.

Their battling qualities, instead of their quality on the ball, their defensive organisation or their devastating ability on the counter, can often be overlooked, but as they showed here they can rough it with the best of them. Very much a case of job done. It's almost time to get very, very excited.

STAR MAN – CONOR COADY

A captain's performance if ever there was one from Coady who revelled in the backs-to-the-wall second half. Eight clearances in total and a couple of vital blocks. Gets an extra point as his distribution was exceptional in the first half – picked out Doherty with inch-perfect rakes on a number of occasions, including in the build-up to the winning goal. It's pinpoint passing that we've all come to expect but shouldn't take for granted. He'll be dreaming of climbing those steps at Wembley.

TWEET OF THE GAME

Tim Spiers ✔
@tim_spiers_Star

I mean bloody nora that was NOT easy. Bristol City cranked the pressure up but Wolves stood firm. Proper rearguard action.

17 Feb 2019

BOURNEMOUTH

(KING PEN 14)

WOLVES
(JIMENEZ PEN 83)

1

1

Bournemouth (4-4-2): *Boruc; Clyne, Ake, Mepham, Smith; Ibe, Lerma, Gosling (c), Fraser; King, Solanke (Mousset 90+1). Subs not used: Begovic, Simpson, Rico, Daniels, Surman, Surridge.*

Wolves (3-5-2): *Patricio; Bennett, Coady (c), Boly; Doherty, Moutinho, Neves, Dendoncker (Traore 77), Otto; Jimenez (Saiss 88), Jota (Cavaleiro 66). Subs not used: Ruddy, Vinagre, Gibbs-White, Costa.*

A truly madcap game with three contentious penalties awarded, a glaring spot kick not given, two goals, 10 bookings, an elbow in the face, a referee losing control, a host of chances – and even the sprinklers came on.

And at the end of it all Wolves came away with a very hard-earned – and satisfactory – point. Teams from outside the top six just don't win at the Vitality Stadium. Burnley were the last to do so back in November 2017. So for Wolves to continue their unbeaten run, which now stands at eight matches in all competitions, as well as starting an appetising week of fixtures with a point and putting any suggestions of being distracted by the FA Cup to bed, meant this was a good point in many respects. Their performance certainly merited it, particularly in a first half in which they were the better side and played some classy, attractive football, before grinding out a result in the second half.

Sadly, though, after an afternoon of thrills and spills, the race for seventh wasn't on the lips of the small band of Wolves fans who'd managed to get tickets for one of the longest trips of the season. If it's implemented incorrectly the introduction of VAR has the potential to ruin the beautiful game of football as we know and love it – but it's because of performances like Roger East's on Saturday that VAR will happen.

The controversy started in the opening minutes. Wolves thought they'd taken the lead when Diogo Jota won the ball back in the Bournemouth box, teeing up Raul Jimenez for a smart finish, but the referee harshly penalised the Portuguese forward for a soft foul. The ref was the centre of attention

30 seconds later – and again Wolves were on the wrong end of his decision. Joao Moutinho unwisely put his foot in on Josh King, but made minimal contact with the Bournemouth man who went down and won the penalty. King sent the penalty into the corner and the hosts were ahead. Mr East wasn't done yet. A few minutes later he denied Wolves a cast-iron spot-kick, missing a blatant hand ball by Chris Mepham when the ball rolled down his arm. Every Wolves player appealed hysterically – usually a sign they'd seen something obvious – but to no avail.

The aggrieved visitors persisted in searching for an equaliser, which they almost found when a Jota cutback was cleared by Nathan Ake and hit Leander Dendoncker, six yards out, before rolling wide. Jota and Jonny Castro Otto were combining to great effect down the left, while an angry Moutinho was as aggressive as he was artistic. The majority of the game was being played in Bournemouth's half and livewire Jota was again causing them problems when he latched on to a Ruben Neves through ball, shrugged off his man and fired a shot across goal, where a despairing Jimenez dive just failed to connect.

As at the start of the first half, Wolves began the second on the front foot and piled on the pressure via Moutinho's searching corners. From successive flag kicks Dendoncker forced Artur Boruc to push over the bar with a powerful header and then Willy Boly nodded on to the roof of the net. A poor Rui Patricio kick invited pressure at the other end but the keeper redeemed himself with a fine low save after Dominic Solanke was cutely played in on goal. It was a crucial moment in an entertaining game between two evenly-matched, attacking sides.

With 20 minutes to go Wolves were again on the attack and Jimenez saw a shot blocked. But once more the game came back to the referee – Moutinho was elbowed in the face by Jefferson Lerma, albeit the Bournemouth man had his eye on the ball. He was only booked amid angry protests from Moutinho's team-mates and then, after treatment, Moutinho himself who was bleeding from the mouth. On came Adama Traore who made an instant impact with a superb cross which Matt Doherty could only glance across goal. And then, finally, a decision went Wolves' way. Doherty looked to shoot from inside the box and was tripped by Adam Smith – this time the referee favoured the visitors and Jimenez coolly sent Boruc the wrong way to score his 12th goal of the campaign.

A madcap game had experienced enough drama and controversy to fill three matches – but it kept on coming. Ivan Cavaleiro hastily tripped Ryan Fraser on the corner of the box and, despite replays showing the contact was made inches outside the area, Mr East pointed to the spot. This time, though, justice was done when King put his penalty wide via the post. The atmosphere was feral now and both teams went for the win. Jimenez almost diverted a Cavaleiro cross in and then Bournemouth ramped things up with a succession of crosses and corners, with Patricio making a stunning save to deny a Solanke header at his near post in the game's last big chance.

The sprinklers even came on in injury time. It was an appropriately wacky end to a wild afternoon.

NUNO

There were many decisions, but the task is so tough for the referee. I haven't seen the images, but I'm always supportive of the referees. In the first 10 to 15 minutes, until the penalty, we started really well, controlling and dominating the game. We had many chances against a tough team, so getting on the front foot early pleases me a lot – until the moment we lost our focus. It was by a decision, but we lost the composure and momentum of the game and allowed Bournemouth to control. It's something we have to work on. After, we had to dig deep. And we did it – we showed character.

FAN VERDICT – NATALIE WOOD

Just two words are needed to describe this game...Roger East! It was without doubt one of the worst refereeing displays I've seen in the Premier League, he was a key character in every major talking point of the game which should never be the case. The sprinklers coming on at the end just about summed up an utterly ridiculous game. It was actually a decent performance against a good Bournemouth team. A draw was a fair result and a good point on the road. The stand-out player would be Jota who continued his good run of form, causing plenty of problems. Dendoncker also had another great game – he is becoming a real key character in our game.

POSSESSION: **45% / 55%** | SHOTS: **10 / 10** | SHOTS ON TARGET: **3 / 2** | CORNERS: **9 / 8** | FOULS: **10 / 15** | BOOKINGS: **4 / 5**

STAR MAN - JOAO MOUTINHO

Had the sheer temerity to be elbowed in the mouth by Jefferson Lerma and was duly booed by the home fans. Moutinho was an angry man – aggrieved by the penalty decision (he was unwise to stick his boot in but it was still a soft decision) and was terrier-like thereafter, snarling and snapping around midfield like an unfed chihuahua. His set pieces were on the money and he was Wolves' most creative influence. Dripping in suave sophistication, soaking in elegance and smothered in style. Hard to believe Wolves paid £5m to buy him – that wouldn't even get you his nipples if Wolves sold him now. Think Rolls Royce, think Cartier, think Caviar, think Joao Moutinho.

TWEET OF THE GAME

Tim Spiers ✔
@tim_spiers_Star

Some ridiculous refereeing decisions made today but Bournemouth improved greatly in the 2nd half and overall it's a good result at a very tough place to come - no non-top six team team has won here since Nov 2017. Two winnable games coming up. Big week ahead.

23 Feb 2019

TABLE

	TEAM	P	GD	PTS
5	ARSENAL	26	16	50
6	CHELSEA	26	16	50
7	WATFORD	27	4	40
8	WOLVES	27	1	40
9	WEST HAM	27	-5	36
10	BOURNEMOUTH	27	-10	34
11	EVERTON	27	-3	33

HUDDERSFIELD TOWN **1**

(MOUNIE 90+1)

 **WOLVES** **0**

JOHN SMITH'S STADIUM, 7.45PM
FEBRUARY 26, 2019 ATTENDANCE: **22,714** (2,323 AWAY)

 Premier League

Huddersfield Town (4-3-1-2): Lossl; Duhaney (Bacuna 45), Kongolo, Schindler (c), Durm; Billing, Stankovic (Kachunga 82), Hogg; Pritchard (Mooy 78); Grant, Mounie. Subs not used: Hamer, Lowe, Zanka, Depoitre.

Wolves (3-5-2): Patricio; Bennett, Coady (c), Boly; Doherty, Moutinho (Gibbs-White 66), Neves, Dendoncker, Otto; Jimenez (Costa 78), Jota (Cavaleiro 66). Subs not used: Ruddy, Saiss, Vinagre, Traore.

Well, at least Wolves won't have to play them next season. Huddersfield have been absolute dross for the past few months, but they've still managed to take six points off Nuno Espirito Santo's team. In their last 14 matches, the Terriers have earned a solitary point against Cardiff. Their last victory in any competition came back in November against, well, you can guess. Talking of 14 matches, this grim surrender continued Wolves' dreadful record against Huddersfield, which now stands at 12 defeats in 14 matches.

It was an evening to forget all round. Even Nuno had an off-night with some strange substitutions. Wolves haven't even managed to score against a team that's let in 50 goals this season. And they've arguably saved their worst two performances of the entire season for matches against a team racing headfirst to the Championship.

Nuno urged his team not to underestimate the Terriers ahead of the game, but his players didn't listen. They were limp in attack, short of ideas and inspiration, they were second best in the tackle and outfought and, at times, outplayed by Huddersfield. They also made uncharacteristic defensive errors. Joao Moutinho and Diogo Jota were their only creative influences but both were withdrawn on 65 minutes. Nuno, again, shunned Adama Traore who remained on the bench come full-time at a raucous John Smith's Stadium.

Huddersfield boss Jan Siewart, chasing his first point as Terriers boss, made a wholesale eight changes from the side that lost 2-0 at Newcastle at the weekend. The first half made a mockery of the recent form of both of these teams. Of the two sides, Huddersfield looked more like one in eighth place than Wolves in what was a turgid and forgettable 45 minutes. The one thing Wolves didn't want to do in the early stages was offer the rock-bottom Terriers any encouragement and get the home fans on-side. Well, that's exactly what they did. The hosts started with purpose and pace, quickly rousing the home supporters. They were first to the majority of loose balls, while Wolves lacked fluency and rhythm. If they managed to string a decent sequence of passes together, they did so laboriously.

Set pieces from Moutinho were their most likely route to goal, as well as the odd lively burst from Jota. Their first shot came on 20 minutes when a Moutinho corner dropped to Matt Doherty whose shot was blocked. Two minutes later the Irishman got a far clearer sight of goal when Jota scampered to the byline and fired across goal, but Doherty couldn't direct it into the net despite half the goal being open.

That was as close as Wolves came. The main problems for were in midfield, with no player doing himself justice. Wolves needed an improvement, but instead it was the Terriers who started the second half with renewed purpose and almost took the lead. First, the ball broke nicely for Steve Mounie whose effort was brilliantly blocked by Willy Boly. From the resulting corner Jon Gorenc Stankovic was afforded a free header but put it too close to Rui Patricio. It was a let-off.

Wolves didn't heed the warning though and Mounie should have broken the deadlock when Ryan Bennett allowed a cross to bounce in the six yard box, but the striker nodded into the side netting. Another Moutinho corner saw Wolves create their first chance of the half, with Boly heading over from a great position. That was Moutinho's last involvement as he and Jota were both withdrawn in favour of Morgan Gibbs-White and Ivan Cavaleiro. Far from improving, Wolves' performance had worsened in the second half but the substitutions sparked a revival of sorts.

The hosts were threatening sporadically with Jonathan Hogg heading just over and then substitute Aaron Mooy shooting wide. Wolves were doing most of the attacking with Cavaleiro and Gibbs-White at the heart of most things, but Huddersfield looked the most likely scorers and Mounie curled a 20-yard effort inches past Patricio's post with five minutes to go. It just wasn't happening for Wolves – and in stoppage time Huddersfield got what they deserved when, after Patricio brilliantly saved from Karlan Grant, Mounie tapped home to send the home fans barmy and have Wolves leaving with their tail between their legs. It was a meek surrender. And, frankly, Huddersfield looked like they wanted it more.

Wolves have enjoyed a season of almost continuous highs and are still in with a great chance of finishing seventh and therefore possibly qualifying for Europe. But one big improvement they will need to make is turning it on against the 'lesser' sides. They've only beaten one of the current bottom five this term (Southampton), drawn against Fulham and lost to Huddersfield (twice), Cardiff and Brighton. Nuno didn't have the answer in his post-match press conference, but it's a recurring problem that needs rectifying – starting this weekend against Cardiff.

POSSESSION: **50% / 50%** | SHOTS: **15 / 7** | SHOTS ON TARGET: **3 / 0** | CORNERS: **3 / 5** | FOULS: **10 / 10** | BOOKINGS: **2 / 2**

STAR MAN - RUI PATRICIO

Despite the defeat Patricio comes out with credit having produced a good all-round performance. Began with a couple of confident punches from corners, there were no problems with his kicking all night and he made a couple of fine saves including from Grant for the winning goal when he was helpless to stop the rebound.

TWEET OF THE GAME

Tim Spiers ✓
@tim_spiers_Star

Not a single shot on target against the team 11 points adrift of safety. Huddersfield have earned 14 points all season - almost half of them have come against Wolves. Both thoroughly deserved wins tbh.

26 Feb 2019

TABLE

	TEAM	P	GD	PTS
5	MAN UTD	27	17	52
6	CHELSEA	26	16	50
7	WATFORD	27	4	40
8	WOLVES	28	0	40
9	EVERTON	28	0	36
10	WEST HAM	27	-5	36
11	LEICESTER	28	-5	35

WOLVES

(JOTA 16, JIMENEZ 18)

2

CARDIFF CITY

0

MOLINEUX STADIUM, 3PM
MARCH 2, 2019 ATTENDANCE: 31,309 (2,968 AWAY)

Premier League

Wolves (3-5-2): *Ruddy; Bennett, Coady (c), Boly; Traore (Cavaleiro 75), Dendoncker, Saiss, Gibbs-White (Moutinho 63), Vinagre; Jimenez, Jota (Doherty 47). Subs not used: Norris, Otto, Neves, Costa.*

Cardiff (4-1-2-1-2): *Etheridge; Peltier, Morrison (c), Bamba (Manga 45), Bennett; Gunnarson; Camarasa, Ralls; Reid (Paterson 59); Niasse (Healey 76), Zohore. Subs not used: Smithies, Bacuna, Arter, Harris.*

At 2pm no-one knew quite what to expect from this game, when Nuno Espirito Santo made one of the boldest team selections of his Wolves tenure. By 4.30pm they were singing "Nuno's the special one" as Wolves cantered to one of their most comfortable victories of the season.

Nuno messed up on Tuesday night at Huddersfield, making some peculiar subs as Wolves crashed to defeat. But this welcome return to winning ways was primarily down to him and a line-up which belonged in the 'brazen' category. Any doubts over whether dropping five of his key performers this season – Joao Moutinho, Ruben Neves, Matt Doherty, Jonny Castro Otto and Rui Patricio – as well as trying Adama Traore in a new position, were well and truly banished.

Just a few days ago Wolves' XI looked set in stone. But Nuno showed his flexibility and his ingenuity with several brave decisions, which all came off. Wolves won 2-0 but the scoreline didn't reflect the opportunities they created (Leander Dendoncker hit a post and the excellent Neil Etheridge made a string of saves) or the silky football they produced.

With wing-backs Ruben Vinagre and Traore flying down the flanks Wolves were football's equivalent of the Red Arrows and Cardiff's defence struggled to cope. Vinagre enjoyed his best game of the season, Traore was back to his explosive best, Raul Jimenez and Diogo Jota combined beautifully for the two goals, Morgan Gibbs-White was bright and inventive and Romain Saiss and Dendoncker marshalled the midfield. John Ruddy, after a nervy start, was solid between the sticks on his first league start of the season and the back three coped well with Cardiff's aerial bombardment. It was a hugely impressive team display and the perfect response to Tuesday.

It was actually Neil Warnock's team who started better, taking the game to a flat-looking Wolves and there was an early scare when Ruddy initially spilled an Aron Gunnarsson shot but then gratefully gathered at the second attempt. Cardiff were spraying it around nicely and troubling Wolves via set-pieces and long throws.

Then two goals in the space of just two minutes completely transformed the afternoon as Wolves sparked to life in sublime style. Their opening goal was a thing of beauty. Willy Boly brought the ball upfield and then Jota, Jimenez and Gibbs-White combined intricately with some gorgeous interplay, slicing through Cardiff with five passes, the last four of which were all one-touch, before Jota coolly sidefooted home. It was a breathtaking move.

Two minutes later it was 2-0. Jimenez robbed Sol Bamba on the touchline, ran inside and chipped for Jota who played back to the Mexican for an easy finish. Cardiff's defence was porous and rampant Wolves set about trying to extend their lead further. They were finding more space than Neil Armstrong, stretching Cardiff via the pace of Vinagre and Traore, with the latter adopting full Roadrunner mode.

Vinagre bounded down the left to cross for Gibbs-White who couldn't divert goalwards, before Dendoncker spurned a wonderful chance when the ball hit his boot from a corner, ricocheted off the post and then Etheridge brilliantly pushed over his rebound. Traore embarked on a George Weah-style run from his own half, leaving both Victor Camarasa and Bamba on the floor, with Bamba fouling Traore and injuring himself in the process to leave the field on a stretcher.

It wasn't plain sailing, though. Ryan Bennett earned his 10th booking of the season to earn a two-match ban (and was lucky to avoid a second yellow card from another sliding foul), while Gunnarsson volleyed inches wide with the last kick of the first half to act as a warning that it wasn't over yet. Traore seemed on a one-man mission to score a wondergoal. Twice he charged from deep as Cardiff's defenders ran scared, but both his shots from outside the box were off target.

Vinagre came close to netting his first goal of the season when his left-footed effort was pushed wide by Etheridge after a fine counter, before Jimenez somehow failed to make it 3-0 when, after being teed-up by Matt Doherty, he shot too close to Etheridge from 10 yards and the keeper made a fine save. The impressive Vinagre again almost netted with a wonderful pacy run down the left and a powerful shot which the excellent Etheridge tipped over. Without him it would have been far more than 2-0.

Nuno's bold and ingenious team selection worked wonders. Wolves got over their 'bottom six' hoodoo in timely fashion – and will now head to Chelsea full of confidence.

NUNO

It was well played in the first half, very well. As the game went on, our mobility started to appear, our talent and combinations. I'm pleased, especially for the manner we scored. I'm not so pleased with the second half because we must do better in situations when we are in front. Credit, though, for the way we defended, until the end of the game, with all the problems Cardiff put you in – throw-ins, corners, through-balls – over and over again. It's good, but we have to improve. It requires a lot of work on the training ground.

FAN VERDICT – GULRAJ KULAR

It kind of felt like Nuno had locked himself in a room with a bottle of vodka and a tactics board and this was the end result. That may be doing the incredible preparatory work he does on a weekly basis a disservice but this was very un-Nuno in terms of how drastic the changes were. What resulted was at times frenzied, untidy and rough around the edges, but also as razor-sharp in attack as at any other point this season. It was a slight throwback to our days under Mick McCarthy when our wings were our breadwinners, with The Golden Arrows flying up and down. Pure, unadulterated pace is a wonderful thing and watching us take advantage of those wide areas was a joy to behold.

POSSESSION: **56% / 44%** | SHOTS: **13 / 12** | SHOTS ON TARGET: **6 / 4** | CORNERS: **7 / 8** | FOULS: **11 / 6** | BOOKINGS: **1 / 2**

STAR MAN – RUBEN VINAGRE

His best performance in a Wolves shirt. More enthusiasm than Liam Gallagher in a swearing competition, more energy than Conor Coady after 15 Red Bulls; this was Vinagre at his bounding best. Only his sixth league start this season but he played without fear and, crucially, combined his penchant for attacking with some good defensive work. Helped stretch Cardiff with his pace and direct approach. Twice came close to scoring but was denied by the excellent Etheridge. And he's only 19 years old.

TWEET OF THE GAME

 Tim Spiers ✓
@tim_spiers_Star

Traore at his explosive best, Vinagre had his best game of the season, Jota and Jimenez combined beautifully for the goals, MGW back in form, Saiss and Donck held it together, back 3 coped with aerial threat and Ruddy was solid after that nervy start.

Absolutely superb, Wolves.

2 Mar 2019

TABLE

	TEAM	P	GD	PTS
4	MAN UTD	29	20	58
5	ARSENAL	29	22	57
6	CHELSEA	27	18	53
7	WOLVES	29	2	43
8	WATFORD	28	-1	40
9	WEST HAM	29	-4	39
10	EVERTON	28	0	36

CHELSEA
(HAZARD 90+2)

WOLVES
(JIMENEZ 56)

1
1

Chelsea (4-3-3): Kepa; Azpilicueta (c), Rudiger, Luiz, Emerson; Kante, Jorginho (Willian 72), Kovacic (Loftus-Cheek 57); Pedro (Hudson-Odoi 62), Higuain, Hazard. Subs not used: Caballero, Christensen, Barkley, Giroud.

Wolves (3-5-2): Patricio; Saiss, Coady (c), Boly; Doherty, Moutinho, Neves, Dendoncker, Otto; Jimenez (Traore 89), Jota (Gibbs-White 81). Subs not used: Ruddy, Kilman, Vinagre, Costa, Cavaleiro.

This was a defensive masterclass for 92 minutes. Sadly for Wolves, the game lasted 94 minutes. Wolves have been a lot of things this season; fearless, attacking, creative, adventurous – but above all they've been excellent defensively. And, as far as an organisational rearguard goes, this was very nearly their finest hour.

In fact, it was almost the perfect away performance. Wolves defended manfully and resolutely, restricting Chelsea's opportunities. Only four teams have conceded fewer goals than Wolves this season. Their organisation has earned them many points – and here it so nearly earned them a famous win. But there was still so much to admire about their performance. Chelsea created a few chances, sure, but none were of the 'clear cut' variety as the solid gold Wolves wall repelled almost everything thrown its way. Blocks, headers, clearances and interceptions were made with apparent ease with each of the back five absolutely outstanding against multi-million pound stars Eden Hazard, Pedro and Gonzalo Higuain. And it was only a pinpoint Hazard shot at the very end that denied them the win.

Wolves are also clinical on the counter-attack and, again, here more than on any occasion that was true as they registered a solitary shot all afternoon and scored from it. It was no surprise that Raul Jimenez was the man to score it – his 14th of the season and his 12th in the league, equalling the Premier League record for a Wolves player (Steven Fletcher, 2011/12) – as he, like Wolves, proved yet again he has what it takes against the big boys. Jimenez's partnership with Diogo Jota is increasingly prolific. All in all

a good day's work, then. It says much for how far Wolves have come that a point at Stamford Bridge is nowhere near being one of their best results of the season.

Nuno will have been confident of earning at least a point given Wolves' record against the top six and a run of 11 wins in 19 matches in all competitions. In a dull first half, though, that result looked like being 0-0 at best. Almost the entire first period was played out in Wolves' half with Chelsea enjoying a whopping 79 per cent possession. For all their dominance, they created very little and Rui Patricio wasn't seriously troubled. It started out as an intriguing tactical battle, with Wolves defending deep and looking to hit the Blues on the counter-attack. As the half wore on, though, there was very little to get excited about and when the whistle blew for the break even a few Chelsea fans were jeering. Nuno will have been impressed with their defensive solidity, but the head coach kept flailing and waving his arms in the air – so much so you wondered if he was taking part in a semaphore competition – whenever Wolves failed to get into the Chelsea third of the pitch.

The status quo continued at the start of the second half. Then on 56 minutes Wolves finally had their first shot – and scored with it. They had searched for a fruitful counter-attack all afternoon and, when it came, it was a thing of beauty. Jota and Jimenez raced clear from their own half, running straight through the middle of the Chelsea defence and combining perfect passes at pace, before it opened up for Jimenez, who received Jota's weighted through ball and beat Kepa Arrizabalaga. Back came Chelsea, with

Patricio smartly pushing wide a Higuain before tipping a Pedro rasper over the bar. Higuain was then inches away from connecting with a corner. Chelsea were mostly being restricting to long shots and crosses by a resolute rearguard. Players were throwing themselves at everything, making a succession of blocks. When Patricio saved brilliantly from Willian's curling shot it looked like Wolves would see it through, but then with, just two minutes left, their hearts were broken when Hazard worked a yard of space and sent a 20-yarder into the bottom corner. They were two minutes away from the ultimate smash and grab – via one shot and one goal. That they couldn't see it through was reminiscent of Arsenal away and felt like a defeat.

Maurizio Sarri disparagingly said Wolves didn't need to be organised to keep Chelsea at bay for so long as they were sat so deep – a classless comment from an under-pressure boss, who isn't exactly one to talk about organisation seen as he struggles to arrange a substitution. The truth is that Wolves were organised with military-like precision. That's not something that comes via a few days' work on the training ground. The unstinting defensive rigidity that Wolves possess stems from the relentless coaching Nuno Espirito Santo and his staff have undertaken from day one, in June 2017.

After losing at Huddersfield you worried they may have gone into next week's mountainous quarter final on a downer, but a hugely convincing victory over Cardiff has been backed up with an impressive point at Stamford Bridge. Confidence is high – and these players look ready to achieve something special.

NUNO

The result could go another way but sometimes you make late goals, sometimes you concede late goals. We'll take a look, but I'm very proud. I'm happy with the performance of my team. It's a tough team to defend against, it requires a lot of work, and the boys were very good. The second half, we started very well, the goal came and then we stayed in shape until the last moment when it was individual quality from a Chelsea player. I'm very proud of how the team worked. It was not only the defence but all the team.

FAN VERDICT – ROB CARTWRIGHT

This was a tactical masterclass from Nuno. The team kept their shape and discipline superbly well and defended as a unit. Chelsea have been on a good run recently and we expected them to come at us from the off. They certainly dominated possession but I was so impressed with Wolves' resolution here. How many times did Chelsea have to turn and play the ball backwards, as they could find no way through? We dealt with everything they could throw at us. They hardly played the ball into our box, with the exception of many crosses that were cleared. To a man they were exceptional. It was a cruel blow to concede the equaliser but it was in all honesty a fair result.

POSSESSION: **76% / 24%** | SHOTS: **22 / 2** | SHOTS ON TARGET: **6 / 1** | CORNERS: **13 / 0** | FOULS: **8 / 14** | BOOKINGS: **1 / 4**

STAR MAN – LEANDER DENDONCKER

Sometimes Dendoncker can be a luxury Belgian chocolate but here he was uncompromising full-fat mayonnaise squeezed all over Chelsea's fancy triple-cooked chips. Full on Doncker Kong beast mode. He can do box-to-box and do it well – but this showed he can do dirty, rugged, no-nonsense defending too. Won no fewer than eight tackles – one of the highest figures of the season from a Wolves player – and made a series of important interceptions while covering a hell of a lot of ground. Excellent.

TWEET OF THE GAME

Tim Spiers ✔
@tim_spiers_Star

Says so much for Wolves that a draw at Stamford Bridge won't be remembered as one of their best results of the season.

Restricted Chelsea's clear-cut chances, unbelievably resolute and disciplined at the back.

At the other end - one shot, one goal. A very good day's work.

10 Mar 2019

TABLE

	TEAM	P	GD	PTS
4	ARSENAL	30	24	60
5	MAN UTD	30	18	58
6	CHELSEA	29	19	57
7	WOLVES	30	2	44
8	WATFORD	30	-2	43
9	WEST HAM	30	-6	39
10	LEICESTER	30	-4	38

WOLVES **2**
(JIMENEZ 70, JOTA 76)

MANCHESTER UNITED **1**
(RASHFORD 90+5)

MOLINEUX STADIUM, 7.55PM
MARCH 16, 2019 ATTENDANCE: **31,004** (4,685 AWAY)

QUARTER-FINAL

Wolves (3-5-2): Ruddy; Saiss, Coady (c), Boly; Doherty, Moutinho, Neves, Dendoncker, Otto; Jimenez (Costa 90), Jota (Traore 87). Subs not used: Norris, Bennett, Vinagre, Gibbs-White, Cavaleiro.

Manchester United (4-3-3): Romero; Dalot, Lindelof, Smalling, Shaw; Matic (Mata 87), Herrera (Pereira 71), Pogba (c); Lingard (McTominay 87), Rashford, Martial. Subs not used: De Gea, Jones, Rojo, Fred.

Smell it, taste it, drink it in – Wolverhampton Wanderers are back in the big time. This wonderful, historic club has been in the doldrums for decades. In the 1950s and 1970s they had one of the finest teams in the land – but since 1981 they've done absolutely naff all in the league and only reached a solitary, measly FA Cup semi-final. Until now. Fosun and Nuno Espirito Santo have transformed everything. Their group of special players have delivered so many memorable days and nights in the past couple of years – but this 'pinch me' win topped the lot by the length of a Diogo Jota run from halfway.

This was the 100th meeting of these two grand old clubs – and from a Wolves perspective it was one of the best. A game for the ages, an atmosphere comparable to nothing we've heard at Molineux for years and years. The barbaric noise after the two goals was so ferocious it could have stripped the gold paint off this grand stadium. Wolves' disbelieving supporters screamed with all the horsepower of a jumbo jet until their lungs could take no more. And on the pitch Wolves lifted off.

The night began with perhaps a surprise from Nuno who selected Romain Saiss over Ryan Bennett at centre-half. The pre-match build-up was as hyperbolic as it gets. The majority of the crowd were in their seats way before kick-off, there were shiny gold and black flags in two stands, blaring music, fire and a lights show. Could anything live up to that? Well, the first half didn't, certainly not in terms of excitement or chances.

Wolves sat deep in the early stages, perhaps paying United too much respect. Matt Doherty and Jonny Castro Otto were full-backs instead of wing-backs, stood in a rigid line of five. That meant United, for all their possession, couldn't carve out an opportunity, but equally with Wolves unwilling to commit many going forward they struggled to work their way up the pitch. Joao Moutinho punted the ball clear in the eighth minute and there was no-one to chase it, as if Wolves were 1-0 up in the 95th minute. However, as at Chelsea last week, Wolves were playing a game of patience. It was cat and mouse, a game of chess. Like a Radiohead album in the 2000s it was interesting, intriguing, perhaps underwhelming at first – but you knew the more it went on it would become epic.

Then a rabble-rousing intervention from captain Conor Coady got Wolves going. He intercepted in midfield and sprayed to Otto, whose cross won a corner. From that Moutinho picked out Ruben Neves on the edge of the box and his first-timer was held by Sergio Romero. Jota then latched on to Doherty's cross but hit his volley into the ground, allowing Romero an easy save, before Otto blocked a Diogo Dalot shot with his elbow in the penalty area – United's penalty appeals were ignored.

Wolves were starting to grow in confidence, committing more players forward, and just before half-time they could and should have taken the lead. Neves played a perfect through ball to the rampaging Jota – he was through on goal but credit to Romero who rushed off his line and blocked from about 15 yards out. Shortly after the break the visitors were again indebted to Romero

who produced a save even better than the one from Jota, extending his frame Superman-style to push Raul Jimenez's free header onto the bar from a Moutinho corner.

With an hour on the clock you wondered if Wolves would rue those two good chances. Moutinho set about making them irrelevant with a curling 25-yarder that the pesky Romero tipped over. The immaculate Moutinho then wriggled his way into the box past two players and passed to Jimenez – he superbly kept possession despite being surrounded and, with his back to goal, squeezed a low shot into the corner to break the deadlock.

But Wolves weren't done there. Seven minutes later they broke via Jota, all on his own in the United half. He brushed aside a Luke Shaw challenge, headed for the penalty spot and struck low and true past Romero with a fantastic finish to make it a scarcely believable 2-0. The noise was almost indescribable. No Wolves fan inside Molineux will ever forget that moment.

United tried to forge a way back into the game. Instead they were initially sent down to 10 men when Victor Lindelof crashed through Jota. After a VAR delay it was overturned to a yellow. The last few minutes were a procession as Wolves' supporters were allowed to enjoy a famous, unforgettable win. Rashford netted in the dying seconds but there was barely time for the restart before the celebrations began. A magical, never-to-be-forgotten night.

NUNO

We did it together! What pleases me more is when I walk down the stands, there are people who say they saw the 1950s and 60s – and they are still coming to the stadium – to give them back this joy, seeing our friends going out of the stadium with this smile, with a lot of beer! Throughout the game the atmosphere was fantastic. The FA Cup is the oldest competition there is. We played well and achieved it with the amazing support of our fans, pushing us and believing in us. We were very organised – we allowed them to have possession but tried to recover in the right areas. It was a very good performance.

FAN VERDICT – CHRIS HUGHES

Nights like this are why we come, week after week, to watch our team. Taking those trips to Carlisle, Crawley and Gillingham in League One. Long trips and late nights, time off work, and not always for a positive result. We did it in the hope that, one day, our club would rise back to where it had once stood, proudly amongst those in the upper echelons of English football. We were absolutely superb all over the pitch from start to finish. Near-perfection all over the park. The biggest shout out has to go to the front two and, as ever, the man who is five foot seven of football heaven, who schooled £90m Pogba in how to control a game.

POSSESSION: 38% / 62% | **SHOTS: 17 / 11** | **SHOTS ON TARGET: 7 / 2** | **CORNERS: 10 / 6** | **FOULS: 12 / 5** | **BOOKINGS: 3 / 5**

STAR MAN – JOAO MOUTINHO

Just take a moment to remind yourself that Joao Moutinho plays for Wolverhampton Wanderers. Not only does this guy have better technical ability than the Cirque du Soleil, he's also a tenacious, tough-tackling midfielder and an inspirational leader. Wolves struggled to get a foothold in the early stages and it was Moutinho who gradually coaxed them upfield, meaning the team grew in confidence and ended the half on top. The rest was history. We know he can pass and tackle but we didn't know he could slide inside two players like an eel down a drainpipe to tee up Jimenez's opener. He also came close to netting a 30-yarder and put a corner on Jimenez's head with Romero pulling off an outstanding save. He's without doubt one of the finest players to ever pull on the famous gold shirt and this, despite some stiff competition, was surely his finest hour this season. Five tackles overall and seven – yes, seven – key passes, the same number as the whole Man United team put together. Bravo Joao, bravo.

TWEET OF THE GAME

 Tim Spiers ✔
@tim_spiers_Star

Genuinely quite emotional, as I'm sure so many of you are. The decades of mediocrity and underachievement, the pain, the heartache, Bolton and Palace in the play-offs, successive relegations, forever failing to live up to those great Wolves teams of years gone by.

No more.

 16 Mar 2019

ANALYSIS

This kind of thing just doesn't happen to Wolverhampton Wanderers. We've become well accustomed to seeing other clubs of a similar size achieve great things and wondered 'why can't that be Wolves?'. Finally, it is. After decades of indifference, of torment, of anguish and of seemingly endless false dawns, their time is now.

We've witnessed numerous magical moments and matches since Nuno Espirito Santo began transforming this perennial Championship outsider and chronic underachiever into one of top-level European football's most exciting 'new boys' inside the space of just 20 months. Cardiff away with two penalties spurned, a carnage comeback against Chelsea at home, outplaying and beating Spurs at Wembley, triumphing in the Battle of Boro with nine men, Bristol City in the last minute – they're momentous memories to never be erased or repressed. This topped the lot.

An FA Cup quarter-final, the most eagerly-awaited tie of the round, live on prime time BBC. There was so much hype, so much expectation – but Wolves lived up to it. They beat grand old Manchester United at a rabid Molineux in front of the watching nation. And they did so convincingly. It was a 'coming of age' performance and result for this blossoming team.

Nuno's game plan was enacted to the letter. They sat deep early on, dismissed the notion of an early United goal and blunted the visitors' potent attack. After feeling their way into the game, via the coaxing influence of the inspirational Joao Moutinho, they grew in belief and confidence. From the 30-minute mark onwards they were undoubtedly the better team. They produced silkier football, they yearned for opportunities and craved victory with a will to win and lustful desire that United simply couldn't match. They combined brains and brawn, artistry and brutality, regimental organisation

> ## "I TOLD THE BOYS TO MAKE HISTORY – MAKE SURE PEOPLE REMEMBER THIS TEAM. IT'S THE BEST GAME OF MY CAREER."
> CONOR COADY

and exquisite elegance. What a team Nuno has assembled.

Everyone played their part. A co-ordinated back line protected John Ruddy like burly bodyguards wearing suits and sunglasses escorting a world-famous rock star through an airport. Leander Dendoncker stayed so close to Paul Pogba he'd be able to pick out the Frenchman's aftershave from a blind smell test. On the flanks, the buzzing Matt Doherty and Jonny Castro Otto were perpetual pesterers in both defence and attack. Between them the magnificent Moutinho and his partner in crime Ruben Neves, the Portuguese artisans, set to work on dismantling United's susceptible defence, picking holes with pacey precision passes. Masters of their craft, Moutinho and Neves, like all the great artists, had substance to back up their style, displaying beaver-like work ethic to tirelessly collect the logs for Diogo Jota and Raul Jimenez to gnash

> ## "IT'S AMAZING – WE CAN DO SOMETHING SPECIAL. I'M VERY PROUD OF THE TEAM."
> RAUL JIMENEZ

ANARCHIC, DISBELIEVING SCREAMS GREETED BOTH GOALS

and gnaw on. Moutinho, after a slip inside the eye of United's mind, teed up Jimenez for the first goal, Neves passed to Jota for the second. Molineux ate it up with a ladle.

Ah yes, the second goal. A few minutes earlier Jimenez had adeptly surprised the excellent Sergio Romero (who must be just about the best back-up goalkeeper on the planet) with a brisk finish on the turn. It was a special moment, but it was beaten by that magnificent second from Jota. Completely on his own in the United half, the undeterred Jota barged his way past the hapless Luke Shaw who was left resembling a DNA double helix. Jota picked his spot and surprised Romero at his near post with a low, true strike that took the roof off Molineux. It was classic Jota. Persistence, courage and robustness, but with the skill and accuracy at the finish. Anarchic, disbelieving screams greeted both goals in a riotous manner rarely heard inside WV1. The wolf pack howled as their heroes feasted on United's bones – the home advantage card had well and truly been played.

> **"IT WAS INCREDIBLE AND A BEAUTIFUL MOMENT FOR US. WE ARE AT WEMBLEY – THE FANS DESERVED IT."**
> RUBEN NEVES

Occasions such as these are commonplace for a club like United. They've won more trophies than any club in the land, they've just beaten PSG in the most remarkable Champions League tie, FA Cup quarter-finals are an annual tradition. Wolves' annual tradition is being knocked out of the League Cup by a lower division minnow. Their new-found status as English football's new kids on the block will take some getting used to, for this is a fanbase far more familiar with failure.

Those lucky enough to watch the glory days of the 1950s have been largely underwhelmed by what they've seen since. The 1970s generation came close and won a couple of League Cups. But anyone who started from the 1980s onwards, brought up on tales of Wolves as the best club in the land, have been almost eternally frustrated by decades of dissatisfaction. Sure there's been great players, cherished memories and success; Championship titles, a few years in the top flight here and there, the odd cup run. But nothing as tangible as this. Wolverhampton Wanderers, after almost four decades in the doldrums, are back where they belong.

Nights like this may become the norm in the coming years, Fosun certainly hope and believe so, but at the moment a giddy, pure, almost childlike excitement has engulfed this club. The suffering has been worthwhile. Wolves, your time is now.

And so on to Wembley where Wolves will face Watford for a place in the 2019 FA Cup final. Win or lose it's been a season – and an FA Cup run – to remember. The teams are also going head-to-head for seventh place and a possible Europa League spot. They're evenly matched and Watford won at Molineux in October, but Nuno's boys will fancy their chances. After all, they've just beaten Manchester United. Clear your diary for the weekend of April 7, it's going to be some ride.

These are the days of their lives – and now Wolves will plot a course for Wembley with a head full of dreams.

> **"THE ATMOSPHERE WAS SPECIAL. NOBODY WILL FANCY PLAYING US – WE PLAYED THE GAME-PLAN PERFECTLY."**
> MATT DOHERTY

BURNLEY
(COADY OG 2, MCNEIL 77)

WOLVES

2

0

Burnley (4-4-2): Heaton (c); Bardsley, Tarkowski, Mee, Taylor; Hendrick, Cork, Westwood, McNeil (Gudmundsson 86); Barnes, Wood. Subs not used: Hart, Lowton, Gibson, Ward, Brady, Vydra.

Wolves (3-5-2): Patricio; Saiss, Coady (c), Boly; Traore (Costa 71), Moutinho, Neves, Dendoncker (Doherty, 59), Otto; Cavaleiro (Jimenez 59), Jota. Subs not used: Ruddy, Kilman, Vinagre, Gibbs-White.

We should have seen this coming. The deadly combination of a match after an international break against a team in the bottom five of the table spelt danger loud and clear – and Wolves succumbed to a disappointing defeat.

Burnley began the day in 17th position after a torrid season. With their final four fixtures looking incredibly difficult on paper, they will have targeted this match as a crucial one to their survival hopes. So what's the one thing you don't want to offer to a motivated team fighting for their Premier League future in front of a passionate and vociferous home crowd? Well, gift them a goal and something to fight for after 90 seconds would be right up there, but that's exactly what Wolves did.

Thereafter, they never fully recovered. Apart from a productive spell shortly after half-time, their usual fluency and potency was absent and they sorely missed the rested Raul Jimenez.

His introduction in the second half helped Wolves' cause, but by then Burnley had the bit between their teeth. They threw their bodies at every cross and through-ball, they sat in deep and defended for their lives. There was no way through and a second goal then killed the match.

The pivotal moment of the match came much earlier in the game, though. Wolves showed two changes from the team that beat Manchester United two weeks earlier – Adama Traore started at right wing-back and Ivan Cavaleiro was up front alongside Diogo Jota. Wolves will have been hoping for an early goal to subdue a motivated side in dire need of a win – but instead

they criminally handed the initiative to the hosts. Chris Wood wasn't picked up from a left-sided free-kick, the striker rounded a stranded Rui Patricio and side-footed goalwards – the ball hit the post and ricocheted into the net off Conor Coady, who was sliding to try and clear it on the line. It was dreadful defending and the worst possible start for Nuno's team.

The goal rocked them in the opening stages, with Wolves' usual assuredness on the ball absent as they struggled to move upfield. Jonny Castro Otto fired a shot from range and Ashley Barnes appeared to block it with his hand, albeit from point-blank range and with his hand by his leg. Wolves' players screamed for a penalty to no avail. Nuno's team improved as the half went on, with Traore the main outlet down the right flank. The Spaniard was full of attacking intent but, with no Jimenez in the middle, his crosses towards the likes of Otto and Jota were meat and drink to a tall Burnley backline. Patricio had nothing else to do for the rest of the half with Burnley happy to sit in and fight for their lead. Wolves sorely missed the focal point of Jimenez in what was an underwhelming half of little goalmouth action or fluid football.

Nuno elected not to change things up at half-time, but saw an improvement from his team, who twice went close in the first five minutes after the restart. Traore raced forward from deep into the heart of the Burnley half and played to Jota on the left – his ambitious curling shot from a narrow angle dropped just wide of the far post. Then Leander Dendoncker galloped down the right, beating a despairing Ben Mee slide and

getting to the byline – he looked up and picked out Cavaleiro, 12 yards out, but he blazed over the bar from a superb position.

With more than an hour gone neither team had managed to register a shot on target in what was a low-quality encounter. The visitors continued to attack but a vociferous and passionate home crowd urged their team forward – they did so to devastating effect to kill the game off. Dwight McNeil edged forward towards the box as Romain Saiss backed off and then drilled a low drive into the corner to make it 2-0 and lift the roof off Turf Moor. There was no way back and it meant Sean Dyche's 300th game in charge of Burnley finished exactly the same as his first – a 2-0 home win over Wolves.

That's three international breaks in a row that Wolves have returned from to slip to a 2-0 defeat against opposition they'll have been confident of beating (Watford and Huddersfield being the others). They just couldn't prise Burnley apart despite dominating possession and play for long spells of an uninspiring encounter and much of that had to do with the absence of Jimenez from the start. Did they also have an eye on next weekend's semi-final? Only the players can answer that, but another below-par performance against Man United on Tuesday will not be tolerated by Nuno.

NUNO

We started very bad, conceding very early in a moment that requires focus, concentration, communication. It's clearly a big mistake from ourselves. Burnley are organised and after we rushed ourselves, we conceded the second goal. It was game over, and there are a lot of things we have to look at. We must be clinical. But first, we must produce better. Burnley are very physical. We must compete in the same way, and against Manchester United, we must compete better than we did here. This is the competition. We must bounce back and raise our standards, and go again.

FAN VERDICT – NATALIE WOOD

A really forgettable away day and, overall, a subpar performance. It is difficult to pick a man of the match, which isn't a rarity this year, but for once it's because there are very few good performances to choose from. We had a tough run of big fixtures before the international break and for some players they had little more than 48 hours back in England before this game, which is always going to have an impact. Burnley frustrated us all afternoon. They were probably one of the poorer teams we have played but they managed to stop us really playing our natural game. We move on from this performance and hopefully respond positively on Tuesday.

POSSESSION: **37% / 63%** | SHOTS: **6 / 8** | SHOTS ON TARGET: **1 / 1** | CORNERS: **1 / 5** | FOULS: **12 / 10** | BOOKINGS: **1 / 1**

STAR MAN – ADAMA TRAORE

Easily the pick of the bunch. Always an outlet on that right flank, he had the measure of Charlie Taylor who spent most of the afternoon looking at the number 37 on Traore's back. A couple of good crosses went unrewarded, with Jimenez not on the pitch to take advantage, and his radar was off at times, but overall he was a menace. Measured his bursts of pace and brushed off challenges with ease. Also carried out his defensive duties. A mystery as to why he was substituted – Wolves tailed off thereafter.

TWEET OF THE GAME

TABLE

	TEAM	P	GD	PTS
4	MAN UTD	31	19	61
5	ARSENAL	30	24	60
6	CHELSEA	30	17	57
7	WOLVES	31	0	44
8	LEICESTER	32	-1	44
9	EVERTON	32	3	43
10	WATFORD	31	-3	43

WOLVES
(JOTA 25, SMALLING OG 77)

 2

MANCHESTER UNITED
(MCTOMINAY 13)

1

MOLINEUX STADIUM, 7.45PM
APRIL 2, 2019 ATTENDANCE: **31,302** (2,961 AWAY)

Wolves (3-5-2): *Patricio; Bennett, Coady (c), Boly; Doherty, Moutinho, Neves (Saiss 84), Dendoncker, Vinagre (Otto 75); Jimenez, Jota (Cavaleiro 73). Subs not used: Ruddy, Gibbs-White, Traore, Costa.*

Manchester United (3-5-2): *De Gea; Young (c), Smalling, Lindelof; Dalot (Pereira 84), Fred (Jones 65), McTominay, Pogba, Shaw; Lingard, Lukaku (Martial 73). Subs not used: Romero, Rojo, Matic, Mata.*

So lightning can strike twice. For the second time in 17 days Wolves beat Manchester United 2-1 at Molineux. Just when you think they might have one eye on Sunday's date at Wembley – and, let's face it, most of us thought that was the case after an opening 20 minutes dominated by United – they go and produce an exhilarating comeback to earn yet another unforgettable win in this special season of wonder and surprises.

It felt like a free hit, it felt like a distraction, but for Nuno Espirito Santo and his players it was anything but. They took it as seriously as any game this season – and produced yet another Molineux night to savour.

Wins over Chelsea, Liverpool and now two against United have all come under the lights in WV1. Last season most of Wolves' unforgettable wins came away from home, but a continuously packed Molineux is being royally treated in 2018/19. What on earth have they got in store for us next?

Nuno made four changes from the XI that lost 2-0 at Burnley. Raul Jimenez and Matt Doherty, rested at Turf Moor, came back into the side, as did Ruben Vinagre and the suspension-free Ryan Bennett. United showed Wolves a deep sign of respect by matching them up with three at the back. The Red Devils made their intentions clear from the kick-off and, at a noisy Molineux where the home supporters predictably directed a few songs about their upcoming Wembley appearance at the away fans, Romelu Lukaku should have netted inside five minutes but put his free header too close to Rui Patricio. The fired-up visitors continued to attack and it was

no surprise when they took the lead via Scott McTominay, who drilled low past a despairing Willy Boly challenge and into the corner via Patricio's fingertips.

The goal seemed to rock Wolves who were making sloppy and basic defensive errors. Shaw cut inside Doherty and Wolves were indebted to Conor Coady for making a goal-saving sliding block, before Jesse Lingard was criminally offered acres of space just six yards out but couldn't beat Patricio with his header. It looked like being a long night, but we should have known better than that.

True to form, seconds after Jimenez fired wide from a narrow angle, they equalised. The tenacious Joao Moutinho won the ball off a dozing Fred high up the field, allowing Jimenez to beautifully thread a pass through two defenders for his partner in crime Diogo Jota who coolly beat David De Gea. It was a classic Wolves goal – and it was the start of a rousing 20-minute spell of attacking football.

Leander Dendoncker should have made it 2-1 but crashed over from six yards after great work from Doherty, while a Ruben Neves half-volley was well saved by De Gea. Jota ran Luke Shaw ragged, as he did for that second goal in the Cup. Shaw learned his lesson this time, choosing to foul Jota instead of letting him scamper free.

Lukaku sent Wolves another warning sign when he fired inches past the post just before the break, but Wolves had earned the 1-1 scoreline at half-time after a spirited and stirring comeback. The open nature of the game continued in the

second half. Patricio produced an excellent save to deny a diving McTominay header as Wolves again failed to deal with a cross from the flanks. At the other end Wolves were looking to counter attack predominantly through Jota, who earned another United booking when Ashley Young brought him down. And just a few minutes later it was deja vu as Young again brought Jota down, after being handed a hospital pass. Referee Mike Dean had no hesitation in dishing out a second yellow and a red.

Wolves had the momentum and the initiative. Jimenez couldn't quite find Vinagre after De Gea inexplicably lost the ball as Wolves looked to take full advantage. They were playing some glorious football at times and Jimenez epitomised their confidence when sending a 'rabona' cross into the box. With 18 minutes remaining Nuno made his first change, sending on Ivan Cavaleiro for Jota and then Jonny Castro Otto replaced Vinagre.

The changes gave Wolves renewed vigour – and they earned a second goal to take the roof off Molineux. Moutinho's cross from the left was diverted goalwards by Jimenez ahead of the rooted De Gea, it bounced slowly towards goal, Dendoncker tried and failed to get a touch but Smalling definitely did as Wolves took the lead. It was diabolical and catastrophic defending but Wolves cared not a jot.

Far from sitting back they should have added another but Cavaleiro smacked against the bar from 12 yards when in on goal. It mattered not. "We're the famous Wolverhampton and we're going to Wembley" they sang at full volume as the game reached its joyous conclusion.

NUNO

What pleases me and the players the most is that we have these nights at Molineux. When United were controlling the game, they kept singing and backing the team – this is what we want in Molineux. Of course, to do it twice against such a difficult opponent, an amazing team, makes the effort and work of the boys really, really good. The approach is always the same, against all the opponents. United started very well, they scored and they were on the front foot. But we reacted well. We stayed in shape, stayed organised. It is not easy to play against Manchester United, but there's no secret. It's work.

FAN VERDICT – CLIVE SMITH

The night started with this as a game we could have done without – but ended as another season highlight. We really were terrific. Games that used to be damage-limitation are now seen as an opportunity to gobble up a top six scalp. The attitude of the players was spot on, not a hint of saving something for Sunday. Every one of them ran their socks off and yet again it was a joy to watch. Going a goal behind did not faze us one bit. We played on the front foot, closing down when they had possession while also using the full width of the pitch as everyone was involved.

POSSESSION: 50% / 50% | SHOTS: 9 / 18 | SHOTS ON TARGET: 2 / 4 | CORNERS: 3 / 5 | FOULS: 5 / 11 | BOOKINGS: 1 / 3 | REDS: 0 / 1

STAR MAN – DIOGO JOTA

His turnaround since starting the season with no goals or assists up to December has been nothing short of remarkable – Jota is now arguably in the form of his career. Six goals in his last six Molineux matches and in his last 14 league games he's scored seven and set up four. Also played a key role in United's downfall, drawing two fouls in quick succession from Ashley Young who was duly sent off. You need to kick him a lot harder than that for Diogo not to get up, Ashley. Also earned a booking off Luke Shaw, who must be doing cartwheels that he doesn't have to face Jota again this season.

TWEET OF THE GAME

Tim Spiers ✔
@tim_spiers_Star

In awe of this team.

Quality, technique, ability, pace etc, yes

But the fearless fighting spirit and courage they show on top of that is something else. They're never beaten. Never overawed.

2 Apr 2019

TABLE

	TEAM	P	GD	PTS
4	TOTTENHAM	31	24	61
5	MAN UTD	32	18	61
6	CHELSEA	31	18	60
7	WOLVES	32	1	47
8	WATFORD	32	0	46
9	LEICESTER	32	-1	44
10	EVERTON	32	3	43

ANALYSIS

If, at the start of the week, you'd asked Wolves supporters if they'd accept two league defeats in exchange for a place in the FA Cup final, the majority would have accepted. But, as Nuno said on the eve of the game, it would be a huge mistake to take their eye off the league. Matt Doherty had also urged Wolves not to let their campaign peter out after Saturday's disappointing defeat at Burnley, where they were powder puff in attack and leaky at the back.

All that was forgotten as, yet again, Wolves bounced back against one of the big boys – and in some style. That's three games against United this season, a draw and two wins for Wolves, who've approached games against the Red Devils in a David versus Golliath manner for what feels like decades. Not anymore.

United changed formation to try and counter Nuno's boys but it didn't work and they were clearly rattled, earning a succession of bookings including two for the red-carded Ashley Young. Molineux lapped it all up. As well as quality, creativity, pace, ability, technique, etcetera, they'd got bottle, spirit and heart by the bucket-load. We saw it against Chelsea at Molineux when they came from behind to beat a top six side and they did it again here to take their tally against English football's premier sextet this season to 13 points from 10 matches. It's a deeply impressive and envious record which hints at another unforgettable campaign in 2019/20. Wolves are no flash in the pan. For the here and now this was not only the perfect build-up for Wembley, it also epitomised Nuno's fearless Wolves – and was the ultimate testament to his famed 'game by game' approach.

Many managers would have been tempted to rest their star players, wrapping them in cotton wool for the semi-final. Nuno's approach was to fight for the ultimate confidence-boosting win, generating momentum and belief just a

"IT WAS A REALLY GOOD GAME AND OUR PERFORMANCE WAS VERY GOOD. THE FIRST STEP TO ACHIEVE SOMETHING IS TO BELIEVE."

DIOGO JOTA

few days after the Burnley defeat threatened to send them to Wembley with their tails between their legs.

The head coach said at his pre-match press conference that it would be a very different encounter to last month's FA Cup game. That was certainly the case in the first 20 minutes when Wolves, unlike when they sat deep and defended three weeks ago, came out on the attack in an open start to the game. Unfortunately that suited United down to the ground and after just 20 minutes they could and should have been 3-0 up.

"WE USED THE CROWD AND THE ATMOSPHERE. IT'S SENSATIONAL AT MOLINEUX - THE BEST IN THE DIVISION."

CONOR COADY

This time Wolves had to weather the storm and, with sloppy United unable to exert their dominance, it was Wolves who took the game by the scruff of the neck.

Nuno more than matched Jose Mourinho at Old Trafford in September – now he's outsmarted Ole Gunnar Solskjaer twice in the space of three weeks.

What a perfect way to prepare for Wembley. See you on Sunday.

NUNO HAS OUTSMARTED SOLSKJAER TWICE IN THE SPACE OF THREE WEEKS

WATFORD
(DEULOFEU 79, 104, DEENEY PEN 90+4)

WOLVES
(DOHERTY 36, JIMENEZ 62)

3

2 (AET)

WEMBLEY, 4PM
APRIL 7, 2019 ATTENDANCE: 80,092 (34,300 WOLVES FANS)

SEMI-FINAL

Watford (4-4-2): Gomes; Femenia (Janmaat 108), Mariappa, Cathcart, Holebas (Masina 98); Hughes (Deulofeu 65) (Sema 112), Doucoure, Capoue, Pereyra; Gray, Deeney (c). Subs not used: Foster, Kabasele, Quina.

Wolves (3-5-2): Ruddy; Saiss, Coady (c), Boly; Doherty, Moutinho (Traore 101), Neves (Bennett 86), Dendoncker, Otto (Vinagre 106); Jimenez, Jota (Cavaleiro 88). Subs not used: Norris, Gibbs-White, Costa.

You'd have to be pretty sadistic to conjure up a crueller way to lose a football match. Wolves were 180 seconds from reaching their first FA Cup final in 59 years – a hoof into the stands, a run to the corner, anything, and they'd have been there.

Instead, Leander Dendoncker tripped Troy Deeney inside the Wolves box. Deeney did the rest and Gerard Deulofeu won it to smash Wolves hearts into smithereens. So much of football is about momentum. Wolves were cruising at 2-0 up, but gradually began to sit deeper and Watford hammered them for 15 minutes. The tide swung their way and Wolves couldn't swim against it. Their FA Cup fairytale turned into a horrifying nightmare from which they couldn't wake.

The day had started with such expectation and excitement. Wembley echoed to the noise of 34,300 Wolves fans singing their gold hearts out in what was a spine-tingling and goosebump-enducing pre-match atmosphere unlike anything this correspondent has heard before.

Only one point separates these sides in the league table and most predicted a close game of football between two evenly-matched sides – which is exactly how the first half panned out. Wolves began on top with Jonny Castro Otto curling wide after just 20 seconds before Joao Moutinho curled a free-kick onto the roof of the net.

Watford defended in big numbers but began to dominate midfield before creating a big chance for Andre Gray, who escaped the shackles of Conor Coady and Romain Saiss but lobbed over John Ruddy and the crossbar from very close range.

It was looking a little ominous – but Dendoncker sparked Wolves into life with a 30-yard rocket which was tipped over by Heurelho Gomes. From the resulting corner Wolves took the lead. Moutinho played it short to Diogo Jota who bent over a come-and-get-me cross to the back stick where Matt Doherty did exactly that, timing his run perfectly to power in a header and send one half of Wembley into ecstasy.

Suddenly Wolves were brimming with confidence. Jota ran from deep past three Watford defenders and curled only fractionally wide as he narrowly avoided scoring a Wembley wondergoal. Back came Watford before the break. A cross was superbly headed by Deeney into Gray's path just 12 yards out – he looked primed to score but Coady produced a monumental block to save Wolves.

They started the second half intent on doubling their lead and the Hornets just couldn't handle Jota. He raced forward on the break and defenders clawed at him like zombies on the last surviving human – Jose Holebas eventually nailed him and Wolves won a free-kick – from which they doubled their lead in sensational style. Doherty swung the ball over for Raul Jimenez who leapt like he was on a trampoline, chested the ball down and volleyed first-time past Gomes with a terrific goal gushing with quality to grace any Wembley occasion.

Wolves continued to look the more likely goalscorers, particularly through the exceptional Jota who had their defenders running scared. The Hornets, though, began to pile on the pressure and it paid off when they pulled a goal back. With 12 minutes remaining a long throw came to substitute Deulofeu who curled a deliciously cute effort into the corner over a helpless Ruddy.

Suddenly Wolves were on the ropes. A succession of corners, crosses and long throws had them pinned deep into their own half. Ruben Neves even hoofed the ball into the air at one point – it was that sort of game now. Watford pushed, pushed and pushed. And Wolves got deeper. Then in the 92nd minute, with Wolves 180 seconds from the final, Watford struck the cruellest of blows.

Dendoncker was judged to have clipped Deeney in the area, Michael Oliver pointed to the spot, VAR agreed and Deeney drove the penalty past Ruddy to take the game into extra-time. Wolves were sick to the pit of their stomach, their supporters stunned and silent.

The players regained their composure and made the stronger start to extra-time but Watford had momentum and belief. They completed their comeback when super-sub Deulofeu raced clear of Otto and Coady before firing across Ruddy in front of the disbelieving Wolves supporters.

Adama Traore, who had replaced Moutinho, had the beating of a tired defence but his crosses couldn't find a white shirt. Then came the big chance – Ivan Cavaleiro was free in the box, he rolled the ball past the keeper but delayed his shot and Watford scrambled it clear. Nuno kicked a water bottle in frustration. There were to be no more opportunities. Watford celebrated wildly as the Wolves players sank to their knees in utter desolation. The FA Cup dream had died.

NUNO

We're in pain. We have to improve and grow so we have another chance to come back to Wembley. We are going to go again. Even though we are in real pain, we are conscious that we should have done better. We had parts of the game playing really well, good football, controlling. It's difficult to play against Watford, because of all the long balls and they have physical players for the second balls. We realised it would be tough in extra-time as the momentum of the game was with Watford. It's difficult to erase the penalty from our minds.

FAN VERDICT - CHRIS HUGHES

Gutting. It hurt at Villa Park in 1998 but that was a game we were never in against a much better side. Here, being, what, two minutes from a place in the final? That stings. Despite us getting the two-goal lead, I always felt Watford were having the better of the game. Both of our goals were against the run of play but it's terrible that we didn't manage the game and see out the victory. Nuno will have to shoulder some of the blame. It was clear that we were retreating into our shell and sitting ever-deeper, inviting relentless Watford pressure. Unlike 1998, as a plodding mid-table second tier club, this group of players have the talent to bring us back here again. This isn't the end, it's the beginning...

POSSESSION: **58% / 42%** | SHOTS: **15 / 11** | SHOTS ON TARGET: **3 / 6** | CORNERS: **7 / 6** | FOULS: **16 / 11** | BOOKINGS: **3 / 2**

STAR MAN – DIOGO JOTA

At times he was awe-inspiring, taking the game to Watford on his own with a series of barnstorming runs deep into their half, holding off the challenges of defenders taller and supposedly stronger than him. Tenacious, courageous and skilful, like Jimenez it was so cruel that Jota was on the losing side. He and his strike partner were actually pretty quiet in the first 30 minutes, shackled by an organised Hornets defence. But he came to life thereafter, firstly with a delightful cross for Doherty's goal and then Jota almost scored a Wembley wondergoal, embarking on a mazy run from deep and curling just wide. He continued in this manner in the second half, frightening the life out of the Watford backline and earning a number of free-kicks including for the second goal. Wolves were never the same after he departed. One of English football's form players right now.

TWEET OF THE GAME

ANALYSIS

There's no way to dress it up, no way to soften the blow. You can't paint lipstick on this hog of a defeat. This hurts – and then some.

At the 79th-minute mark of this FA Cup semi-final, Wolves were 2-0 up and heading for the club's first final for 59 years. They were under pressure, sure, but they were repelling Watford's advances with a string of blocks and clearances. Then a moment of magic from the right boot of Gerard Deulofeu flipped the game on its head – and Wolves never recovered.

What took place over the next 41 minutes was almost unexplainable, other than to point to the momentum Watford generated from that moment thereafter. Nuno's Wolves just don't let leads like this slip. They didn't necessarily lose their heads, or forego their discipline, or hand victory to Watford on a plate. No matter how hard they tried, they just couldn't find the plug to stop the water sinking down their FA Cup drain. With Diogo Jota, Ruben Neves and Joao Moutinho all substituted, they lacked the creativity and inspiration they craved and, while Watford's substitute was their match-winner, Wolves' subs couldn't make the same impact.

It'll take a long time to get over this. They were on the brink of history, of greatness, of immortality. There were no villains, no poor performers – they gave absolutely everything to reach the final, but Watford took their momentum and ran with it. Wolves just had no answer. It's been a magical FA Cup run, but to the long list of semi-final heartaches this club has suffered – 1973, 1979, 1981 and 1998 – you can add 2019.

Wolves will surely never have a better opportunity than this to reach a final and that's what hurts the most. Leander Dendoncker's trip on Troy Deeney was clumsy and Wolves could have no arguments with the decision, which was backed up by VAR. The Belgian was close to tears afterwards

as he admitted it was a "stupid foul". He didn't see Deeney coming, like Wolves didn't see the Watford juggernaut coming – and you cannot dispute that they deserved to win this game.

If the quarter-final victory over Manchester United was one of the greatest victories in Wolves' recent history – and many players including Conor Coady and Matt Doherty felt it was the best of their career – then this was surely the most torturous defeat. In the stands the atmosphere in the Wolves end, so ear-bleedingly raucous before kick-off (has Wembley ever been louder?) was reduced to silence that would make a morgue sound rowdy.

They had arrived in London quietly confident of seeing their team create history, turning one corner of the capital into a sea of gold and black, having watched Manchester City unconvincingly edge past Brighton a day earlier. Many of them believed Wolves' name was on the trophy.

This will take time to get over, but get over it Wolves must. Allowing the season to peter out would be something else entirely and Nuno will be furious if his players do so. If Watford win the Cup the dream of Europe will vanish, but if Wolves were to miss out on finishing seventh and Manchester City win the trophy, it would be a huge waste.

> "IT WAS A STUPID FOUL IN THE LAST SECONDS OF THE GAME. I SHOULDN'T HAVE TOUCHED HIM, BUT IT'S TOO LATE."
>
> LEANDER DENDONCKER

In defeat they can be deeply proud of their magnificent run to the semi-finals, the club's first since 1998. Reaching this stage was a considerable achievement and victories over Liverpool and Manchester United will live long in the memory.

They must learn lessons in defeat – and channel the pain and anger into a revival in the coming weeks. Revenge of sorts at Vicarage Road in late April may go some way to doing that. Who knows, it may be Wolves, not Watford, who end up in Europe after all.

SOUTHAMPTON
(REDMOND 2, 30, LONG 71)

3

WOLVES
(BOLY 28)

1

ST MARY'S STADIUM, 3PM
APRIL 13, 2019 ATTENDANCE: 31,308 (3,262 AWAY)

Southampton (5-4-1): Gunn; Valery (Stephens 84), Yoshida, Bednarek, Vestergaard, Bertrand; Sims (Romeu 61), Ward-Prowse, Hojbjerg (c), Redmond; Ings (Long 61). Subs not used: McCarthy, Targett, Armstrong, Austin.

Wolves (3-5-2): Patricio; Saiss, Coady (c), Boly; Doherty (Traore 60), Moutinho, Neves (Gibbs-White 70), Dendoncker, Otto; Jimenez, Jota (Costa 87). Subs not used: Ruddy, Bennett, Vinagre, Cavaleiro.

It must be incredibly difficult to rouse a team after a blow as crushing as last weekend. But whatever happened to Wolves eight days ago, there was no excuse for this defensive capitulation.

Nuno Espirito Santo's team will have desperately wanted to immediately bounce back from their semi-final nightmare. Instead they contrived to produce arguably the worst defensive display since the Portuguese head coach rolled into town in the summer of 2017. Southampton scored three but it should have been far more. Wolves dithered, they hesitated, they gave the ball away, they didn't keep their shape or discipline. They played like strangers at the back. Their defensive performance, as with their succumbing to Watford last weekend, was most un-Wolves-like under Nuno.

There were numerous culprits and an excessive number of individual mistakes. Going forward wasn't as much of an issue – in the first half they responded to conceding an unforgivable early goal, just as they had at Burnley, with a bright attacking display that hinted they could score a few goals themselves. Attack was the best form of defence and Wolves enjoyed 70 per cent possession overall, but once Saints had restored their lead on the half-hour they could afford to sit deep and soak it all up. The main problems were at the other end – and Wolves got exactly what they deserved.

The Saints came into the game in decent form with three wins in their past five, which had seen them climb five points clear of the relegation zone. For Wolves, then, the game was reminiscent of their last away trip to Burnley, facing a struggling team arguably in a false position. However, they took that notion a little too literally – as at Turf Moor they fell asleep at the back and conceded inside 90 seconds.

Josh Sims got in behind Willy Boly and Jonny Castro Otto down the right and was able to pick out Nathan Redmond with a low ball into the six-yard box – he nipped in ahead of a dithering Romain Saiss to slam home with a minute-and-a-half on the clock. It was a desperately poor goal to concede.

Diogo Jota and Raul Jimenez began to trouble the Saints' back line with the latter shooting at Angus Gunn from 18 yards. Leander Dendoncker then saw a close range effort blocked after great work from Otto. It was all Wolves – a deserved equaliser soon followed. The trusty right boot of Joao Moutinho bent a corner towards Boly who, under pressure, planted a perfect header into the corner for his second goal of the campaign.

That should have been the foundation for Wolves to take charge. Instead they capitulated. Redmond struck again inside two minutes, latching on to a defence-splitting pass and, being kept onside by Conor Coady, dinked cutely over Rui Patricio for his second of the game. Wolves were rocked. Ruben Neves misplaced a basic pass in his own third and the impressive Sims fired across goal from a good position. Then after yet another poor pass Sims was played in again, this time all on his own, but fired past the advancing Patricio and wide. It could and should have been at least 3-1 – Wolves were all over the shop.

After the break Wolves huffed and puffed with plenty of pressure and a couple of corners, but they weren't blowing the Saints door down. Nuno called for Adama Traore who made an instant impact, sprinting past two defenders and sending over a decent cross, which was cleared.

Their big chance arrived on 69 minutes – but Raul Jimenez blew his lines. A corner was nodded back into the six-yard box – a defender merely helped it on to the boot of Jimenez, who had a free volley from just eight yards, but his effort was shanked so far wide it went out for a throw.

Southampton made them pay for spurning it when substitute Shane Long, criminally being kept onside by a motionless Traore who was two or three yards deeper than his team-mates, beat Patricio. Wolves' defensive incompetence continued but Southampton didn't add to their tally and the closing stages were a procession.

The result continued their poor record versus struggling sides – against the current bottom five they've played eight, won two and lost five. A Wembley hangover? Maybe, but Wolves haven't won away from home in the league since February 2 and this defeat shared hallmarks with losses at Burnley and Huddersfield.

It would be such a shame if their season petered out from here. It's been a magical campaign – and Nuno has five games left to oversee the conclusion it deserves.

Things can quickly turn around again and you'd back this Wolves team to do so, as they have time and again.

NUNO

I think it was a bad game, a bad performance. Since the beginning of the game, our defensive organisation was not at our best. The only moment we played the way we can play was after the moment we conceded (the opener) until the moment we equalised. The game was there for us, but we conceded in a way we cannot concede. The game became harder and the second half was bad. A bad performance. We are a team that wants to compete in every game, and we didn't compete at our best. We need to regroup, analyse, look at the game and react for the next one. We have to regroup and face the last challenges with optimism.

FAN VERDICT – ADAM VIRGO

Overall it wasn't good enough. There were a couple of spells individually that were decent but as a whole it was way below the standards we've set this season, especially from a defensive point of view. Confidence is a huge thing in football and any sport for that matter. Last week in the semi-final clearly took a lot out of us physically and mentally which could have made a difference to our performance. It's natural to be affected by what happened last week, we're all human. One to forget and move on from. Hopefully the week in Marbella will do the players some good.

POSSESSION: 31% / 69% | **SHOTS: 12 / 17** | **SHOTS ON TARGET: 6 / 2** | **CORNERS: 4 / 9** | **FOULS: 13 / 8** | **BOOKINGS: 1 / 3**

STAR MAN – RUI PATRICIO

Wolves conceded three times but you couldn't really look at Patricio for any of them. He's had absolutely no protection from a leaky defence and indeed helped keep the score down, especially with an excellent save from point blank range to deny Maya Yoshida shortly after Southampton's third goal.

TWEET OF THE GAME

Tim Spiers ✓
@tim_spiers_Star

Wembley hangover or not, that's no excuse for the basic defensive errors we saw time and again today. Probably the worst defensive performance under Nuno. Five games left to give this special season the ending it deserves #wwfc

13 Apr 2019

TABLE

	TEAM	P	GD	PTS
5	MAN UTD	33	19	64
6	ARSENAL	32	25	63
7	LEICESTER	34	1	47
8	WOLVES	33	-1	47
9	EVERTON	34	2	46
10	WATFORD	32	0	46
11	WEST HAM	34	-10	42

 **WOLVES**

 **BRIGHTON**

 0

 0

Wolves (3-5-2): *Patricio; Bennett, Coady (c), Boly; Doherty (Traore 83), Moutinho, Neves, Gibbs-White (Dendoncker 73), Otto (Vinagre 66); Jimenez, Jota. Subs not used: Ruddy, Saiss, Costa, Cavaleiro.*

Brighton (4-4-1-1): *Ryan; Bruno (c) (Bernardo 70), Duffy, Dunk, Bong; March, Stephens, Propper (Kayal 10), Izquierdo; Gross; Murray. Subs not used: Button, Burn, Jahanbakhsh, Andone, Locadia.*

It would be a crying shame if Wolves' fabulous season ended with a whimper, but unless they can rediscover their spark in the next week that's exactly what will happen.

From the very first minute of this incredibly frustrating afternoon it was abundantly clear that Brighton were playing for a 0-0 draw. Wolves, though, just couldn't find a way through the wall of garish green shirts. That wasn't due to a lack of effort or endeavour, far from it. They hit the woodwork twice and dominated possession and play. What Wolves did lack was a little ingenuity and nous in the final third. Joao Moutinho's set-pieces were their best route to goal, especially in the second half when they created opportunities against opposition with fewer attacking ambitions than any team seen at Molineux this season.

It was reminiscent of last season's goalless stalemate against equally defensive-minded Sunderland. Indeed, the more possession Wolves enjoy in a match (68 per cent here) the less likely their chances seem to be of winning.

Ryan Bennett and Morgan Gibbs-White were handed starting berths as Nuno Espirito Santo made two changes from the team that lost 3-1 at Southampton. Brighton arrived at Molineux desperately low on form and confidence after five successive defeats in all competitions without scoring a single goal. The visitors lined up in a deep-lying 4-5-1 formation and set out denying Wolves space and freedom in the final third. They were more than happy to let Wolves have the ball – and Nuno's team enjoyed 80 per cent possession in the opening 20 minutes – but keeper Mat Ryan wasn't forced into action

during one of the dullest 45 minutes witnessed at Molineux this season.

Wolves' early route to goal looked like being via the lively Gibbs-White, who was a boundless ball of energy in midfield, recycling possession briskly and looking for pockets of space and that piercing through ball. Chances, though, were at a premium. Gibbs-White floated a decent ball to Diogo Jota but he couldn't get a shot away under pressure. Then Jota played a delightful one-two with Raul Jimenez and burst into the box, but again a Brighton defender snuffed him out. The in-form Jota was Wolves' liveliest attacking threat. He wriggled into some space 20 yards out and fired across goal and just wide. And then on the stroke of half-time he latched onto a deflected Ruben Neves long-ranger and toe-poked the ball onto the top of the bar from just a few yards out. That was as close as Wolves came during an agricultural half of football that failed to raise the noise levels at a sun-kissed Molineux.

As for nervous Brighton, their half could be accurately summed up by one moment – the biggest noise the away fans generated was when their team won a throw in Wolves' half.

The second half continued in much the same pattern although Brighton looked a tad more adventurous. Indeed, Beram Kayal's 25-yard thunderbolt skimmed just a few inches over Rui Patricio's crossbar. Wolves were lacking a spark – Moutinho's corners were a threat but dogged Brighton were scrambling them clear.

Nuno injected pace via Ruben Vinagre who replaced Jonny Castro Otto in the 67th minute

and instantly had the right idea when he bombed to the byline and crossed to Jimenez, whose looping header came to nothing. Moutinho's corner was cleared to Jimenez whose 15-yard half-volley spank wasn't too far over, but with time running out Wolves weren't getting anywhere. Leander Dendoncker replaced Gibbs-White, whose influence had waned after the break and within seconds of his introduction the Belgian almost broke the deadlock – Jimenez clipped it to Jota who sent a header bouncing off the post, it rebounded to Dendoncker but from point blank range he was somehow denied by a sprawling Ryan in the Brighton goal.

Wolves had their tails up now but they just couldn't find a way through. Nuno's final roll of the dice came seven minutes from time with Adama Traore replacing Matt Doherty. Moutinho's free-kick was met by Jimenez who headed towards Dendoncker – he nodded at Ryan from a great position. It just wasn't happening for Wolves. Vinagre and Traore were the best route to goal in the closing stages but there was no way through and Brighton escaped with the goalless draw and the point that they came for.

Counter-attacking at pace is Wolves' forte – when teams sit deep and try to frustrate them, they sometimes don't have enough in their ranks to break them down. That will have to change next season when there'll be no element of surprise against Premier League managers who will see them coming. For now, though, there's an immediate task at hand – reviving a slightly forlorn Wolves for the final four games of the season. If that doesn't happen by this time next week, seventh place will surely be out of reach.

NUNO

We had chances, we had combinations, we tried. We had a lot of the ball and tried to move with intensity but it was not to be. That's football. It's very difficult to break a team down, Brighton defended well because their main objective was not to concede.There was good goalkeeping and then the ball that hit the post could go in but didn't. Our fans were pushing, the boys were trying. The ball just didn't go inside of the net.

FAN VERDICT – RUSS EVERS

Stats don't always tell the story but here we had 68 per cent possession, 22 shots to five, five of which were on target to Brighton's none, plus 14 corners to one. We hit the woodwork twice and on another day a 3-0/4-0 home win would not have surprised any of the 31,000 sun worshippers at Molineux. Brighton defended deeply and well and were experts at time wasting but we should have been able to put them to bed. However, it was not to be and at least we got back to a clean sheet and maintained the unbeaten home run. At least Arsenal in midweek will try to attack us!

POSSESSION: 68% / 32% | **SHOTS: 23 / 5** | **SHOTS ON TARGET: 5 / 0** | **CORNERS: 14 / 1** | **FOULS: 0 / 8** | **BOOKINGS: 0 / 1**

STAR MAN – JOAO MOUTINHO

The best player on the pitch. Constantly looked to get on the ball and make things happen. A pass accuracy of 95 per cent and he was Wolves' most likely route to goal, especially via his teasing set pieces which led to the majority of Wolves' chances. Controlled the midfield. Surely player of the season? His consistency is metronomic.

TWEET OF THE GAME

Tim Spiers ✔
@tim_spiers_Star

Brighton just won a throw and their fans went mental

                                        20 Apr 2019

TABLE

	TEAM	P	GD	PTS
6	MAN UTD	33	19	64
7	WATFORD	34	0	49
8	LEICESTER	35	1	48
9	WOLVES	34	-1	48
10	EVERTON	34	2	46
11	WEST HAM	35	-10	43
12	NEWCASTLE	35	-9	41

WOLVES
(NEVES 28, DOHERTY 37, JOTA 45+2)

ARSENAL
(SOKRATIS 80)

3

1

Wolves (3-5-2): Patricio; Bennett, Coady (c), Boly; Doherty, Dendoncker, Neves, Moutinho (Gibbs-White 90), Otto; Jimenez (Traore 82), Jota (Cavaleiro 78). Subs not used: Ruddy, Vinagre, Saiss, Costa.

Arsenal (4-3-3): Leno; Maitland-Niles, Sokratis, Koscielny (c), Monreal; Xhaka, Torreira (Guendouzi 59), Ozil; Mkhitaryan (Kolasinac 59), Lacazette, Iwobi (Nketiah 71). Subs not used: Cech, Mustafi, Elneny, Willock.

Tired? On the beach? Not a chance. Instead of wilting or going through the motions with just a few games to go, fearless Wolves instead roused themselves and produced one of their most impressive victories of the entire season.

They played the occasion perfectly, allowing Arsenal to control the ball and then taking full advantage of their defensive frailties to score three times in the first half and, ultimately, win the game. Coming on the back of three successive disappointing results it was a remarkable turnaround. The hapless Gunners left the door ajar but Wolves crashed through it via a wave of fluent attacking play and the game was over after 45 minutes.

Nuno kept faith with 10 of the players who had failed to break Brighton down a few days earlier, with Leander Dendoncker replacing Morgan Gibbs-White in the only change. In contrast, Arsenal boss Unai Emery made no fewer than seven changes from their 3-2 defeat at home to Crystal Palace, with top scorer Pierre-Emerick Aubameyang out injured. The Gunners came into the game with a poor away record, having won only six times on the road all season. Wolves, meanwhile, were unbeaten at fortress Molineux since January 2. The first half accurately reflected these facts.

It was actually a pretty dire opening 15 minutes, with Arsenal dominating possession (around 80 per cent) but doing absolutely nothing with it. Wolves were playing it tight and cagey but doing little going forward. As a spectacle it was so bad it had you wishing Brighton were the opposition.

Then Wolves burst to life. It was Diogo Jota who sparked some noise from the home crowd with a gallivanting run from his own corner flag to the Arsenal half. Then the mercurial Ruben Neves got the ball rolling with an incisive pass from deep which led to Matt Doherty teeing up Joao Moutinho for a superb effort from 20 yards which curled just wide. Wolves were motoring now and Raul Jimenez prodded over the bar from a long Ryan Bennett throw.

Then that man Jota stretched his legs to scamper forward from deep, playing to Jonny Castro Otto, who was cynically wiped out just outside the box. It may have prevented a goal – but Wolves needn't have worried. From the resulting free-kick Neves clipped it powerfully up and over the wall and past a helpless Bernd Leno. Molineux erupted – Wolves were doing it again against a top six side.

Jimenez fired wide and Neves clipped a deflected free-kick over as Wolves, so passive in those opening 15 minutes, kept their boot to Arsenal's throat. Soon after it was 2-0. Yet again Jota was the inspiration, taking Otto's pass and crashing one into the six-yard box, forcing Leno to push the ball behind for a corner. From that, Moutinho played it short to Otto, whose whipped cross saw Doherty get ahead of a flailing Leno to head home for his eighth goal – by far the most prolific season of his career (plus seven assists to boot).

Wolves weren't done there. Before half-time they made it a scarcely-believable 3-0 and it was no surprise to see Jota add his name to the scoresheet, producing another trademark run from deep, skipping past Sokratis before firing under Leno, who made another gaffe to allow the ball to roll beneath him. Molineux buzzed amid a sense of disbelief and wonder at half-time.

The Gunners, whose only real opportunity in the first half came when Alexandre Lacazette fired over from the right of the six-yard box, had to change something and they switched formation for the second period to 3-5-2. It had little effect. Indeed, it was more of the same with Arsenal controlling and dominating possession – and Wolves carving out the meaty chances. The more Arsenal pushed forward, the more Wolves looked likely to add to their lead on the break.

Jimenez raced down the right and picked out Jota who, if he'd controlled the ball would surely have slammed home, but the ball bounced off him. The impressive Otto was in the thick of the action again when he played the ball across the box for Jimenez, who set his sights from a narrow angle but drove across goal and wide. Arsenal pressed and pressed but to no avail. Ryan Bennett and Lacazette tangled legs in the box but referee Stuart Attwell judged it wasn't a penalty – and then Bennett brilliantly threw his body at the ball to block Lacazette's shot from close range.

It looked like being a cakewalk but Arsenal pulled one back with 10 minutes to go when Sokratis headed home a Granit Xhaka corner to give them the faintest glimmer of hope. A couple of uncomfortable set pieces aside Arsenal offered just a minimal threat thereafter and Wolves saw out four minutes of stoppage time with no problems at all. Molineux was in full hero-worship mode at full-time. Rightly so.

NUNO

Fantastic for the players. Credit to them – a fantastic performance. Our fans came here in large numbers. It was the largest attendance we have had this season, so thank you to them. It was another good night at Molineux – I'm very proud of how the players engage themselves and commit themselves. We give everything we have each game. That's what makes me proud, the belief we have in ourselves. Playing against any team is difficult, but Arsenal have very good players. The first moment we broke, we were lucky enough to have this moment of quality. That put us on the front foot, so well played.

FAN VERDICT - GULRAJ KULAR

As sure as clockwork, the victory against a top six side arrives. To be quite honest, this wasn't like any of the other games we've had against the big guns, in a number of ways. There was much good about Wolves and honourable mentions go to the back three and the wing-backs in particular. But the vast majority of the credit has to go to Diogo, who dragged us up from our bootstraps like a disciplinarian parent and whipped us into shape, with his drive, determination and outstanding ability to pummel his way past opponents. He really is unstoppable, against the highest class of opposition as well. It's no longer Ruben Neves' exit I fear now...

POSSESSION: **30% / 70%** | SHOTS: **11 / 11** | SHOTS ON TARGET: **3 / 1** | CORNERS: **5 / 5** | FOULS: **12 / 9** | BOOKINGS: **2 / 3**

STAR MAN – JONNY CASTRO OTTO

His finest hour in a Wolves shirt? Defensively sound, full of running, rarely gave the ball away, produced important tackles and interceptions – and then going forward he was a revelation. Like an amorous puppy who hasn't yet discovered his no-go areas, incessant Otto just couldn't be shaken off by the Arsenal defence. A continual, unabating, positive presence in the opposition half. Vinagre is supposed to be the left wing-back who attacks with wild abandon, but Otto adopted that role here, linking sublimely with Jota on a number of occasions. Fouled for the free-kick which led to the first goal and then swung over a peachy cross for Doherty's second. Bravo.

TWEET OF THE GAME

Tim Spiers ✔
@tim_spiers_Star

Wolves have beaten Arsenal for the first time in FORTY YEARS.

Twenty miserable matches played since they beat the Gunners in 1979 #wwfc

24 Apr 2019

TABLE

	TEAM	P	GD	PTS
4	CHELSEA	35	21	67
5	ARSENAL	35	23	66
6	MAN UTD	35	13	64
7	WOLVES	35	1	51
8	WATFORD	35	0	50
9	EVERTON	35	6	49
10	LEICESTER	35	1	48

ANALYSIS

When Wolves last beat Arsenal, Margaret Thatcher had been Prime Minister for four months. It's been 40 long years since the Gunners were downed by the men from Molineux – a barren run of 20 winless matches. As he's proved so often in the past two years, Nuno Espirito Santo loves breaking a Wolves hoodoo.

The odds on them beating Arsenal here were far greater than them beating Brighton, but regular Wolves watchers knew which was the more likely victory. That's 16 points earned against the big six now, compared to 10 against the bottom six. Arsenal had 71 per cent possession but couldn't muster a solitary, measly shot on target until they scored a mere consolation from a late corner. Sure they played some pretty stuff, but it was chilled out house over a 9am Ibiza sunrise kind of pretty. Note perfect, sure, but no zest, nothing piercing or penetrating. In contrast Wolves were brash punk rock, producing razor-sharp two-minute attacks on the senses. And Arsenal couldn't cope.

The magnificent Diogo Jota tore them to shreds with his now trademark gallivanting runs from deep. It was two such runs that led to a free-kick for the first goal and a corner for the second until Jota went it alone to net a third before the first half was up.

Jota is a superstar, not just in the making, but right now. He's enjoying a phenomenal second half of the season, so much so that he's making a late run for player of the year. Since the switch to 3-5-2 on December 5, when Jota scored his first of the season against Chelsea, he's netted eight goals in 11 Molineux appearances. Wolves were flacid and passive in the opening stages of this game and it was Jota who sparked them – and the quiet home fans – into life when he bombarded from his own corner flag into the Arsenal half, before playing a part in all three goals. He is Wolves' fearless, undaunted, audacious daredevil.

Jota still wasn't man of the match, though. That accolade belonged to Jonny Castro Otto and there was a strong supporting cast too. Like Wolves, Ruben Neves had endured a below-par couple of weeks and, like Wolves, he enjoyed a return to form here. Coincidence? Nope. When Neves is on top of his game, Wolves invariably are too. His passing range was more adventurous and, in possession, he was further up the field too. A beauty of a free-kick went up and down quicker than Zebedee at the Hacienda to beat a despairing Bernd Leno dive and open the scoring. It means he's scored more goals (four) this season than had touches in the opposition penalty area (three).

Defensively Wolves were excellent. In sharp contrast to their horror show against Southampton a couple of weeks ago, they were disciplined, organised and defiant. The Gunners couldn't find a way through. Unsung hero Ryan Bennett produced one of his best display of the season, which included a goal-saving block and more clearances (six) and interceptions (four) than any of his team mates. Romain Saiss gave some excellent displays when he replaced Bennett in the side, but Wolves do tend to look more solid – and certainly more rigid and organised – when Bennett plays. He, Conor Coady and Willy Boly know each other's games inside out.

And then the reliable, consistent Matt Doherty managed to nab his eighth goal of the season. It was only five years ago he wasn't a regular in League One. Throw in seven assists and you've got the season of a lifetime for the Irishman.

So, after a disappointing couple of post-Wembley results, Wolves are very much back on track. They travel to Watford this weekend to launch a revenge mission – and will move a giant step closer to securing seventh if they complete that mission. What a season it's been. Now for the icing on the cake.

> **"I'M REALLY HAPPY TO SCORE AND ALSO FOR THE TEAM'S PERFORMANCE. AFTER THE FIRST 10 MINUTES WE CONTROLLED THE GAME."**
> RUBEN NEVES

WHAT A SEASON IT'S BEEN – NOW FOR THE ICING ON THE CAKE

WATFORD
(GRAY 49)

WOLVES
(JIMENEZ 41, JOTA 77)

1

2

VICARAGE ROAD, 3PM
APRIL 27, 2019 ATTENDANCE: 20,323 (2,100 AWAY)

Watford (4-2-2-2): Foster; Femenia, Cathcart (Success 82), Mariappa (c), Holebas; Doucoure, Capoue; Hughes (Kabasele 74), Pereyra; Gray, Deulofeu. Subs not used: Gomes, Janmaat, Mesina, Sema, Chalobah.

Wolves (3-5-2): Patricio; Bennett, Coady (c), Boly; Doherty, Moutinho, Neves, Dendoncker, Otto; Jimenez (Cavaleiro 87), Jota (Gibbs-White 90+7). Subs not used: Ruddy, Saiss, Vinagre, Costa, Traore.

Twenty days doesn't exactly render this particular dish cold, but revenge was still oh-so sweet. Wolves struck a potentially decisive blow in the 'battle for seventh' with a gutsy win to exact some retribution three weeks after their Wembley nightmare.

Let it never be said that this team lacks character. They possess it by the truck-load and have responded admirably in this, their litmus test of a week as they look to secure potential European football at Molineux for the first time in almost four decades. There was despondency after the defeat to Southampton and the draw against Brighton. Following big, big wins over Arsenal and Watford there is euphoria again and deep pride at this team's success. It's taken some serious guts to rouse themselves, physically but also mentally, to engineer this late flourish to the campaign.

Whatever happens in the last two matches it's been a never-to-be-forgotten season, but with a game against already-relegated Fulham to come at Molineux, what a fantastic opportunity they have to put the icing on this golden cake and finish 'best of the rest', before praying Manchester City can do them a favour and open a door to Europe. They were lionhearted here. Nuno forever talks of needing to "compete" in every game and boy did they have to do that against a pumped-up Watford team.

There was plenty of needle in this one, on and off the pitch, but Nuno's team stood their ground and gained a foothold, allowing their quality to shine through especially via the prolific Diogo Jota and Raul Jimenez who yet again proved the difference in attack.

Wolves were unchanged, while Watford were without the suspended Troy Deeney – who stuck by his comments about Jimenez's mask in his pre-match programme notes – so Gerard Deulofeu partnered Wolverhampton-born Andre Gray up front.

Given how closely matched they've been this season, it was no surprise there was barely anything to choose between the sides in a tight first half, played out in a fraught atmosphere. Ruben Neves crunched Wembley match-winner Deulofeu with a fair ball-winning tackle which left the Spaniard limping, but he was soon to cause Wolves a number of problems.

Deulofeu had the game's first real opportunity when he was played in behind Willy Boly but, to the delight of the travelling supporters behind that goal, he fell over and scuffed his shot. Then Wolves broke at pace, predictably via the superb Jota who took on two players and slotted to the overlapping Leander Dendoncker on the right. He played across the six-yard box for Jimenez, but the Mexican couldn't quite connect.

The menacing Deulofeu then burst through the heart of the Wolves defence and looked set to fire goalwards before Ryan Bennett stole the ball off his toes in the nick of time. From the resulting corner it really should have been 1-0 to the hosts but Will Hughes sent a free header over the bar from just four yards after Wolves failed to clear.

The game was opening up – and Wolves struck before half-time in clinical fashion. After superb work from the excellent Jonny Castro Otto and Neves in the build-up, keeping play alive, Jota whipped a cross towards his strike partner Jimenez and he made no mistake with a planted six-yard header.

With a good half's work under their belt Wolves will have been hoping to keep things steady. Instead they gift wrapped an equalising goal to the Hornets. Just four minutes into the second half Bennett sent a pass back to his own goal, not spotting the lurking Deulofeu. Rui Patricio did well to smother at his feet but Gray was there to smash into the net from the edge of the area, past a helpless Boly on the line. It was a kamikaze mistake.

Wolves responded well with Jota heading Matt Doherty's whipped cross over from six yards, before Doherty shanked at the ball from Ben Foster's unconvincing clearance. Jota then sent another teasing cross towards Dendoncker, arriving late, but it just evaded the Belgium international. Conor Coady threw himself at the ball to block a well-struck Hughes shot, while a Joao Moutinho boomer from range deflected just over. It was too close to call – but then Wolves struck again with just 12 minutes left. Neves swung over a cross from deep to the back post where a flailing Foster missed the ball and Jota guided a cracking finish into the net to send the 2,200 away supporters into ecstasy.

Patricio's goal wasn't seriously troubled again, with Wolves defending with organisation and calm. Jota surely should have earned a penalty when being taken down by Christian Kabasele late on but it mattered not. "We're all going on a European tour" the away fans sang. Wolves are a gigantic step closer to doing just that.

POSSESSION: 57% / 43% | SHOTS: 10 / 11 | SHOTS ON TARGET: 1 / 4 | CORNERS: 4 / 5 | FOULS: 10 / 11 | BOOKINGS: 3 / 2

STAR MAN – DIOGO JOTA

It's a team game. There's no 'I' in team. The strength of the wolf is in the pack. But come on, all slogans aside, would Wolves be seventh in the table without the form of Diogo Jota? In his past 21 appearances since Nuno switched to 3-5-2 on December 5, Wolves' intrepid No.18 has scored 10 goals and set up a further five (all for Jimenez). But that doesn't tell half the story. His rambunctious exuberance is so often the inspiration behind galvanising Wolves up-field and that was no different at Vicarage Road where he tormented the home defence with a series of punchy runs from deep. An assist, with a perfect cross to Jimenez. A goal, with a cool finish on the volley. Outstanding, yet again.

TWEET OF THE GAME

Tim Spiers ✓
@tim_spiers_Star

Neves swings a massive cross from deep BEN FOSTER GOES WALKABOUT and Jota SLAMS into the empty net for 2-1 TO WOLVES WITH 12 MINS TO GO

27 Apr 2019

TABLE

	TEAM	P	GD	PTS
4	CHELSEA	35	21	67
5	ARSENAL	35	23	66
6	MAN UTD	35	13	64
7	WOLVES	36	2	54
8	EVERTON	36	6	50
9	WATFORD	36	-1	50
10	LEICESTER	35	1	48

ANALYSIS

This was one of the more satisfactory victories of an unforgettable season that could still have a fairytale finish.

First things first, though. The three points guaranteed Wolves will finish in the top half of the Premier League and, therefore, achieve the club's ultimate aim of 2018/19. Surviving relegation was the priority first and foremost. But a top-10 finish was the lofty ambition – and Wolves have delivered with two games to spare.

Yes, Nuno has been handed the kind of war chest that even a number of Premier League bosses can only dream of, but, having money, as anyone who sat through 1990 to 2002 under Sir Jack Hayward can testify, doesn't equal success.

It has to be spent wisely. West Ham and Fulham spent more than Wolves last summer but neither of those clubs have achieved their

targets this season. Nuno, who deserves so much credit, is clearly irked by what he perceives to be a lack of recognition, saying in a terse post-match press conference: "We've achieved mathematically staying in the Premier League, nobody said that. Now we achieved mathematically that we stay in the top half of the table, nobody's mentioning that. And last season we were playing in the Championship." You can't argue with that.

A top 10 finish is his – and Wolves' – reward and having achieved one target, another is now within their grasp. One victory is all Wolves may need to secure seventh and, tantalisingly, possible qualification for the Europa League. An offer of having to beat a relegated team to all-but finish seventh is a generous one that Wolves should take. Should they do so, Wolverhampton will turn blue for the day on May 18.

They're in this enviable position thanks to a courageous, battling victory at Vicarage Road, an afternoon which tested their mettle to the limit. In terms of quality there is precious little to separate Wolves and Watford. Mental attributes such as bravery, fearlessness and fortitude were required – fortunately for Wolves those characteristics are not in short supply. They produced organised and brave defending, meticulous passing from midfield, relentless work rate on the flanks and then fireworks up front via the electric duo of Raul Jimenez and Diogo Jota.

Jota has been nothing short of phenomenal since the switch to 3-5-2. Up to that point he'd played 14 games in all competitions and failed to provide a single goal or assist. Since then – 21 appearances, 10 goals, five assists. He galvanises Wolves and sometimes single-handedly coaxes them upfield via those trademark barnstorming ventures from deep.

His telepathy with Jimenez has left many a Premier League defence perplexed – if they can replicate this over the whole of next season, who knows where they can fire Wolves.

A word too for Ruben Neves who, after a difficult couple of weeks, has returned to form. Ben Foster called Neves' assist for the winner a "lump" into the box, which is a bit like saying the Venus de Milo is a "couple of limbs short of being a decent statue". Neves' perfectly-placed piercing pass, which befuddled Foster and his helpless defenders and landed on Jota's left boot, was Wolves' finest assist of the season.

Two games to go then and plenty to play for. If Wolves can put a timely end to their bottom six hoodoo and finish their Molineux campaign off in style, they can still have their perfect ending to 2018/19.

> **"I HAD ONE CHANCE BUT I HAVE MY REVENGE AND I SCORE – IT WOULD BE AMAZING IF WE CAN GO TO THE EUROPA LEAGUE."**
> RAUL JIMENEZ

WOLVES
(DENDONCKER 75)

FULHAM

1

0

MOLINEUX STADIUM, 3PM
MAY 4, 2019 ATTENDANCE: 30,456 (1,080 AWAY)

Wolves (3-5-2): *Patricio (Norris 90+3); Bennett, Coady (c), Boly (Kilman 90+3); Doherty, Moutinho, Neves, Dendoncker, Otto (Vinagre 90+3); Jimenez, Jota. Subs not used: Gibbs-White, Traore, Costa, Cavaleiro.*

Fulham (3-5-2): *Rico; Christie, Le Marchand, Ream; R Sessegnon (Ayite 83), Anguissa (Elliott 88), Chambers, Cairney (c), Bryan; Babel, Mitrovic. Subs not used: Fabri, Mawson, S Sessegnon, Nordtveit, Kebano.*

On May 4, 2013, Wolves were relegated to League One. On May 4, 2019, Wolves all-but secured seventh place and possible European football.

Seventh heaven – and an almost perfect league season – is now within touching distance. Wolves stormed to the Championship title during a season none of us will ever forget, but if they finish seventh and qualify for Europe, having also reached the FA Cup semi-finals, it will surpass 2017/18 in terms of an awe-inspiring achievement. No wonder they're awarding Nuno titles. Sorry, Doctor Nuno.

Wolves are now on 57 points from 37 matches, giving them the third highest tally of a newly-promoted team in a 38-game Premier League season, behind Sunderland (58, 1999/2000) and Ipswich (66, 2000/01). It'll be the freedom of the city next for Nuno. And who knows what's next for Wolves – the sky is the limit.

They were unchanged for the third game in a row, while relegated Fulham were in confident and carefree mood having won three games on the spin. It was no classic at Molineux, with the game having a distinct end-of-season feel. Large periods were played out in a near-silent atmosphere as Wolves struggled to lift the tempo.

Diogo Jota's magnificent recent form has put him centre of attention and the first 15 minutes were all about the Portuguese forward. Twice he wriggled into the box and twice went down under challenges, but on both occasions referee Jonathan Moss turned down Wolves' penalty appeals. It looked like there was contact for the

first tackle, but very little for the second and indeed Jota was booked for diving.

Wolves then produced what would be the standout move of the half, with Joao Moutinho playing beyond the back-line for Raul Jimenez, who cutely flicked towards Jota – he drove a 15-yard shot towards the bottom corner but was expertly denied by keeper Sergio Rico.

Moutinho was again the architect a few minutes later when harrassing his man to win the ball back just outside the Fulham box, before playing to Jota who fizzed an effort across goal and inches wide. Wolves' next chances came via, you guessed it, maestro Moutinho whose whipped cross reached Leander Dendoncker and he crashed a header against the crossbar. Willy Boly then flashed a header wide from a corner taken by, yes, Moutinho, as Wolves dominated without generating much in the way of tempo or momentum. That was about it for a fairly tepid 45 minutes in which too few of Wolves' star performers came to the fore.

Wolves went straight on the attack at the start of the second half and that man Jota, for the third time, was desperately close to scoring. Conor Coady brilliantly won the ball back with a rabble-rousing tackle, Jimenez sprinted from deep and then Jonny Castro Otto fed Jota, who drilled fractionally wide of the post left-footed. That got them going in the stands and suddenly Wolves had purpose and urgency in their play.

However, it was Fulham who then fashioned the best opportunity of the game for either team when Ryan Sessegnon was played in behind

Otto and squared the ball for front-runner Aleksandar Mitrovic, who ballooned a free shot into the North Bank from 12 yards. Back came Wolves with three chances inside two minutes. A Ruben Neves screamer from range was tipped wide by Rico, before the keeper saved Matt Doherty's goalbound header with his leg. Moutinho had crossed to Doherty for that chance and from his resulting corner Jimenez flashed a header past the post.

It was all Wolves now – and with just 15 minutes remaining their persistence paid off. That man Moutinho slipped in Doherty down the right and he perfectly picked out Dendoncker, arriving late eight yards out, to slam into the net in front of an ecstatic South Bank. Wolves piled forward in search of a second with Jota doing everything bar finding the net. His rasping half-volley was tipped onto the bar by Rico and then there was just about time for Will Norris and Max Kilman to get onto the field with seconds to go, before the full-time whistle blew and Wolves' wonderful home season drew to a close.

You can only marvel at the character they have displayed to bounce back in their last three games. Individually and collectively, this team has courage, valour and pride – they seem to lift each other's standards. Recruitment in people, not just players, has been vital to this.

Wolves will finish as high as they have since 1980, their attendances are higher than they've been since 1970 (and every crowd has been above 30,000 for the first time since the 1940s) and they will end the season unbeaten at Molineux for four months. Halcyon days, indeed.

NUNO

It was our last game at home this season and Molineux has given us so, so much this season. They deserve nothing less than what we did. How we did it is important, and I think we played good. It was very, very good for us. Every minute is important, but the home factor is definitely so, so important. We did it at home and Molineux was so behind the team. They have pushed us so much and helped us so much, so we cannot thank them enough. The FA Cup final still has to be played. It would be stupid to think about the Europa League.

FAN VERDICT – NATALIE WOOD

It wasn't a classic game by any stretch of the imagination but we got the job done. We controlled it from the start and looked by far the better team. Bar one chance for Fulham it was all Wolves and we finally got our reward – a great goal and well deserved. Moutinho yet again was a class above. It was great to sign off our final home game with a win and more importantly a win against a bottom six team! It was a good team performance and a well deserved victory. Hopefully we will go into next weekend having confirmed seventh.

POSSESSION: 39% / 61% | SHOTS: 19 / 6 | SHOTS ON TARGET: 6 / 2 | CORNERS: 7 / 1 | FOULS: 10 / 15 | BOOKINGS: 1 / 3

134

STAR MAN - JOAO MOUTINHO

Ran the show. Directly created six – yes, six – chances via either perfectly whipped crosses or delightful through balls. Was also involved in the build up to the winner when he played in Doherty. Creative and tenacious in equal measure. The master of ceremonies and a master of his craft. In 30 years' time when experienced manager Max Kilman has just guided Wolves to a fifth European Super League title, fans will still turn up to China Airlines Molineux and tell their kids: "I saw Joao Moutinho in a Wolves shirt."

TWEET OF THE GAME

Tim Spiers ✓
@tim_spiers_Star

Highest league position since 1980

Highest Molineux average attendance since 1970

Heady days. And you get the impression it's only the start #wwfc

                                    4 May 2019

TABLE

	TEAM	P	GD	PTS
4	CHELSEA	36	21	68
5	ARSENAL	36	20	66
6	MAN UTD	36	13	65
7	WOLVES	37	3	57
8	EVERTON	37	8	53
9	LEICESTER	36	4	51
10	WATFORD	36	-1	50

DR NUNO

Before kick-off Nuno was presented with an honorary degree from the University of Wolverhampton. The Wolves boss was made an honorary doctor of sport after the university rewarded Nuno for his contribution to sport in the region. Vice-Chancellor, Professor Geoff Layer, said: "We are delighted to recognise a leader who has brought pride and recognition to our city on an international scale."

Nuno took to the field – hat, gown and all – for the official ceremony amid cries of "there's only one Doctor Nuno" from the Wolves supporters.

"Molineux, thank you!" he said. "I want to thank the University of Wolverhampton to give me this honour and privilege of this honorary doctorate, it means so much to us. When I say 'us' I mean everybody that works so hard to achieve what we have achieved – especially you, the fans, thank you so much for your support. It's a privilege and an honour to receive the doctorate.

"It goes beyond me – it's all the people that work; the players, the staff, employees at Compton and Molineux, the fans. It's a commitment to do something together. I feel very welcome in Wolverhampton. It has been two years and every day has been a day of warm reception. People have treated me really well and it's always been our intention to give something back to the city and the club. We're committed to it. Sport can change lives. Being engaged in a team sport, you are able to feel what is human nature and because sport is truly global you can make an example for others to follow and this team spirit and unity should engage us in life also."

LIVERPOOL
(MANE 17, 81)

WOLVES

2

0

ANFIELD, 3PM
MAY 12, 2019 ATTENDANCE: **53,331** (2,900 AWAY)

Liverpool (4-3-3): Alisson; Alexander-Arnold, Matip, Van Dijk, Robertson (Gomez 84); Fabinho, Henderson (c), Wijnaldum (Oxlade-Chamberlain 88); Salah, Origi (Milner 63), Mane. Subs not used: Mignolet, Lovren, Shaqiri, Sturridge.

Wolves (3-5-2): Patricio; Bennett, Coady (c), Boly; Doherty (Traore 80), Neves, Dendoncker, Moutinho (Gibbs-White 84), Otto (Vinagre 84); Jimenez, Jota. Subs not used: Ruddy, Kilman, Costa, Cavaleiro.

The overriding feeling from the Wolves players trudging out of Anfield was one of disappointment. Given the play they'd had, the chances they'd created, they thought they should have taken at least a point. Considering they were at the home of the Champions League finalists who end the Premier League having earned 97 points this season and lost just a solitary game, that's quite a statement, but it's entirely in keeping with the bold and fearless approach with which Wolves have taken on the league's biggest and best this season.

After a first half in which they occasionally looked a little overawed, or at the very least just not themselves, Wolves approached the second period with adventure. They'd hit the bar via the exceptional Matt Doherty at the end of the first half and in the second they went close on several occasions in what was one-way traffic at times in front of the Kop. Ultimately, a special result to end a special season wasn't to be theirs, with an excellent Liverpool team ending their campaign with yet another victory, albeit not the title they so craved at the start of the day.

Nuno went with his strongest XI possible, naming the same team as for the last four matches. Doherty was back at the ground where he made his Wolves debut some eight years ago. Here he made his 252nd appearance for the club.

Divock Origi had the game's first shot in anger when he drilled at Rui Patricio. Otherwise it was a fairly tepid start – until the Reds took the lead in the 17th minute when Trent Alexander-Arnold

played a one-two to skip past Jonny Castro Otto and cross low for Sadio Mane, who couldn't miss from six yards.

A surreal few minutes then took hold at Anfield as news reached the stadium that Brighton had scored at the Amex against Manchester City. The whole place went berserk with the celebrations as frenzied as if Liverpool had scored a last-gasp winner. Then as City equalised and soon took the lead, the Wolves supporters were the ones cheering and chanting "City, City".

On the field, the game, surely as a result, died a death. With the home team affected by the chaos in the stands, Wolves began to venture forward with more confidence and conjured up the move of the match to go within inches of equalising. Otto scampered down the flank and cut the ball inside where Raul Jimenez dummied for Diogo Jota, who fed Doherty – and his 18-yard effort smashed off the crossbar.

Nuno's team attempted to take the game by the scruff of the neck at the start of the second half – there was more gumption about them and they were showing less respect for the Reds.

As news of a third Manchester City goal spread around Anfield, it felt like a result was there for the taking. Doherty, who was enjoying a very productive half in behind Andy Robertson, passed to Jimenez in a great position 12 yards out, but the Mexican scuffed his shot well wide. Wolves were now dominating the game and they should have equalised when Doherty lifted a piercing pass over the top, where Jimenez dummied for Jota, who was through on goal –

but Alisson raced from his line to smother the shot. Jimenez then flicked Otto's cross towards Jota and his point-blank-range header was saved by Alisson.

As City scored a fourth, the away supporters – who had adopted the role of wind-up merchants with no little relish – sang "Raheem Sterling, he's top of the league" to a chorus of boos from the home fans. It was Liverpool – against the run of play – who doubled their lead via the same combination for their first goal, with Mane converting Alexander-Arnold's cross, albeit from an offside position.

The clinical finishing of Mane was the reason Wolves didn't get a result – and a more prolific touch in front of goal is something Nuno & Co will be looking to add to this quality-rich squad in the summer. That's for another day, but what is unquestionable is that Wolves have the platform and the foundations from which to do something even more impressive than they've done in 2018/19. This valiant performance was yet more proof, not that it was required, that Wolves are here to stay.

All eyes now turn to the FA Cup final, where Manchester City can open the door to the club's first European campaign since 1980/81. This club and this team has shown time and again that nothing fazes or intimidates them. They take challenges in their stride, methodically and sensibly. Squad additions are needed but no player will be signed on a whim, or to make up the numbers. Whatever the Wembley result it's been a season to cherish. Wolves returned to the big time with a bang – they've played scintillating football and won many fans in the process. What on earth have they got in store for us next?

NUNO

It's been a fantastic season, and the bond we have as players and staff with the fans is the most important thing we have. Together we are stronger. Last week against Fulham we had a good moment in our stadium. They have come again to support us, and we appreciate it. Tomorrow, we start again, looking at the future. We are very proud of what we have achieved, and we are especially proud with how we did it. The belief of the boys is what makes this possible, so what we've achieved is thanks to the commitment and hard work of them. Now, we want to go again. What we did, let's enjoy and appreciate it. But let's work on it to become stronger.

FAN VERDICT - ROB CARTWRIGHT

Liverpool are the best team I've seen at Molineux this season but they were fortunate to win here. In between their goals Wolves were on top, controlling midfield if not possession. In the second half we took the game to the Reds and started to create a number of chances. I did feel we could give another 10 per cent in this game – we were on top for long periods without really going for it. A few players looked jaded. No surprise with the smallest squad in the league and an unchanged team for the last four games. Conor Coady was awesome and the whole defence did well.

POSSESSION: **59% / 41%** | SHOTS: **13 / 7** | SHOTS ON TARGET: **5 / 2** | CORNERS: **4 / 1** | FOULS: **3 / 11** | BOOKINGS: **0 / 2**

STAR MAN - MATT DOHERTY

His 252nd appearance in a Wolves shirt as he ended the campaign where it all started for him, having made his debut at Anfield back in 2011. An average first half when he gave the ball away too often ended with him almost scoring with a great effort which hit the crossbar. After the break he terrorised Liverpool with a bold display of attacking intentions. Consistently got in behind Andy Robertson and picked out Jimenez and Jota for two big chances with perfect passes. What a season he's had – end product galore (eight goals and eight assists in all competitions) and a humongous contribution to the team effort.

TWEET OF THE GAME

Tim Spiers ✔
@tim_spiers_Star

Spoke to a few players and they're all frustrated Wolves didn't get a result against the Champions League finalists who end the season on 97 points. Which is pretty standard for Wolves this season tbh. Here to stay ay they

12 May 2019

TABLE

	TEAM	P	GD	PTS
4	TOTTENHAM	38	28	71
5	ARSENAL	38	22	70
6	MAN UTD	38	11	66
7	WOLVES	38	1	57
8	EVERTON	38	8	54
9	LEICESTER	38	3	52
10	WEST HAM	38	-3	52

END OF SEASON AWARDS

MORE THAN 1,400 FANS AND STAFF DESCENDED ON THE TELFORD INTERNATIONAL CENTRE FOR THE CLUB'S END OF SEASON AWARDS – A CELEBRATION OF WOLVES REACHING 'SEVENTH HEAVEN'. AS FOR THE PLAYER OF THE SEASON, THERE WAS ONLY ONE WINNER...

PLAYER OF THE SEASON
JOAO MOUTINHO

PLAYERS' PLAYER OF THE SEASON
RAUL JIMENEZ

TOP GOALSCORER
RAUL JIMENEZ

GOAL OF THE SEASON
DIOGO JOTA v CARDIFF

YOUNG PROFESSIONAL OF THE SEASON
RUBEN VINAGRE

ACADEMY PLAYER OF THE SEASON
LEWIS RICHARDS

WOLVES FOUNDATION PLAYER OF THE SEASON
JOHN RUDDY

WOLVES WOMEN PLAYER OF THE SEASON
EMMA CROSS

EXPRESS & STAR FAN OF THE SEASON
STEVE GREEN

RACHAEL HEYHOE FLINT AWARD
KEVIN ROGERS

WOLVES UNDER-23s 2018/19

IT WAS ALSO A SUCCESSFUL SEASON FOR THE WOLVES UNDER-23 SIDE WHO WON PROMOTION TO THE TOP LEVEL OF UNDER-23 FOOTBALL. THEY DID SO IN THE MOST DRAMATIC OF CIRCUMSTANCES, COMING FROM 2-0 DOWN TO BEAT MANCHESTER UNITED IN THE LAST GAME OF THE CAMPAIGN.

Rob Edwards' young charges needed three points to secure the title but with just 10 minutes remaining were 2-0 down. An own goal got them back in the game on 80 minutes before Niall Ennis equalised with two minutes remaining. Then in stoppage time Sadou Diallo completed an astonishing late comeback and sparked wild scenes of celebration from the players, staff and 350 Wolves fans who had made the trip to Manchester. Jeff Shi also attended and later called it his favourite game of the entire season.

Rob Edwards said at full-time: "It's an unbelievable rollercoaster of emotions and one of the best feelings I've had in 20 years of professional football. It was incredible how they turned it around. They showed something there, they're going to be good players. They're going to have good, long careers if they keep that. I'm proud. At 2-0 down we showed belief and character, I've seen a lot from these players, but I haven't seen that. To be 2-0 down to a top team, with unbelievable individuals, shows our lads have a bit about them. They were incredible scenes to score that one late on."

STATS

GOALKEEPERS

RUI PATRICIO
APPEARANCES 37

JOHN RUDDY
APPEARANCES 9

WILL NORRIS
APPEARANCES 0 (1)

DEFENDERS

CONOR COADY
APPEARANCES 46

RYAN BENNETT
APPEARANCES 38 (2)
GOALS 1

WILLY BOLY
APPEARANCES 41
GOALS 4
ASSISTS 1

KORTNEY HAUSE
APPEARANCES 2

MATT DOHERTY
APPEARANCES 41 (4)
GOALS 8
ASSISTS 8

JONNY CASTRO OTTO
APPEARANCES 38 (1)
GOALS 1
ASSISTS 1

RUBEN VINAGRE
APPEARANCES 10 (11)
ASSISTS 1

RYAN GILES
APPEARANCES 1

MAX KILMAN
APPEARANCES 0 (1)

MIDFIELDERS

JOAO MOUTINHO
APPEARANCES 39 (5)
GOALS 1
ASSISTS 8

RUBEN NEVES
APPEARANCES 38 (2)
GOALS 5
ASSISTS 4

LEANDER DENDONCKER
APPEARANCES 24 (2)
GOALS 2

ROMAIN SAISS
APPEARANCES 19 (7)
GOALS 2

MORGAN GIBBS-WHITE
APPEARANCES 9 (22)
ASSISTS 1

ELLIOT WATT
APPEARANCES 1

PEDRO GONCALVES
APPEARANCES 0 (1)

FORWARDS

RAUL JIMENEZ
APPEARANCES 40 (4)
GOALS 17
ASSISTS 7

DIOGO JOTA
APPEARANCES 32 (5)
GOALS 10
ASSISTS 7

HELDER COSTA
APPEARANCES 18 (12)
GOALS 2
ASSISTS 2

ADAMA TRAORE
APPEARANCES 12 (24)
GOALS 1
ASSISTS 2

IVAN CAVALEIRO
APPEARANCES 9 (20)
GOALS 5
ASSISTS 2

LEO BONATINI
APPEARANCES 2 (7)
GOALS 1
ASSISTS 1

BENNY ASHLEY-SEAL
APPEARANCES 0 (2)

NIALL ENNIS
APPEARANCES 0 (1)

APPEARANCES COUNT ALL COMPETITIONS, SUBSTITUTE APPEARANCES IN BRACKETS

31030
AVERAGE MOLINEUX ATTENDANCE FOR THE SEASON, THE CLUB'S HIGHEST SINCE 1970

4 GOALS SCORED BY RUBEN NEVES

16 POINTS WON AGAINST THE 'BIG SIX', ONLY MANCHESTER CITY AND LIVERPOOL WON MORE

3 TOUCHES IN THE OPPOSITION BOX BY RUBEN NEVES *(2,441 OUTSIDE THE BOX)*

£26900000
PRIZE MONEY RECEIVED FOR FINISHING SEVENTH

(PLUS £3.2M FOR REACHING THE FA CUP SEMI-FINALS)

0 GOALS CONCEDED IN THE CARABAO CUP (IN SIX MATCHES) SINCE NUNO BECAME HEAD COACH

21 YEARS SINCE WOLVES' LAST FA CUP SEMI-FINAL

6064
PREMIER LEAGUE MATCHES PLAYED WITHOUT A TEAM FAILING TO COMMIT A SINGLE FOUL, UNTIL WOLVES MANAGED IT AGAINST BRIGHTON AT MOLINEUX

16 COMBINED TOTAL OF GOALS AND ASSISTS FROM MATT DOHERTY IN ALL COMPETITIONS

78 GAMES PLAYED BY MANCHESTER UNITED SINCE THEY HAD LOST AFTER SCORING FIRST, UNTIL WOLVES BEAT THEM 2-1 IN APRIL

42 YEARS SINCE A WOLVES PLAYER HAD SCORED A TOP-FLIGHT HAT-TRICK *(JOHN RICHARDS AGAINST LEICESTER)* BEFORE *DIOGO JOTA* SCORED THREE, ALSO AGAINST LEICESTER

7 WOLVES' PREMIER LEAGUE POSITION WAS THEIR HIGHEST LEAGUE FINISH SINCE 1980

2 PREMIER LEAGUE OCCURRENCES OF SUCCESSIVE 4-3 VICTORIES AGAINST THE SAME OPPOSITION *(WOLVES V LEICESTER, 2003 AND 2019, LIVERPOOL V NEWCASTLE, 1996 AND 1997)*

40 YEARS SINCE WOLVES HAD BEATEN ARSENAL *(A RUN OF 20 WINLESS MATCHES)*

10 *PLAYERS CALLED UP FOR SENIOR INTERNATIONAL DUTY*

---

21 PLAYERS USED BY NUNO IN THE PREMIER LEAGUE

9 NUNO SELECTED THE SAME XI FOR WOLVES' FIRST NINE MATCHES, A PREMIER LEAGUE RECORD

17 GAMES LOST TO INJURY OR ILLNESS BY THE ENTIRE FIRST-TEAM SQUAD

4170
MINUTES PLAYED BY CONOR COADY – THE ONLY TOP-FLIGHT PLAYER TO PLAY EVERY SINGLE MINUTE OF EVERY GAME IN ALL COMPETITIONS

11 RUI PATRICIO'S SQUAD NUMBER, CHOSEN AS A MARK OF RESPECT FOR RETIRED FORMER NO. 1 CARL IKEME

3 LAST MINUTE WINNERS (AGAINST WEST HAM, NEWCASTLE AND LEICESTER)

304 GAMES PLAYED IN THE TOP FLIGHT BY WOLVES WITHOUT WINNING THREE IN A ROW, BEFORE WINS OVER CHELSEA, NEWCASTLE AND BOURNEMOUTH IN DECEMBER

17 RAUL JIMENEZ SCORED 17 GOALS IN ALL COMPETITIONS, THE MOST BY A WOLVES TOP-FLIGHT PLAYER SINCE JOHN RICHARDS IN 1981

3 MANAGER OF THE MONTH NOMINATIONS FOR NUNO ESPIRITO SANTO, WHO WAS ALSO NOMINATED FOR MANAGER OF THE YEAR

14 *POINTS WON AFTER FALLING BEHIND, THE THIRD HIGHEST TOTAL IN THE LEAGUE*

£32000000
FEE PAID FOR RAUL JIMENEZ, SMASHING THE CLUB'S TRANSFER RECORD

7 KEY PASSES MADE BY JOAO MOUTINHO IN THE FA CUP WIN OVER MAN UNITED – *THE SAME AS THE ENTIRE UNITED TEAM*

57 WOLVES' POINTS TOTAL WAS THE HIGHEST BY A NEWLY-PROMOTED PREMIER LEAGUE TEAM FOR 18 YEARS

0 DEFEATS AT MOLINEUX IN THE LAST 11 HOME GAMES OF THE SEASON IN ALL COMPETITIONS

94 SECONDS IVAN CAVALEIRO HAD PLAYED IN THE PREMIER LEAGUE BEFORE SCORING HIS FIRST GOAL *(WITH HIS FIRST TOUCH)* AGAINST SOUTHAMPTON

34300
WOLVES FANS AT WEMBLEY FOR THE FA CUP SEMI-FINAL

11 GOALS SCORED IN THE LAST 10 MINUTES OF MATCHES *(ONLY ARSENAL, CHELSEA AND LIVERPOOL SCORED MORE)*

AUG 11 EVERTON (H) 2-2 (NEVES 44, JIMENEZ 80)
AUG 18 LEICESTER CITY (A) 2-0
AUG 25 MANCHESTER CITY (H) 1-1 (BOLY 57)
AUG 28 SHEFFIELD WEDNESDAY (A) 0-2 (BONATINI 53, COSTA PEN 85) *EFL CUP R1*
SEP 1 WEST HAM UNITED (A) 0-1 (TRAORE 90+3)
SEP 16 BURNLEY (H) 1-0 (JIMENEZ 61)
SEP 22 MANCHESTER UNITED (A) 1-1 (MOUTINHO 53)
SEP 25 LEICESTER CITY (H) 0-0 (1-3 ON PENS) *EFL CUP R2*
SEP 29 SOUTHAMPTON (H) 2-0 (CAVALEIRO 79, OTTO 87)
OCT 6 CRYSTAL PALACE (A) 0-1 (DOHERTY 56)
OCT 20 WATFORD (H) 0-2
OCT 27 BRIGHTON (A) 1-0
NOV 3 TOTTENHAM HOTSPUR (H) 2-3 (NEVES PEN 68, JIMENEZ PEN 79)
NOV 11 ARSENAL (A) 1-1 (CAVALEIRO 13)
NOV 25 HUDDERSFIELD TOWN (H) 0-2
NOV 30 CARDIFF CITY (A) 2-1 (DOHERTY 18)
DEC 5 CHELSEA (H) 2-1 (JIMENEZ 59, JOTA 63)
DEC 9 NEWCASTLE UNITED (A) 1-2 (JOTA 17, DOHERTY 90+4)
DEC 15 BOURNEMOUTH (H) 2-0 (JIMENEZ 12, CAVALEIRO 90+4)
DEC 21 LIVERPOOL (H) 0-2
DEC 26 FULHAM (A) 1-1 (SAISS 85)
DEC 29 TOTTENHAM HOTSPUR (A) 1-3 (BOLY 72, JIMENEZ 83, COSTA 87)
JAN 2 CRYSTAL PALACE (H) 0-2
JAN 7 LIVERPOOL (H) 2-1 (JIMENEZ 38, NEVES 55) *FA CUP R3*
JAN 14 MANCHESTER CITY (A) 3-0
JAN 19 LEICESTER CITY (H) 4-3 (JOTA 4, 64, 90+2, BENNETT 12)
JAN 26 SHREWSBURY TOWN (A) 2-2 (JIMENES 75, DOHERTY 90+3) *FA CUP R4*
JAN 29 WEST HAM UNITED (H) 3-0 (SAISS 66, JIMENEZ 80, 86)
FEB 2 EVERTON (A) 1-3 (NEVES PEN 7, JIMENEZ 45, DENDONCKER 66)
FEB 5 SHREWSBURY TOWN (H) 3-2 (DOHERTY 2, 45+6, CAVALEIRO 62) *FA CUP R4 (R)*
FEB 11 NEWCASTLE UNITED (H) 1-1 (BOLY 90+5)
FEB 17 BRISTOL CITY (A) 0-1 (CAVALEIRO 28) *FA CUP R5*
FEB 23 BOURNEMOUTH (A) 1-1 (JIMENEZ PEN 83)
FEB 26 HUDDERSFIELD TOWN (A) 1-0
MAR 2 CARDIFF CITY (H) 2-0 (JOTA 16, JIMENEZ 18)
MAR 10 CHELSEA (A) 1-1 (JIMENEZ 56)
MAR 16 MANCHESTER UNITED (H) 2-1 (JIMENEZ 70, JOTA 76) *FA CUP QF*
MAR 30 BURNLEY (A) 2-0
APR 2 MANCHESTER UNITED (H) 2-1 (JOTA 25, SMALLING OG 77)
APR 7 WATFORD (N) 3-2 (DOHERTY 36, JIMENEZ 62) *FA CUP SF*
APR 13 SOUTHAMPTON (A) 3-1 (BOLY 28)
APR 20 BRIGHTON (H) 0-0
APR 24 ARSENAL (H) 3-1 (NEVES 28, DOHERTY 37, JOTA 45+2)
APR 27 WATFORD (A) 1-2 (JIMENEZ 41, JOTA 77)
MAY 4 FULHAM (H) 1-0 (DENDONCKER 75)
MAY 12 LIVERPOOL (A) 2-0

FAN VERDICTS

THE EXPRESS & STAR'S FAN VERDICT CONTRIBUTORS HAVE FOLLOWED WOLVES UP AND DOWN THE COUNTRY AND, AS LOYAL SUPPORTERS OF MANY YEARS, ENJOYED SOME OF THEIR HAPPIEST MOMENTS AS WOLVES FANS IN 2018/19. HERE THEY SUM UP THEIR THOUGHTS ON AN UNFORGETTABLE SEASON.

ROB CARTWRIGHT

WE ARE BLESSED AND PRIVILEGED TO BE ABLE TO WATCH NUNO PUT HIS STAMP ON THE HISTORY OF WOLVERHAMPTON WANDERERS. IT'S NOT JUST RESULTS, BUT THE STYLE OF FOOTBALL. ALSO, THE WAY HE HAS DEVELOPED AND IMPROVED PLAYERS AND THE WAY HE GIVES YOUTH A CHANCE.

WITH OUR FIRST TASTE OF EUROPEAN FOOTBALL FOR 39 YEARS BECKONING, WOLVES MUST NOW BE THREE YEARS AHEAD OF THEIR PLAN FOR SUCCESS. THAT IS DUE TO NUNO AND HIS SUPERB BACKROOM TEAM. HE IS A MAN OF FEW WORDS, HE LETS HIS PLAYERS DO HIS TALKING ON THE PITCH AND LONG MAY THAT CONTINUE.

GAME: SPURS 1-3 WOLVES

PLAYER: JOAO MOUTINHO

UNSUNG HERO: RYAN BENNETT

GULRAJ KULAR

A TOTAL, UNEQUIVOCAL, UNMISTAKEABLE, RIP-ROARING SUCCESS. A SLIGHT TINGE OF FRUSTRATION GIVEN OUR RESULTS AGAINST THE BOTTOM SIX, BUT THIS IS BUT A MERE SPECK ON THE MOST WONDROUS COPYBOOK OF MY TIME SUPPORTING THE CLUB.

I'LL NEVER FORGET THE 2-1 VICTORY OVER MANCHESTER UNITED IN THE FA CUP FOR ATMOSPHERE, QUALITY OF PERFORMANCE AND THE SENSE OF 'ARRIVAL' AT THE HIGHEST LEVEL OF THE GAME.

GAME: WOLVES 2-1 MAN UNITED (FA CUP)

PLAYER: JOAO MOUTINHO

UNSUNG HERO: WILLY BOLY

ADAM VIRGO

ABSOLUTELY BRILLIANT. TO FINISH SEVENTH AND GET TO AN FA CUP SEMI-FINAL IN OUR FIRST SEASON BACK IN THE PREMIER LEAGUE IS FANTASTIC. THE FACT WE'RE NOW IN THE EUROPA LEAGUE IS ALSO BEYOND BELIEF. I'M STILL IN ABSOLUTE SHOCK THAT WE'LL ACTUALLY BE GOING ON A EUROPEAN TOUR AND I, JUST LIKE ANY WOLVES FAN, CANNOT WAIT.

GAME: WOLVES 2-1 MAN UNITED (FA CUP)

PLAYER: JOAO MOUTINHO

UNSUNG HERO: LEANDER DENDONCKER

NATALIE WOOD

FIVE YEARS AGO WE'D JUST GOT PROMOTED FROM LEAGUE ONE AND IT FELT LIKE THE START OF OUR REBUILD – IT'S SAFE TO SAY I NEVER IMAGINED IN A MILLION YEARS THAT WE'D NOW HAVE FINISHED SEVENTH IN THE PREMIER LEAGUE, QUALIFIED FOR EUROPE AND GOT TO AN FA CUP SEMI-FINAL.

I'VE WATCHED WOLVES HOME AND AWAY FOR MANY YEARS AND THIS SEASON HAS BEEN BY FAR THE MOST MEMORABLE. IT FEELS LIKE THIS IS JUST THE BEGINNING, WHICH IS WHAT MAKES IT EVEN MORE EXCITING.

GAME: SPURS 1 WOLVES 3

PLAYER: JOAO MOUTINHO

UNSUNG HERO: CONOR COADY

CLIVE SMITH

IF WE ARE HONEST, IT'S GONE BETTER THAN ANY OF US EXPECTED. OUR PREVIOUS EXPERIENCE OF THE PREMIER LEAGUE HAD BEEN ABOUT DAMAGE LIMITATION AND MUST WIN SIX-POINTERS AND WE HAD VERY FEW POSITIVE MEMORIES. THIS TIME IT WAS DIFFERENT.

WITH SUCH A YOUNG AND INEXPERIENCED SQUAD IT HAS BEEN A DELIGHT TO WATCH THEM GROW AND IMPROVE DURING THE CAMPAIGN. BEING SO COMPETITIVE AND ABLE TO PLAY SUCH GOOD FOOTBALL HAS MADE IT A WONDERFUL SEASON – WE HAVE NOT LOOKED OUT OF PLACE.

GAME: WOLVES 4-3 LEICESTER

PLAYER: RAUL JIMENEZ

UNSUNG HERO: MATT DOHERTY

RUSS EVERS

A SEASON THAT STARTED WITH AN ENORMOUS AMOUNT OF HOPE AND A LITTLE BIT OF BELIEF THAT ULTIMATELY SURPASSED THE EXPECTATIONS OF MOST WOLVES FANS – AND CERTAINLY CAUGHT THE REST OF THE FOOTBALL WORLD COLD.

TWO VISITS TO WEMBLEY AND NUMEROUS VICTORIES AND BRAVE PERFORMANCES AGAINST SOME OF THE VERY BEST, ALL CULMINATING IN THE PURCHASE OF A MAP OF EUROPE!

GAME: MAN UNITED 2-3 WOLVES (U23s)

PLAYER: JOAO MOUTINHO

UNSUNG HERO: MATT DOHERTY

CHRIS HUGHES

IT'S BEEN ALMOST PERFECT. AT THE START OF THE SEASON I'D HAVE SETTLED FOR 17TH OR ABOVE IN THE LEAGUE, JUST TO CONTINUE THE BUILDING PROCESS. TO HAVE SEWN UP SEVENTH WITH A GAME TO SPARE AND BEEN ONE TIRED DENDONCKER CHALLENGE AWAY FROM AN FA CUP FINAL WAS AN IMMENSE PERFORMANCE.

THROW IN MAN CITY'S CUP FINAL WIN SEALING A EUROPA LEAGUE QUALIFYING PLACE FOR NEXT SEASON AND WE'VE GONE INTO THE REALM OF DREAMS.

GAME: WOLVES 2-1 MAN UNITED (FA CUP)

PLAYER: JOAO MOUTINHO

UNSUNG HERO: RYAN BENNETT

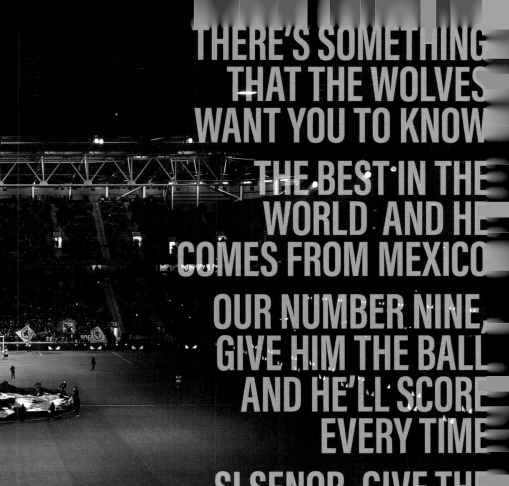

THERE'S SOMETHING THAT THE WOLVES WANT YOU TO KNOW

THE BEST IN THE WORLD AND HE COMES FROM MEXICO

OUR NUMBER NINE, GIVE HIM THE BALL AND HE'LL SCORE EVERY TIME

SI SENOR, GIVE THE BALL TO RAUL AND HE WILL SCORE

OH JOAO MOUTINHO, HE LOVES A VINO

HE CAME FROM MONACO, TO WANDERERS

HE'S 5 FOOT 7, OF FOOTBALL HEAVEN

SO PLEASE DON'T TAKE MOUTINHO AWAY

WRITER: **TIM SPIERS**

EDITORIAL DESIGN AND PRODUCTION: **SIMON HILL**

PHOTOGRAPHY: **SAM BAGNALL**

AMA SPORTS PHOTO AGENCY:
MATTHEW ASHTON
ROBBIE JAY BARRATT
MOLLY DARLINGTON
MALCOLM COUZENS
JAMES WILLIAMSON
JAMES BAYLIS
DAVE BAGNALL

ADDITIONAL PHOTOGRAPHY:
TIM THURSFIELD
STEVE LEATH
DAVID HAMILTON
JAMIE RICKETTS

PRINTED BY:
precisioncolour**printing** limited

PUBLISHED BY:
THE MIDLAND NEWS ASSOCIATION LTD

WITH THANKS TO:
WOLVERHAMPTON WANDERERS F.C.
UNIVERSITY OF WOLVERHAMPTON
JOE EDWARDS
LEIGH SANDERS
MARK SHIPP

MNA Media

Express & Star

ON MAY 18, MANCHESTER CITY'S 6-0 THRASHING OF WATFORD IN THE FA CUP FINAL MEANT WOLVES QUALIFIED FOR EUROPE FOR THE FIRST TIME IN 39 YEARS, EARNING A PLACE IN THE EUROPA LEAGUE FOR 2019/2020.

WITH THE CLUB SET TO BECOME THE FIRST IN THE UK TO INSTALL RAIL SEATS IN AN ENTIRE STAND, PLUS A GROUNDBREAKING TRIP TO CHINA PLANNED FOR THE SUMMER, A NEW MEGASTORE OPENING IN SHANGHAI AND PLANS TO EXPAND COMPTON PARK – NOT TO MENTION AMBITIONS OF BECOMING A TOP SIX CLUB AND BEYOND – THERE HAS RARELY BEEN A MORE EXCITING PERIOD IN THE HISTORY OF WOLVERHAMPTON WANDERERS.

PLANS ARE ALSO BEING DRAWN UP TO EXPAND MOLINEUX AND THE CLUB RECENTLY UNVEILED A SPECTACULAR VISION FOR WHAT THE STADIUM MAY LOOK LIKE IN YEARS TO COME. THE IMAGES OFFERED A BREATHTAKING AND TANTALISING GOLDEN GLIMPSE INTO THE FUTURE OF A CLUB THAT HOPES – AND BELIEVES – IT CAN RECREATE AND EVEN SURPASS THE GLORY DAYS OF THE 1950S. THERE WILL BE HIGHS AND LOWS, GOOD DAYS AND BAD, BUT ONE THING'S FOR SURE... IT'S GOING TO BE ONE HELL OF A JOURNEY.